Miracles of Book and Body

BUDDHISMS

Janet Gyatso, Charles Hallisey, Helen Hardacre, Robert Sharf, and Stephen Teiser,
series editors

*Available from Princeton University Press

Miracles of Book and Body

BUDDHIST TEXTUAL CULTURE AND MEDIEVAL JAPAN

Charlotte Eubanks

UNIVERSITY OF CALIFORNIA PRESS
BERKELEY   LOS ANGELES   LONDON

University of California Press, one of the most distinguished university presses in the United States, enriches
lives around the world by advancing scholarship in the
humanities, social sciences, and natural sciences. Its
activities are supported by the UC Press Foundation
and by philanthropic contributions from individuals
and institutions. For more information, visit
www.ucpress.edu.

University of California Press
Berkeley and Los Angeles, California

University of California Press, Ltd.
London, England

Library of Congress Cataloging-in-Publication Data
Eubanks, Charlotte D. (Charlotte Diane), 1971–.
    Miracles of book and body : Buddhist textual culture
and medieval Japan / Charlotte D. Eubanks.
        p. cm.
    Includes bibliographical references and index.
    ISBN 978-0-520-26561-5 (cloth : alk. paper)
        1. Buddhist literature, Japanese—History and criticism.
    2. Folk literature, Japanese—History and criticism.
    3. Books and reading—Religious aspects-Buddhism.
    4. Buddhism—Japan—History—1185–1600.
    5. Movement, Psychology of—Religious aspects—
Buddhism.   I. Title.
BQ1029.J32E93   2011
294.3'85—dc22   2010013953

Manufactured in the United States of America

20   19   18   17   16   15   14   13   12
10   9   8   7   6   5   4   3   2   1

This book is printed on Cascades Enviro 100, a 100% post
consumer waste, recycled, de-inked fiber. FSC recycled
certified and processed chlorine free. It is acid free, Ecologo
certified, and manufactured by BioGas energy.

In memory of my brother
John
May you be peaceful and at ease

CONTENTS

ILLUSTRATIONS

NOTE ON SUTRAS

This book references sutras by their briefest common English title. This list provides the accession numbers for the sutras in the *Taishō Shinshū Daizōkyō*. All references to the canon provide volume number, *Taishō* accession number, page, register, and lines (e.g., T 14.475.549c10 refers to the tenth line, third [c] register of page 549 of *Taishō* text number 475 [the *Vimalakīrti Sutra*], which can be found in volume 14).

Brahma Net Sutra	T. 1484
Diamond Sutra	T. 235
Flower Ornament Sutra	T. 279
Greater Heart Sutra	T. 220
Heart Sutra	T. 251
Lotus Sutra	T. 262
Nirvana Sutra	T. 374
Sutra of Immeasurable Life	T. 360
Sutra of Immeasurable Meanings	T. 276
Sutra of Meditation on the Bodhisattva Universal Virtue	T. 277
Sutra of Meditation on the Buddha Amitāyus	T. 365
Unflawed Pure Light Great Dhāranī Sutra	T. 1024
Vimalakīrti Sutra	T. 475

NOTE ON *SETSUWA*

This book gives the full Japanese title for *setsuwa* collections on their first appearance in the text, alongside an English translation (e.g., *Nihon Genpō Zen'aku Ryōiki, A Wondrous Record of Immediate Karmic Retribution for Good and Evil in Japan*). Thereafter, the book uses a standard English version of the title, shortened in the case of particularly lengthy titles.

ENGLISH TITLES

A Collection of Sand and Pebbles (see *Shasekishū*)

A Collection of Spiritual Awakenings (see *Hosshinshū*)

A Collection of Treasures (see *Hōbutsushū*)

A Companion in Solitude (see *Kankyo no Tomo*)

Miracles of the Lotus Sutra (see *Hokke Genki*)

One Hundred Sessions of Sermons (see *Hyakuza Hōdan Kikigakishō*)

Tales from Times Now Past (see *Konjaku Monogatari*)

The Three Jewels (see *Sanbō Ekotoba*)

A Wondrous Record of Immediate Karmic Retribution (see *Nihon Genpō Zen'aku Ryōiki*)

Hōbutsushū 宝物集, compiled probably no later than 1180, compiler uncertain. *A Collection of Treasures.*

Hokke Genki 法華験記, compiled 1040–44 by Chingen 鎮源. Known by a variety of titles, including *Dainihonkoku Hokkekyō Genki* 大日本国法華験記 and *Honchō Hokke Genki* 本朝法華験記. *A Record of Miracles of the Lotus Sutra.* Shortened title: *Miracles of the Lotus Sutra.*

Hosshinshū 発心集, compiled 1214–15 by Kamo no Chōmei 鴨長明. *A Collection of Spiritual Awakenings.*

Hyakuza Hōdan Kikigakishō 百座法談聞書抄, compiled ca. 1110, compiler uncertain. Also known as *Hokke Shuhō Ippyakuza Kikigakishō* 法華修法一百座聞書抄, *Daianji Hyakuza Hōdan* 大安寺百座法談, and *Hokke Hyakuza Kikigakishō* 法華百座聞書抄. *Notes Taken While Listening to One Hundred Sessions of Sermons.* Shortened title: *One Hundred Sessions of Sermons.*

Kankyo no Tomo 閑居友 (sometimes rendered *Kango no Tomo*), compiled 1222 by Keisei 慶政. *A Companion in Solitude.*

Konjaku Monogatari 今昔物語, probably compiled by 1120. Also known as *Konjaku Monogatarishū* 今昔物語集. *Tales from Times Now Past.*

Nihon Genpō Zen'aku Ryōiki 日本現報善悪霊異記, compiled ca. 823 by Kyōkai 景戒 (sometimes rendered Keikai). Commonly known as *Nihon Ryōiki* 日本霊異記. *A Wondrous Record of Immediate Karmic Retribution for Good and Evil in Japan.* Shortened title: *A Wondrous Record of Immediate Karmic Retribution.*

Sanbō Ekotoba 三宝絵詞, compiled 984 by Minamoto no Tamenori 源為憲. Commonly known as *Sanbōe* 三宝絵. *Illustrations and Explanations of the Three Jewels.* Shortened title: *The Three Jewels.*

Shasekishū 砂石集 (sometimes rendered *Sasekishū*), compiled 1279–83 by Mujū Ichien 無住一円. *A Collection of Sand and Pebbles.*

ABBREVIATIONS

DZZ   *Dōgen Zenshi Zenshū*
HZ   *Hyakuza Hōdan Kikigakishō*
NKBT   *Nihon Koten Bungaku Taikei*
NKBZ   *Nihon Koten Bungaku Zenshū*
NST   *Nihon Shisō Taikei*
SNKBT   *Shin Nihon Koten Bungaku Taikei*
SNKBZ   *Shin Nihon Koten Bungaku Zenshū*
SNKS   *Shinchō Nihon Koten Shūsei*
T   *Taishō Shinshū Daizōkyō*
YSG   *Yōkyoku Sanbyaku Gojūbanshū*

ACKNOWLEDGMENTS

Several institutions were instrumental in supporting me as I worked on this manuscript. I would like to thank Jim Heisig, Paul Swanson, and Ben Dorman of Nanzan University and the Shubunken staff for providing lodging, library access, office space, and stimulating conversation during several stages of the research for this book. The Devaney Fellowship, Gambil Family Endowment, Reynolds Fellowship, and Teaching East Asia Center at CU-Boulder all provided much-appreciated funding during the initial periods of research and writing. My home institution of Penn State funded further research in Japan and generously awarded a semester of teaching release as I completed the manuscript. Thank you also to Shigemi Nakagawa for extending library privileges at Ritsumeikan. Keller Kimbrough, Kagitani Kimiko, Reiko Tachibana, Kimiko Suzuki, Dana Kletchka, Kat Staab, Whitney Izzo, Greg Kordas, and everyone at the North American Coordinating Council on Japanese Library Resources have my endless thanks for assistance with crafting permissions letters and creating digital files for the artwork.

Special thanks to Abe Yasurō, Keller Kimbrough, Terao Kazuyoshi, Erin McCarthy, and Hayo Krombach for their curiosity and probing questions as I was formulating the shape of this book. Stephen Teiser, Charles Hallisey, Laurel Rasplica Rodd, Stephen Miller, Bruce Holsinger, Andy Cowell, Ed Rivers, and an anonymous reader reviewed earlier drafts of this manuscript, and their comments have strengthened it immeasurably. Any errors or oversights remain my own. Sincere thanks as well to the peer writing group at Penn State, particularly to Eric Hayot, Jonathan Eburne, Hester Blum, Sophia McClennen, Chris Castiglia, and Christopher Reed, who sharpened my thinking and pushed me to clarity. Finally, a warm thanks to Reed Malcolm for deftly shepherding this book from manuscript to bound volume.

The Nanzan Institute and the Johns Hopkins University Press have kindly granted permission to reprint parts of this book that were first printed in their publications. A portion of chapter 4 originally appeared in the *Japanese Journal of Religious Studies,* and a version of the conclusion was first printed in the pages of *Book History*.

A few personal notes of thanks to those who are last in print but first in my heart: to my family, who first taught me to care about sacred words, and to my partner Etta, whose reserves of strength are astounding, and who brings joy and wonder to every day.

Introduction

The Cult of the Book and the Culture of Text

SOMETIME IN THE LATE 1190s the Japanese Buddhist monk Myōe (1173–1232) decided that a shaved head was not a reliable enough symbol of a person's devotion or true intentions. Thus, as a sign of his sincerity, he picked up a dagger and sawed off his right ear, spattering blood over the various ritual implements arrayed before him. According to his disciple Kikai, Myōe's logic in choosing to cut off his ear was as follows: "If he plucked out an eye, he would grieve over not being able to see the scriptures. If he cut off his nose, snot would dribble on the scriptures. If he severed a hand, he would be in agony over forming the mudras. But if he cut off an ear, he would still be able to hear."[1] Myōe's guiding logic in choosing which portion of his body to damage pivoted on the material reality of his physical access to the sutras: seeing them, holding them, keeping them clean, and hearing them.

By marking himself in such a drastic way, Myōe hoped to accomplish two things. First, he wanted his permanent, though intangible, internal commitments reflected on the external reality of his physical body, available for all to see for as long as his body should last. Second, he believed that by altering his physicality in such a painful way, he might also be able to alter the sacred writings of Buddhism. He believed profoundly, perhaps even fanatically, in a correlation between body and text. Following the incident, Myōe avidly and repeatedly searched the Buddhist sutras, looking for lists of beings in attendance at the historical Buddha's sermons and hoping to find his name recorded there.

In other words, Myōe believed that his sacrificial act may have accomplished a feat of textual transubstantiation and that he might find his name forcibly inserted into the sutras he so diligently studied, as if severing his ear could suture his name. Significantly, after dismembering himself, Myōe had a dream in which an Indian priest came to him, verbally acknowledged his chosen marking as the act of a bodhisattva, and then gave him two pieces of paper with seals attesting to the merit of his deed. In a way, Myōe finally got what he wanted: written proof that the Buddha recognized him, individually and by name, as a worthy disciple.[2]

Myōe's story suggests an intense interest in the correlation between devotional body and sacred text in medieval Japan. His narrative underscores the importance of excavating a sense of Buddhist textual culture as a crucial tool for understanding Buddhism's incredible spread from India throughout South and East Asia to Japan and, once on the archipelago, its permeation of Japanese culture between the ninth and thirteenth centuries. While Myōe's act was indeed an extreme one, his performance of excess resonates deeply with, and draws its inspiration from, persistent Buddhist ideas about the status of the physical body, the efficacy of the sutras, and the power of devotion to compose and recompose the human frame. These ideas are ingrained at the level of the sentence, the phrase, and the word, observable in rhetorical patterns that Buddhist scriptures (sutras) and various sutra-inspired literary genres frequently echo and elaborate. Some of the most common figures that this study explores include the notion that the body is a vessel that may be filled either with purity or with filth, the trope that suggests that remembering something is analogous to holding it in the hands, the equation of sacred text with bodily relic, and the concept that a paradigmatic act of reading involves centripetal movement around the text, spinning around the sutra like stars around a pole rather than "skimming" over its surface like a rock skipped across water. My aim is to identify and explore formal aspects of Buddhist rhetoric that are particularly tenacious—persisting across linguistic, temporal, geographical, and generic bounds—and that can therefore speak more generally to Mahāyāna Buddhist notions of the power and presence of the written word.

At its heart, this book is about trying to understand how a Japanese monk at the end of the twelfth century could strike upon the fascinating conviction that cutting off his ear might miraculously rewrite scripture. To speak in more expansive terms, however, this book is also an examination of the imaginative life of sacred text, seeking to answer questions about how Mahāyāna Buddhist scriptures imagine themselves to work as literary narratives, and about how these ideas get taken up in the popular imagination, for instance, in miracle tales attesting to the efficacy and power of sutras. While extreme, Myōe's act was not an aberration. Myōe, after all, was neither the first religious figure, nor the only one of his time, to act on a deeply held belief that moments and habits of devotional intensity could bridge human body and sacred text, pointing to them not as discrete from one another but rather as nodes along a shared material continuum. This book will introduce many of these people, some decidedly "real" in the historical sense—Kūkai (774–835), Chōgen (1126–1203), Dōgen (1200–1253), and Nichiren (1222–82), for instance—some clearly literary Everymen—the chanting hermit, the Unbelieving Man—and yet others who represent fanciful composites of the real and the ideal.

By exploring the texture of Buddhist language about textuality—reading it closely for patterns and resonance, describing it "thickly" in the context of a specific medieval genre (*setsuwa,* or "explanatory tales"), examining how it informs ritual action—this study documents the various ways in which characters (whether historical or fictional) in medieval narratives responded to the urgings of figurative language, often literalizing that rhetoric in the specificities of their practice. For instance, a medieval copyist might respond to scriptural assertions of a golden-skinned buddha by writing the word "buddha" in gold ink every time he encounters it in the sutra he is reproducing.

My interest, then, is in the "form" of Buddhist texts, in both senses of the word. On the one hand, this study ponders the formal elements of Buddhist literature (primarily sutras and setsuwa) looking for the rhetorical logic crystallized in the elements of metaphor, metonym, tone, and synecdoche and tracing the implications of narrative strategies, including metafictional gestures in which the text reaches beyond itself to include the reader as character. On the other hand, this study is also concerned with the concrete forms that these figurative, literary gestures engender, including a range of calligraphic practices (gilded sutras, sutra text in the shape of stupas, etc.), as well as various material formats for text such as the scroll, the booklet, the CD, and the sutra library. The flow of this book reflects this methodology. Early chapters begin by reading widely in a given genre (sutra or setsuwa) to identify figurative patterns and to uncover how those genres work on the level of language. Later chapters then closely explore specific literary passages that take up, amplify, transmit, or redirect those patterns before ultimately examining instances in which the figurative patterns erupt into the material world. In this way I chart the trajectory of what Gregory Schopen has called the Mahāyānic "cult of the book" as it takes shape in medieval Japan.[3]

If, as Schopen and others have argued, Mahāyāna Buddhism (as imagined in the pages of sutras and as practiced in much of East Asia) can be characterized as a "cult of the book," then it behooves us to pay close attention to the specific language those books (the sutras) employ, the material formats in which their devotees may encounter them, and the particular ways in which these linguistic and material aspects signify as they travel across continents, centuries, and tongues. These are precisely the types of query that studies of textual culture seek to answer. By "textual culture" I mean to indicate three interrelated lines of inquiry. On the linguistic level, textual culture refers to the particular rhetorical tools by which a text or set of related texts (here, Mahāyāna sutras and the Japanese miracle tales they inspire) seeks to shape the conditions of its own reception and reproduction. These tools may include direct commands that the text makes of its readers, promises it resolves for those who treat it properly, and threats made against those who would defame it. More subtly, a text may employ narrative flow and figurative language to guide its readers into a position of receptivity and engagement. On the material level, textual culture speaks to the various forms that text assumes in a given time and place (here, medieval Japan), including techniques of calligraphy and illumination, for instance, or a choice between types of container such as scroll, booklet, or codex. On the level of performance, textual culture concerns the conventions, techniques, and practices that people utilized (or imagined utilizing) to engage with texts. In our case, these include reading, chanting, circumambulation, memorization, and the giving of offerings.

Although Japanese scholars have recently begun to explore questions of textual culture, their work primarily concerns developments dating to the Tokugawa period (1600–1868) or later.[4] Likewise, a number of Western-trained scholars have produced several masterful studies of Chinese and Japanese print culture, but these, too, tend to deal mostly with the early modern period.[5] One of the major contributions of this book, then, is that it seeks to extend our understanding of textual culture back into the premodern period. In this endeavor, I draw on a full range of textual studies scholarship, a field that has developed largely out of the interaction between modern bibliographical studies (the thought processes undergirding the creation of critical editions) and the thorny realities of medieval European texts. As developed in this realm, the scholarship of textual culture weaves itself from three main strands: the history of the book, the sociology of text, and the ontology of the written word.

Historians of the book[6] seek to understand when and how major revolutions in the material form of written knowledge occurred and to describe the cultural impacts of those material changes. Motivated especially by the turn to digital and virtual media, these scholars historicize this contemporary revolution with respect to the two most recent major switches in bookish materiality: the move from the rolled scroll to the bound codex, and the move from the manuscript to the printed book. Because revolutions in European book culture frequently link to the rise of a literary vernacular, histories of the book often function simultaneously as national histories.[7]

A second angle onto textual culture has developed out of theoretical concerns adhering to the production of critical editions.[8] Scholarship on the "textual condition" or the "sociology of text," as this field is sometimes called, focuses on the production of literary texts and particularly on the instability of the material text as it undergoes changes in format, punctuation, page layout, page breaks, illustration or illumination, paper quality, size, shape, and so forth. By focusing attention on these details and the social conditions that give rise to their appearance and interpretation, this line of study attempts to understand the ways in which "a 'text' is not a 'material thing' but a material event or set of events, a point in time (or a moment in space) where certain communicative interchanges are being practiced."[9]

Finally, a third approach to textual culture inquires into the "ontological status" of literature,[10] the problematic locale of which can be easily apprehended by considering the prototypical question "If the *Mona Lisa* is in the Louvre, where are *Hamlet* and *Lycidas?* What is the essential physical basis of a literary work of art?"[11] In other words, a sculpture consists of stone, and a painting consists of canvas and pigment, whereas a poem does not consist (or does not consist only) of any single instance of black ink on white paper. Part of the issue is that a work of literature typically exists in multiple copies and variants in a way that sculptures and most paintings do not.[12] In addition, a poem may exist in other registers that are independent of material form (for instance, a memorized poem or a poem that exists only in the moments of its oral performance).

What each of these realms of inquiry shares is an attention to the relationship between the language of a text (its "linguistic code," the literary tropes it employs), the material form of a text (its "bibliographic code" of ink color, paper quality, etc.), and the way these two factors combine in social, ritual, or liturgical contexts to produce meaning. In the course of this book, I make several innovations into these theoretical concerns. First, by attempting to explore not Japanese textual culture but *Buddhist* textual culture (primarily as articulated in Japan, a cultural inheritor of Indic and Sinic practices), this book attempts to think about textual culture as an enterprise that exists before, beyond, and between nation.[13] To that end, my arguments pursue a transnational, transcultural, diasporic notion of textual culture and practice that privileges modes of spiritual engagement over and above those of national identity and language. In this way, I seek to understand the "mystery of the Sacred Word"[14] in tandem with an appreciation of how that mystery might be parsed into written letters (whether Chinese or Japanese), intellectual sense, and the full range of embodied sensual engagement that constitutes faith.

Second, while "textual condition" scholarship focuses critical attention on modern works of literature (primarily poetry), the ideas generated by this field of inquiry suggest interesting approaches that can be brought into dialogue with anthropological and performance-based models of communication,[15] both of which afford a better purchase on textual conditions and traditions that diverge from modernist high literary aesthetics. This book brings anthropological, performance-based, and textual approaches into conversation with one another, manipulating, changing, and extending them as necessary, in order to consider religious text as a species of the literary that coheres at the nexus of ritual, liturgy, and the aesthetic.

Third, studies of the "ontology" of text likewise have typically focused on certain kinds of literature, most often poetry and, more specifically, poetry composed in the heavily Christian cultures of Europe and North America. In this book, I think through the notion of textual ontology in a Buddhist context. I devote one chapter (the first) exclusively to parsing the ontological status of sutras, and later chapters proceed by examining practices of sutra memorization, chanting, and copying in order to illustrate the ways in which Buddhism posits the voice as a "musical shuttle" (to borrow a term from Walt Whitman) that has the power to weave together the page and the embodied mind as interpenetrating locales for the inscription of sacred text.[16] Thus, I argue that, in addition to the page, one of the other places a sutra may be said to "exist" is in human memory.

Finally, this book negotiates the tension between what David Kastan has called the "platonic" and the "pragmatic" views of textuality, the former of which concerns the work as transcendent of all material forms and the latter of which scrutinizes a text as always associated with specific material iterations (paper, ink, binding, etc.).[17] While, platonically speaking, a text is not commensurate with any one of its material forms and therefore exists in a world apart, practically speaking, in order to be seen or heard, it must manifest as a material object. The coming chapters begin with a more platonically inflected approach: How do Mahāyāna sutras ask to be read? How do they seek to direct and shape the ways in which their devotees encounter them? What literary tools do sutras employ to insist on their existence beyond the written page? But even these more abstract questions quickly point to evidence of textual anxiety—what Roger Chartier has called the "fear of obliteration"[18]—which can only speak to an awareness of the transience and mutability of material forms, of text as embodied in particular material objects. Sutras worry about being burned, forgotten, excerpted and abridged, appropriated by other religious groups, and so forth. Thus, this study becomes increasingly concerned with the "pragmatic" aspects of textual experience, exploring the ways in which medieval sermons establish texts (particularly didactic texts such as sutras and, to an extent, setsuwa) as acting on, in, and as bodies.

SUTRAS THROUGH *SETSUWA*

My primary source for speaking about Buddhist textual culture in medieval Japan is the genre of setsuwa (literally "explanatory tales"). Often used in sermons to illustrate points of doctrine, setsuwa were also compiled into a number of literary collections between the ninth and thirteenth centuries in Japan, the same time span during which Buddhism moved beyond the court and came to permeate all levels of Japanese society. Most scholars who have written about setsuwa have connected them to oral and folkloric traditions, placed them in a chronology of Japanese national literature, mined them for hagiographic or quasi-historical information about certain people, places, and practices, or used them to chart the growth and development of Japanese popular religious culture.[19] In addition, there have been several excellent annotated translations of setsuwa into English with introductory material that provides important social and cultural context.[20] Each of these approaches is valuable in its own right, and this study takes much information and inspiration from all of them while being oriented along somewhat different lines.

To put it succinctly, my interest lies with textual culture as a Buddhist enterprise assuming particularity in medieval Japan; setsuwa are the records that provide the most elaborate and well-attested evidence of this cultural interaction. I argue that "explanatory tales," as a popular genre, record various attempts by Japanese devotees to understand and to capture the essence of Buddhist scripture, often in a vernacular and colloquial language. Although there are literary precedents for explanatory tales in both India *(jātaka* and *avadāna)* and China *(zhi guai* and Buddhist miracle tales, often denoted by the titular *yan ji),* medieval Japan produced the most richly varied and enduring tradition.[21] When viewed alongside canonical sutra texts, these popular stories throw into sharp relief cultures and practices of reading, and they suggest particular ways of understanding the relation between reader and written text. In essence, I treat setsuwa as a repository, constituent, and matrix of "textual community." As Martin Irvine notes, "A textual community is formed by the two dimensions of the social function of texts, which are as inseparable as the two sides of a sheet of parchment—a received canon of texts [here, sutras] and an interpretive methodology articulated in a body of commentary [here, setsuwa] which accompanied the texts and instituted their authority."[22] Though elucidating textual culture is my foremost objective, this study also comprises the first synchronic view in English of setsuwa as a genre. Thus, I devote an entire chapter (chapter 2) to situating Buddhist setsuwa as a literary genre with its roots in the performance of sermons.

While I treat the genres of setsuwa and sutras at greater length later, it may be helpful to provide some brief context at the outset. The first sutras entered Japan in the form of classical Chinese-language translations, and so they have remained, despite an awareness of both the presence of Sanskrit originals and the potential for translation into Japanese. This situation has impacted the textual culture of sutras in Japan in several ways. Perhaps most immediately, in a practical sense, it meant that there was a considerable gap between sound and sense. George Tanabe describes the situation succinctly, noting that the chanting of Chinese-language sutras in Japan "produces sounds that cannot be recognized as regular spoken language. The *Heart Sutra,* for example, is popular in East Asia as a Chinese text about emptiness, a fundamental Mahāyāna teaching, but when it is chanted in Japan, each Chinese character is given a Japanese pronunciation without any change in the Chinese grammatical word order of the text. The audible result is neither Japanese nor Chinese, but a ritual language unto itself."[23] While chanting the sutras remained an important part of liturgy and an aesthetic pursuit in its own right, for instructional purposes sutra chanting was accompanied with sermons (Jp: *sekkyō,* "explaining the sutras," or *seppō,* "explaining the dharma").[24] Few of these sermons were recorded in toto, and so our best records of medieval sermonizing come to us in the form of literary collections of setsuwa.[25]

The word *setsuwa,* as applied to literature, is a relatively modern coinage and has been used to indicate an entire range of literature, both oral and written.[26] Thus, some collections classified by modern scholars as setsuwa are not explicitly Buddhist, being oriented more toward stories related to a particular locale (Yoshino or Uji, for instance) or compiling more broadly stories detailing the arts and courtly culture (as with Ōe no Masafusa's *Gōdanshō* of

1111). To speak more precisely, then, I am concerned with what Japanese scholars, at their most prolix, call "Buddhist setsuwa literature" (Jp: *bukkyō setsuwa bungaku*). Thus, in the pages of this study, the word *setsuwa* should be taken to refer to collections that treat obviously Buddhist material and that link themselves to the public venue of the sermon. Some collections, such as *A Wondrous Record of Immediate Karmic Retribution for Good and Evil in Japan* (ca. 823), state their desire to act like a preacher, "pull[ing] people forward" with their words and guiding them onto the Buddhist path (NKBZ 10: 245). Others, like *The Three Jewels* (984) and *A Companion in Solitude* (1222), bring sermon material to recently tonsured women. Some, like *Notes Taken While Listening to One Hundred Sessions of Sermons* (ca. 1110), are based on a transcription of multiday sermonizing events, while yet others comprise compilations of a preacher's favorite material (*A Collection of Sand and Pebbles,* compiled starting in 1279 and put into complete form in 1284) or include parenthetical remarks that may name the preacher from whom the compiler heard the story (*A Collection of Spiritual Awakenings,* 1214–15).

In seeking to understand the textual culture of sutras through the lens of medieval Japanese setsuwa, we must be sensitive to some important points. First, setsuwa are an admittedly didactic genre. They seek to instruct and to ✓ guide thought, speech, and action down very particular paths. Their attempts to persuade and encourage exert a steady pull on their narratives, and thus any depictions of textual engagement (reading, writing, chanting, etc.) must be taken with a grain of salt. A second, and related, point is that setsuwa speak to the exemplary, the miraculous, and the ideal. Thus, their narratives are not absolutely reliable as records of "what actually happened." They are, rather, articles of faith and conviction in the modal sense: nuanced evocations of ✓ what *could* have, *should* have, *ought* to have, or *may* have happened. It is this modal sense that I seek to remind us of when I speak of "the imagination" or "the imaginary."

A third consideration has to do with the extent to which setsuwa can be described as a "popular" genre. On the one hand, the poetic conventions of aristocratic culture clearly leave their mark on many setsuwa collections, most obviously those compilations generated during the genre's heyday in the late tenth to early twelfth century. During this period, most compilers of setsuwa collections—and arguably most readers of them—were of aristocratic origin and remained associated with the courtly culture of the arts. What this means is that setsuwa compilers were writing for, and as, people who had a finely trained eye for metaphoric detail and a density of allusion. The earliest extant collections (*A Wondrous Record of Immediate Karmic Retribution for Good and*

Evil in Japan) and the last one I survey here (*A Collection of Sand and Pebbles*) do not weave such an intricate brocade, but these are atypical. Thus, while many of the narratives preserved in setsuwa collections were undoubtedly utilized in public sermons, it is not clear to what extent the compilers embroidered their texts as they recorded them for more restricted, aristocratic audiences.

There is no reason to assume, however, that the metaphors I discuss here, even if perhaps less rhetorically complex in more widely popular contexts, were any less poignant. For instance, sutras may speak of the dharma as a gentle soaking rain, as in the "Medicinal Herbs" chapter of the *Lotus Sutra*. Clearly taken by the sensuality of the image, elite authors could revel in this evocative liquidity, as Genshin (942–1017) does when he writes on the essence of the "Medicinal Herbs" chapter: "The vast sky / doesn't choose where to rain / but / each grass and tree gets wet / with a difference."[27] Rural farmers soaking in warm baths while reciting buddhas' names, however, surely felt the metaphor at work just as viscerally.[28] Again, while the courtier Fujiwara no Yorimichi (992–1074) constructed an entire villa (the Byōdōin) around a body of water, based on the metaphor of the dharma as a raft that carries one to the other shore of nirvana, pedestrians enjoying monk-constructed bridges surely were impacted by the metaphor in equally sensual, if more utilitarian, ways.[29] Given the ubiquity of Buddhist participation in these sorts of public works projects in medieval Japan and their connection to almsgiving campaigns, there is good reason to suppose that, even in the least literary and most impromptu of sermons, Buddhist figural language played an important and enduring role in communicating the teachings to a broad popular audience.

As a genre, setsuwa makes sweeping commedia-like gestures, providing glimpses of courtiers and beggars, the young and the elderly, the lusty and the restrained, the naively intuitive and the aesthetically polished. And in the performance context of public Buddhist services, setsuwa played to a wide audience indeed. Konishi Jin'ichi notes, for instance, that the congregations for such services were "all inclusive: both sexes, all social classes, and laity as well as clergy were in attendance. . . . Public Buddhist services provided the people with one form of entertainment during [the early medieval] period." And he even suggests that on such occasions temples became something like "city colleges where people learned new Chinese loanwords and characters in the course of being entertained" and edified.[30] While appealing to popular audiences, then, written setsuwa also modulate among elite traditions of Japanese poetic discourse and attendant norms of composition (humility topoi, allusive variation, and citation from Chinese-language sutras with their references to Indic terms, concepts, places, and persons). There is no simple way to parse elite from popular here; there are only subtle variations in the techniques used to negotiate and shuttle among these various modes and their attendant hierarchies of authenticity.

In the final analysis, sutras and setsuwa work together to leverage people into a position of spiritual receptivity and to instruct them how to engage in the devotional praxes of reading, reciting, copying, and worshipping sutras. Both genres maintain that sustained contact with Buddhist scripture has the power to bring about miraculous changes in the devotee's physical reality, drawing attention to the materiality of sutra texts and their physical reception in the human body. Setsuwa on the topic of sutras reveal that sutra reading was (and remains) a visceral process, sensual and fantastic, involving an almost chemical reaction between body and sutra text in the course of which both are transformed in specific ways (the sutra may come alive, for instance, and the body may fill with light or be cured of illness).

CONCERNING MIRACLES

If setsuwa are "explanatory tales," then more often than not what they seek to explain are instances and eruptions of the miraculous. My understanding of miracles draws from the work of two scholars of the unusual in medieval culture. Caroline Walker Bynum's treatment of miracles associated with the Eucharist in medieval Europe is useful in thinking about the ways in which miracles, while never to be expected, may nevertheless be courted. Prayer, fasting, self-mutilation, going without sleep—all are methods by which a practitioner might situate herself in a position of receptivity to the miraculous. Similar techniques apply in medieval Japan: wakefulness, prayer, pilgrimage, training of the memory—all of these are known methods through which a devotee might seek a miraculous sign. Of course, doubt and suspicion may also elicit the miraculous, in which case the strange and shocking event is meant not to encourage further suspicion but rather to allay it.

Again, Robert Campany's discussion of anomaly accounts in medieval China is instructive. He points to the taxonomic drive behind recording instances of the anomalous and the role of "human agents within communities" in sorting events and objects into typical and atypical "with reference to some reigning worldview, system, or ideology."[31] As Campany reminds us, remarking the atypical constitutes a way of describing the world and therefore exploring accounts of the anomalous from particular times and places can help us sketch the contours of that culture's concept of the cosmos and how it works.

I want to clarify further two specific attributes of miracles as I understand
them here. First, miracles typically elicit positive responses. As Campany notes,
anomalies may be received in a variety of fashions: they may be suppressed,
ignored, ridiculed, and so forth. Miracles, as depicted in sutras and setsuwa,
are a specific kind of anomaly to which the recipient responds with elation
and welcome, or at least the relief of being given a second chance. Second,
miracles are not aberrations. They are, rather, instances in which the core workings of the world are revealed in a sudden and (miraculously) observable fashion. In this sense, like Buddhist-inflected *zhi guai* (strange tales) of medieval
China, the setsuwa of medieval Japan "aim to domesticate Buddhist tradition . . . , to weave it tightly into the fabric of [Japanese] society and implant
it into the very landscape . . . , demonstrating its efficacy on [Japanese] soil
despite its foreign provenance"—in the case of Japan, a doubly foreign provenance from India and then China.[32]

Setsuwa relay numerous accounts of miracles associated with the reading,
memorization, worship, and circulation of Buddhist scripture, thereby validat-
ing the accuracy of the teachings those scriptures contain, displaying the efficacy of the sutras (both as abstract teachings and as concrete objects), and
claiming for them an authority that, while foreign, is anchored firmly to Japanese soil. Miracles are instances in which abiding concepts about the true nature of reality show forth in stark, sensually confirmable ways, like the tip of
a volcanic island jutting suddenly above the ocean's surface, thereby revealing
the workings of unseen tectonic plates deep below. Geology can tell us where
to expect new islands, though we may still be surprised and amazed by particular instances of their appearance. Similarly, rhetorical patterns and narrative structures can alert attentive readers to the immanence of miracles of book
and body, though we may still wonder over the curious particularities of individual stories.

LITERARY BUDDHISM

Buddhism, even when restricted to Mahāyāna Buddhism, is an enormous subject, and there is always the danger of treating it as monolithic. There is, of
course, any number of ways of dividing this gigantic rock into more manage-
able portions, and by far the most common method of division is sectarian in
nature. This is the tack favored by historians and religious studies scholars and
others who wish to speak of Tendai, Shingon, Kegon, Pure Land, or Zen Buddhism. In this book, however, I take a different approach. I am, by training
and avocation, a literary scholar, and as such I have focused this study on the

literary aspects of Mahāyāna Buddhism. In considering sutras, my first con- ✓
cern is how those texts use language, the figures they employ, the narrative ex- ✓
pectations they engender, the readers they imagine. As Alan Cole has noted, ✓
despite a "stable resistance to thinking about" Mahāyāna sutras in literary
terms, these texts do in fact operate "at a fairly sophisticated level of symbolic
exchange," and it makes sense to pay close attention to how they function *as
literature*.[33] To that end, the first chapter of this book focuses on excavating ✓
some of the symbols and structures through which sutras build themselves into
narratives of meaning, paying special attention to the metacommentary that
sutras offer about how they should be read and about the place of reading vis-
à-vis other methods of textual engagement, such as recitation and circumambulation. By the same token, I understand the medieval Japanese genre of ✓
setsuwa as a literary effort to come to terms with, and to celebrate, the notions of textuality and literariness that sutras posit.

My choice to foreground the rhetorical and to downplay the sectarian has
solid precedent. While some sutras are more popular in certain Buddhist
schools than in others (the *Sutra of Meditation on the Buddha Amitāyus* in
Pure Land schools, for instance, or the *Vimalakīrti* in Zen schools), none is
the exclusive property of any particular sect, and some sutras, particularly the
Lotus, are ubiquitous. Setsuwa are similarly cross-sectarian in nature. *Notes
Taken While Listening to One Hundred Sessions of Sermons,* for instance, consists of sermons delivered by preachers from at least three different sectarian
orientations (Tendai, Hossō, and Kegon); *The Three Jewels* discusses rites and
ceremonies held at Mount Hiei (Tendai), Yakushiji (Hossō), Hokkeji (Shingon Ritsu), Daianji (Shingon), and Tōdaiji (Kegon) among others; and
through his *Collection of Sand and Pebbles* the nominally Rinzai Zen monk
Mujū accepts Hōnen's (1133–1212) Pure Land recitation of the *nenbutsu* on
a par with Enni's (1202–80) seated meditation, speaking as a "voice for pluralism."[34] While they may be put to sectarian uses, then, sutras and setsuwa ✓
are manifestly trans-sectarian genres.

DEFINING THE "MEDIEVAL"

Temporally speaking, the setsuwa considered in this study span the ninth
through the thirteenth centuries in Japan; the first major Buddhist collection
(A Wondrous Record of Immediate Karmic Retribution) was compiled in the
820s, and the last *(Collection of Sand and Pebbles)* was completed in the 1280s.
Historians of Japan will recognize this range as corresponding to the Heian
(794–1185) and Kamakura (1185–1333) periods. I have chosen to refer to

this temporal period as "medieval" (Jp: *chūsei*) for several reasons. First, however imprecise the mapping may be, the term "medieval" means something to the general reader, whereas "Heian" and "Kamakura" communicate little to a reader not already familiar with Japanese history. The other option, "ninth through thirteenth centuries," I employ on occasion, but what it offers in precision it lacks in concision, and I generally opt for the more economical "medieval." More specifically, in using "medieval" I point to literature and the literary as the basis of this study. "Heian" and "Kamakura" are place names referring to the political capitals of Japan, and to use them as temporal categories to parse literature suggests that literature is a handmaiden to history, inevitably determined by political contingencies. To be sure, a relation between changing historical realities and literary developments exists but, as a specialist in literature, I prefer to think of it as more of a reciprocal exchange. By rejecting "Heian" and "Kamakura" in favor of "medieval," I mean to signal that literature provides the foremost element under consideration in this study.

Further, my interest is to identify and examine abiding concepts, figures, and metaphors in a body of literature (setsuwa) pertaining to textual culture. Particular stories may appear in multiple collections spanning centuries—both *The Three Jewels* of 984 and *Tales from Times Now Past* (ca. 1120) repeat stories from *A Wondrous Record of Immediate Karmic Retribution* (ca. 823), for instance—suggesting a sustained interest in specific ideas and a stability to ways of expressing those ideas in language. Rather than entertain a diachronic attitude, such as might be inhered in the use of "ninth through thirteenth centuries," I intend the term "medieval" to gesture to this relatively stable, underlying "shape."[35] This usage of "medieval" typifies some scholarly writing on Japanese literature. For Konishi Jin'ichi, whose work has been influential in shaping literary periodization of Japanese works in the West, the core identifying characteristic of medieval literature in Japan consists of a mature relationship to continental culture—primarily the influences of Buddhism and Chinese poetry—which had been accepted, adapted, and integrated with indigenous norms. Rajyashree Pandey similarly observes that, "In Japan there was no written literary tradition predating the advent of Buddhism, and the introduction of a written script from China went hand in hand with the encounter with Buddhist canonical writing," resulting in a "religo-aesthetic tradition, in which aesthetics could not be defined outside of Buddhism."[36] This tradition, she argues, dominates medieval poetics, a contention that many have endorsed but few have explored in detail.

Finally, my usage of "medieval" coincides with recent work on specific types of Japanese Buddhist praxis. For some time it was common to posit a break in Buddhism between its earlier incarnations in the sixth through twelfth centuries and a "new" "Kamakura" Buddhism that increasingly stressed simplification of praxis, salvation in doxis, and a tendency to cohere around powerful individual personalities. These changes in Buddhism, the argument goes, were spurred by two key factors: the advent of *mappō* (the final age of the dharma) in 1052 C.E. and the political shift from aristocratic to warrior rule, which involved a relocation of the capital from Heian to Kamakura and entrained widespread cultural upheaval. Many studies over the past twenty years, however, point instead to numerous points of continuity between "Heian" and "Kamakura" Buddhism and maintain that many of the presumed changes to Buddhism in the Kamakura period had long-established precedents in earlier centuries.[37] Setsuwa, and the general liturgy of public Buddhist services in which setsuwa were employed, are but one of the many sources that suggest the power of this continuity, the broad brushstroke of which is "medieval."

A NOTE ON SOUTH ASIAN AND CHINESE MATERIALS

As coming chapters will show, Japanese setsuwa make specific claims about the benefits of textual engagement, about the text as a sort of body, and about the possibilities of embodied reading. In this, the authors of Japanese tales were not creating out of thin air but were interpreting, adapting, and extending concepts, structures, ideas, and tropes that came to them from Chinese and Indian Buddhist literature. Sutras were one genre of Buddhist writing that traveled from India to Japan, via Chinese translations and sometimes the good graces of Korean envoys, and portions of sutra narratives at times found expression in vernacular miracle tales. Such is the case, for instance, with the story of the "Himalaya Boy" (Jp: Sessen Dōji), which I discuss at length in later chapters and which can be found in the *Nirvana Sutra*. Minamoto no Tamenori, author of *The Three Jewels* (984), chose the story to appear in the opening section of his setsuwa collection, where it is part of a sequence of tales treating the former lives of the Buddha.

In fact, stories of the Buddha's former incarnations (Sk: *jātaka*) and the larger literary class to which such stories belong, karmic biographies (Sk: *avadāna*), featured prominently among the earliest strata of Indian Buddhist literature to be translated into Chinese, starting in the middle of the 3rd century C.E., where they continued to be used as materials for sermonizing.[38] In China, these stories combined with native narrative forms, most prominently that of "strange tales" (Ch: *zhi guai*), to produce, between the fourth and the tenth centuries C.E., a vibrant genre of miracle tale literature. These Chinese collections of miracle tales were circulating in Japan by at least the eighth century, and a number of the stories in the earliest extant Japanese setsuwa collection (*Nihon Genpō Zen'aku Ryōiki, A Wondrous Record of Immediate Karmic Retribution for Good and Evil in Japan,* ca. 823) seem to be based upon textual antecedents from a Chinese collection (*Mingbao Ji, Records of Supernatural Retribution,* ca. 653–55).

My point, then, is not to show how all these genres (sutra, *jātaka, avadāna*) worked in India or China, but simply to point out that some of the concerns I locate in the Japanese tradition had been raised earlier, in Chinese and South Asian works. Any Chinese or South Asian texts I reference in this study, therefore, have been selected simply and strictly because the ideas they express receive important attention and elaboration later, in Japan. Thus, though I do at times make brief reference to South Asian materials and practices, I do so simply for the purpose of suggesting areas of resonance, possibilities of continuity, and opportunities for potential future research.

OVERVIEW

Each of the succeeding chapters approaches the relation between book and body from a different angle, with the central question remaining: how does Buddhist rhetoric, as materialized on the written page, work on human bodies? Perhaps not unexpectedly, as I wrote this book, I began to think of its structure as analogous to that of a human body. Chapters 1 and 2 function like the skin, that most public of surfaces, the external membrane that encloses us, represents us to the world, and provides the sensual plane of our interactions with others. These "skin" chapters explore the generic dimensions of the two key genres shaping Buddhist discourse in medieval Japan: the sutras and the "explanatory tales" (setsuwa) that seek to interpret the sutras into specificity, the here and now of named people and places, of (usually) Japanese people on (often) Japanese soil. The first chapter examines the metafictional elements of sutras, the way these elements work together to create agency and presence, and the directives toward which sutras turn this authority when they ask their devotees to accept, keep, read, recite, copy, worship, and expound them. The second chapter explores setsuwa as an art form that moves between literature and performance, and establishes a medieval context for setsuwa texts.

To continue the analogy, chapters 3 and 4 are what medieval Japanese might term the *shinkan* (literally, "heart and liver") of the study. They are what bring it internal life and vivacity, the specificity of the interior. These chapters focus on setsuwa that concern sutras and their devotees. Chapter 3 explores how setsuwa sketch an inverse relation between body and text, such that as the body decays in sickness and death, text begins to cohere and unify: composition balanced against decomposition. Chapter 4 builds off this discussion, describing the various ways in which the sutra fragment is able to incorporate into a humanoid form (that is, both *in* and *as* a human body). This chapter considers statuary, chirographic practice, and literary evidence to argue that, in the medieval imagination, the voice served as a "musical shuttle" coursing between body, mind, and scroll.[39]

The conclusion then provides the skeletal structure, the spine. In it I examine a pivotal metaphor for textuality in the Buddhist tradition, that of "turning the wheel of the dharma" (Sk: *dharma cakra pravartana;* Jp: *tenbōrin*) The study culminates in an appraisal of Buddhist technologies of reading that typically spin text around a central axis, suggesting the same motion as, though perhaps a greater freedom of movement than, the twisting of flesh around the spine and evoking a similarly embodied practice.

My argument proceeds from the idea that the written text of the sutras and ✓ the human body are comparable sites. As Myōe understood, both book and text are fragile, mutable, subject to decay and decomposition—in short, they are exemplary sites for encountering central Buddhist teachings on suffering, impermanence, and detachment. I argue further that the human body and the ✓ sacred text are not distinct from one another, but rather occupy interpenetrating spheres. Sacred text can and does take on human form, and humans can and do transform their physical bodies into both the implements necessary to write down sacred text (skin as paper, blood as ink, bones as stylus, hair as brush tip) and ultimately into repositories of sacred text. *Miracles of Book and Body: Buddhist Textual Culture and Medieval Japan* shows that, through extended devotional activity, the body becomes a sutra scroll around ✓ which the skin wraps itself like a silk brocade cover.

ONE

The Ontology of Sutras

THE FINAL CHAPTER OF THE *LOTUS SUTRA* opens on a very curious scene. The bodhisattva Fugen (Sk: Samantabhadra), long abiding in the eastern quarter of the cosmos, has heard that a buddha is preaching the *Lotus Sutra* on Earth. He arrives, with a multitude of beings trailing him, at the foot of the historical Buddha. After circumambulating the Buddha seven times, he announces, "I have come to listen receptively. I beg of the World Honored One to preach [the *Lotus Sutra*] to us!"[1] He immediately follows this request with a question: "After the extinction of the Thus Come One, how may a good man or good woman attain this" *Lotus Sutra?*[2] The Buddha provides a brief answer to Fugen's question, and the bulk of the remainder of the chapter is then given over to the various vows Fugen makes to guard and protect anyone who accepts, keeps, reads, recites, copies, explains, or practices this scripture. In the course of these lengthy praises, Fugen goes so far as to maintain that if a person "forgets a single phrase or a single gāthā [verse] of the *Lotus Sutra,* I will teach him, reading and reciting together with him,"[3] so that he is able to remember it.

What is curious about this scene is that Fugen asks for something he clearly does not need. He arrives in great excitement and requests to hear a sutra that he presumably has not heard before. And yet a mere paragraph later—and still having heard nothing of the sutra—he vows to help other beings study the sutra, which he clearly already has completely memorized, down to the last phrase and verse. In the tiny gap of white space between Fugen's request and his question there is narrative slippage, a textual fissure that allows us to peer more deeply into the motivating concerns and pivotal themes of the sutra. On a narrative level, Fugen's false request produces a litany of desperation rather than the expected preaching of the *Lotus Sutra*. Each of Fugen's vows begins with the prefatory phrase, "In the last five hundred years, in the midst of a muddied, evil age ... if there is anyone ... "[4]

Thus, Fugen's dramatic last-minute appearance underscores two fundamental things about the *Lotus Sutra*. First, it will be exceedingly difficult for any of us who live in this degenerate later age to encounter the sutra, and, second, we can never be certain that the text we have encountered is precisely the *Lotus Sutra* because what we have *of* the sutra consists largely of narrative *about* the sutra: we hear of its powers and its rarity, we hear bodhisattvas and buddhas from other lands praise it, we hear what happens to those who slander it, and so forth. Many of these narrative gestures concentrate on increasing readerly desire while constantly obscuring the object of that desire. Is the sutra called the *Lotus Sutra*—the book I can hold in my hands and read aloud— the same thing as the teaching called the *Lotus Sutra*—the thing Fugen was so eager to hear? I would argue that by denying the simple satisfaction of readerly desire, texts like these involve their readers in an insatiably desirous relationship to writing and, in doing so, thematize the reader-text relationship, marking this as one of the crucial concerns that the text is trying to explore and for which it is trying to script the rules of engagement.

Other scholars, on whose work I build here, have explored the various complicated and compelling ways that Mahāyāna sutras cut across oral and written modes of discourse, navigate between aural and visual sense worlds, and perhaps even disrupt various norms of mainstream Buddhist traditions.[5] This last point, concerning a distinction between Mahāyāna and "mainstream" Buddhism, is tied into an abiding concern in modern scholarship with the origins of the Mahāyāna in India—not the intellectual focus of this book, but an issue that requires some clarification before we can move forward.[6]

IMAGINING THE ORIGINS OF THE MAHĀYĀNA

The last half century has seen multiple attempts to theorize or generalize the origins of the Mahāyāna and to define the core concerns that caused it eventually to split from the Buddhist mainstream. Survey materials, textbooks, and encyclopedia entries often characterize the Mahāyāna as a reform movement that arose out of "dissatisfaction" with perceived "shortcomings in the Theravada tradition," such as a primary concern with "individual salvation" rather than the liberation of all beings.[7] Hirakawa Akira, starting in the 1950s, offers a second approach, stressing the importance of laity and the centrality of stupa worship in the formation of the early Mahāyāna.[8] Though his theses have been heavily criticized and largely disproved, his work may be credited with generating sustained academic conversation about the shape of early Mahāyāna. Responding to Hirakawa, several scholars, particularly beginning in the 1980s and 1990s, advanced a third argument: that the Mahāyāna was "the work of a predominantly monastic order of meditators engaged in strenuous ascetic practices, people asserting, in short, that the Buddha is to be found in and through the realization of the dharma, not the worship of relics."[9] Importantly, this third position re-centers the focus, from stupa to dharma, and reasserts the centrality of the Buddhist teachings as contained in the written sutras. In this sense, it bears a surface similarity to Gregory Schopen's early work on the "cult of the book," which provides a fourth angle on Mahāyāna origins: that the Mahāyāna distinguished itself by establishing cultic centers organized not around stupas, but rather around written sutra texts that were recited, worshipped, honored, and circumambulated.[10]

It is absolutely essential, however, to decouple the question of origins from the culture of books. In his later work, Schopen moves beyond the analysis of the linguistic record (what sutras say) to an analysis of the material record (what given, datable sutra texts look like). He points out that sources do provide evidence of a working "book-cult" in India—manuscripts whose "covering boards or first leaves were often heavily stained and encrusted from continuous daubing with unguents and aromatic powders," for instance—but that this "evidence is almost a thousand years later than it should be" (at least according to his earlier thesis).[11] That is, although the linguistic text of sutras, composed between the first and fifth centuries C.E., seems to call for book worship, material evidence for such worship dates to no earlier than the eleventh to fifteenth centuries C.E. in India. Arguing in a similar vein, Jan Nattier has noted that passages concerning sutra worship are often interpolations, sections and phrases that were stitched into the sutras in their later versions, and she concludes that "the emergence of the Mahāyāna ... does not begin with the cult of the book, but rather culminates in it at some point."[12] The book-cult, then, while perhaps not part of the story of Mahāyāna origins, is nevertheless an aspect of Mahāyāna that became increasingly important over time, and which achieved particular significance in Chinese-language translations of the sutras and in East Asian cultures (such as Japan) that relied on these translations. An examination of the Mahāyāna "cult of the book" thus will tell us not about the Great Vehicle's origins in India but about the movement in some of its localized, East Asian forms.[13]

In addition to distinguishing between the early years of Indian origins and later developments in the sinophone Buddhist sphere, we also need to make a distinction between "what sutras want" and "what sutras were given." Answering the question of what sutras want (for the purposes of this study) is a matter of examining what they ask for, in the Chinese translations that were consulted most often in medieval Japan—what they ask for, *but may or may not have gotten*. Inquiring into what sutras were given is a matter of examining the material record, which will provide evidence concerning when, where, and how sutras' desires were actualized. In response to the first question— "What do sutras want?"—we know that the Chinese translations of Mahāyāna sutras that were circulating in medieval Japan asked for a wide variety of things, including worship, circumambulation, and offerings; they asked to be read, recited, memorized, and held. In response to the second question—"What were sutras given?"—we know that by at least the tenth century in Japan they were being worshipped, read, recited, copied, expounded upon in sermons, and memorized. A similar array of praxes surrounding Mahāyāna sutras may have developed as early as the third or fourth century in China and as late as the eleventh to fifteenth centuries in India. As will become clear, throughout this study references to sutras treat only the first of these questions, the one concerning the abstract, idealized nature of desire as discernable in the linguistic record, while I use Japanese sources (texts written in Japan, using either the Japanese or the Chinese language) to examine questions about the actualization of sutras' desires and traces these actualizations leave in the material record.

To be clear, then, I come to Mahāyāna sutras specifically from the vantage point of medieval Japanese explanatory tales (setsuwa). My general purpose in this and succeeding chapters is to outline the textual attitudes of a certain body of literature that began in India, was translated into Chinese, and was then reinterpreted in Japan. Rather than speaking of the Indian origins of the Mahāyāna, I am interested in the idea of Mahāyāna textual culture as constructed by the authors of Japanese setsuwa. As a medieval genre, setsuwa are an often-miraculous form of literature that assumes sutras are living beings who may incorporate themselves into human form. Thus, my main interest in sutras has to do with exploring three questions. First, how did sutras come to be alive, that is, what narrative tools propel them into life? Second, now that they are alive, what do they want: as living beings, what are their requirements, their equivalent of food and shelter? And finally, what is the nature of the reader-text relationship they propose; in other words, what happens to human beings who decide to give sutras what they ask for? In short, I am interested in examining the rules and the stakes of sutra engagement and how we, as humans and as readers, play into them.

First, how is it that sutras come alive? Mahāyāna sutras use a variety of literary techniques that modern readers might most readily associate with metafiction. Taken collectively, these metafictional strategies impact the ontological status of Mahāyāna sutras in some important ways. The issue of textual ontology can be generally glossed with the oft-quoted question: "If the *Mona Lisa* is in the Louvre, where [is] *Hamlet?*"[14] In other words, where, how, in what plane of action does a literary text exist? I suggest that by obscuring the authorial hand and complicating any notion of a simple origin in oral discourse, Mahāyāna sutras cut themselves off from their point of creation and establish a unique ontology for themselves. Instead of mooring themselves to an external source, as most literature does, Mahāyāna sutras seek to take the authority that might otherwise be invested in an author or in a speaker and invest it in themselves. We see this most plainly in the argument that sutras contain the entire body of the Buddha, and that they are, in fact, the entity that gives birth to buddhas. Mahāyāna sutras thus frame themselves as textual constructs that are alive and eerily self-aware.

Moving forward, now that sutras have a certain sentience, what do they want? I argue that sutras are, in essence, a nervous genre. Aware of their vulnerabilities to the ravages of time and convinced they are always in danger of dying, they evince a strong reproductive drive. Mahāyāna sutras are careful to include within themselves instructions about how they should be propagated, promises of reward for those who agree to do the propagating, and threats to inflict pain on those who do not comply. In short, having successfully placed themselves in a position of agency, sutras speak from this position, demanding very particular things from their readers, only one of which is actually to be read.

Finally, what is the nature of the reader-text relationship that Mahāyāna sutras propose? Here I explore the persistent rhetoric of the "vessel" or "container" through which the mind (Jp: *kokoro*) of the devotee becomes metaphorically linked to two other Buddhist sites: the stupa and the scroll. This word "mind" needs some explanation. Buddhism recognizes six "sense organs" (Jp: *rokkon*, literally the "six roots"): the eye is the sense organ that perceives form; the ear, sound; the nose, scent; the tongue, flavor; the body, the "touch" of external stimulus; and, finally, consciousness perceives dharma, itself a multivalent term that in its more specific instances indicates the Buddhist teachings, and at its most expansive encompasses the true nature of reality, the "laws" of the universe. The salient point here is that "consciousness" is embodied, firmly situated in the flesh. This means that the "mind" (Jp: *kokoro*) is at once the rational and logical center of thought (what in English we might associate with the "brain"), and it is part and parcel of the fabric of our bodies and sensual perceptions (what in English we might associate with the "heart"). This "mind" has a physical locale: it resides somewhere in the region of the chest, a detail that will prove important in the discussions that follow. Whenever I use the word "mind" in this book, this is the entity to which I refer. Considering the reader-text relation, then, ultimately I argue that what Mahāyāna sutras seek is nothing short of a mutually beneficial symbiotic relationship with the human body. In this relationship, the human body serves as a host organism for the sutra-as-symbiont. It is precisely this symbiotic relationship that establishes the ground rules of Mahāyāna textual culture and that becomes the subject of so much miracle literature in medieval Japan.

THE SUTRAS

In this chapter I will be toggling between several early Mahāyāna sutras with the aim of creating a synchronic sketch of the genre as a whole and paying particular attention to what sutras say about their own textuality. All of the sutras I survey here were known in medieval Japan through their classical Chinese translations. My point in treating them as a group is to suggest the degree to which their themes and strategies overlap. I treat Mahāyāna sutras as a literary genre rather than as the intellectual property of any given spiritual school or group of schools. This approach reflects my grounding in setsuwa, a genre that transgresses sectarian bounds.

My basic criterion for deciding what sutras to include in this chapter is whether or not a given sutra appears in setsuwa. The *Lotus Sutra* clearly receives the lion's share of attention, with the Pure Land sutras following in a collective second place and the others considerably further behind. Properly speaking, the *Flower Ornament Sutra,* which I discuss at length below, did not attract much attention in Japanese setsuwa literature, possibly because its length made many forms of popular devotion (memorization, for instance) quite difficult. Nevertheless, when it does appear in the literature, it makes a powerful impact: Myōe (the monk who severed his ear) was a devotee of the *Flower Ornament Sutra.* Further, the sutra is particularly germane to this discussion because it is largely given over to describing the special characteristics of bodhisattvas, distinctions that helpfully illuminate the function of memory in the preservation of sacred text. The only other anomaly is the *Heart Sutra.* Because of its extreme brevity, this sutra was widely memorized and chanted even by illiterate believers.[15] Although the *Heart Sutra* appears frequently in setsuwa literature, its 276 written characters say little about textual culture, so I omit it from my discussion in this chapter.

One distinguishing characteristic of Mahāyāna sutras is that they were composed in the early centuries of the Common Era, nearly half a millennium after the historical Buddha's death. Nevertheless, they all stage themselves as oral discourses, generally with the historical Buddha serving as the main character. The *Lotus Sutra* is typical in this regard and begins by placing the Buddha at Vulture Peak on the Indian subcontinent addressing a vast audience. The sutra centers on a series of lengthy dialogues between the Buddha and various interlocutors, the course of which produces a number of famous parables such as the parable of the burning house, which I mention in passing below. The *Lotus* was translated into Chinese a number of times, most famously by a team of translators led by Kumārajīva (344–413), and it is his translation (T 262) that I refer to in this study.

The *Sutra of Immeasurable Life* and the *Sutra of Meditation on the Buddha Amitāyus* (Jp: Amida) also situate the Buddha in the center of the Indian subcontinent at Vulture Peak in the realm of King Bimbisāra. In the *Sutra of Immeasurable Life,* our historical Buddha, speaking to a large audience primarily through his chief interlocutor and disciple Ānanda, describes how the buddha Amida achieved enlightenment, reiterating that buddha's vows and painting a detailed picture of his Pure Land. This sutra has many translations into classical Chinese, and I refer here to the one by Samghavarman (active third century, T 360). The *Sutra of Meditation on the Buddha Amitāyus* addresses similar subject matter from a different vantage point. While the Buddha has been at Vulture Peak, the son of King Bimbisāra has killed his father and imprisoned his mother, Queen Vaidehī. When Queen Vaidehī calls on the Buddha to aid her, he appears in her prison cell along with Ānanda and he teaches her to visualize the Pure Land of Amida. I reference the translation by Kumārajīva (T 366).

The *Diamond Sutra* and *Nirvana Sutra* move the locale northeast, closer to the base of the Himalayas. The *Diamond Sutra* places the Buddha at the Jetavana Grove in Śrāvastī. The subject consists largely of a dialogue between Buddha and his disciple Subhūti concerning the true nature of reality. Again, I reference the Kumārajīva translation (T 235). The *Nirvana Sutra* stages itself at the nearby town of Kuśinagar under a pair of teak trees in whose shade the Buddha has laid himself down to die. The sutra consists mostly of conversations the Buddha has with his disciples Kāśyapa and Mañjuśri, and a lengthy dialogue with the bodhisattva Lion's Roar, in which he clarifies earlier teachings and explains the nature of nirvana. My references are to the translation by Dharmakṣema (385–433, T 374).

The *Vimalakīrti Sutra* and the *Flower Ornament Sutra* depart from the previous patterns in that the Buddha is not the undisputed main speaker in either. The *Vimalakīrti Sutra* opens with the Buddha at the Amra Gardens in Vaishali near the northeast edge of the Indian subcontinent. Most of the narrative, however, concerns the layman Vimalakīrti, who has taken ill and who uses the opportunity of his illness to preach on a number of topics, most prominently the evanescence of the body. I reference Kumārajīva's translation (T 475). Similarly, although the *Flower Ornament Sutra* begins by placing the historical Buddha on the Indian subcontinent in the eastern kingdom of Magadha, the bulk of the discourse is carried out by "transhistorical, symbolic beings" who often speak through the power of the Buddha.[16] The actual orator at any time may be the Buddha, two buddhas (the speaker and the Buddha who underwrites him), or even a myriad of buddhas all speaking in unison and often all sharing the same name. Early chapters wend from one topic to the next, though most are concerned with the special characteristics of bodhisattvas. The final chapter, which dwarfs most of the others, follows the progress of the devotee Sudhana as he enters into and pursues the bodhisattva path. The scripture was translated, in whole or in part, multiple times into classical Chinese. The one I reference is the lengthier Śikṣānanda (652–710) translation (T 279), though I also consulted the earlier Buddhabhadra (359–429) version (T 278).

As several scholars have pointed out, while Mahāyāna sutras typically situate themselves as the direct discourse of the historical Buddha, they are in fact later compositions. This raises important questions about the literary nature of these texts and the particular ways in which they understand their fictions of place, presence, and orality. In the following sections I take up these arguments, examining the narrative strategies sutras employ and characterizing the genre as a metafictional enterprise.

MAHĀYĀNA AND METAFICTION

Though metafictional elements have occasionally been identified in earlier works, metafiction is most closely associated with postmodernism, and the word itself was not coined until 1960, so it may seem odd that I am characterizing many Mahāyāna sutras, texts that were written in the first centuries of the Common Era, as metafictional. I use the term in the sense articulated by Patricia Waugh, who defines metafiction as "writing which self-consciously and systematically draws attention to itself as artifact in order to pose questions about the relationship between fiction and reality."[17] While she characterizes metafiction as explicitly postmodern, many of the specific techniques she discusses as its core strategies can be found in abundance in Mahāyāna sutras. In addition to its rhetorical style, metafiction also concerns itself with a critique of genre, often calling attention to its own literariness by parodying or departing from oral convention. Thus, metafiction is both a set of narrative strategies and a reaction against a certain temporal frame, a desire to shake things up, to use literature as a way to depart from convention and, by critiquing convention, to create something new. While some may balk at my use of the word "fiction" to describe sacred texts, the point I mean to stress is that Mahāyāna Buddhism was born out of just such a desire to shake things up and that, furthermore, it chose written scripture—literature—as the primary tool through which to orchestrate that upheaval.[18]

Where did Mahāyāna sutras come from? Did they originate in the teachings of the historical Buddha, kept, as some traditional sources maintain, beneath the sea under the watchful eye of the Dragon King until such time as land-loving beings were ready for them? Are they the latter-day revelations of inspired mystics? Or are they the conscious construction of "wily authors"?[19] I think the last two speculations are the more tenable and, in both of these scenarios, Mahāyāna sutras are "fiction" in the sense that they were created and fashioned by human hands. Over the next several pages I will examine the ways in which metafictional strategies obscure the authorial hand while implicitly critiquing the notion that Mahāyāna sutras originate in the oral discourse of the Buddha. By invoking these strategies, sutras invest themselves with authority and begin to address their audiences directly, asking their readers to treat them in certain ways.

Let me be clear. By using the tools of fiction to think about sutras, I do not mean to question either their efficacy or their validity. Rather, I wish to point out two things. First, sutras as we have them today possess a complex textual history that we, as yet, understand imperfectly. Second, sutras employ a rich range of rhetorical and literary techniques. Drawing concerted attention to these may help us to understand better both the medium and the message: how sutras work and what they say. Approaching sutras in this way is a bit like taking apart a pocket watch. The objective is to understand how the watch functions, not to deny the forward march of time whose movement the watch was created to make visible and quantifiable. Assuming that sutras were created in order to make certain things visible, let us then look closely at how they do so.

Mahāyāna sutras make use of a host of metafictional narrative techniques, some of which operate at a surface level while others cut straight to the core of the Mahāyāna as a particular Buddhist path. As one of the more superficial techniques, many sutras make intertextual allusions to other sutras: the *Flower Ornament Sutra* references a sutra named *Voice of the Cycles of Teaching of All Buddhas* (T 10.279.381c19); the *Nirvana Sutra* glosses passages from the *Contemplation Sutra* (T 12.374.474a27 ff. and T 12.374.565.604 ff.) and the *Lotus Sutra* (T 12.374.471a28 ff.); while the *Lotus Sutra* alludes to the *Sutra of Immeasurable Meanings* (T 9.262.2b8), which appears to have been composed after the *Lotus Sutra* in the wake of this imaginative citation. These intertextual references establish a given sutra as a member of a recognized genre of texts. Further, these allusions often serve as the stepping-stone for the sutra at hand to claim its own supremacy, defining itself as containing all the previous teachings *and* going beyond them.

In addition, Mahāyāna sutras often include as part of their narrative passages detailing the reception of that narrative. These descriptions are sprinkled liberally throughout the text, and most sutras conclude with a scene of joyful reception. In fact, these scenes are such a staple of the genre that the *Nirvana Sutra* defines "sutra" as any text that "begins with 'Thus have I heard,' and ends with 'were overjoyed, did obeisance, and departed'" (T 12.374.451b22–23). In this way sutras establish what reactions they anticipate from their audiences. As readers, we are expected to receive the teachings with great happiness, to worship and make offerings to them, to vow to protect them, and to promise to teach them elsewhere in the world. Lest we forget, our role is almost always scripted for us in the final paragraphs of the sutra, so that as we turn from its closing lines to face the world outside, we remember the charge we have been given.

THE TROUBLE WITH ENTRUSTMENT

In a somewhat more complex gesture, Mahāyāna sutras typically include scenes in which the narrative is named and entrusted. In these interludes, the main character (the historical Buddha) charges a secondary character (usually Ānanda, but sometimes Kāśyapa or another disciple) with the duty of preserving and propagating the story in which they both appear. Imagine, for a moment, reading the final chapter of a novel in which a secondary character turns to the protagonist and asks him, "What's the name of this book we're

in, and how would you like me to circulate it after you die?" When the naming and entrustment scene is successful, and when it occurs near the end of
the text, it activates the traditional opening of sutras ("Thus have I heard")
and reminds readers that they have been consuming a frame narrative. Readers can now identify that "I," who disappeared after line one, as a specific character in the story.[20]

This frame narrative also establishes something of a phantom link between
the sutra's authority and its purported origin in the word of the Buddha. The
other metafictional strategies, however, largely work to undermine this tentative link and, in fact, naming and entrustment scenes are at times quite problematic. The *Nirvana Sutra,* for instance, is virtually a case study in everything
that can go wrong with entrustment.[21] Put another way, the sutra showcases
a variety of ways in which a written sutra, by disrupting the smooth functioning of entrustment, can stop being merely the object that is passed around
(orally entrusted by one person to another) and can instead begin to seize authority for itself.

When the *Nirvana Sutra* opens, the Buddha is on his deathbed. Myriad
beings appear, all grieving and wailing that once the Buddha has passed into
extinction, the teachings, too, will begin to die. Responding to these worries,
Buddha encourages the monks in the assembly not to despair, because "I now
entrust [Jp: *fushoku*] all the unsurpassed true dharma to Mahākāśyapa. This
Kāśyapa will henceforth be the one on whom you may rely. Just as the Thus
Come One is the refuge of all beings, so it is with Mahākāśyapa. He is now
your refuge."[22] The monks, however, have something else in mind and they
make a counterproposal, arguing, "If this dharma treasure is entrusted to
Ānanda or any other monk, it will not abide for long. Why is this? Because
all of the voice-hearers including Mahākāśyapa will die. . . . Thus, you should
entrust this unsurpassed buddha dharma to all the bodhisattvas."[23]

At this point in the *Nirvana Sutra* narrative, the Buddha has not even suggested Ānanda as an option, though he was widely regarded in pre-Mahāyānic
tradition as the monk who had heard and remembered more of Buddha's
teachings than any other. The monks' point, though, is that any one of them
may die at any moment, so it would be far safer to entrust the teachings to all
of the advanced practitioners rather than any single person. The Buddha re-
covers quickly from this criticism and praises the monks' forethought, noting that he had already considered this contingency. He accepts their proposal
and formally announces that he hereby entrusts the dharma to all bodhisattvas. The narrative continues, however, as if this protest had never been
lodged, and a few pages later Kāśyapa formally vows to "protect and hold the

true dharma," expounding it widely to all other beings and beating down those who do not have faith in it in the way that hail or frost beats down the tender grasses (T 12.374.382c20–23).

What we have here, in somewhat muted form, is something like a deathbed squabble over the inheritance. To whom will the treasure of the dharma be handed down? At this point, the treasure under discussion is the entire dharma, and not just any single named sutra, so whoever receives the formal assignment stands to become the next leader of the assembly. One faction stands behind Ānanda, another behind Kāśyapa, and yet another espouses pluralism. Though the Buddha, as developed in this sutra, agrees to pluralism in principle, in practice he anoints Kāśyapa. At least for now.

The troubles are not over. Though Kāśyapa may have been chosen as the receptacle for all previous teachings, the Buddha is clearly beginning another sermon. Although naming and entrustment scenes usually happen near the end of sutras, Kāśyapa moves preemptively in this case, asking the Buddha, "O World Honored One, what is this sutra to be called? How should bodhisattva-mahāsattvas make offerings to it and hold it?" (T 12.374.385a2–3). Kāśyapa here positions himself as the keeper of all the Buddha's teachings, up to and including this final dispensation. The Buddha, appearing to accept Kāśyapa's bid, names the sutra that he is in the process of delivering and then returns to his sermon, making a number of provocative points that seem to contradict some of his earlier teachings. Kāśyapa cannot help but point out several of these glitches, and eventually his persistence seems to annoy the Buddha, who replies somewhat testily, "If you have doubts in what I say, you should not be the one to accept [the teaching]!" (T 12.374.397b11), and he counsels Kāśyapa to throw off the deceptions of Māra, the Evil One. Kāśyapa does so and finally agrees to accept the teachings as given. The issue of entrustment appears to be resolved. The sermon draws to a close, and the layman Cunda is chosen to present the last offerings.

At this point, however, Mañjuśri stands up, says that he has some questions, and engages the Buddha in a lengthy conversation, an addendum to the sermon, which Kāśyapa occasionally interrupts. The Buddha concludes the sermon a second time, saying, "Mañjuśri and the rest of you, you should expound the great dharma widely, to all people. Now, I entrust this dharma to you [Mañjuśri] and, when Kāśyapa and Ānanda arrive, you should entrust this true dharma to them, too."[24] Haven so spoken, he lies down on his right side, succumbing again to the pain of his bodily illness.

This second entrustment scene raises a rather thorny question, under which is hidden an equally thorny textual problem. Where has Kāśyapa gone? At several points earlier in the sutra there have been references to the notion that, although virtually all beings in the cosmos appear to be gathered around the Buddha's deathbed, Kāśyapa and Ānanda are missing. In truth, Ānanda has not yet shown up as an active character in the narrative, but, as we have already seen, Kāśyapa has been serving for dozens of pages as Buddha's main interlocutor. He has already been entrusted with (a truncated version of) the *Nirvana Sutra,* he has already clashed with Manjuśri over who will receive the final teaching, and, to make matters particularly perplexing, the Buddha was *just talking to him.* In fact, after a few more chapters (dominated by a dialogue between Buddha and Manjuśri), Kāśyapa will interject himself into the conversation once again, seeming to have been present and listening all the while.

What this snag in the narrative tells attentive readers is that the text of the ✓ *Nirvana Sutra* that we now have is clearly a composite document, one that has been stitched together from at least two separate sources. It is ironic that the entrustment scene is the segment of the narrative that most obviously exposes the seams in that narrative's textual history. If the conventional work of the entrustment scene is to provide a clear point of oral origin for the written text of the sutra, that is manifestly *not* how this particular entrustment scene works. I would not go so far as to call it a parody of convention, but it is definitely a departure, and a critical one at that.

As if this were not enough, there is a third entrustment scene, this one properly situated very near the end of the narrative, but no less troubling for its place of prominence. Following the second entrustment, the Buddha engages in a series of intensive dialogues, first with Manjuśri and Kāśyapa, and then with the bodhisattva Lion's Roar. Buddha and Lion's Roar agree that Ānanda is the best candidate to receive the final teachings and make the final offering, and they discuss his memory skills at length. Buddha entertains several more questions from the assembly and then asks for Ānanda, presumably preparing to entrust him with the entirety of the *Nirvana Sutra.* Ānanda, however, has never arrived. One of the assembly informs Buddha that Ānanda has been waylaid by Māra, who has turned himself into sixty-four thousand billion likenesses of Buddha, each of which is preaching a different doctrine. Ānanda is "greatly pained" by this and by his inability to break free, and, though he stays his mind on the Thus Come One, strangely no one has come to his aid (T 12.374.600c25–26).

Manjuśri then makes what could be interpreted as a power play, assuring the Buddha that certainly, among all the beings congregated, there is at least one capable of receiving and retaining the teachings. He persists, "Why ask where Ānanda is?" (T 12.374.601a10). Buddha lectures Manjuśri at length about Ānanda's special qualities, and particularly his power of memory, before concluding, "That is why I ask where Ānanda is, [because] I desire for him to accept and hold this *Nirvana Sutra*."[25] Buddha sends Mañjuśri to rescue Ānanda and Ānanda returns, but he is never formally entrusted with the teachings and never takes a vow to preserve or propagate them. In narrative terms, all his appearance has done is to cast doubt on Mañjuśri and Kāśyapa's powers of memory (which are inferior to his own) and draw attention to the fact that, at the sutra's close, Buddha still has not settled the question of who should be entrusted with preserving the teaching or if, in fact, different disciples hold responsibility for different portions of it. If Ānanda is, indeed, the Buddha's choice (or one of the Buddha's choices), then Ānanda will have to depend on the cooperation and memory skills of his fellow disciples since he, in fact, never heard any of the sutra with whose preservation he may have been charged.

Scenes like these reveal that Mahāyāna sutras draw on the narrative conventions of oral delivery and transmission while undermining some aspects of that structural logic. The point is that the way Mahāyāna sutras were created (through a writing process that at times resulted in a composite text) and the way they suggest they were created (through the transcription of a perfect memory of an entrusted verbal teaching) do not match up.[26] It seems certain that at least some Mahāyāna sutras were stitched together from a number of disparate texts into a single literary document that comes apart at the seams when read attentively from beginning to end. Entrustment scenes can reveal these seams and some of the stitchwork done to conceal them. What they do not reveal, however, are the identities of the tailors: early Mahāyāna sutras have no (named) authors. Thus, they are severed both from a verifiable history of oral discourse and from an identifiable act of literary fabrication. Instead, they float free from both these traditional locales of textual authority.

THE ANXIETY OF TEXT

If Mahāyāna sutras occasionally advert to unsettling questions about their textual pasts, in another metafictional strategy they are much more overtly anxious about their ability to survive into the future. A substantial portion of many Mahāyāna sutras consists of rhetoric built to engender fear that the narrative will be corrupted, destroyed, or otherwise lost to circulation. In the *Sutra of Immeasurable Life*, for instance, the Buddha maintains matter-of-factly that, in the ages to come, "all scriptures and paths will perish, but out of compassion and pity, I will especially preserve this sutra and maintain it in the world for a hundred years more."²⁷ Similarly, in the *Lotus Sutra* the Buddha enunciates a lengthy verse concerned with the fragility of the teachings, studded throughout with lines like, "If after the Buddha's extinction / in the midst of an evil age / one can preach this scripture / that is difficult. . . . / If after the Buddha's passage into extinction / in the midst of an evil age / to read this scripture for but a moment / that is difficult. . . . / If after my extinction / one can hold this scripture / and preach it to even one person / that is difficult."²⁸ Part of what makes these actions so difficult is the simple passage of time, during which memories fade, pages rot, and lineages of oral transmission tangle and break.

Mahāyāna sutras also worry about enemies other than time. The *Lotus Sutra* speaks of human adversaries who "malign the scriptures," acting on "hatred and envy" (T 9.262.15b26–27). The *Vimalakīrti Sutra* admits to similar anxieties, as when the Buddha instructs Maitreya to "employ supernatural powers to propagate sutras such as this, spreading them" throughout the world "and never allowing them to be wiped out [Jp: *danzen*]."²⁹ The *Nirvana Sutra* provides the most explicit and extended nightmare of textual desecration. The Buddha suggests to Kāśyapa that a mere eighty years after his passage into Nirvana,

> there will be many evil monks who will abridge this sutra and cut it into
> many pieces, so that the color, fragrance, beauty, and flavor of the true
> dharma are lost. All these evil monks . . . will insert worldly phrases, grand
> and decorative, but devoid of the essential. Or they will chop off the begin-
> ning and add it to the end, chop off the end and add it to the beginning,
> or put the beginning and end in the middle and the middle at the begin-
> ning and end. You should know that evil monks such as these are friends
> of Māra.³⁰

This violent editorial cutting and pasting will obstruct beings' access to the scripture, Buddha argues, keeping them from getting at its true meaning.³¹ Like Roland trying to control the arrangement of his corpse on the battlefield, the Buddha wants his textual corpus to maintain a certain shape and order, lest the evidence be misread and his deeds misunderstood. The imagery supports the notion of a great physical battle in which sutras are unstrung, sliced and chopped, then sewn back together into unsatisfying semblances of their former selves.

Passages such as these work to establish an overarching atmosphere of desperation, and they stress the importance of the recipient in transmitting and preserving the text in these violent times. In addition to elaborating an anxious tone, these passages also suggest an important characteristic of sutras as material objects, namely, that they are not capable of sustaining themselves. With the Buddha having died, the sutras are in danger of dying, too, unless someone else makes special, even supernatural, efforts to preserve them. Even when these efforts are made, however, beings find them "difficult," and inevitably the sutras will all eventually perish. The world will pass through a spiritual dark age, which will end only when another buddha appears to start the cycle turning again.

THE SUTRA LIBRARY

Happily, there is an inverse to this nightmare. If the *Nirvana Sutra* imagines the tatters in which a material copy of a sutra may end up, the *Vimalakīrti Sutra* provides an equally extreme account of the opposite, a fantasy of completely perfect preservation. In the thirteenth chapter of the *Vimalakīrti Sutra,* the Buddha offers the following story. Long, long ago there was a buddha named Medicine King who lived and taught in a world called Great Adornment. His chief patron was a king who had one thousand sons, one of whom was named Moon Parasol. One day Moon Parasol, observing all the various offerings of his father and brothers (flowers, incense, banners, music, etc.), wonders to himself what the best of all offerings is. Suddenly, a heavenly being appears in the sky and tells him the most superior is the offering of the dharma. Neither Moon Parasol nor his father knows how to make this offering, so they ask Medicine King to explain. He says, "Good man, the offering of the dharma means the profound sutras preached by all the buddhas. The people of the world all find them difficult to believe and difficult to accept, for they are wonderfully subtle and difficult to see, clean and pure and without stain. . . . They are contained in the storehouse of the bodhisattva and are sealed with the *dhāraṇī* seal."[32] Moon Parasol, the Buddha tells us, was one of his former incarnations and thus, in delivering the teachings of the *Vimalakīrti Sutra,* the Buddha completes the offering of the dharma that he, as Moon Parasol, desired to make. I will deal more closely with this sort of pretextual history soon, but for the moment let us concentrate on the issue of textual perfection.

In this story, the buddha Medicine King speaks of a vast storehouse filled with text, in other words, a library. The holdings of this library consist of every sutra ever given, each of which is preserved whole, with no smudges or stains, and each of which is stamped with a seal that marks it as genuine. This library

is not exactly open to the public, however, because it exists inside the bodhisattva who has achieved such an advanced spiritual stage that he has the
power of perfect recall (Sk: *dhāranī*). The bodhisattva's memory is thus a library that only he can read. This is just as well, because normal, worldly people
have trouble seeing such a bright, clear text (a frustrating experience perhaps
remotely akin to trying to read a glossy page under a high-powered fluores-
cent light). The offering of the dharma, therefore, consists of making the perfectly preserved sutras visible to everyday beings by expounding upon them
in sermons. These sermons form the basis of various individually named sutras.

The *Flower Ornament Sutra* contains a similar passage that helps delin-
eate between the perfect, and perfectly sealed, sutras of the bodhisattva and
the sutras that we, as human beings, might hope to encounter in this world.
In a section explaining the tenth and final intuition of a bodhisattva on the
path to enlightenment, the sutra states that the Buddha's wisdom "exists
within the body of every living being," a fact that often goes unrecognized,
literally "unseen."[33] The sutra glosses this situation as follows: "It is as if there
were a single sutra scroll . . . and on this scroll were recorded all things in the
multi-thousand-fold world, [leaving] nothing not [recorded]."[34] This sutra
scroll is then envisioned as existing within a mote of dust, and in fact every
mote of dust is similarly possessed of a sutra scroll. Sutras, therefore, are
everywhere, millions upon millions of them within our very bodies, but they
are obscured and hidden, illegible to the vast majority of living beings. We
have a sutra library inside of us, but we do not have access to its holdings. Rendering the sutra scrolls legible requires nothing short of an act of readerly
fission in which a person possessed of "penetrating wisdom" and a "pristine
pure divine eye" (T.9.278.624a8)—in other words, a buddha or very advanced
bodhisattva—trains the sacred optic on the mote of dust and splits it asunder,
releasing the sutras into the world, where they can now be of benefit to living
beings.

There is a distinction to be drawn, then, between the sutra as "text" and the
sutra as "work." Editors of critical editions have long noted the various discrepancies that occur between different copies of a single work of literature.[35]
A copy may be illustrated or not, include marginalia or not; it can be produced
as manuscript or as type, in different fonts, on different substances, with various page and line breaks; some authors, like Walt Whitman, published numerous versions of a single poem; and so forth. Proponents of textual studies assert that each of these differences, though they may at times seem to be
superficial, exerts a subtle pull on the work, creating a greater or lesser sense

of variability and pointing to the instability of literature as an art form. Thus the famous question comparing the singularity of *Mona Lisa* with the bewildering multiplicity of *Hamlet*.

Peter Shillingsburg provides a useful set of terms for grappling with the realities of textual dispersion. According to his terminology, a piece of literature that might be expressed in any number of forms (in folio or quarto, on vellum or paper, in various editions, etc.) but that is not reducible to any single one of those expressions should be termed the "work." Distinct apprehensions of the work that are expressed in words and punctuation form the "linguistic text."[36] This linguistic text, in turn, may be housed in any number of material forms or physical "containers."[37] The combination of linguistic text and physical container forms the "material text." While the work and the linguistic text exist in the abstract as inaccessible and intangible, the material text (any single iteration of the work expressed in language and contained in some physical form) is available to human senses. We only ever read material texts.

To gloss this terminology with respect to the literature at hand, the sutra as a linguistic text (a string of words and line breaks) exists abstractly in this world and may survive by lodging itself in a container, the most popular being memory or some sort of external surface (leaves or paper). This physically lodged material text is subject to the ravages of time and the violent attacks of editors or rivals and, even given the best efforts of its devotees, will eventually fade and die. The sutra as work, however, continues to exist, perfect and undamaged, and this abiding teaching is at least one of the concepts encompassed in the Sanskrit word *dharma*. In later chapters of this book I will tend to bracket the idea of the "dharma," the perfect "work," since it is inaccessible to the average believer. Instead, I will be focusing on the "material text," which is complicated enough. After all, this text can comprise any of the physical, material copies of that work that may be written on leaves, carved into bark or stone, brushed onto silk or paper, or inscribed on the surface of the mind. It is these interconnected surfaces that so intrigued the authors of medieval miracle literature and that found their ways into the sermons of medieval priests. Unless otherwise specified, then, I intend the word "text" to refer to the material text as housed in a specific container.

REMEMBERING PREHISTORY

A number of Mahāyāna sutras contain within them stories of the Buddha's past lives. Occasionally, in yet another metafictional narrative move, these sutras tell us that the Buddha, over the course of one of these previous incarnations, has encountered the very sutra that he is currently preaching. In the *Lotus Sutra,* for instance, the Buddha explains to the assembly of monks that, in a certain kingdom long ago, there was a buddha named Victorious Through Great Penetrating Knowledge who often gave sermons to the king and his sixteen sons.[38] Hearing the dharma expounded for the fourth time, all of the sixteen princes, along with myriad other beings in the kingdom, renounce their worldly riches and take up vows, embarking on a path of formal practice. Following a hiatus of twenty thousand *kalpas,*[39] during which the princes have been perfecting their training, the buddha preaches again, this time finally delivering the long-awaited sutra entitled, of course, the *Lotus Sutra.* After expounding the *Lotus* for eight thousand *kalpas,* Victorious Through Great Penetrating Knowledge retires to a quiet chamber where he spends eighty-four thousand *kalpas* in meditation. In the meantime, those assembled have one of three responses: joyful acceptance (the sixteen princes), a wait-and-see attitude (some of the other voice hearers), and doubt (everyone else). The sixteen princes commit the sutra to memory, then preach it widely. Eventually they all become buddhas, the sixteenth of whom is none other than the historical Buddha Śākyamuni, who is telling his audience this story about his past.[40] In other words, readers of the *Lotus Sutra* encounter a narrative in which the orator of the narrative tells a story about how he heard the story from someone else. The story that the "someone else" told, the story that the Buddha is now telling, and the narrative that we are now reading all have the same title.

One point these narrative backstories make is that the Buddha is not the author of any particular sutra, nor is he the wellspring from which the work originates. He is, rather, the latest in a long line of enlightened beings who have committed themselves to memorizing and spreading copies of the text. Another implication of these stories has to do with narrative drift. When the Buddha features as a character in his own narrative, the line between story and storyteller blurs. He claims to have memorized the sutra, the same sutra with the same title that he is now preaching, when he was a young ex-prince, but with two major (and unacknowledged) alterations. First, material has been added: the story of the sixteenth prince could not have been present in the sutra that the sixteenth prince originally heard, and therefore our text includes a later addition. Second, material has clearly been deleted. English translations run roughly four hundred pages, complete with notes. One would have to preach quite slowly indeed for this text to require eight thousand *kalpas* to transmit.[41] Thus, the particular relation between the text of the *Lotus Sutra* and the abiding work remains ever in question, but in a promising and alluring way: the story can expand to include audience members as characters.

Three variations on the motif suggest how this metafictional strategy can encompass figures other than the Buddha, drawing an increasing range of beings into the textual organism. The first variation involves a question. The *Nirvana Sutra* includes a lengthy dialogue between the Buddha and the bodhisattva Lion's Roar, during the course of which Lion's Roar asks the Buddha about the accuracy of a typical metaphor that describes nirvana as a flame blown out. Rather than answer the question, the Buddha responds that ages ago a buddha named Well Gained delivered a teaching of the *Nirvana Sutra* that took three billion years. At that time, "I, along with you, was among those congregated. I asked that buddha this same question. At the time, that Thus Come One was in right samādhi for the sake of all beings and did not reply. Excellent, great one! You do well to remember this incident."[42] Lion's Roar plays, in this textual generation, the same role that the Buddha played in the last generation with the unspoken promise being that, in a future iteration, Lion's Roar will be the buddha to whom the question is posed. While still operating within a very elite circle—a bodhisattva who is the chief interlocutor of a living buddha—this narrative move creates more room for play in the borders of the text.

The second variation works with the issue of expanding text in a different way, by using nominal sameness to refract time and space into an endless hall of mirrors. The Buddha, still speaking to Lion's Roar, recalls hearing a sutra called the *Nirvana Sutra* delivered by a buddha named Śākyamuni, who was born to a king and queen with the same names as the historical Buddha's mother and father. This doppelgänger buddha has disciples who also share names with the Buddha's disciples Śāriputra and Ānanda. After listening to that buddha preach the *Nirvana Sutra,* the Buddha Śākyamuni (our historical Buddha) makes the following vow: "If in ages to come I attain buddhahood, the names of my father, mother, country, disciples, and attendants shall be [the same], and I shall expound the dharma and teach, all just as it is with the World Honored One now. Nothing will differ."[43] That is why, the Buddha says, "I am now expounding the *Great Nirvana Sutra* in this place" (T 12.374. 540a20). The nominal sameness indicates a more profound identification of the here and now with the there and then. Time and space twist back on themselves, and the entire assembly is caught in a plot loop that repeats until everyone has played the lead part.[44]

The third iteration of this motif suggests that what is true for the Buddha-role is also true for all members of the assembly. Many Mahāyāna sutras claim that they are difficult to hear, that the default position is to doubt the teachings. These sutras often go on to claim that a listener will need to have cultivated a store of "good roots" (Jp: *zenkon*) before he or she will be able to accept the teachings.[45] The *Lotus Sutra* takes this one step further, arguing, "If there is one who believes and accepts this scripture dharma, that person has already, in times gone by, seen buddhas of the past, honored and made offerings to them, and has already heard this dharma."[46] In other words, if anyone is able to accept these teachings the first time they hear them, that should be a sign that they have, in fact, heard them before and have done so in the direct presence of a buddha. The *Lotus Sutra* thus assumes that there are very important things about our past lives that we have forgotten. On a more positive note, these passages also provide a way for any reader to write themselves into the narrative, even if only as an unnamed and unremarked extra, one of those myriad of beings who walked away doubting the first time (or the first million times) around.[47] Accepting the sutra quickly here and now proves retroactively that we must have been there, then.

The different varieties of this textual history motif all work to slice open the closed world of the narrative and to implicate the reader by drawing him or her into a lineage (actually, a repeating loop) of textual transmission. If the Buddha was the perfectly receptive listener in a previous audience, as proven by his ability to store and replicate the teaching, then we have the attractive option to serve in turn as the voice of the dharma. It may take us an incalculable length of time to reach his skill level, but eventually we can assume his position, our image mapped perfectly onto his. The motif, at least one variant of it, even accounts for the troublesome specter of narrative drift by encouraging its readers to take a vow to achieve enlightenment as a buddha named Śākyamuni. In short, the narrative encourages its readers to swear to become a character, preferably the main character, in the narrative being read.

TEXTUAL GENESIS

The metafictional strategies surveyed thus far accomplish two main effects. First, they establish readerly desire for the sutra through a strategy of obscuring the object of that desire. Sutras suggest that their teachings exist on two planes: that of the work (which is largely inaccessible but perfectly preserved) and that of the text. Any given text is characterized by narrative drift and contains large sections that consist of metalanguage about the teaching, both of which techniques raise concerns about the location of the teaching itself. These concerns are amplified by repeated claims that the sutra as text may be damaged and will become extinct. Any devoted reader who is drawn into the textual project will want the sutra but will have problems ascertaining where, exactly, that sutra is, meaning that a devotee can never stop searching for the fuller text (ultimately, the work) to which he or she is devoted.

Second, these metafictional strategies have unmoored sutras from traditional points of authority (the author or orator). Troubled entrustment scenes reveal fissures and contradictions within the text and suggest that it has been imperfectly preserved, while textual prehistories defer oratorical creation into an ever-receding past (often, several pasts) that slips further and further over the horizon and ultimately is not visible. Mahāyāna sutras provide a response to this impasse by inverting the process of authorship, claiming that sutras are the generative entities that produce buddhas rather than the other way around. Very early in its narrative, the *Diamond Sutra* claims that "all of the buddhas and all of their teachings of supreme perfect enlightenment spring forth from this sutra."[48] Similarly, the *Vimalakīrti Sutra* maintains that "the enlightened intuition of all the buddhas is born from this sutra" (T 14.475.556a29). Claims like these extend the hyperbole by which many Mahāyāna sutras claim places of supremacy for themselves, asserting that this sutra (whether "this sutra" is the *Lotus,* the *Nirvana,* the *Diamond,* or the *Vimalakīrti Sutra*) is the king of all sutras, that it supersedes all others, and that it represents the culmination and pinnacle of the Buddhist teachings. The next logical step for hyperbole of this sort, and one for which the various scenes of textual prehistory have prepared the reader, is the claim that "this sutra" is not simply the most powerful and comprehensive of all sutras, but that it is also the birthplace for all buddhas, the place from which all enlightened intuition (Sk: *bodhi*) springs.

TEXTUAL ONTOLOGY

The rhetorical claim that sutras give birth to buddhas tells us a great deal about what might be called the "ontological status" of sutras in the Mahāyāna Buddhist tradition. In 1956 René Wellek and Austin Warren opened the question of the ontological status of literature by noting that, in contrast to most of the plastic arts, a literary work of art was not coterminous with its artifact (words on a page), nor could one say that a work of literature was "an individual experience or a sum of experiences" (whether of author or readers), but rather "only a potential cause of experiences." They sought to understand literary ontology as "dynamic" and "intersubjective," existing in a network of "collective ideology."[49] These highly abstract notions largely divorced literature from its material matrix. In the early 1980s James McLaverty, among others, sought to reunite literature with its artifactual iterations, arguing that "the existence of works of art as print and paper is not less but more important"[50] than scholars had recently taken it to be, an idea that gave birth to the field of textual studies and to thinkers such as Peter Shillingsburg, whose idea of the "work" and the "text" I have already discussed above. The current state of the field understands literary works "both as artificial objects and as conceptual entities."[51] That is, literature simultaneously exists in two interrelated places: on the printed page, and in the minds of a community of readers and authors who continue to think about the piece of literature and its meanings.

One crucial limitation of current understandings of textual ontology, at least in terms of trying to understand Mahāyāna sutras, is that they treat text largely as an object connected, however tenuously, to an author. While each Mahāyāna sutra must have been authored by someone (or a group of someones), these people are never mentioned, obscured behind the fiction of a narrative "I" that is itself unstable. A second limitation of these theories is that they treat literary texts as objects, dynamic and fluctuating to be sure, but devoid of agency. This understanding (which, to be fair, was articulated primarily in reference to Romantic poetry) may work perfectly well for many literary texts, but Mahāyāna sutras take the question of textual ontology to another level on which sutras, through a variety of literary techniques, seize agency for themselves and begin acting not just as "conceptual entities" but as embodied ones.

Approaching the question of ontology from a somewhat different angle, then, scholars of Buddhism have long argued that Mahāyāna understands the sutra as a site of living presence. As the *Lotus Sutra* puts it, "Wherever [this sutra] may be preached, or read, or recited, or written, or whatever place a roll of this scripture may occupy, in all those places one is to erect a stupa of the seven jewels, building it high and wide and with impressive decoration. There is no need even to lodge a śarīra [relic] in it. What is the reason? Within it there is already a whole body of the Thus Come One."[52] Assertions like these have led Gregory Schopen to argue, famously, that Mahāyāna Buddhism is a "cult of the book," that devotion to the material form of sutras (scrolls, for instance) fundamentally defines Mahāyāna Buddhism and marks it as distinct from earlier Buddhist traditions.[53] To gloss this detailed thesis rather quickly, sutras provide the germ, the seed, the catalyst that transforms a normal human into an enlightened being: the seed of the teachings, planted in the fertile soil of the mind, grows to fruition in the form of *bodhi,* the "enlightened intuition" that marks a buddha as a distinct species of life. The sutras, therefore, are a generative site, capable of producing not just one buddha, but presumably an unlimited number of them. In the end, sutra trumps buddha. Any place that a sutra has existed (even if only as a passing vocalization) is an even more vital site than the birthplace of the Buddha, the tree under which he gained enlightenment, the locale of his first sermon, or the grove in which he passed into nirvana.

Thus, sutras are revealed to be very complicated textual entities that, having obscured the authorial role almost entirely and having conjured the vision of oral delivery only to undermine it, take upon themselves the trappings of presence and the rhetoric of embodiedness. As the dominant half of the sutra-buddha binary, sutras inhabit a position of strength from which they can leverage their readers into action. As Paul Harrison has noted, "it is certainly the case that Mahāyāna sutras burst their bounds, that they range all over the place, unsystematic, exaggerated and larger than life. In short, they possess a kind of organic roughness and wholeness and vitality that is descriptive and constitutive of a total world, a world which obeys different laws from the one we normally inhabit, but into which we can enter."[54]

WHAT A SUTRA WANTS

As textual beings possessed of a certain agency (the power to invite us into their world), sutras issue very specific injunctions telling the reader what she or he is meant to do with their text. The typical demands require devotees to listen, accept, hold, read, recite, and expound the sutra for other people. Many sutras also require believers to write it down and make copies of it.[55] With the exception of writing, all of these commands appear in all of the sutras I survey here: the *Lotus Sutra,* the *Vimalakīrti Sutra,* the *Nirvana Sutra,* the *Diamond Sutra,* the *Flower Ornament Sutra,* and the two Pure Land sutras (which are the ones that omit writing). The *Lotus Sutra* has garnered by far the most attention with respect to these textual commands, and its tenth chapter outlines the so-called "five varieties of dharma preacher" (Jp: *goshu hōshi*), namely: those who accept and keep the sutra, those who read it, those who recite it, those who explain it to others, and those who copy it in writing.[56] These methods of textual engagement are not unique to the *Lotus Sutra* but are typical of most Mahāyāna sutras. (Even sutras that do not request any of these things, such as the extremely short *Heart Sutra,* commonly find themselves being memorized, chanted, copied, and expounded upon.) By treating this group of sutras together, I want to emphasize the very textual nature of Mahāyāna culture as a whole.

Most strings of textual commands begin with the injunction to "listen," which, in the context of Mahāyāna sutras, must be viewed with a certain amount of skepticism. As discussed above, these sutras were not composed until several centuries after the Buddha's death, even though they stage themselves as oral discourses that were delivered by the Buddha during his lifetime. What this reveals is that Mahāyāna sutras address themselves simultaneously to two audiences. Members of the assembly form the first (fictive) audience, and their reactions to that teaching provide the first models for correct and incorrect response patterns. The second audience comprises everyone who was not present to hear the oral teaching but who has, in the course of succeeding years, come into contact with the sutra through the medium of the written text and its expositors. While these later beings cannot "listen" to the teaching in the same way that the first audience did, they are nevertheless charged with similar duties of textual devotion.

The *Diamond Sutra* contains a scene that showcases this two-audience phenomenon quite clearly. The Buddha engages in a lengthy discussion, at the end of which his disciple Subhūti responds, "World Honored One, just now I have been able to hear scriptural canons like this one, and I do not find it difficult to believe, understand, receive, or hold it. But if, in the age to come five hundred years from now, there is a being who is able to hear this sutra, believing, understanding, accepting, and holding it, this person is indeed most rare."[57] The disciple Subhūti here nominally addresses the Buddha, expressing concern about beings living in a degenerate age, but his words also speak to a second audience, challenging those readers who live in such a degenerate age to be that "most rare" person who will fully engage the sutra that has become available through the conduit of written text.

Other than the command to listen, the key distinction to be drawn with respect to injunctions of textual engagement pivots on the proximity to enlightenment, rather than temporal proximity to the supposed moment of oral delivery. Sutras direct their instructions toward specific types of being. In the following pages I will examine the vocabulary of textual engagement, suggesting that advanced spiritual beings (buddhas and bodhisattvas) receive subtly different instructions from those given to the much larger, less spiritually advanced contingent of monks, nuns, laymen, and laywomen. These differences primarily affect the command to "hold" the sutras, though the level of spiritual attainment has ramifications for some of the other categories of textual engagement as well.

Somewhat confusingly, Mahāyāna sutras maintain the fiction of orality while also speaking of themselves as material texts whose prose has been divided into chapters, whose verse comes in lines, and whose words have been recorded in writing. Ultimately, I suggest that this modulation between oral and written reflects the reproductive cycle of sutras, which may phase between written and oral forms as they move from one generation to the next. Human beings may first encounter a sutra either in the context of a sermon or in the form of a material text (a scroll, for instance). Regardless of what form the sutra assumes in this initial contact, it asks to be accepted, held, read, and recited (that is, internalized) before being either expounded or copied (that is, reproduced for a new generation of potential believers).

ACCEPTANCE

The first thing Mahāyāna sutras ask of all beings, regardless of their spiritual acumen, is to accept the sutras' teachings. Acceptance forms the basic threshold, passing over which beings enter into the bodhisattva path. As noted earlier, however, sutras generally assume that the default position is doubt. When Subhūti suggests that latter-day people who accept the *Diamond Sutra* will be rare, the Buddha heartily agrees, noting that if a person in that age is "neither surprised nor frightened nor afraid . . . that person is rare indeed."[58] In fact, many beings choose not to commit themselves to accepting the teachings, and the second chapter of the *Lotus Sutra* records that fully five thousand members of the assembly (all of them either monk, nun, or laity) simply stood up and walked out, a sign of their "deep and grave roots of sin and overweening pride."[59]

A large part of acceptance, then, consists of emotional maturity and humility: the ability to face things that are frighteningly new and to consider that one might have something to learn from them. The importance of this attitude holds, regardless of temporal position (whether attending the assembly or encountering the sutra five hundred years later), and it becomes easier the further one advances spiritually. The *Vimalakīrti Sutra* maintains that one thing that characterizes a bodhisattva is that, "when hearing a sutra they have not heard before, they do not doubt it,"[60] while the *Flower Ornament Sutra* stipulates that bodhisattvas who still find themselves reluctant to praise excellent teachings and cause others to accept them are guilty of "conceited action."[61] These claims reinforce one another. The more spiritually advanced a being is, the easier it will be for him or her to accept the teachings; the ease with which a being accepts the teachings indicates the degree of his or her spiritual advancement.[62]

In addition to emotional maturity and confidence, the act of acceptance requires an attitude of faith. Sutras suggest that beings must be open to the new teachings and must be willing to accept them as true. Of course, this sort of faith is hard to come by, particularly in degenerate later ages, so to support the dharma preacher in his labors, the Buddha promises to send him "magically conjured" monks, nuns, laymen, and laywomen who will "hear the dharma, accept it in faith and follow it obediently without turning back,"[63] thus providing a model for other, unconjured beings to emulate. Of course, Mahāyāna sutras themselves virtually burst at the seams with precisely these sorts of conjured audiences. In their pages laymen and laywomen of all backgrounds, monks and nuns, advanced practitioners, Hindu deities, forest spirits, dragons, and even flesh-eating demons sing the praises of Mahāyāna scripture and accept their teachings as supremely valid.

The sutras are rather grim about other methods for causing beings to accept the teachings on faith, but they do offer a second course of action should pure faith not be an option, namely: harnessing desire. In the burning house parable from the *Lotus Sutra,* a father tries to rescue his sons from an inferno, but they are too distracted by the pleasures of their play to heed him. Devising an "expedient means" (Sk: *upāya;* Jp: *hōben*), he offers them magnificent carriages if only they will follow him outside. Glossing this parable as an allegory, Buddha claims that living beings "are all my children. / Yet now these places [where they live] / have many cares and troubles / from which I alone / can save them. / Even though I teach and command, / they do not accept [my words] on faith / but are profoundly addicted / to their tainted desires."[64] The sutras do not offer their readers carriages or fanciful toys for their allegiance. Instead, they promise any number of other boons: fragrant skin, good breath, straight teeth, mental clarity, eloquence, and the promise of enlightenment, to name but a few.

We might therefore understand the transaction sutras offer as a kind of gift exchange. In return for our acceptance (whether motivated by pure faith or tainted desire), they offer to bestow us with various rewards. While many of these rewards are physical in nature, the most precious of all is the gift of the dharma. The perfect dharma (the "work") remains inaccessible to normal human beings but is available, in however imperfect a form, in the sutra texts. What this economy of exchange entails, then, is that the sutras give us themselves and we, in turn, give them the gift of accepting that gift. For this exchange to come off, readers must accept a subordinate position (the son role). Accepting the sutra as true, believers must simultaneously accept the sutra as dominant: the sutra is the rich and wise father, and we are the obedient children. This posture of confident humility has been choreographed countless times in the sutras as audience members kneel, bow their heads, and bring their raised palms together in supplication, whereupon they receive the teachings "on the crown of the head."[65]

Most commonly, sutras yoke the act of "accepting" the sutras to the act of "holding" them by using a compound verb (Jp: *juji*). The semantic range of this term is enormous, and translators typically take one of two tacks, either treating each element of the compound separately or fusing them into a single semantic whole.[66] The first approach yields translations such as "receive and keep," "accept and hold," or "absorb and retain," while treating the term as a compound has resulted in the English equivalents "uphold," "possess," "remember," and "memorize." I want to suggest that the reason this term is so very slippery is that, in fact, it means different things when applied to different kinds of beings who may access the sutra in different ways. The meaning of the term shifts subtly in tandem with the subtle shifts in subject (the being who accepts and holds) and in object (the thing being accepted and held).[67] Is the being in question a buddha, a bodhisattva, a devoted monk or nun, or a layperson? How watertight is their memory, how firmly planted their good roots? Do they hold the sutra as "work" or as "text?" Do they meet the sutra verbally or in writing? The answers to these questions help determine more precisely what it is that sutras want when they demand to be "accepted and held."

The question of strong memory lies at the crux of understanding the command to "accept and hold" the sutras. Who, then, possesses this memorial power? The *Flower Ornament Sutra,* which is almost wholly dedicated to cataloging and describing the characteristics of bodhisattvas, clearly asserts that the power of total recall belongs only to buddhas and especially advanced bodhisattvas. According to this sutra, one core quality of buddhas is that they are all "endowed with mnemonic powers [Sk: *dhāraṇī*] able to accept and hold all buddha dharmas."[68] Any buddha can at any time access any of the sutras as perfectly preserved works simply by consulting his own flawless and complete memory. For all other Buddhist practitioners, total recall remains an alluring vision—the *Vimalakīrti Sutra* describes perfect memory as a lush castle garden containing a grove of dharma trees (T 14.475.549c10)—and it remains a skill to be pursued over any number of lifetimes.

Aside from buddhas, bodhisattvas are closer than any other kind of being to attaining the state of total recall. Again according to the *Flower Ornament Sutra,* bodhisattvas engage in ten stages of concentration, the first of which focuses on "developing a boundless heart-mind [capable of] accepting and holding all the buddha dharmas without forgetting any."[69] When bodhisattvas master the tenth concentration level, they become capable of "accepting and holding the buddha dharmas of past, present and future" and, having access to all the dharmas, they can "enter into them without impediment."[70] Bodhisattvas have to work for this absolutely free, unhindered access to the dharma, and the ability comes only after countless lifetimes of cultivation, in particular cultivation of the mind, which they must purge from distraction and expand greatly until it is "boundless" (T 10.279.213b5) and "deep" (298c5), with the capacity to contain all dharma. While bodhisattvas begin their training in mental concentration like other beings—with access to the "text" (or "teaching," Jp: *kyō;* T 10.279.127c10)—they end with access to the "work" (or "dharma," Jp: *hō*).

The *Flower Ornament Sutra* describes in great detail just such a journey √ from text to work. Its lengthy final chapter follows the pilgrimage of the ideal devotee Sudhana. Having heard Manjuśri preach, Sudhana vows to take up the bodhisattva path. Seeing that Sudhana is wholeheartedly committed, Manjuśri instructs him to travel south in search of a teacher. This Sudhana does, studying under scores of masters, sometimes apprenticing with them for as long as twelve years. Each of the beings Sudhana meets on his journey acts as a conduit, pouring into him all of the teachings that they have heard, retained in perfect memory, and come to embody.

The later stages of this pilgrimage are particularly relevant to my argument √ because now that Sudhana is sufficiently advanced, his teachers often do not talk to him very much at all. Rather, they establish physical or mental contact with him—placing their hand on his head or holding his gaze—and cause him to see things directly. In one of these scenes, for instance, the teacher rubs Sudhana's head with his right hand. Instantly Sudhana sees multitudes of buddhas, each in his own land, stretching in every direction. Simultaneously standing before each of them, he hears their sermons and explanations and finds himself able to "completely penetrate every sentence and every verse, keeping [the teachings] distinct, accepting and holding them without confusion."[71] Here Sudhana shows his ability to listen to multiple sutras at once and to transcribe each of them perfectly into his memory, without dropping a single word or transposing a single verse. Later in his journey a teacher performs a miracle for Sudhana in which he sees, pouring forth as light from her pores, "the vigorous energy to accept and hold the dharma-cycles of all buddhas."[72] This crucial vision shows Sudhana how to move from cataloging individual sermons to accessing the entire dharma library. By the end of his journey Sudhana has become a bodhisattva. Memorizing teachings (text) has turned him into a √ storehouse of the dharma (work).

For buddhas and advanced bodhisattvas, holding takes place in the mind, and the object so held is the dharma in its entirety. This is what "accept and hold" means for them. Many Mahāyāna sutras employ slightly different Chinese characters to express more precisely this kind of mental holding. The *Vimalakīrti Sutra*, for instance, always distinguishes the bodhisattvic act of mental holding with the term "hold completely" (Jp: *sōji*), and other sutras also make use of this term. In the *Nirvana Sutra*, for example, Buddha explains that the sutra of that same name has always existed in unchanging form. In earlier ages, though, it was unnecessary to preach the sutra, to bring it forth into textual form, because beings were "less greedy and had much wisdom. All the great bodhisattvas were malleable and easy to teach. They had great virtue and held completely without forgetting, like great elephant kings."[73] For bodhisattvas, the mind is the sense organ that retains the dharma, holding it tightly like a strong elephant might grasp something with its trunk. Lesser beings—those who are greedy and not so wise—do not have this pliability or strength of mind and must, in a sense, be hammered at with the tool of individual sutra texts if an impression is to be made.

ON FRAGMENTS AND HANDS

On the whole, sutras leave a significant gap between figures like Sudhana and the vast majority of more typical devotees. While sutras do allow that some of these less single-minded beings will be able to memorize some portion of sutra text, they often suggest that even these comparatively minimal accomplishments must be buttressed by the vow of a bodhisattva or buddha who promises either to extend his powers of memorization to the devotee or to appear to the devotee in person to help him or her memorize the text. (In later chapters I will explore in detail how medieval Japanese authors take up these possibilities.) If sutras recognize the limitations of common memory, what does the command to "accept and hold" signify for those at the other end of the spectrum: monks, nuns, and laity possessed of only normal powers of mind? Generally, Mahāyāna sutras offer two humbler options.

One possibility is to memorize a fragment of the sutra text. At several points in its narrative, the *Lotus Sutra* extols the great merit accruing to one who "accepts and holds so much as a single four-line verse of this scripture" (T 9.262.54a18–19). The merit so gained far outstrips the merit to be garnered from countless lifetimes of other sorts of offerings and, in fact, is only outstripped itself when the dedication stretches to encompass the entire sutra. The *Diamond Sutra* makes similar claims as to the efficacy of this practice, and it offers precisely two four-line verses, both uttered by the Buddha. The first one reads: "Should one try to see me in form / or seek me in sound / this person follows a false path / and will not attain sight of the Thus Come One."[74] If this first *gāthā* describes improper methods of seeing, the second *gāthā* provides the inverse: "All things are conditioned phenomena / like dreams, illusions, bubbles, and shadows / like dew or, again, like lightning. / You should regard them as such."[75] Both of these verses capture succinctly the larger message communicated by the sutra as a whole, which concerns itself with criticizing the limitations of conceptual thought and language. The *Diamond Sutra* takes pains to point out a slippage that has delighted semiologists and deconstructionists for decades. Namely, the word is not the thing, and to imagine that the thing you seek (the Buddha, for instance) can be encompassed in language, concept, sound, or form constitutes a grave error, an illusion no more lasting than dew or lightning.

The rhetoric of "even a four-line verse" functions on the logic of synecdoche, part standing in for whole, but not just any part will do. Sutras never encourage devotees to choose four lines of prose, for instance. Sutra verse (Sk: *gāthā*) seems to have a special power, as fragment, to suggest the contours of the whole from which it was drawn. This special power appears to short-circuit any fears or anxieties that sutras normally have about being cut up, pulled apart, reassembled, or abridged. The shortest complete unit of a *gāthā* is four lines, and *gāthā* of this length are like the arm of a starfish. The whole is better, but the part is good enough because it contains, as it were, the genetic map necessary to regenerate the other arms.

Sutras provide a second, humble method, and that is to take the metaphor of "holding" literally, to actually, physically hold the material text of the sutra in your hands. The *Flower Ornament Sutra* instructs bodhisattvas who are active in the world to use various everyday events as triggers for the dedication of merit. When washing the hands, for instance, bodhisattvas "should wish that all beings / have pure clean hands / to accept and hold the buddha dharma."[76] This would keep them from damaging the sutra with oils or smudging it with dirt, but this act of respect also acknowledges that the material text of the sutra is a great treasure. As Śāriputra asserts in the *Vimalakīrti Sutra*, "One who takes this sutra in his hand has thereby acquired the storehouse of the jewels of the dharma."[77] Sutras typically use this image of the storehouse to describe the advanced bodhisattva's mind. While the bodhisattva holds all of the dharma in memory, one who possesses a sutra as a material object held in hand similarly holds part of that dharma, the key that can eventually unlock the library. Later in that same scripture Maitreya vows, "If in ages to come there are good men and good women who seek the Great Vehicle, I will see to it that sutras such as this one come into their hands, will lend them powers of memorization, and will cause them to accept and hold, read and recite, and expound them widely to other beings."[78] Here we begin to see how the mimesis of holding the sutras in one's hand can transform into the more perfect grasp of total recall, as the devotee moves through the later steps of memorizing the sutra and then explaining it to others, growing their collection one sutra at a time.[79]

Given that sutras often include injunctions to revere, worship, make offerings to, and circumambulate the sutra scroll—in other words, taking seriously the idea that Mahāyāna Buddhism is, in fact, a "cult of the book"—this physical holding of sutras is a central ritual concern of the religion as a whole. Additionally, physically holding the sutras is mimetic of the mental holding accomplished by advanced bodhisattvas. Significantly, sutras typically link the act of "accepting and holding" to the act of "reading and reciting," so that the words and phrases of the sutra move slowly from the hand to the mind by way of the eye and mouth. If all buddhas are born from sutras, then, by ingesting sutras and storing them within the mind, the reader catalyzes his or her own spiritual transformation.

Virtually all beings are capable of transcribing the sutras onto the mind. Bodhisattvas simply accomplish this at a faster rate and without the need for an external material text to prompt them and correct their memory. Thus, what a sutra wants when it asks a certain being to accept and hold it varies with the varying capabilities of that being. At its simplest, holding may entail only possession: keeping a physical copy of a single sutra on hand and protecting it from the elements. At its most intricate, holding requires a feat of memorization resulting in perfect access to the entire dharma. A large, vaguely defined territory of absorbing and remembering text lies between these two extremes.

TO READ AND RECITE

The next devotional response that sutras typically ask for is chanting (Jp: *dokuju*). Once again, the two elements of this compound at times appear separately, in which case the first element (Jp: *doku*) means "to read" and the second (Jp: *ju*) "to recite." As a general rule, buddhas and very advanced bodhisattvas recite sutras, study and analyze them, and preach them widely, but they are less often to be found reading them, unless doing so for the sake of other beings. Others who do not possess the power of instantaneous total recall might learn to recite sutras through a process of repeated reading. This suggests that the key difference between reading and reciting has to do with the material location of the text being vocalized. When devotees pronounce the words of sutras that they know by heart, they are reciting the text, and when they must rely on an external prop (say, the sutra as written in a scroll), they are reading.

One goal of reading is clearly memorization. Some sutras indicate this by including the specific command to "memorize" (Jp: *fu*) as part of the devotional sequence. For instance, the buddha Amida's twenty-ninth vow reads, "If, when I attain buddhahood, bodhisattvas in my land should not acquire eloquence and wisdom in accepting and reading the sutras, in memorizing, reciting, holding, and expounding them, may I not attain perfect enlightenment."[80] Other times, the goal of memorization becomes apparent only when the practice of reading goes astray. Near the beginning of the *Lotus Sutra* the disciple Manjuśri reminds Maitreya (who is destined to be the next buddha in this world) about his problematic past. In an earlier incarnation Maitreya was a bodhisattva known as Seeker of Fame. His mind was marred by pride, and, "though he read and recited a multitude of sutras, he derived no profit from them, completely forgetting most."[81]

Memorization, therefore, is the bridge that allows the sutra to move from an external source (the Buddha's voice or the sutra scroll) to an internal one, the mind. When the mind is inadequately prepared, however, all that is so painstakingly written there may be erased. Medieval Japanese literature becomes fascinated with this process of writing and erasing the mind, a theme I will take up at length in later chapters.

In addition to moving the sutra inside the body, the process of repeated reading and recitation also refines and clarifies the text. The *Nirvana Sutra* offers a helpful metaphor for how this happens. The Buddha explains, "When washing dirty clothes one first washes with ash water, and then with clean water. If one does this, the clothes become clean. The concentration and wisdom of bodhisattvas is also like this. O good man! It is as a person first reads and recites, and later the meaning comes forth."[82] Clean clothes, bodhisattvic knowledge, and meaning do not just appear; rather, they must be gained through repeated action. Reading a sutra is like washing dirty cloth with lye, and reciting a sutra is like rinsing away both lye and dirt to reveal the clean cloth underneath. Repeating the action enough times, the launderer comes to understand the warp and woof of meaning.

Furthermore, this interaction between reader and text (launderer and cloth) is almost alchemical, and the reader, too, undergoes a slow transformation. Earlier in the *Nirvana Sutra,* the Buddha has offered a different metaphor that more clearly highlights this subtle alteration in the reader. Here, the Buddha likens reading and reciting to the work of a goldsmith: "O good man! For example, with a goldsmith, from the day when he begins to learn his art up to those of his hoary old age, moment follows moment and what has come before passes away and does not last. But by repeated practice, what he makes is wonderful. Due to this, the person earns praise as the best goldsmith. Reading and reciting the sutras is just like this, good man."[83] In this case the metaphor concerns the goldsmith rather than the gold, though surely he smelts his metal over fire to remove its impurities just as the washer uses lye to leach the dirt. What changes in this metaphor, though, is the person who manipulates the substance (the goldsmith, the reader). Moment by moment as he hones his craft, time and dedicated practice transform him from apprentice to master, his title primarily dependent upon the degree to which he has internalized his craft and purged himself of error.

When sutras ask to be read and recited, therefore, what they want is to be internalized. The repetition of reading and reciting leverages the sutras from "out there" to "in here" and, as the laundering and goldsmithing metaphors indicate, memorizing the sutras works on the mind analogous to the ways that bleaching works on cloth or smelting on metal. It wipes out impurities: the mind becomes a perfectly smooth surface on which the fabric or gold of the sutras can shine in its most highly burnished state. This melding of subject and object, of reader and what is being read, propels the devotee onward toward buddhahood, moving him or her from apprentice to master.

SPREADING THE WORD

Finally, sutras require that their devotees propagate them, either by preaching or through creating written copies. The eight sutras I survey here all employ a standard pattern according to which they encourage their audience to accept, hold, read, recite, and then expound the sutra, teaching it to others. Everyone, from buddha and bodhisattva to lay believer, is expected to engage in this activity, and a certain missionary zeal imbues the exhortation to "expound the buddhas' words widely for the sake of the multitude of beings" (T 12.365.341c18). It does not matter whether the teachings expounded upon come directly from the Buddha's mouth or in the form of a written sutra; the efficacy, and the command, remain the same. In one instance, one of the historical Buddha's disciples listens to his teachings, then goes into the nearby village to share them with the townspeople (T 14.475.541a14–16). In another instance, a degenerate monk has abandoned his vows but continues to meditate on the meaning of the scriptures he has read and recited. When approached and asked about the teachings, he delivers a sermon (T 12.374.383b28–29). Again, a king may sit upon his throne, holding a copy of the sutra in his hand and expounding upon it to his assembled court (T 12.374.371a23–25). And finally the *Lotus Sutra* maintains that, in an evil age, there is even merit to be gained in "secretly preaching so much as a single phrase to a single person" (T 9.262.30c27). When sutras ask to be preached or expounded, what they want is for their believers to take the text that has been internalized and to reintroduce it into the world. Like so much seed cast upon the wind, even a single phrase of the sutra may find itself lodged in fertile soil.

The other way many sutras ask to be reproduced is in script. Sutras ask all varieties of being to engage in this activity, and, as later chapters will show, medieval Japanese literature is particularly interested in the kinds of merit that can be gained from copying out even a minimal portion of text or simply from wetting the inkstone to allow a literate person to write out a single word of a sutra. Combining a number of now-familiar motifs, the *Lotus Sutra* claims that, after the Buddha's extinction, "If there is a person who accepts and keeps, reads and recites, understands and expounds, or writes down or copies out even a single *gāthā* of the *Lotus Sutra* or who shall look with veneration on a scroll of this scripture as if it were the Buddha himself," it should be known that this person has already served myriad buddhas in earlier times.[84] In a slightly later chapter from the same sutra, a host of bodhisattvas speaking in unison vow to "cause living beings to write and copy this scripture, to accept and keep, to read and recite it, [and] to expound its meaning" to others.[85]

While accepting, holding, reading, and reciting all track the trajectory of the sutra as it moves from an external source into the devotee's mind, preaching and copying reverse the direction, now moving the text back out into the larger world, where it may encounter other potential devotees. We can see this process of propagation at work in the somewhat more flexible location of writing in the devotional sequence. Whereas each of the other varieties of sutra devotion typically maintains its same place in the sequence (listen-accept-hold-read-recite-preach), the act of writing may appear in one of two locations, either at the end of the list, alongside preaching, or at the very beginning. I would suggest that this indicates a logical cycle of textual engagement. Though rare, some sutra passages do explicitly acknowledge that while any variety of devotion may be practiced on its own, the ideal devotee would move through all of these stages in turn.[86] In this cycle of textual devotion, the believer accepts the sutras and then embarks on a lengthy process of memorizing and nurturing them through contemplation and internalization before passing the teaching on to other potential believers via the spoken or written word.

When sutras ask their devotees to accept them, to internalize them in memory, and then to bear them forth again into the world, they treat the human body (particularly the mind) as a special type of container that they call a "dharma vessel" (Jp: *hōki*). Like all other living entities, individual sutra texts are fragile and destined to die. No single copy of a sutra, whether held in memory or written on paper, can defeat time (though, as an aside, it is worth noting that the world's oldest known, dated, printed text is a copy of the *Diamond Sutra* from the year 868). Therefore, if sutras are to last in this world, they must find a way to replicate themselves. The list of wants I discussed above speaks precisely to this reproductive drive and indicates the enormous role that humans must play. Leaving aside rather fantastic notions of demons, dragons, goddesses, and mythical animals such as the *garuda* and *kinnara,* in the day-to-day waking reality of this degenerate age, sutras are a highly specialized niche species that relies heavily on the human body. Sutras seek a symbiotic relationship with the human body that serves as their host or, as they put it, "vessel."

A capacious memory is the single most important characteristic by which sutras identify their ideal host organism. While a fully enlightened being, a buddha, provides the "supreme dharma vessel,"[87] other less enlightened beings are capable of containing viable amounts of dharma (the smallest measure of which would be one four-line *gāthā*). As I discussed earlier, the Buddha's disciple Ānanda has frequently been identified as the human who comes closest to approximating the ideal. In the *Vimalakīrti Sutra,* the Buddha praises Ānanda for being "foremost in hearing, in concentrating and in holding all" the teachings he has heard, while still noting that Ānanda's powers pale in comparison to those of bodhisattvas, of whom he remarks, "though the deepest places in the sea can be fathomed," bodhisattvas' powers of memory cannot be measured.[88] Again, in the *Nirvana Sutra,* both the bodhisattva Lion's Roar and the Buddha describe Ānanda as a watertight container. Lion's Roar notes that expounding sutras to Ānanda is "like pouring water and filling another vessel," and Buddha praises Ānanda, saying, "hearing a sutra once, he never asks me about it again. It is like pouring water into a single vessel."[89] Sutras frequently describe the Mahāyāna dharma in liquid terms, figuring it as an ocean of teachings, a great cloud filled with moisture, or a monsoon-like rain, so that preaching the dharma is like pouring water into the narrow aperture of the ear.

While Ānanda holds claim to the position of ideal dharma vessel among humans, others can perform this same function in a more limited capacity, and, though they have clear preferences, Mahāyāna sutras seem to take the "any port in a storm" view. As Buddha explains to his disciple Kāśyapa in the *Nirvana Sutra,* "Imagine that you have three vessels. The first is perfect, the second leaks, and the third is broken. When one wishes to put milk, cream, or butter into them, which would one use first?"[90] Kāśyapa responds in the expected order and Buddha decodes the allegory, saying that bodhisattvas are the perfect vessel, *śrāvaka* (individual practitioners who may be uninterested in spreading the teachings to others) are the leaky vessel, and *icchantika* (beings who seem to be impervious to the teachings) are the broken vessel. Though their capacities differ widely, each of these vessels is capable of containing at least some dharma-milk, even if only a few ounces cupped in a shard or even if only for a limited duration before it all leaks away. While any vessel will do in a pinch, clearly sutras prefer a vessel that is whole, that can contain their full measure, and that holds the promise of one day emptying its contents into another vessel before it cracks and crumbles with time.

What is it, then, that makes a vessel "complete," capable of containing the vast storehouse of Mahāyāna teachings? In a particularly rich episode from the *Vimalakīrti Sutra,* the layman Vimalakīrti criticizes the Buddha's disciple Purna, who has been expounding older, pre-Mahāyānic teachings to a group of young aspirants. Vimalakīrti instructs Purna, "You should first enter into meditation and observe a person's mind before expounding the dharma to that person. One does not put rotten food in a precious vessel. You must determine what thoughts are in the minds of these monks. Do not treat precious lapis lazuli as though it were mere glass!"[91] He goes on to reveal that in past lives these young monks vowed to follow the Mahāyāna path; thus, to fill them with inferior teachings is inappropriate and misjudges their capacities. As this story indicates, the primary factor in determining memory volume has to do with mental attitude. First, one must make a vow to pursue the Mahāyāna teachings, and then one must prepare a place to receive them.

This dedication and clearing of the mind is precisely what the Dragon King's daughter is able to accomplish with such startling speed in her famous appearance in the twelfth chapter of the *Lotus Sutra.* According to the story, the Buddha's disciple Manjuśri has been expounding the teachings in the dragon palace under the sea, where his best disciple has been the eight-year-old daughter of the Dragon King. Mañjuśri praises her, exclaiming, "She has attained *dhāraṇī* and is able to accept and hold completely the deep and subtle treasure-houses of all the buddha dharma. . . . What she recalls in her mind and expounds with her mouth is subtle and broad."[92] Another disciple, Śāriputra, objects, declaring, "A woman's body is filthy; it is not a dharma receptacle."[93] In mimetic defense of her own accomplishments, the young girl suddenly appears and gives the Buddha a jewel, which he accepts straightaway. She points out to Śāriputra that when one is prepared to accept a gift, the actual exchange moves quite quickly, and she provides visual confirmation of this by transforming herself into a male buddha. The point of this amazing display is that although the mind is physically embodied, it is not defined by that body. Rather the opposite. Once the dharma has lodged within the mind, it is capable of working on the body from the inside out.

Mahāyāna sutras thus understand the human mind as a vessel into which they can pour themselves. While the ideal vessel is watertight, in the sense that none of the teachings leak out, its barriers do appear permeable in other ways. Given enough time, presumably even a miniscule volume begins to affect both the mind and the larger physical container (the human body) that surrounds it. The greater the volume of internalized text, the speedier and more noticeable the transformation. This almost chemical reaction that occurs through the permeable membrane of the mind—although definitely a by-product of the process and not its main objective (which is the preservation of sutras)—is nevertheless pleasurable and interesting, and it is a theme that medieval Japanese explanatory tales return to time and again.

SCROLL AND STUPA

In its capacity as vessel, the human body (or, more precisely, the embodied sense organ of the mind) functions in ways comparable to two other types of Buddhist container: the stupa and the scroll. Stupas contain relics of a once-living buddha (bones, ash, etc.), while sutra scrolls contain wisdom, the germ of enlightened intuition that transforms a being into a buddha. As discussed above, Mahāyāna Buddhism seeks to elevate the place of the scroll as a container of the dharma. While implicit in many sutras, the assertion of the scroll's primacy is particularly strong in the *Lotus Sutra,* which instructs adherents to "make offerings to the sutra scroll, venerating it, holding it in esteem, and singing its praises" (T 12.262.38b19–20), just the same as if it were a living buddha who had just finished delivering a teaching. Similarly the *Diamond Sutra* suggests circumambulating the sutra while scattering offerings of flower and incense (T 8.235.750c22–23). These passages place a great deal of emphasis on the container—the offerings are not given to the sutra but specifically to the sutra scroll—thus insisting metonymically on the identification between the concrete, material thing of the scroll with the more abstract sutra contained therein.

If Mahāyāna Buddhism recognizes the human mind as a similar sort of container for the sutras, then logically we would expect sutras to give comparable directives to revere, respect, and make offerings to people who are recognized dharma vessels and to commemorate their presence through the building of stupas. In other words, we would expect sutras to draw correlations between the stupa-as-container, the scroll-as-container, and the mind-as-container. This is, in fact, precisely what we see. In the *Nirvana Sutra* the Buddha tells his disciple Kāśyapa that he has included two *gāthā* in the sutra specifically for the purpose of ensuring that those who protect the sutra will be praised. The first of these verses maintains, "To any person versed in dharma, / no matter whether young or old, / offerings should be made; / one should respect and worship him / as the Brahmin worships fire."[94] Even more specific, the *Lotus Sutra* declares that any place where anyone has accepted, held, read, recited, preached, or copied the sutra, "whether in a place where sutra scrolls are lodged, or in a garden, or in a grove," or in any other place, there one should erect a stupa in recognition of the fact that this place is "a Platform of the Path" on which buddhas have achieved unsurpassed supreme enlightenment.[95]

Thus Mahāyāna Buddhism recognizes any place where a sutra has existed as a locale of enlightenment, whether the sutra existed in memory, in writing, or in spoken language. Like any literary work, sutras require physical form if they are to be accessible to people. Earlier Buddhist traditions stressed the entrustment and oral transmission of sutras, meaning that sutras were always bound up with the physical form—the memory and the body—of the person expounding them. Ideally, this orator would be a buddha and locales of his important life events would be marked with a stupa that identified the location of his physical trace (pieces of his corpse, items he had touched, ground he had trod). Mahāyāna Buddhism adopts the stupa, and the rhetoric of physical presence, but leverages the locale of that presence away from the Buddha's body and into the words (the "linguistic text") of the sutra. These words can exist in one of two almost endlessly reproducible media: the written text (as in a scroll) or the memory (as in a human mind). The fusion of the container (body or scroll) with the linguistic text of the contained (the sutra) creates a material locale of embodiedness that accrues the praise, veneration, worship, and offerings previously accorded to the Buddha.

As a type of container, the human body is particularly valuable because it is alive and therefore capable not just of containing the sutra, but of engaging the sutra as a living organism. Typical symbiotic relationships in the natural world offer three economies of exchange: parasitism, in which the symbiotic relation negatively impacts the host organism; commensalism, in which the host is largely unaffected; and mutualism, in which both symbionts benefit from the relationship. Sutras are at pains to show that they offer humans a mutually beneficial symbiotic relationship in which buddha-like respect and veneration is but one of many potential boons. For hosts who agree to accept them without doubt, Amidist sutras such as the *Contemplation Sutra* and the *Larger Sutra of Immeasurable Life* promise release from evil karma (T 12.365.345c14) and rebirth in the Pure Land (T 12.360.272c8), where believers can meet Amida face-to-face and be free of all hunger, illness, and pain. The *Nirvana Sutra* promises similar boons, including long life (T 12.374.382c25), and even suggests that belief in the sutra can change one's physical appearance, causing strength to increase daily and one's appearance to steadily improve (399b5–7). Finally, the *Lotus Sutra*, most loquacious in this regard, claims that it shall reward anyone who is able to encourage others to listen to its teachings with breath that never stinks, a mouth and tongue never diseased, teeth ever straight and white, lips never scarred, a nose never out of joint, a full and round face, and a perfectly formed male member, among other things (T 9.262.47a8–19). Many, and perhaps most, of these promises must await future incarnations to come to fruition, thus reducing the immediate allure of sutras' boons and potentially placing sutras in a tenuous position as they search for new hosts.

Of course, should persuasion fail to do the trick, sutras also occasionally employ a tactic of intimidation, placing threats in the mouths of characters that appear in the narrative as would-be protectors of the teachings. Facing the Buddha's death, a number of figures (laity, goddesses, and disciples) in the *Nirvana Sutra* vow to crush any being who slanders the Mahāyāna teachings "as hail does grass" (T 12.374.367c26, 368b16, 382c22). In the same sutra the Buddha himself proclaims that those who speak ill of the *Nirvana Sutra* in particular will suffer illness, financial ruin, friendlessness, and tyranny, such that they shall be "like a bird whose wings are broken and who cannot fly."[96] With similar vindictiveness, the *Lotus Sutra* threatens those who malign it with deafness, dumbness, blindness, poverty, destitution, and general decrepitude, their bodies stinky, scabby, and covered with boils (T 12.262.16a3–7). Thus sutras promise to smite those who would slander or reject them or who would seek to part them from potential symbionts. Sutras offer a clear message to would-be hosts: "Accept me and live, perhaps in improved circumstances; reject me and suffer."

WHAT SUTRAS NEED

Given that they are willing to offer, and to threaten, so much, sutras clearly need a great deal from their symbiotic relationship with humans. Whereas the cycle of textual devotion I examined earlier describes what sutras *want,* in this final section I would like to turn to consider what it is that sutras *need,* their basic requirements for survival. In the natural world, for example, a host organism might provide its symbiont with any of several necessities of life, including nutrients, locomotion, shelter, or a place to incubate its young. As with its natural models, the human mind offers sutras many of these things, none of which sutras are capable of achieving on their own as material texts.

The first thing sutras need to continue to be viable in the world is shelter and protection. As we have already seen, sutras consistently proclaim the immanence of their extinction, whether at the hands of time, enemies of the faith, or overzealous editing. In this atmosphere, sutras not only want to be accepted, held, and internalized in the mind of a believer; they *need* it to survive as a literary species. This is why they so often include narratives about model beings who take great vows to protect, preserve, and guard the teaching.[97] At times sutras even include scenes in which former enemies see the light, as when, in the *Nirvana Sutra,* a host of demons declares that they "now love Mahāyāna and protect Mahāyāna," vowing to subdue all non-Mahāyānists and to guard the teachings and all those who work to ensure that "the true dharma shall not die out."[98] Elsewhere in the *Nirvana Sutra,* the Buddha tellingly proclaims that bodhisattvas must guard and protect their own bodies, caring for them properly, lest they be unable to make copies of the sutra, keep it safely in memory, chant it, and preach it widely to others (T 12.374.497c9–11). This passage frames the preservation of the body as a necessary step toward the ultimate goal, which is preservation of the sutras.

Cleverly, sutras often draw attention to the human side of the equation. Absorbing the sutras and providing them a safe haven, the human body acquires a certain magnetism, drawing in a host of beings (bodhisattvas, demons, goddesses, and so forth) who vow to protect and support the human *as vessel* of the dharma. In this somewhat solipsistic logic, sutras promise that supernatural beings will protect us if we protect them. Sutras thus seem to be offering humans precisely what they themselves need: shelter.

The second thing that sutras need from their exchange with humans is locomotion, and this is tied closely to their third requirement for survival, which is reproduction. In the "Fortitude" chapter of the *Lotus Sutra,* for instance, 8,500 people vow "to preach this scripture broadly in other lands," while some chapters later, in "Entrustment," the Buddha charges his auditors, saying, "You must all accept and keep, read and recite, and broadly proclaim this dharma, enabling all beings universally to hear it and know it."[99] This is the closest Buddhism comes to a missionary imperative, and the propagation of faith has primarily to do with the movement and reproduction of text. As I discussed earlier with respect to sutras' wants, in the cycle of textual devotion the preaching and copying of sutras begins to move internalized text back into the external world, where it can encounter new hosts in the next generation of its diasporic spread.

In conclusion, in this chapter and the chapters to come I understand sutras as living textual entities. My goal thus far has been to examine the origins of this phenomenon by locating and tracing the techniques by which sutras identify themselves as the germ of Buddhist life. Through the concerted use of metafictional strategies, sutras unmoor themselves from both the authorial hand and the oratorical mouth, taking those powers unto themselves and drawing on the rhetoric of embodiment to invest themselves with a living palpability. Thus birthed into the world, they find they are subject to the same realities of death and decline as all other beings, and they survive from generation to generation by cultivating a symbiotic relationship with a human host organism in whose mind the sutras may lodge.

To the degree that a believer (a host, or "dharma vessel") engages them, the sutras live physically within that believer's body. Humans provide shelter, protection, locomotion, and a reproductive mechanism, ensuring that individual sutra copies do not disintegrate before they are able to replicate themselves, and that the species, the textual line, survives in this age of darkness. In return, sutras promise an array of benefits, including relief from illness, enhanced mental faculties, eloquence, and a more pain-free incarnation in one's next existence. Medieval Japanese vernacular literature refracts and reflects on the nature of this symbiotic relationship by creating a plethora of narratives in which the human body disintegrates into textual fragments and, now reversing the image, textual fragments incorporate themselves into human bodies.

Another implication of this symbiotic relationship is that the gendered position of the reader becomes very complex. We are meant to serve as womblike containers into which the seed of the teachings can be inserted. And we are meant to gestate those teachings, transforming ourselves before inserting the seed into others. This suggests a perhaps uncomfortable array of positions that we as readers must assume in relation to the sutra text, ranging from lover (receptacle of seed) to child (the new being born of that seed) and finally seducer (inseminating others). This may be one reason that explanatory tales often stress the reproductive capabilities and genital status of their protagonists, speaking in particular of prepubescent girls, sexually active monks, well-endowed *hijiri* (wandering ascetics), genitally malformed nuns, and so forth.[100]

They key thing to glean from this symbiosis, however, is that Mahāyāna Buddhism understands paper (silk, bark, leaves, stone, or any other external writing surface) and the human body (which houses the memory organ of the mind) as intertwined locations for the inscription of sacred text. Reading is the process that allows the sutra-as-germ to break through into the membrane of the mind, while writing performs the inverse, as the body breaks open to produce the next iteration of scripture. Medieval Japanese setsuwa literature takes up this economy of flesh and text with considerable gusto, providing the material for an extended meditation on the particular ways in which one culture, distant in both time and place from the classical Indian subcontinent, made sense of and continued to build upon the rhetorical figures and life cycles of Buddhist textual culture.

TWO

Locating Setsuwa in Performance

ON THE TWENTY-SIXTH DAY of the Sixth Month of 1110, the otherwise unknown priest Kyōshakubō delivered a sermon before an audience of high-ranking aristocrats in the imperial capital of Heian. His sermon was part of a multiday event organized in accordance with a vow made by one of the imperial princesses. Seated before the assembly, he opened his address with the following words: "The heart of the Dhāraṇī [chapter of the *Lotus Sutra*], on which I will lecture today, is that this chapter tells how the bodhisattva Medicine King, the bodhisattva Brave Donor, the four deva kings, and various other beings each uttered a vow and taught a [protective] *dhāranī* for the sake of guarding holders of the sutra [Jp: *jikkyōsha*]. Though you have heard this many times already, there is no such thing as not receiving merit from this *Lotus Sutra,* even if the title only brushes your ear in passing or you intone it, mouthing it in jest."[1]

Kyōshakubō then cites a brief passage from the sutra in Chinese, which he glosses by means of a lengthy vernacular tale, a setsuwa. Though I will discuss this tale more fully in chapter 4, briefly, a man casts aspersions on the efficacy of the Buddhist teachings but happens to come into possession of a copy of the *Lotus,* which he shoves into his closet. Years later, when he dies and goes to judgment, he is spared reincarnation in hell simply for his unintentional act of protecting the sutra from the elements. Kyōshakubō concludes his sermon by praising his audience members, who, he observes, have followed the urgings of their hearts and committed themselves to holding, reading, and reciting the *Lotus,* and to supporting a multiday preaching event. The merit they have gained, he argues, is beyond the power of language to express.

Passages like these help us to position setsuwa alongside sutras as the two textual bases for the thriving medieval performance genre of sermonizing (Jp: *sekkyō* or *seppō*). As "explanatory tales," setsuwa explore the teachings and efficacy of the sutras and, in so doing, they fulfill the request that many sutras make to be expounded upon and clarified. Notably, Kyōshakubō commends his listeners for responding to four of the five injunctions the *Lotus Sutra* specifically makes when it asks its devotees to accept and keep, read, recite, copy, and expound it for the sake of other beings, and other sermons in the collection suggest that copying the sutra was another of the event's goals. Setsuwa thus both explain the sutras and, simultaneously, respond to the injunctions that those sutras levy. In addition, setsuwa act as a bridge, ferrying meaning from classical Chinese to the vernacular and describing a connection between sacred text and human body.[2] Kyōshakubō moves quickly from a telegraphic, Sinicized citation of the sutra to a substantial Japanese-language narrative, and his sermon is typical in its usage of physical, sensual tropes. Instead of simply hearing the sutras, their sounds "brush the ear," and instead of simply intoning them, we "mouth" their words, suggesting the corporeal nature of the interaction.

IMAGINING THE MEDIEVAL

Complementing the previous discussion of sutras, this chapter refocuses the question of textual presence onto the premodern genre of setsuwa. Like sutras, setsuwa are hyperaware of their position as written objects and, as performed texts, they seek to transcend the page and engage their readers on a corporeal level. In Japan, setsuwa scholarship tends to focus mostly on the orality of the tales, the ways in which they reflect the development of the Japanese language, and their connection to folkloric, popular cultural traditions. While useful in terms of developing a literary canon, this scholarly lens sets somewhat anachronistic and romanticized constraints on our understanding of the genre, defining it more in terms of protonationalism, rather than as a religious and rhetorical project.[3]

One of my major goals in this chapter, therefore, is to decouple setsuwa from the more modern question of national identity and focus instead on examining setsuwa in their medieval performance context, articulating a sense of how monks (and very occasionally nuns) sought to explain the complexities of Buddhist doctrine to lay audiences. If I see Buddhism as a transcultural phenomenon, a textual diaspora stretching across what would become national boundaries, this view is validated by the structure of setsuwa collections, which frequently organize their tales along a temporal and geographical vector as Buddhism stretches from its origins on the Indian subcontinent, across the breadth of the Asian continent, and finally to the islands of Japan. While the archipelago maintains its cultural distinctiveness, setsuwa envision Japan as a part of a larger, pan-Asian, Buddhist cultural sphere.

Another remarkable, and related, trend in Japanese setsuwa scholarship is the tendency to speak of setsuwa collections in a sensualized, often eroticized, manner. In this treatment setsuwa texts (and particularly their manuscripts) are something of an exquisite corpse, or sometimes an elusive beauty, into which the scholar must breathe new life. This way of viewing medieval texts can be readily observed in non-Asian contexts as well and has, I think, to do with certain modern conceptions about the oral nature of medieval textuality, a kind of literary "presence" that has been lost (or perceived as lost) in this post-Gutenberg age of rapid mechanical reproduction. As the sermon I alluded to above should suggest, setsuwa collections do in fact concern themselves with questions of somaticity, sensuality, and ontology to such an extent that the text-flesh relation forms one of the most consistent themes of the genre. A second task of this chapter, then, is to consider the prefaces and colophons of setsuwa collections: those places where the compilers speak most openly about their intentions and motivations. A close reading of these passages reveals some interesting things about how compilers wished their collections to work, if not always *as* a body, at least *on* the body, most often as medicine, healing sound, or sustenance, but also at times in violent and erotic ways.

In short, this chapter will begin to explore the very particular ways in which setsuwa as a genre thinks through the text-flesh relation, the liminal position that setsuwa holds with respect to orality and writing, and the importance of the performance setting to setsuwa mechanics. My working theses are, first, that setsuwa collections comprise the record of a major performance genre in medieval (especially twelfth- and thirteenth-century) Japan. Second, setsuwa seek to interact with their audiences in physical, sometimes highly sensual ways, perhaps responding to perceptions of a certain life force emanating from the sutras that they complement. And, third, setsuwa detail the various ways in which believers in medieval Japan sought to understand and cultivate the union of human body and sacred writ, providing an intriguing chapter in the book of Buddhist textual culture. In pursuing these theses, this chapter begins by introducing the nine setsuwa collections I will explore and explaining the rationale for choosing these particular texts. I then move through a series of close readings of prefaces and colophons, in which setsuwa compilers describe their textual project as either embodied or as acting on the body. Finally, I provide a more complete sketch of the medieval sermonizing scene in which setsuwa tales were employed.

AVADĀNA, ZHI GUAI, AND SETSUWA

While some of the material found in setsuwa no doubt has its origins in oral narrative—folklore, stories about native deities (Jp: *kami*), legends associated with specific locales and place names such as was collected in the gazetteers (Jp: *fudoki*) of the eighth century, and so forth—there can be no doubt that the Japanese genre of "explanatory tales" was influenced by Indian and Chinese narrative forms. Chief among these influential forms were the Indian "karmic biography" (Sk: *avadāna*) and its subset of "birth stories" (Sk: *jātaka*, stories of the Buddha's former incarnations), and the Chinese "strange tale" (Ch: *zhi guai*) and its particular manifestation in accounts of miracles (Ch: *yanji*).

Avadāna is a major genre of Indian Buddhist literature that was produced from at least the second century B.C.E. and continued to see new compilations until at least the eleventh century in India, and later in outlying areas such as Sri Lanka, Nepal, and Southeast Asia. The form was a mainstay of Buddhist missionary activity throughout the continent: as Joel Tatelman notes, "It can hardly be random coincidence that *avadānas* and other narrative works form a major part of the holdings of monastic libraries as distant from each other in time and space as early twentieth-century Laos and first-century Afghanistan."[4] *Avadānas* are both entertaining and didactic (aimed particularly at illustrating the workings of karma), and, according to John Strong, "were and still are used by Buddhist preachers in popular sermons."[5] Whereas *jātaka* tales feature the historical Buddha as protagonist, *avadānas* are less exclusive, commonly detailing the life and actions of a lay believer. Most *avadāna* and *jātaka* have a three-part structure comprised of a frame narrative set in the present, a flashback narrative, and a "juncture" in which the protagonist in the flashback scene is revealed to be none other than a former incarnation of one of the people in the present-tense frame narrative. In some instances, however, *avadāna* narratives will "shrink the 'story of the past' almost to nothing, while the 'story of the present' becomes the true *raison d'etre* of the tale," in which case attention shifts "away from deeds in previous births to actions in the here-and-now."[6]

As I mentioned in the introduction, *avadāna* compilations were, along with sutras, among the earliest Indian Buddhist texts to be translated into Chinese where, Donald Gjertson argues, they combined with a native narrative form, "strange tales" (Ch: *zhi guai*), resulting in the birth of dedicated collections of Buddhist miracle stories. The so-called "strange tales" (Robert Campany's "anomaly accounts" is another apt translation of the term *zhi guai*) are widely heterogeneous in their subject matter, though they generally describe events or objects that were somehow felt to be either unnatural or supernatural and thus in need of interpretation. Typically the accounts are quite brief and very much focused on the local terrain.

As we will see in the stories that follow, setsuwa recapitulate a number of the narrative strategies, structures, and preferences of the Indian "karmic biography" and the Chinese "anomaly account." From *avadāna*, which in Mahāyāna contexts were often organized around illustrating the six perfections of the bodhisattva, setsuwa inherit repeating tropes of self-sacrifice, a structural tendency toward temporal doubling (in which the present moment serves as a narrative frame for a past event), and an abiding thematic concern with past lives and the workings of karma. Again, influenced by Chinese miracle tales and anomaly accounts, setsuwa show a tendency to focus attention on presenting and then explaining the cosmological workings behind unusual events.[7] From these Chinese genres, setsuwa also inherit a trend toward downplaying both the elevated status of the main character and the "revelation scene" in favor of focusing on the present-moment moral choices of a quotidian character (a lay believer or a nonbeliever) who inhabits a specifically local time and place. And, like both the Indian "karmic biography" and the Chinese "miracle tale," Japanese "explanatory tales" tended to find use in sermons.[8]

Setsuwa, however, does chart its own territory as a Japanese genre. For instance, when collections refer explicitly to material from India or China (as in *Tales of Times Now Past,* discussed below), it is often as a part of a different tripartite structure, one that is aimed at situating Japan at the cutting edge of Buddhist expansion, the current location of the Buddhist event horizon. Setsuwa also provide important evidence about the ways in which medieval devotees sought to shape Buddhist belief and practice to local norms and preferences.

THE TEXTS

Though I will be making occasional reference to other texts and genres, nine main setsuwa collections serve as the backbone for this study.[9] The first three represent the earliest extant setsuwa texts, which span the course of three centuries: the *Nihon Genpō Zen'aku Ryōiki* (*A Wondrous Record of Immediate Karmic Retribution for Good and Evil in Japan,* ca. 823), the *Sanbō Ekotoba*

(*Illustrations and Explanations of the Three Jewels,* 984), and the *Hokke Genki (A Record of Miracles of the Lotus Sutra),* which was compiled between 1040 and 1044. The next two centuries saw a marked uptick in setsuwa production as Buddhism came to permeate the fabric of Japanese society, and I have chosen six representative texts, three from the twelfth century and three from the thirteenth. These are the *Hyakuza Hōdan Kikigakishō* (*Notes Taken While Listening to One Hundred Sessions of Sermons,* ca. 1110), the massive *Konjaku Monogatari* (*Tales from Times Now Past,* by 1120?), the heavily literary *Hōbutsushū* (*A Collection of Treasures,* by 1180?), the intensely personal *Hosshinshū* (*A Collection of Spiritual Awakenings,* 1214–15) and *Kankyo no Tomo* (*A Companion in Solitude,* 1222) collections, and the somewhat wry *Shasekishū* (*A Collection of Sand and Pebbles,* 1279–83). For easier reading, I will generally refer to the collections by abbreviated English titles (*The Three Jewels,* for instance, rather than *Sanbō Ekotoba*). Specialist readers may refer to the setsuwa finding list at the front of this book, which gives the full Japanese titles, along with their kanji, authors, and likely dates of compilation.

I have chosen to concentrate on these nine collections for a number of reasons. First, unlike many other collections that are often included under the scholarly rubric of "setsuwa," these nine works organize their explanatory tales in service of a consistently Buddhist project. The tales serve to elucidate a referenced sutra passage, refer to a given Buddhist rite or ceremony, include a moral reference explaining how the setsuwa may be used to clarify points of Buddhist doctrine, express the story of personal religious awakening, or are presented expressly as materials for use in sermons.

Second, as Kojima Takayuki has somewhat playfully noted, setsuwa collections may be roughly divided into two main types: the "taciturn" and the "loquacious."[10] I have chosen to focus on these nine compilations because, generally speaking, they are loquacious. They provide self-referential hints and suggestions, include colophons, or contain extensive prefatory notes so that enough may be known, or guessed with relative certainty, about their origins to sustain critical speculations about, and inquiry into, relationships between the written collection, its compiler, and the compiler's intended audience. The one exception to this rule is *Tales from Times Now Past,* which includes no prefaces but which stands as the most widely influential setsuwa collection of all time, providing the core material for countless literary works in Japan, up to and including film and manga in the current century.

Finally, *A Wondrous Record of Immediate Karmic Retribution* represents the first Japanese setsuwa collection and *A Collection of Sand and Pebbles* the last explicitly Buddhist one, with the others more or less evenly spaced through the intervening centuries, so that, taken together, these nine texts may be said to cover the full arc of setsuwa production during the medieval period in Japan.

A WONDROUS RECORD OF IMMEDIATE KARMIC RETRIBUTION

The *Nihon Genpō Zen'aku Ryōiki (A Wondrous Record of Immediate Karmic Retribution for Good and Evil in Japan)* was compiled circa 823 C.E. and, as its title suggests, is particularly concerned with the karmic cycle of sin and retribution. The setsuwa are recorded in classical Chinese, the lingua franca of classical and medieval Japanese Buddhism, though the prefatory notes indicate that the compiler intended the stories' use in ritualistic and oratorical contexts, at which time they most likely would have been rendered into colloquial Japanese. For the most part, the setsuwa in this collection are very short and unadorned, little more than plot summaries giving important details and providing a closing moral. The collection evinces little internal organization, with stories seeming to have been written down more or less as the compiler recalled them.

The compiler Kyōkai (sometimes rendered Keikai) was a low-ranking Hossō school monk who resided at the Yakushiji temple in the recently abandoned old capital of Heijōkyō.[11] Though his exact sources are unknown, it seems certain that the setsuwa in this collection represent an amalgam of stories he had read in various Chinese sources to which were added renditions of local and contemporary incidents that lent themselves to a Buddhist explanation. As Donald Gjertson and Kyoko Motomichi-Nakamura have pointed out, several of the stories in the *Wondrous Record* bear a striking resemblance to tales included in the *Mingbao ji,* a collection of some fifty-seven sketches compiled in seventh-century China by the government official and devout layman Tang Lin (b. 600?).[12] In eight instances Kyōkai has done little more than change proper nouns, relocating stories from China to Japan and suggesting that they happened to Japanese people. Thus, while the title of the collection calls attention to itself as a *ki* (suggesting a written record of historical events), one must be sensitive to fictionalized elements.

THE THREE JEWELS

The next extant setsuwa collection, the *Sanbō Ekotoba (Illustrations and Explanations of the Three Jewels),* did not appear for another century and a half, quite possibly because between the eighth and tenth centuries the state generally discouraged clerics from venturing outside the monastic complexes, mostly located in and around the imperial capitals, thus placing severe limitations on oratorical opportunities. The fifth article of the Sōniryō (Regulations for monks and nuns), promulgated in 701, expressly forbade monks and nuns from leaving the temple complex, gathering crowds of commoners, and preaching to them. The regulations were adopted as part of the legal machinery of the *ritsuryō* system of government, which remained in place, at least nominally, until the tenth century.[13]

The Three Jewels was completed in 984 against the fading backdrop of this system of government, and it is a much more polished and organized piece of writing than its successor. The work is neatly divided into three sections, each of which is thematically devoted to one of the "Three Jewels" of Buddhism: the Buddha, his teachings, and the sangha of believers. The first section consists of setsuwa that illustrate the various perfections (of patience, meditation, and wisdom, for example) that the historical Buddha achieved as a result of experiences in his many past incarnations. The second section offers setsuwa that describe the teachings and miraculous acts of various Buddhist luminaries, especially famous monks and nuns of Japan, while the final section uses the setsuwa format to explain the origins of a number of Buddhist ceremonies and rituals, activities that draw the sangha together.

The collection was created by Minamoto no Tamenori (d. 1011), an aristocratic scholar, lay believer, and expert in Chinese poetry.[14] The project was commissioned by the imperial family and composed expressly for the use of an ailing imperial princess who died shortly after being presented with the text. The collection, written in a Japanese that is occasionally quite poetically sophisticated, represents an attempt to bring Buddhism to the princess, who had taken the initial vows of a nun though she was too frail to enter fully into Buddhist life. As an *ekotoba* (illustrated writing) it was originally intended to pair drawings with prosaic explanations so that the graphic and the chirographic provided mutual commentary, but the illustrations either were never completed or have been lost in the intervening centuries. At any rate, this format suggests that the collection was meant to be perused slowly, carefully, and often. One imagines the ill princess, confined to her chambers, reading and rereading the collection as a textual proxy that gestured toward the wider Buddhist world that she was largely unable to see or hear in person.[15]

MIRACLES OF THE LOTUS SUTRA

Completed approximately sixty years after *The Three Jewels,* the *Hokke Genki (A Record of Miracles of the Lotus Sutra)* is, as the title indicates, wholly devoted to documenting miraculous occurrences associated with the powers of that sutra. The text is known by different titles, reflecting lines of textual transmission, each of which insists that the tales "record" real events. Two of the other titles—*Dainihonkoku Hokkekyō Genki* and *Honchō Hokke Genki*—both situate the tales as specifically occurring in "this court" *(honchō),* the "great country of Japan" *(dainihonkoku).*[16] In addition to distinguishing the collection from various continental texts that detail miracles of the *Lotus Sutra* experienced in China, the titles suggest a growing desire to situate Japan as a Buddhist country that not only inherited textual traditions from the continent but could speak back to those traditions from its own cultural vantage point.

Setsuwa from this collection feature protagonists with a wide range of formal commitment to the Buddhist faith: they may be famous monks or nuns, novices who have taken the introductory vows, or lay believers whose devotions are at best distracted and inconsistent. The one thing that binds them all together is a shared faith in the *Lotus Sutra,* a faith that is rewarded when the sutra saves them from suffering in hell, rescues them from an earthquake or a collapsed mine, or helps assure their rebirth in the heavenly realms. The collection was compiled between 1040 and 1044 by a Tendai priest named Chingen who was associated with a temple in the Yokawa district of Mount Hiei, the most powerful center of esoteric Buddhism in classical Japan. Mount Hiei lies just northwest of the then-capital Heiankyō, and priests who lived there often maintained open contact with the aristocratic culture of the city. Probable audiences for the text thus include not only clerics (who would have used the tales in sermons) but also aristocratic lay devotees and other city dwellers who may have used the collection's "records" of successful rebirth as a goad to their own faith and as an inspiration for their own devotions.[17]

ONE HUNDRED SESSIONS OF SERMONS

Although it took Japan approximately two and a quarter centuries to produce its first three (still-existing) setsuwa collections, the 1100s saw the creation of some seven or eight compilations,[18] the earliest of which was the *Hyakuza Hōdan Kikigakishō (Notes Taken While Listening to One Hundred Sessions of Sermons).* Like most premodern texts, this piece has a rather complex textual history, in this case one of particular interest because of its origins in a performance context. Briefly, a certain imperial princess (exact identity unknown) organized one hundred days of consecutive preaching.[19] The event, which also involved the creation of at least one handwritten sutra, took place in a wing of the imperial palace and eventually stretched to three hundred days, drawing talented preachers (Jp: *nōsetsu*) from a variety of sectarian backgrounds. Each speaker was responsible for ten days' worth of oration, and the collection, much truncated and damaged over the years, preserves twenty days of material, representing the sermons of nine different men.

The collection as we have it today went through a number of intermediate stages. Working backward from the manuscript that was discovered by Son-oda Shūe in 1916 at Hōryūji, Satō Akio and Yamagishi Tokuhei have reconstructed a probable history for the text. The extant manuscript consists of one scroll, written front and back in a rather hurried hand of katakana and kanji. This single scroll, done by a Hōryūji monk, mentions that it is a copy of a manuscript that consisted of at least two scrolls done by a monk (possibly by the name of Toei) at the nearby Daianji. Yamagishi and Satō speculate that Toei was in attendance at most, if not all, of the sermons and that the manuscript represents his written "notes" (Jp: *shō*) of the event. They also suggest that the Toei manuscript may have contained a more complete record of the sermons and that, given that it was written mostly in kana, it may have circulated for a time among ladies at the imperial court. Much of this theory remains conjecture, however, as the beginning and end of the scroll (which would normally contain more information about its origin) are badly damaged and, incredibly, the three-hundred-day event does not show up in courtiers' diaries or official historical records of the time.[20]

Nevertheless, *One Hundred Sessions of Sermons* provides an important window onto the practices of Buddhist sermonizing in medieval Japan. As compared to most other setsuwa collections, the stories here are much expanded, including extended dialogue, glosses of Chinese terminology and technical language, sporadic notes about what sutras are chanted and when bells are rung, and occasional references to ongoing ritual activities such as the joint creation of handwritten sutra scrolls. Furthermore, each setsuwa is explicitly linked to a particular sutra and to a particular chapter or subsection of that sutra, so that it becomes possible to speak in a more detailed manner of the relationship between canonical sutra text and the commentary that a setsuwa offers on that text. Thus, the text, damaged though it is, illuminates an entire performance context of ritual activity in which setsuwa play a key role in sustaining faith and igniting the imagination. Toward the end of this chapter I will sketch this performance context more fully.

TALES FROM TIMES NOW PAST

If *One Hundred Sessions of Sermons* represents a text firmly rooted in oral performance, the *Konjaku Monogatari (Tales from Times Now Past)* returns us to a more overtly written, literary project. Because it has no prefaces, it is impossible to state with certainty exactly when, why, or by whom the massive collection was created. Tradition long attributed the thirty-one volumes to the aristocrat and Buddhist layman Minamoto no Takakuni (1004–77), but more recent scholarship has shown this to be highly unlikely, as a number of the tales are known to have originated several years after his death. This has led to speculation that the project may have been the product of collaboration, perhaps by a team of men (aristocratic and/or clerical) working in tandem, along the model of the editorial teams that created the great poetic anthologies of the Heian court. Contemporary scholarship places the "completion" of the text to within a few decades of Takakuni's death, citing 1120 as "a not unlikely approximate date."[21]

The collection is incredibly ambitious in its scope, tracing the origin of Buddhism and its movement across the continent to Japan. The first five volumes are set in India and detail the life and times of Buddha. The next five volumes shift to China and the focus, though still clearly on Buddhism, widens slightly to include some more secular tales and histories. The last twenty-one volumes comprise a full commedia of Japan, beginning with the transmission of Buddhism to that country and continuing the explicitly Buddhist theme for some ten volumes (sutra miracles, descriptions of the Pure Land, tales of karmic retribution, etc.) before turning to secular anecdotes concerning aristocrats, warriors, and craftsmen, and ultimately concluding with a one-volume gazetteer of anomalous events in the provinces. Some portions are missing and perhaps were never completed, such as the planned volume on imperial politics. It seems clear that *Tales from Times Now Past* was meant to serve as something of a central warehouse of Buddhist tales, an almost encyclopedic reference work. In this capacity it draws material from a number of earlier collections both Chinese (the *Mingbao ji*, for instance) and Japanese (*A Wondrous Record of Immediate Karmic Retribution* and *Miracles of the Lotus Sutra,* among others), sometimes providing alternate or more elaborate retellings, thus giving some indication of the popularity of certain setsuwa and their ability to remain in circulation over a span of several centuries.[22]

A COLLECTION OF TREASURES

Like *Tales from Times Now Past,* the *Hōbutsushū (A Collection of Treasures)* was long attributed to a known historical figure, the famous *waka* poet, warrior, and courtier Taira no Yasuyori (fl. 1157–1200). Yasuyori found himself

on the losing side of the civil wars that ushered in the transition from aristocratic to military rule in the late twelfth century. He was exiled to Kikaigashima, "the island of demons," at the southern tip of the Japanese archipelago, before being pardoned and returning to the Heian capital, where he took
the tonsure and entered the Buddhist path. Modern researchers, however, have
begun to doubt Yasuyori's authorship, and Yamada Shōzen, one of the foremost scholars of the collection, has suggested that whoever the real compiler
was concealed himself behind a cleverly constructed narrator who was made
to resemble Yasuyori in many of his life experiences.[23] If this is the case, then
A Collection of Treasures represents an entirely new textual innovation for setsuwa: their placement within an intentionally fictionalized context. Tellingly,
that context is one of temple-based sermonizing.

A Collection of Treasures begins with the return of its narrator from exile
and his arrival in the capital. He pays a visit to an old friend who tells him
about the miraculous statue of Śākyamuni Buddha that has been installed at
Seiryōji, a temple to the northwest of the city, and which is rumored to have
been done from life. The narrator goes to the temple and, finding a great
crowd assembled in the main hall, slips into a side room where he begins to
recite the *Lotus Sutra*. When he hears the priest enter the main hall, he listens
through the wall to the cleric's speech about the statue. As the day continues,
some of the assembled pilgrims begin to discuss what they value in life before
the priest takes over the conversation and speaks through the night about the
true treasure that is Buddhism.

The setting of the collection as the transcription of a sermon is alluring and
does have precedent, as texts like *One Hundred Sessions of Sermons* suggest,
but it is almost certainly a literary fiction. The scaffolding of the text is simply too apparent as the monk churns with dogged persistence through the regular suspects of Buddhist oratory: how rare it is to meet the dharma; the doctrines of emptiness and transience; the six paths of reincarnation; the various
pains of human existence; piety, merit, and reclusion; the three jewels of the
Buddha, dharma, and sangha; each of the precepts (against killing, theft, intox-
ication, etc.); the practices of confession, charity, and visualization; and finally
the power of the *Lotus Sutra* and a description of the Pure Land. Through a
study of various manuscripts of the collection, Koizumi Hiroshi has shown
that some sections appear to have been fully fleshed out while others remain
either in a skeletal form or in some intermediate state (for example, with a
string of related *waka* that the compiler may have meant to edit into a flowing narrative at some later point).[24] Based on his research, Koizumi posits that

the first version of the collection was in circulation by 1188, after which it underwent a series of revisions and supplementations.

A COLLECTION OF SPIRITUAL AWAKENINGS

With the *Hosshinshū (A Collection of Spiritual Awakenings)* we tread once again on firmer ground: the traditional attribution of the collection to the famous poet Kamo no Chōmei (1155–1216) seems accurate, as do the dates of composition, between 1214 and 1215. To a degree not seen in previous collections, *A Collection of Spiritual Awakenings* is deeply colored by its author's personal experience, and the text comprises an intimate read of Chōmei's life as he looks back at his own individual history, particularly his stumbling progress on the Buddhist path. The collection also reflects Chōmei's training as a *waka* poet, his fairly intimate knowledge of the Kamakura military government and their imperial rivals at the court of Emperor Gotoba, and his long tenure as a semirecluse in the mountains around the Heian capital.

There are no early manuscripts still extant, but material from different textual lineages suggests that the text was slightly unstable. In particular, Chōmei (or perhaps someone else) seems to have added material to the end of the collection, perhaps circulating first one copy and then an expanded version at a later date. Again, it is likely that over the centuries each person who copied the manuscript saw fit to make slight alterations, reflecting his or her own needs and tastes, and we do know that our current version differs somewhat from bits and pieces of *A Collection of Spiritual Awakenings* that were cited in the 1603 Jesuit dictionary *Nippo Jishō*. Unlike some other setsuwa texts that disappeared from circulation, sometimes for centuries at a time, Chōmei's collection remained popular and influential from the time of its conception in the early thirteenth century to the present day.[25]

Aside from language that is sometimes beautifully poetic in texture, *A Collection of Spiritual Awakenings* holds particular value for the lengthy meditations with which each tale or group of related tales typically concludes. These reprises, which are sometimes two or three times as long as the setsuwa they gloss, represent an outgrowth of the telegraphically short morals that earlier collections contain, and they provide a fuller picture of how at least one medieval person made sense of setsuwa tales as Buddhist texts that connected to a larger field of spiritual thought and practice. The author provides no overt organizational scheme other than a tendency to return to moments of religious awakening, and the tales flow one into the next by way of a loose, almost *renga* (linked verse)–like poetic connection.

The penultimate collection I study here, the *Kankyo no Tomo (A Companion in Solitude),* was long attributed to the powerful Tendai abbot and famous *waka* poet Jien (1155–1225), a tribute to the beauty, polish, and light-handed pathos of the collection. Recent scholarship, however, has proved fairly conclusively that the compiler was actually a much less well-known Tendai monk named Keisei (1189–1268). Though a scion of the Kujō clan, a branch of the politically influential Northern Fujiwara, Keisei was dropped as a child, leading to a permanent deformity of the back. Thus, he entered the priesthood at a young age. He remained quite well connected socially, however, securing funds for a trip to China, from which he returned with some two hundred Buddhist scrolls. His traveling done, Keisei settled into the rhythms of a mountain-dwelling Buddhist recluse, though he maintained communication with friends and relatives in the capital. Eventually he received a commission from a noblewoman (probably a relative) for the completion of a setsuwa collection that was to guide and inspire her in her practices as a novice on the Buddhist path.[26]

The dominant thread in the collection concerns the lives and practices of Buddhist recluses and mountain dwellers, people who, like both Keisei and his patroness, had renounced the world in order to live in peaceful meditation. But *A Companion in Solitude* is delicately woven from a number of other thematic threads as well. The moment of religious awakening, the issue of gender in any woman's attempt to overcome the five obstructions[27] and advance on the Buddhist path, instances of lay devotees' rebirth in the Pure Land, and the contemplation of dead and decaying bodies all appear frequently throughout the collection. While most of the setsuwa are quite short, they are full of finely drawn detail and sensitive emotional observations. The collection is unique in being termed a *tomo,* literally a "friend," a term that presents the written text as a living presence that was to perform the role of guide on the Buddhist path.

A COLLECTION OF SAND AND PEBBLES

The last major collection that I cover in this study was completed in 1283, some sixty years after *A Companion in Solitude.* The *Shasekishū (A Collection of Sand and Pebbles),* however, is very different in tone, scope, and audience. Rather than being composed by a socially connected cleric for an aristocratic audience in the immediate environs of the capital, *A Collection of Sand and*

Pebbles is a more provincial and much less formal work. The compiler Mujū Ichien (1226–1312) was a Rinzai Zen monk, and his setsuwa collection evinces much of the humor and dry wit often associated with that school of Buddhism. For Mujū laughter is as powerful a source of religious awakening as poetic sorrow. His stories often begin on a wry and humanist note, with headings such as "The Monk Whose Wife Tried to Kill Him," and may take comic unexpected turns, as when, in the midst of a death rehearsal ceremony, the layman dressed as the buddha Amida farts, leading the laymen costumed as Amida's attendants Seishi and Kannon to collapse in a fit of giggles.[28] Mujū's comic and quotidian turn presages trends that became more pronounced in the later medieval period and its literary affection for instances of the low overcoming the high (Jp: *gekokujō*). His collection also suggests the other literary venues that setsuwa themes and tropes would come to occupy after the 1200s, when the setsuwa genre gave way to newer literary forms, such as companion tales (Jp: *otogi zōshi*) and vernacular tracts (Jp: *kana hōgo*). Finally, *A Collection of Sand and Pebbles* indicates a growing sensitivity to differing motivations and objectives underlying the performance of sermonizing. For Mujū, the paradigmatic distinction has to do with whether one preaches to earn reward (payment or, more nebulously, reputation) or one preaches to spread the teachings of Buddhism. As others have argued, the late twelfth century also witnessed other shifts in motivation and objective, with the growth both of more "histrionic" styles of sermonizing aimed at "entertainment" and, counterbalancing that, the establishment of formal lineages of preaching, such as the Agui school, which I examine below.[29]

Aside from being a good storyteller, Mujū was the head priest of the Chōbōji temple, which lay off the Eastern Sea Road (Tōkaidō), the main highway connecting the aristocratic capital at Heian with the military capital at Kamakura. Though he may well have had dealings with various authorities in the military structure, most of Mujū's parishioners were rather lower-ranking and even included families of local beggars. According to Mujū's Tokugawa period (1600–1868) biographers, he taught a young man named Tokuwaka how to do *owari manzai,* a special New Year's dance in which a person would go from house to house handing out pine branches, dancing, and accepting alms. Tokuwaka and his brother lived with their father (their mother having died) and eked out a living as street and garden sweepers, an occupation that marks them as clinging to the very lowest rungs of the social ladder.[30] Mujū's collection speaks much less directly about textual culture (and much more about preaching and other forms of performance), which probably has as much to do with his personal preferences for humor and his desire to bring new material into the setsuwa tradition as it does with the social makeup of his congregation and their presumed literacy levels. After all, sutras do not require that one be literate in order to worship them.

As the title suggests, the *Collection of Sand and Pebbles* is a "collection" in the most expansive sense, drawing almost at random from personal experience, the sermons of others, hearsay, and local gossip to form a text that is very loosely organized into thematic units. Any given heading may contain a single setsuwa or may be vastly expanded as Mujū connects story after story in something approximating a stream-of-consciousness fashion. During the composition itself Mujū was forced to set the text aside several times, sometimes for the better part of a year, before picking it up again, making his collection more like the *Wondrous Record of Immediate Karmic Retribution,* with its impulsive and surprising links between stories, than the streamlined, aristocratic productions of *The Three Jewels* and *A Companion in Solitude.*[31]

A SNAPSHOT OF THE GENRE

As is readily apparent, the setsuwa collections considered in this study represent a wide variety of organizational schemes, audience orientations, textual histories, languages of composition, and levels of formality. It is partially due to this remarkable variety that setsuwa have not received widespread critical attention in the West, though they are the subject of a booming field of academic inquiry in Japan. Still, one can point to some generic trends. First, with the exception of the earliest compilation, *A Wondrous Record of Immediate Karmic Retribution,* and the last one examined here, *A Collection of Sand and Pebbles,* all of the collections spin out of centers of aristocratic culture in or near the imperial capital of Heiankyō (modern Kyōto). Thus, though they may take as their protagonists people from a wide range of social classes, these texts reflect most strongly the cultural milieu of the nobility and the premium that culture placed on artistic sophistication as well as its awareness of the emotional highs and lows of amorous pursuit and the sometimes harsh realities of politics.

We can also make some generalizations regarding authorship, which breaks down into roughly three categories. Texts compiled by laity *(The Three Jewels, Tales from Times Now Past,* and *A Collection of Treasures)* tend toward the encyclopedic. These highly structured collections are the product of a social class flush with education, leisure time, and financial resources, and their textual projects seem particularly interested in netting the sum total of Buddhism in neatly abstracted form. Texts compiled by clerics for professional purposes

(A Wondrous Record of Immediate Karmic Retribution, Miracles of the Lotus Sutra, One Hundred Sessions of Sermons, and *A Collection of Sand and Pebbles)* tend to be less well-integrated and more narrowly focused on themes that would attract interest and would inspire or maintain faith. These collections appear to be handbooks of tales for use in sermonizing. Finally, two of the texts *(A Collection of Spiritual Awakenings* and *A Companion in Solitude)* are intensely personal in nature and appear to have been composed, at least initially, for an exclusive audience, either the author himself or a specific individual to whom he was related. These provide the most richly poetic passages, at times a dense brocade of allusion and metaphor, and they also supply more extended meditations on the meanings of the setsuwa they convey.

CHASING MEDIEVAL MANUSCRIPTS

Modern Japanese setsuwa scholars tend to use a consistent rhetoric of embodiment to describe the texts with which they work. Komatsu Kazuhiko, for instance, writes that "events are the seed [Jp: *tane*] for setsuwa and ideas their womb [Jp: *botai*],"[32] a figuration that invokes the mechanics of sexual reproduction. Writing twenty years later, in 2001, Komine Kazuaki employs the exact same metaphor, though he specifies a different surrogate, when he writes that in the medieval period, "everyday conversations carried with them a significance as the wellspring or womb [Jp: *botai*] from which *setsuwa* were born."[33] In his choice of everyday conversation as the maternal body inside of which setsuwa grow, Komine echoes the assertions of Furuhashi Nobuyoshi, who has claimed that setsuwa have a "life span" (Jp: *seimei*)[34] that is specifically linked to and dependent upon human speech, as if setsuwa were a living substance passed along through word of mouth. Other setsuwa scholars, such as Komatsu Kazuhiko and Satō Akira, also identify setsuwa as an oral genre that is "stilled in writing" and can "reemerge in performance."[35]

A somewhat more troubling metaphor for setsuwa characterizes the scholarly search for meaning in terms of an actively sexual conquest, employing the term *kaimami* to describe philological attempts to "peek between the fence slats," admiring setsuwa manuscripts as if each were an attractive lady who, according to the classical literary trope, the suitor-scholar is forbidden to see but whom he is nevertheless intent on ravishing, by force if necessary. For instance, Komine Kazuaki describes his excitement on first getting to touch the written form of an archived setsuwa manuscript in the following words. "I feel as if the living form and voice [of the setsuwa] float up toward me. Once they are spoken, transformed into voice, these written texts take on meaning, striking the listener's breast, plucking at the heart strings, so that one can truly understand and feel for oneself their meaning."[36] The passage comprises an eerie reenactment of Kaoru's conquest of Oigimi in *The Tale of Genji* and even references the strings that the woman touches, here translated in the metaphorical sense of "heart strings" but literally "koto strings," the koto being the musical instrument Oigimi was playing when she first attracted Kaoru's attention, leading eventually to his unwanted intrusion and (to modern, legal eyes) sexual assault of her.[37]

This language of embodiment and sensual conquest is not peculiar to Japanese scholarship but rather is emblematic of modern philological approaches to, and imaginations of, medieval manuscripts. Writing on the literature of the European Middle Ages, for instance, Paul Zumthor has noted, "Every relationship we maintain with a text involves some latent eroticism. Only this dynamism puts the critical reader in a situation comparable to that of the medieval reader or listener, whose whole body, not only his visual and auditory faculties, was engaged in the reception of the text."[38] For Zumthor, erotic sensation provides an avenue to (or perhaps evidence of) an increasingly authentic experience on the part of the critic who is willing, even excited, to engage with the manuscript on physical as well as mental levels.

Though Zumthor is imminently aware of the shortcomings of this sort of romanticism as a critical approach,[39] he nevertheless seems unable to resist employing the occasional metaphor. For instance, in describing the inherent otherness of medieval texts, he notes, "It is through erudition that the discovery of otherness must pass. And from otherness comes the pleasure; there is pleasure only in the Other, a concrete, historical Other. Pleasure carries a trace of history: if my object is a loved woman, history is there in the very fact that she exists, *hic et nunc*. If the object is a medieval text, I must come to know its body; but that body will be uncovered for me only after my information is as complete as it can be."[40] Learning difficult and obscure medieval languages, familiarizing oneself with the history and religion and politics of medieval societies: all of these scholarly pursuits are for Zumthor a way of "uncovering" the text, as if each bit of linguistic and cultural knowledge strips away one more layer of clothing from the body of the text, ultimately leaving it naked before the scholarly eye. In an analytical survey of scholarship on medieval European manuscripts, Sarah Kay has pointed out the ubiquity of this erotic approach, noting, "One of the meanings of 'philology' is a loving attention to manuscript remains."[41]

I take seriously these modern scholarly figurations of medieval manuscripts and setsuwa texts precisely because the medieval compilers of setsuwa themselves often provided strikingly physical metaphors for describing their textual projects. In order to approach setsuwa in a way that is both accurate and sensitive to the nuances of medieval rhetoric, it is necessary to be explicit about the figurative ramifications of chosen metaphors and to untangle the sometimes violent romanticism of modern scholarship from the precise language of medieval setsuwa prefaces. Furthermore, setsuwa collections' choices of specific metaphorical language and figurative tropes are one of the few medieval sources to focus consistently on the dynamics of the preaching event. It is therefore important to document this rhetoric as accurately and as thoroughly as possible so that our analyses of Buddhist oration, which necessarily involve a certain amount of speculation and guesswork, nevertheless represent medieval conceptions of the relationships between speaker and audience, textuality and physicality, as precisely as possible.

In ways similar to (though by no means identical with) the rhetoric of contemporary scholars, medieval setsuwa compilers tend to describe their collections in terms of human physicality, at times working off a symbolic economy of ingestion, at other times identifying the textual corpus with the human body in ways that suggest a gentle undertone of the erotic. Often setsuwa compilers signal these brief passages of self-reflexivity by employing phrases such as, "It is my earnest wish that . . . " or "It is my hope . . . ," or simply by appending the auxiliary verb *mu,* which indicates personal volition. Though many setsuwa collections (such as *Tales of Times Now Past*) contain no such remarks, when they do exist they are most often found in either the compiler's prefatory remarks or the colophon.

SWALLOWING FOOD AND MEDICINE

One of the most common ways setsuwa compilers conceptualized their literary projects was as a type of food or medicine, a substance to be ingested. In the closing sentences of *A Collection of Sand and Pebbles,* Mujū Ichien notes that his "true intention" (Jp: *hon'i*) is that the setsuwa in his collection serve as "seeds for the awakening of the heart of enlightenment and as nourishment for the practices of the Buddha's teachings" (NKBZ 52: 615). Whether ingested in the form of raw "seeds" of enlightenment or as fully grown, harvested, and prepared "nourishment," setsuwa are active substances that, once they have gained entry into the human body, will work to sustain that body like food.

Also working with the metaphor of physical ingestion of the Buddha's teachings via the mediating force of setsuwa, Minamoto no Tamenori, compiler of *The Three Jewels,* describes his collection in actively medicinal terms. In the preface to his second volume, which focuses on the treasure of the dharma, Tamenori notes, "The Buddhist teachings which remain to us are just like medicine left by a physician. How is it that anyone could not be cured of the sickness of the passions? They are like jewels hidden [in one's garment] by a friend. In the end we shall surely awaken from the dark stupor of desire. . . . The sound of the [Buddhist] law is just like that of a poison drum: hearing it only once, the enemy, spiritual ignorance, is killed. The names of the sutras are just like the saplings of medicinal trees: barely recite them and the disease of endless transmigration is lifted" (SNKBT 31: 74–75, 76). In all of these similes, the Buddha's teachings represent a starting point: a medical regimen to be followed, a jewel to be discovered, a drum to be struck, or a sapling to be nurtured. To be effective, each needs its own intermediary: a nurse to tend the ill, a friend to hide the jewel, a drummer to beat the drum, or a gardener to tend the tree. I would argue that Tamenori here is suggesting that setsuwa— whether as recounted aloud by priests for a listening audience or presented in summarized format to be read by a captive one—represent the fulfillment of that potential: the medicine taken, the jewel found, the drum beaten and heard, the sapling grown and harvested. Ingesting the materials of setsuwa, whether orally (as medicine or purgative poison) or aurally (as drumbeats or the recited names of sutras), the audience is physically transformed from the inside out, cured of the "sickness" of their ignorance, purged of the "disease" and "stupor" of their passions. Importantly, Tamenori's similes conflate the imagery of ingestion with that of aurality, thus suggesting that his audience must actively ruminate on words that come into them through their ears.[42]

Tamenori is asking the ill princess who is his primary audience to act as a complicit agent in her own embodied transformation. Here setsuwa are understood to be active substances that infiltrate the human body, working to alter it on the physical level. Even if the ultimate transformation is a spiritual one, it is described in somatic terms. Nor is Tamenori alone in utilizing medicinal metaphors to describe the curative powers of Buddhist oration. Writing two centuries later the compiler of *A Collection of Treasures* echoes this understanding of the Buddhist teachings as a medicine that, aurally ingested, can cure "the three poisonous illnesses of greed, anger, and ignorance" (SNKBT 40: 172).

In a culturally generalized sense, of course, this metaphor of the Buddhist teachings as medicinal substances relates both to the performance of sickness in the *Vimalakīrti Sutra* as well as to the "Medicinal Herbs" chapter of the *Lotus Sutra*. These two texts were, not incidentally, among the most familiar Buddhist writings in classical and medieval Japan. The *Vimalakīrti Sutra* was understood to have medicinal value in its own right, as was celebrated in the Vimalakīrti service held at Yamashinadera (Kōfukuji) in Nara. As part of the service, recitations of the sutra were believed to be effective for instantaneously curing illness.[43] Read aloud, the sutra is ingested aurally as medicinal and curative, a substance able to transform and heal the human body. The "Medicinal Herbs" chapter of the *Lotus Sutra* likewise belongs to the same figurative network of images, dealing as it does with a comparison of the Buddha's teachings to a gentle rain that falls, its "infusions reaching everywhere. The grass and trees, the shrubs and forests, and the medicinal herbs—whether of small roots, stalks, branches, and leaves, or of middle-sized . . . or of large—and also all trees, great and small, whether high, intermediate or low, all receive some of it."[44] In this soft rainfall of the Buddha's teachings, his words shower equally, gently, and persistently on all things, soaking into them, being ingested by them, bringing them the nourishment required for renewed growth. When setsuwa compilers tap into this metaphor of curative sound, they understand their collections as carrying out, or at least making possible, this same sort of healing.

Chingen, compiler of *Miracles of the Lotus Sutra,* works through his ideas about the position of setsuwa vis-à-vis the human body and sacred text from a strikingly different angle, by inverting the image of healing in favor of a much more violent procedure for achieving wholeness. Mentioning the work (no longer extant) of a Song-era Chinese Tendai monk, he establishes precedents for a collection of tales concerning miracles of the *Lotus Sutra,* and he laments that earlier examples do not include any stories from Japan. In seeking to remedy that lack, Chingen notes that some tales were easy to gather, since they still regularly came up in conversation, while others, hidden in written histories and books, were much harder to find. He compares his textual search to that of Sessen Dōji, the "Himalaya Boy" who offered his own body to feed a hungry demon in return for half a *gāthā* of scripture. Like Sessen Dōji, who wrote the resulting complete verse all over nearby rocks and trees before preparing to be eaten, Chingen rejoices that his efforts have not been in vain and have resulted in *Miracles of the Lotus Sutra.* He ends the preface by asserting that his goal in creating the collection was not personal erudition but the hope of curing "the darkness of ignorance" in all beings (NKBT 7: 510).

GARDENING

Another popular way of conceptualizing setsuwa collections was to speak of them as seeds planted in gardens. In addition to comparing it to food and medicine, for instance, Tamenori also describes his *Three Jewels* as a seed that, introduced in the proper soil, generates an internalized landscape of spiritual fecundity. In his opening preface he writes that, having considered the fact that "the seeds of buddhahood arise through karmic connections, I have carefully gathered and written down the leaves of words of the forest of virtue and planted deeply the upright roots of the sapling of supreme enlightenment, whereupon the jeweled strand of my heart has broken and scattered over the precious gems of these words and the rain of my tears flows to the base of the watery stalk. It is my hope that, with this aspiration, [many] may be led along the path, even in ages to come" (SNKBT 31: 7). In this densely figurative landscape, the human heart serves as the fertile ground into which the seeds of buddhahood are planted. Sprouting leaves and developing a willowy stem in this springtime of the soul, the small sapling receives its water in the form of rapturous tears.

In addition to presenting a beautiful metaphor for religious awakening and growth, Tamenori's comments also pose an intricate meditation on the relationship between textuality and spirituality. The image of a seed that grows in the human heart is not only a Buddhist one—in which case the seed is the kernel of buddhahood—but one intimately connected to Japanese poetic conceptions. The *Kokinwakashū (A Collection of Waka Ancient and Modern)*, an imperially sponsored poetry anthology completed in 914, opens with the following sentence: "Taking the human heart as its seed, Japanese poetry has grown into countless leaves of words" (NKBT 8: 93). In this metaphor, Japanese poetry performs a complex melding of human sentiment, spoken word, and written word as the welling forth of emotion in the poet's heart leads to the verbal composition of leaves of song, hundreds upon hundreds of which are gathered in written form in the anthology that itself figures as a lush forest.

Tamenori thus situates his setsuwa collection in the context of poetic expectations. His description is itself ornately poetic, depending upon an intricately woven net of semantically related words (Jp: *engo*) to express its full range of meaning, the sense of which is communicated as much on the levels of imagery and sensational response to beauty as on those of logical or grammatical association. The related words—"tears," "rain," "watery stalk," and "flow"—work together to bind the sentence into a poetic whole as each image calls forth the expectation for the next. The composer's tears allegorically translate into a gentle rain that nourishes the poetic seed of buddhahood, now sprouted into a willowy stalk around which the gathered waters flow. Furthermore, the word *mizukuki* (watery stalk), when used in an adverbial phrase, can also refer to calligraphy written in a beautiful, flowing hand so that the water that flows around the sapling of enlightenment is associated not only with rain and tears but also with writing, as if the setsuwa compiler's salty tears flowed not from his eyes but from the tip of his brush.

Finally, Tamenori's description also draws on the imagery of a strand of jewels, representative of his heart, which breaks and scatters over the text, itself a collection of gems. Mary Carruthers, in her *Book of Memory,* discusses the image of the strand of pearls as a mnemonic device in medieval European (and particularly Christian) culture, in which case the jewels represent the treasure of the scriptures. Though Buddhist sutras are also commonly counted among the "three jewels" of Buddhism (to which Tamenori refers in his title), the suggestions implied by the image of a scattered strand of jewels in this case do not conform to Carruthers's hypotheses concerning memory, pointing rather to a sensation of emotional eruption more than one of calm recollection. In classical Japanese verse, poets often utilized the image of a broken strand of jewels in order to suggest the emotional and physical turmoil of erotic love. The *Man'yōshū (A Collection of Ten Thousand Leaves),* the progenitor of all Japanese poetry anthologies, contains a series of poems, all of which seize on this actively erotic suggestion. A typical offering reads: "The jeweled strand of my soul / broken and scattered with / the ending of our love— / even though we both should die / never shall we meet again."[45] Drawing on the ambiguity of the word *tama,* which can mean either "jewel" or "soul/spirit," the poem suggests an upwelling of passion that disorders the soul, much as the broken strand of a necklace sends its jewels scattering over the floor. In this light, Tamenori's connection to the text takes on a tinge of the erotic, and his emotional outburst, though it provides the tears that water the young tree of enlightenment, is as much a phenomenon of the senses as it is of the spirit.

The compiler of *A Collection of Treasures* draws on a similar associative net of botanical imagery in the comments with which he closes his setsuwa collection. The final tale in the series, which is studded throughout with *waka* poetry, refers briefly to the Indian practice of writing sutras on the backs of leaves from the *tāra* tree (SNKBT 40: 350), thus implicitly connecting the Buddhist practice of sutra copying with the Japanese practice of poetic composition as "the leaves of words." After making this flitting reference, the priest strikes a small bell, indicating the end of both his sermon and the setsuwa collection that documents it. The compiler (perhaps the word "author" is fitting here) then concludes with a few words of his own, explaining his intentions in composing *The Collection of Treasures.* He writes:

Originally, I longed for the scent of flowers and enjoyed the autumn
foliage, gathering and writing down the leaves of words of many people
[i.e. the *waka* that appear throughout the collection] and scattering them
here and there in the way of the *Kokinshū.* . . . . These poems soothe even
the hearts of fearsome gods invisible to the eye, and make gentle the hearts
of fierce warriors, just as is written in the preface of the *Kokinshū.* Truly,
thinking on this, and with the kind favor of [the Shintō gods of poetry]
Sumiyoshi and Tamatsushima, I have put my strength into [progressing
along] this path crowded with people and I have prepared enough to create
this single volume of writing. I have joyfully taken down these tales told
before the Buddha [icon] and they should be called *A Collection of Treasures.* (SNKBT 40: 350–51)

The author here points to the power of poetry to emotively transform the individual human heart, calming it and turning it into a landscape that is capable of supporting Buddhist growth. By including these remarks as part of the
colophon to his written setsuwa collection—all of which he has framed as the
transcription of a preaching event—the compiler implicitly aligns his act of
writing setsuwa with the devotional acts of sutra copying and Buddhist oration, as well as with the poetic act of composition, and he presents his writings as an offering to the Buddha, a practice that invokes both the sutra-based
argument that the offering of the dharma is the highest offering and the Japanese practice of composing poetry at shrines and temples and then offering
the transcripts to the chief enshrined deity.

SALT GATHERING

Other medieval setsuwa compilers also draw heavily on poetic tradition and
the ornate language of poetic association in order to frame their compositional
acts in a highly literate and emotionally concentrated context. Rather than
working with botanical metaphors, these men focus instead on the pathos-
ridden form of the salt gatherer. Keisei, for instance, concludes his *A Companion in Solitude* with the following: "When I started to write down these
two volumes of notes . . . I was ashamed and even thought I ought to put away
my inkstone, but when I considered the saturated robes of the divers and that
I had already let it be heard that I would finish gathering up this salty seaweed,
somehow I was able to pick up my brush again. It is my hope that [this col-
lection] be offered before forgiving eyes and that it not be spread about [to
encounter] other than understanding hearts" (SNKBT 40: 452–53).

In this passage Keisei figures himself as a salt gatherer. Generally among the poorest and most destitute, these seaside dwellers specialized in diving, plunging into the cold depths of the sea in order to cut strands of kelp free from their roots at the ocean's bottom. Using bonfires of driftwood and dried reeds to extract the salt from the seaweed, the gatherers eked out a meager hand-to-mouth existence. The associative net of imagery in this case draws together the words for "salty seaweed," "diver," "gather up," and "saturated robes" in order to call up vivid imagery of this melancholy coastal scene. Keisei deftly turns this literary landscape into a metaphor for his own writing by suggesting a poetically common potential double meaning in which the word *kakiagu* indicates both the act of "gathering" seaweed (Jp: *kaku,* literally "raking together") and the act of "writing" (Jp: *kaku,* homophonous, but written with a different character). In this sense, Keisei identifies himself with the divers, hoping that "forgiving eyes" will be able to find the salt of the Buddhist teachings that he, in a topos of humility, feels that he has so crudely extracted from the collected seaweed of his setsuwa.

Mujū Ichien, in his preface to *A Collection of Sand and Pebbles,* summons this same net of images. Using a pun on the phrase "reeds and canes" (Jp: *yoshi ashi*), which is homophonous with "good and bad" (Jp: *yoshi ashi,* written with different characters), Mujū cleverly weaves the language of his own sense of purpose into the imagery of the oceanside topos. He writes, "Following my memories of things seen and heard just as they have arisen, I have let my hands gather where they will, bringing together the salty seaweed without regard for the good or bad, without separating out the reeds and canes of the bay at Naniwa" (NKBZ 52: 19). Several sentences later he explains the title he has chosen for his collection through the following analogy: "Those who wish for gold sift through sand to find it, and [those who wish to] polish jewels break open rocks to collect them. Thus [I call these writings] *A Collection of Sand and Pebbles*" (NKBZ 52: 20). Employing rhetorically self-abasing language, Mujū places himself in the role of a humble salt gatherer while also alluding to the process of extraction that both he and his readers will need to undergo, metaphorically breaking open the rock of his setsuwa collection to find the gems of the Buddhist teachings or burning away the dross of the seaweed in order to harvest the salt held within.

Both Keisei and Mujū thus figure themselves as salt gatherers. Though each of the passages is carefully gender neutral, in classical Japanese literature the diver is almost always female and her character is often tinged with more than a little erotic appeal. The Noh play *Ama* (The diver), for instance, features an encounter with the ghost of a female diver. She recounts her own personal history, first telling how she conceived a son with a certain visiting minister of state (who then returned to the capital with the child, but not with her) and then continuing with the story of her death. Having tied a rope about her waist, she dives deep into the sea to retrieve a precious jewel, asking the people in the boat to pull her up when they feel a tug on the line. Just as she is running out of breath, she finds the jewel lying on the bottom of the sea. Realizing that she will lose consciousness before reaching the surface, she takes her knife, slices a gash in her body just under her breast, inserts the jewel into her chest, and tugs on the rope. After being hauled back into the boat, she regains her senses just long enough to tell those present to pull back the fold of skin below her breast and to reach into her chest cavity to find the jewel she has hidden there.

The jewel in question is a famous religious artifact said to contain an ever-present image of the historical Buddha, and the diving woman has retrieved it in exchange for the promise that her son will be educated and introduced into the courtly ranks. Thus, the revelation of the jewel within her breast suggests a referral back to the birth of her son, while the searching fingers that probe her chest cavity might be linked back to the moment of sexual union. Though the Noh play itself dates to no earlier than the mid-fourteenth century, it is based on the earlier medieval collection *Sanshū Shido Dōjō Engi (The Sacred Origins of the Holy Places of Shido in Sanuki Province)*. As with Minamoto no Tamenori's imagery of the broken strand of jewels, Keisei and Mujū's use of the diver as a metaphor for their editorial activities also summons up an erotic subtext. For these male authors this subtext implies a shift of both class and gender, suggesting a greater fluidity in the economy of desire and a more marked humility in the process of pursuit than that allowed for by the metaphorics of *kaimami* pursuit.

PREACHING

While in the case of salt gathering it is the compiler who takes on specific physicality, other setsuwa collections figure the written compilation itself as an embodied presence. For instance Kyōkai, author of *A Miraculous Record of Immediate Karmic Retribution,* describes his text as a physical proxy, an embodied stand-in for his own priestly figure. Concerned with how his work will be accepted by people in times and places distant from his own, Kyōkai clarifies his intentions in creating the collection, writing, "In editing this collection of strange and miraculous events, I want to pull people forward with my spoken words, seize their hands and lead them forward, cleanse their feet and guide them on, so that all of us together may leave this world and be born in the western paradise, living together in the jeweled hall of heaven" (NKBZ 10: 245). In other words, Kyōkai seems to want his writings to work as a human body interacting with other human bodies. He wants the words of his compilation to enter into people, pulling them forward by force; he graces his collection with hands so that it may grasp hold of the hands of others, wash their feet of evil, and guide them to physical rebirth in the western paradise. In short, Kyōkai's collection is meant to act like a preacher, speaking to and physically touching people, guiding them along the Buddhist path.

Minamoto no Tamenori intended his *The Three Jewels* to work in a similar way. Compiled for the express use of an ailing imperial princess, Tamenori's collection was meant to serve as a physical proxy. Unable to attend lectures and sermons on her own, too sick to visit sacred architectural locales or worship their devotional images in person, she was presented with Tamenori's text as a substitute: if she could not go to them, the priests, services, and devotional settings would come to her, in textual format. Tamenori is very careful to ensure that the princess not feel alone in this, pointing out that there are no buddha or bodhisattva bodies left for any of us to see (except in the form of relics) and encouraging her in the belief that "since the Three Jewels are all one and the same, you should revere and worship them all equally" (SNKBT 31: 136). Contemplating the texts of Buddhism therefore accrues the same amount of merit as attending Buddhist services, an act that Tamenori promises will erase all of one's sin and allow one actually to see the Buddha's physical form in its entirety.

MATCHMAKING

Finally, both Mujū and Kamo no Chōmei describe their setsuwa collections as matchmakers or go-betweens, that is, as older women (Jp: *nakadachi,* which is gender-specific) who take on the responsibility of pairing others with appropriate mates. In the preface to his *Collection of Spiritual Awakenings,* Kamo no Chōmei includes the following remarks: "I have fathomed my own shallow heart and, without searching for any particularly deep dharma, I have jotted down things I have seen and heard, quietly placing [these notes] to the right of my cushion. Regarding that which is noble, I sincerely hope that they act as karmic connections, and regarding that which is foolish, I have sought to fashion myself a renewed matchmaker" (SNKS 44). Placing his collection to the right of his cushion, near his armrest where he could pick it up and peruse it at ease, Chōmei hopes that the wise portions of his text may serve as a direct link connecting him to the Buddha, and that those portions that may yet reflect his ignorance might nevertheless negotiate on his behalf. In his figuration he searches and consults with the text as a man might seek the counsel of an older woman in order to find a suitable bride.

Writing nearly seventy years later, Mujū elaborates on this basic image of the text as a marital go-between in his preface to *A Collection of Sand and Pebbles*. "Those who wish to look upon [this collection] without ridiculing its clumsy expressions shall be enlightened concerning the doctrines and teachings of Buddhism. Those who do not scrutinize its unevenness shall learn to discern karmic cause and effect. It shall serve as a matchmaker, leading them from the village of birth and death; it shall be as a friend, accompanying them to the city of Nirvana. Such are the wishes of a foolish old man."[46] Mujū embroiders upon Chōmei's rather plain image of the text-reader relationship as a marital consultation, expanding the sphere of familiarity and allowing for a more widespread textual intimacy. No longer simply for the purposes of its compiler's personal self-improvement, Mujū's text is addressed, even in this instance, to a larger audience.

In the patrilocal marital culture of thirteenth-century Japan, the reader and the compiler of setsuwa texts find themselves in a feminized position, as in the salt-gathering metaphor. If the image of the text is that of a go-between, the image of the reader is that of a new bride for whom the textual matchmaker has secured a lifelong committed relationship to the Buddhist teachings, requiring that the reader/bride relocate to a new home. Mujū's figuration functions as a spatial metaphor in which the believer processes along the Buddhist path, leaving behind the familiar world of birth and death for the shining capital of Nirvana.

SETSUWA AS LIVING TEXTS

Obviously, setsuwa compilers conceived of their texts in a variety of ways and according to a wide range of figurations. At times, compilers imagined their collections as substances to be ingested, either orally (as food or medicine) or aurally (as drumbeats or recited words). Setsuwa may also serve to implant and nourish the seeds of buddhahood, transforming the believer's heart into a lush landscape of trees of enlightenment, leaves of words, and streams of tears. They may serve as guides or mentors, as friends, matchmakers, or forceful priests. Finally, setsuwa sensationalize—and may also sexualize and feminize—the listening or reading body, figuring it as a new bride or as a diver dripping with the salt of the sea.

In short, setsuwa act both *on* the human body and *as* a human body. In contrast to modern scholarly rhetoric, medieval Buddhist descriptions do not focus on the birth or sexual conquest of setsuwa; rather, they focus on the ability of setsuwa to harbor within themselves (as salt or gems, gold or seeds) the teachings of the Buddha. Though metaphorical descriptions of setsuwa collections do at times flirt with the language of the erotic, setsuwa are never figured as bodies to be conquered and are not subject to amorous conquest. (Recall here that the image of the diver is offered not as a metaphor for the setsuwa text but as a metaphor for its compiler!) Instead, setsuwa may excite in their readers and compilers an intense passion for spiritual growth. Thus, the erotic is linked not to academic discovery but to religious maturation. Finally, while setsuwa most certainly do have life, setsuwa never die. It is not they who are reborn when we read them aloud, but we who (ideally) are activated and animated when we come into contact with them.

SETSUWA IN PERFORMANCE

While setsuwa collections mostly concern themselves with supplying examples of what to say, they also provide glimpses of when, where, and how their tales were used in the context of Buddhist services. The extraordinary *Notes on One Hundred Sessions of Sermons* provides us the richest record in this regard, and it tells us that by the early 1100s there was a network of clerics who had been identified as particularly talented preachers (Jp: *nōsetsu*). These men could be engaged to provide sermons as part of Buddhist ceremonies that, as in the case of *One Hundred Sessions of Sermons,* might involve the creation and dedication of a sutra, most often the *Lotus.*[47] In the *One Hundred Sessions of Sermons* setsuwa, preachers often reference parenthetically quotes, titles, and excerpts of sutras, suggesting that it was also common practice to read aloud one or more sutra passages before the sermon commenced and to key the sermon both to the merit-producing project of the sponsoring patron and to specific material from the sutras read.

While *One Hundred Sessions of Sermons* provides a snapshot of a successful sermonizing event at the imperial court, where proper etiquette was de rigueur, it is much more common for setsuwa to suggest the norms of their underlying performance context through stories about services that were somehow unusual. For instance, Kamo no Chōmei's *A Collection of Spiritual Awakenings* relates the story of an official government steward of Sanuki province in a setsuwa that also appears in *Tales from Times Now Past* and *A Collection of Treasures,* meaning that the tale was in active circulation for at least a century between the early 1100s and the early 1200s. Despite his high birth and clan association—the steward is a member of the Minamoto, an offshoot of the imperial line—this man knows nothing of Buddhism, "not even its name" (SNKS 132). He takes great delight in killing animals, catching fish, and maiming people, and he is the terror of his domain. One day, riding home from the kill, he happens across a crowd standing outside a house straining to listen to something going on inside. He asks one of his retainers what is happening. His man explains that it is a Buddhist dedication ceremony, to which the steward responds that he has never seen such a thing before. He dismounts his horse and, still in his hunting gear, pushes through a crowd of people standing in the street. Squeezing into the courtyard garden, he finds himself amidst a throng of seated people who start to flee when they see him.

The steward shoulders his way up to the presiding priest (Jp: *dōshi*), plops down on the ground, and demands that the cleric explain what has been happening. The monk, "sorely afraid, summarized his sermon thus far: the vows made by Amida, the joys of the Pure Land, the pains of this world, the condition of transience, and so forth" (SNKS 134), to which the steward listened closely. Then, rough-spoken and impulsive as ever, he proclaims that he has been moved and demands that the priest shave his head on the spot. When the priest suggests that he wait a few days, the steward sees this as a challenge to his resolve and draws his sword. The layman sponsoring the service nearly faints and the priest shakes uncontrollably but loans the steward vestments, shaves the man's head, and ordains him immediately.[48]

As with *One Hundred Sessions of Sermons,* we can discern a set of liturgical norms operating in the background of this story, and in fact the steward's exaggerated actions help to draw out some of these expectations. First, a lay believer (in this case, a provincial landowner) has arranged for a Buddhist service to be held in conjunction with his donation of some unspecified object (perhaps a statue or a sutra). Second, the dedication service is a public affair that draws a large crowd. Third, at least some of the assembly seats itself at a level below that of the orator, on the ground in the garden. This helps his voice to carry, even to the street outside. Next, the officiating priest, after taking care of the dedication portion of the service, also delivers a lengthy sermon in which he covers a number of standard topics. Finally, while he is speaking the members of the crowd (who, in any case, are not to have shown up with flecks of blood on their clothing) are supposed to remain seated, still, and quiet, rather than interrupting with questions as the steward does.

Setsuwa from other collections underscore many of these same expectations. A story from *A Companion in Solitude,* compiled about a decade later, features a destitute monk who disguises himself as a madman and lives under a bridge, begging for food in the market. One day a powerful minister of state with spiritual leanings orders a Buddhist service to be held and summons a very well-thought-of priest to officiate. On the day of the service the beggar monk shows up in the garden. The nobles, seated inside behind their screens of state, think that he has come too early in expectation of receiving some of the food offerings.[49] Before they can shoo him away, however, he climbs up on the elevated platform, where the officiating priest would normally sit, and delivers a heart-wrenching sermon that leaves everyone in tears. When the noble patron requests to meet him face-to-face, the monk runs off madly and disappears (SNKBT 40: 376–77). Mujū Ichien, writing in a similar vein in the 1280s, devotes an entire section of *A Collection of Sand and Pebbles* to setsuwa about preaching events, most of which have gone awry in one way or another: one preacher makes lewd and suggestive comments, while another seats himself on an old drum (no platform being available) and falls in. In other stories the officiating priest is unaware of the significance of the item over whose dedication he is presiding; he is able to perform the dedication portion of the service with ritual correctness but is completely inept at extemporizing a sermon to conclude the ceremony; or he delivers an ill-prepared or pandering sermon for the sole purpose of gaining the donation.[50]

What these stories suggest is that during the twelfth and thirteenth centuries there was a growing awareness around liturgical expectations and a set of popularly acknowledged norms had developed. According to these norms preachers looked and acted a certain way. They were seated in specific places with respect to their audience members, and they directed their remarks toward suitable subjects. When their sermons, studded with setsuwa as well as sutra references, were successful, these men could bring the house to tears and move audience members to make vows or even take the tonsure.

LITURGY AND THE AGUI LINEAGE

Thus, a set of loosely cohered expectations for preaching events may well have been in place for a century or longer before it was finally codified in the last decade of the thirteenth century, shortly after the composition of *A Collection of Sand and Pebbles*. Two men are largely responsible for standardizing the first formal liturgy for Buddhist preaching: the Tendai monk Chōgen (1126–1203, sometimes rendered Chōken), whose sermons Kamo no Chōmei had heard, and his son Seikaku (1167–1235, also rendered Shōkaku or Shōgaku). Chōgen's father, Fujiwara no Michinori (d. 1159), had been an active collaborator with Emperor Goshirakawa (r. 1155–58) during the political turmoil of the Heiji Disturbance, a tenure that ended in suicide for Michinori. Of Michinori's seventeen sons, at least eleven left political life and took vows as Buddhist monks, from which position they carved out names for themselves as deft scholars. Chōgen, along with his son and disciple Seikaku, seems to have been particularly gifted with eloquence, and both men garnered reputations for being "elegant" speakers whose sermons were famed for their beauty and the "texture and design of their composition."[51] While the main Agui temple perched atop Mount Hiei amid scores of other Tendai structures, father and son lived and trained at a branch temple that had been established downslope in the northern reaches of the Hiean capital, from which they were better able to maintain contact with the noble audiences for their sermons.

The Agui lineage, founded by Chōgen and Seikaku, attempted to systematize sermonizing practice beginning in the late twelfth century. Seikaku compiled the school's first key text, the *Genzenshū (A Wellspring of Words)*, which gave condensed background on important Buddhist figures and sites and provided a list of appropriate topics that could serve as talking points on given occasions such as the death of a parent or child, the taking of the tonsure, the dedication of a new devotional image, and so forth. In 1298, sixty years after Seikaku's death, his successor and disciple Shinjō (sometimes rendered Shinshō) penned a compendium of the school's practices. This volume, entitled *Hōsokushū (A Collection of Rules [for Preaching] the Dharma)*, deals with issues of protocol, etiquette, and the ordering of services. Clearly Shinjō witnessed Seikaku in action at a variety of preaching venues (there are several references to "on one occasion Seikaku . . . "), and the rulebook reflects Shinjō's attempt to discern a standard liturgy.

FORMALITY LEVEL

One of the first things Shinjō does in *A Collection of Rules for Preaching the Dharma* is to distinguish, based on Seikaku's teachings, two levels of formality for Buddhist preaching events. In the case of more formal "ceremonies" (Jp: *hōe*), the officiating priest (Jp: *dōshi*) sits atop a raised platform (Jp: *kōza*), unless he is in intimate audience with nobility, in which case, in deference to rank, he seats himself on a round straw mat and speaks to them through screens of state. In less formal "services" (Jp: *butsuji*) the officiating priest sits closer to ground level (Jp: *heiza*). This distinction indicates the importance of establishing the mechanics of speaker-audience interaction. In the more formal instance, the audience occupies the floor and looks up at the orator, who sits with the altar and devotional images behind him. This means that the audience's view of the preacher will be framed by Buddhist icons (usually a triad) that face the audience from over the orator's shoulders. In the less formal instance, this visual framing—and its attendant hierarchy—would be less dominant. Additionally, the acoustics of the more informal service must have been less satisfactory, particularly for members of larger audiences, who might have found their line of sight to be obscured by pillars, sliding doors and panels, and even walls, as suggested in the setsuwa about the rude hunter cited above.

While in the case of simpler services the officiating priest might play all the roles, more formal ceremonies could entail quite an elaborate cast of characters. Under the officiating priest, who was chiefly in charge of conducting the ritual (the dedication of a new image, for example), one might find a monk whose specific role was to read the sutras with the proper Chinese intonation (Jp: *kyōshi*), another to read Sanskrit text (Jp: *baishi*), a third to vocalize beautifully melismatic passages (Jp: *shōmyōshi*), and a fourth to provide the closing lecture or sermon in which setsuwa would have been employed (Jp: *kōshi*). These men might be attended by any number of other monks, often young disciples with preparatory duties (lighting incense, placing candles, ensuring the venue was properly prepared, etc.). Regardless of the level of formality, the chief officiant was to be seated in proximity to the patron (Jp: *danna*), with the remainder of the audience arrayed as circumstances allowed.

THE LITURGY

In terms of the actual order of events, Shinjō begins with the arrival of the palanquin at the hall (which may be a temple or home chapel). All monks involved in the service enter the structure by rank, with the officiating priest last, giving his disciples time to prepare the hall by lighting incense and candles. The priest and congregants perform obeisance, bowing toward the devotional images a minimum of three times in recognition of the Three Jewels (the Buddha, the dharma of his teachings, and the sangha of believers). Then, right foot first, the officiating priest mounts a central dais.[52] He faces away from the audience and toward the devotional images, with a sutra rest immediately in front of him and a small gong (Jp: *kei*) and ritual implements on either side. Settling himself, he strikes the gong with his right hand. Shinjō notes that as soon as the officiating priest bows for the first time, the assembled laity "should be seated and quiet, to remain so from this point forward."[53]

Preliminaries accomplished, the purpose of the service (for instance, the dedication of a newly produced sutra) is announced with a slow, chanted cadence, the end of the sentence dropping in pitch and volume. The *Heart Sutra* is recited as an offering to local deities and the priest invokes various buddhas, bodhisattvas, and native Shintō deities, calling on their protection. He then dedicates the merit of the service to the salvation of all beings, especially the patron. If the patron has provided a document detailing his or her reasons for holding the ceremony (Jp: *hyōbyaku*), the priest reads this aloud, concluding with a formal prayer or request (Jp: *ganmon*). Shinjō instructs, "Read this quietly, with the portion containing the specific request in a slightly louder voice, but not as loudly as when preaching."[54] The priest finishes by reading aloud the year and date, rerolling the document, and placing it to the side. If the occasion of the ceremony is the dedication of a new sutra, the priest reads all or part of that sutra (which is on the desk before him) at this point.

Having concluded this portion of the service, the priest now changes audiences, from the divine to the human. Facing his listeners, he intones the title of the scripture to be explicated and the sutra passage for the day. Following this, he delivers some celebratory words (Jp: *kyōge*) in which, among other things, he may praise the powers of the sutra from which he (or another officiant) has just read, or he may speak about the qualities of one or more of the buddhas whose images are installed in the temple. Moving into the sermon proper, he may homilize on the topic of meritorious acts and the cultivation of one's good moral roots, or cover any of the other many subjects addressed in setsuwa collections. Judging from the material in *One Hundred Sessions of Sermons,* at times the connection between the sermon and the sutra text is quite explicit, while at other times the link is more distant, even tenuous. The orator signals the conclusion of the sermon with a dedication of merit. He then strikes the gong and descends the platform to accept donations, which may include cloth, brocade, swords, oxen, horses, and so on.

STANDING BETWEEN

As we can see from Shinjō's description, Buddhist sermonizing events (whether the more formal ceremonies or the less elaborate services) have several discrete parts that speak to different audiences. In each of these liturgical moments the presiding cleric functions as a pivot, standing between the devotees seated below him and the powerful beings (buddhas and sutras) to which he raises his eyes. In the first portion of the liturgy the officiant speaks from his own position as a ritual specialist, invoking buddhas and deities and drawing their attention to the specific time and place of the event. Much of this portion of the service would be linguistically opaque for all but the most highly educated lay devotees, as much of it was spoken in another language (Chinese, Sanskrit, or Japanized versions of these) and addressed to other orders of being (buddhas and deities).

Having established a connection with these powerful forces, the presiding priest next introduces the wishes, vows, acts, and intentions of the believer sponsoring the event. In his person and through his words he creates a connection between the lay believer and the objects of that believer's devotions: the buddhas and the sutras. While he is not yet addressing his human audience, the officiant at this point in the service at least uses their words (more precisely, the words of the sponsor) to communicate. In the final portion of the service, in which preaching and the use of setsuwa come to the fore, the orator finally speaks in a loud, clear, conversational voice, addressing his human audience in their own spoken vernacular. Here, his words represent the teachings of the buddhas and the sutras rendered legible, readied for human consumption in the form of setsuwa.

As the next two chapters will show, miracles of book and body form several of the major recurring motifs in setsuwa collections. Setsuwa thus reveal that an elaboration of the "cult of the book" was a fundamental component in attracting and retaining believers in ninth- through thirteenth-century Japan. The collections function as a receptacle of descriptions of textual devotion and also as a matrix for incubating new understandings of the text-body relationship. In this respect they provide a vital lens onto premodern book culture, throwing into sharp relief practices of devotion, situating reading as one among a spectrum of methods for engaging text, and suggesting particular ways of understanding the relation between human reader and written text.

THREE

Decomposing Bodies, Composing Texts

LET US RETURN NOW TO THE STORY of Myōe (1173–1232), the Japanese monk who chose to cut off his ear as a sign of his deep devotion and with whose example I began this book. As I suggested in the introduction, Myōe's act, although a singular one, could not have been wholly unexpected in medieval Japan, simply because his bodily self-sacrifice responds to and is contextualized by Buddhist metaphors, tropes, and figures that were pervasive in scripture and in the visual, literary, and musical arts of his time. Myōe's act performs, in essence, an excruciatingly literal reading of the scriptures, and it reflects the particular ways in which those scriptures were interpreted in medieval Japan. For Myōe, cutting off his ear was a way of seeking a miracle: he hoped that carving off his own flesh would rewrite the scriptures and that he would find his name listed among those who had attended the historical Buddha's sermons so many centuries ago. For those of us here and now, standing at a remove of several more centuries, Myōe's act itself is miracle-like. It is an instance in which the inner workings of an entire world become startlingly clear, starkly apparent, and sensually confirmable. The sharp intake of breath, the heat on our skin, the prickling at the back of our necks: our somatic responses on reading his story tell us that Myōe's act still speaks, even if we may have trouble deciphering its message. This chapter sifts through the literary evidence and seeks to reconstruct, at least in part, the shape and texture of the world of ideas in which Myōe moved.

Though Myōe chose a particularly painful path, the tropes of self-sacrifice and especially dismemberment have long been part of the bedrock of Buddhist symbolism and metaphor. Going all the way back to the *jātaka* tales of ancient India, stories about earlier incarnations of the being that was to become the historical Buddha, we hear of the man who would be Śākyamuni sacrificing himself to tigers and feeding himself to demons in order to demonstrate his grasp of the doctrine of compassion or to gain access to even a fragment of Buddhist scripture. In many of these tales voluntary dismemberment or sacrifice either initiates contact with the texts of Buddhism or serves as indubitable proof that the protagonist has translated these teachings into physical form, embodying them in his thoughts, words, and deeds.

These self-sacrificial episodes were well known in Japan from the earliest decades of Buddhism's tenure there. For instance, they are depicted on the Tamamushi no zushi, a miniature Buddhist shrine of about 230 centimeters in height that was fashioned during the Asuka period (552–645). The shrine's exterior is decorated with "body sacrificing" (Jp: *shashin*) motifs, including an image of the Buddha throwing himself off a cliff to feed a hungry tigress and one of him feeding his body to a demon in exchange for the second half of a sutra verse. The tales remained popular over the centuries, showing up, among other places, in the setsuwa of the tenth-century collection *The Three Jewels* and the twelfth-century *Tales from Times Now Past,* and inspiring the acts of people like Myōe, with whom Keisei, compiler of *A Companion in Solitude,* was acquainted. (In 1232, Keisei served as the officiant at Myōe's one-hundred-day memorial service.)

WRITING THE BODY

Continuing this study's concern with the interrelationship of physical corpus and textual corpus in medieval Japanese literature, this chapter will focus on exploring setsuwa of bodily sacrifice and corporeal dissolution as instances of performative writing. Peggy Phelan offers perhaps the most concise definition of this method of writing, which, she argues, enacts "the affective force of the performance event again. . . . Performative writing is solicitous of affect even while it is nervous and tentative about the consequences of that solicitation. Alternately bold and coy, manipulative and unconscious, this writing points both to itself and to the 'scenes' that motivate it."[1] Though Phelan plays with the legal language of citation and summons ("solicitation"), her notion of performative writing pivots on an understanding of the value of transience (what she calls the "unmarked"), and, in writing performatively, Phelan notes her desire to transgress the "rules of the written document" through "the act of writing toward disappearance, rather than the act of writing toward preservation."[2]

Though Phelan does not refer here either to medieval textuality or to spiritual practice—her notions originate from the tensions she feels in her dual position as performance artist and theorist—her ideas nevertheless suggest ways to begin understanding the fluid relationship between body and text that setsuwa construct and to begin exploring the techniques through which these highly emotional, and sometimes shocking, narratives seek to leverage their readers into a painful awareness of the fragility of their human frames. In this chapter and the next I will be arguing that setsuwa, as a type of writing, repeatedly turns to the twinned tropes of text and flesh as a way of actively soliciting emotional and physiological responses from its audiences, and that these collections not only preserve a record of oral sermon literature but also continue to function in an actively devotional context in which they seek to further contemplative practice.

In addition to the notion of performative writing, the idea of the fragment is important to this chapter, for the fragment represents a piece of a larger whole and thereby suggests the potential of unity and the possibility of rejoining (re-membering) that which has been divided. The relationship of part to whole, as symbolized in the fragment, is crucial to a number of concerns that were widespread throughout the medieval period in Japan[3] over such things as *kyōgen kigo* (the use of secular forms of writing to express larger religious truths), or *waka soku darani* (the belief that the *waka* form of Japanese poetry could be read as a *dhāranī* —here, a sort of Buddhist incantation), *sokushin jōbutsu* (the idea that a person could become a buddha in this very body), and *hongaku shisō* (the Tendai school doctrine that each being contains within itself buddha nature).[4] One of the more striking characteristics of this persistent medieval Buddhist concern with the relationship of part to whole is the degree to which it was at once focused on the production of language, and particularly the assembly of written texts, while simultaneously being mediated through a human body that was subject to transformation on both physical and spiritual levels. Religious concerns with fragmentation and unity thus played themselves out metaphorically and, at times, literally on the physical corpus of Buddhist devotees.

This chapter and the next focus on miraculous accounts of book and body in medieval Japanese Buddhism. There are two main trajectories involved: first (the subject of this chapter), the often violent, self-sacrificial dismemberment of the human body into textual fragment, and, second (the subject of the next chapter), the salvific incorporation of textual fragment into embodied being.

Through close readings of setsuwa concerning bodily decomposition and textual incorporation, as well as considerations of ritual practices such as sutra copying (Jp: *shakyō*) and meditation on putrefaction (Jp: *fujōkan*), these two chapters argue that medieval Buddhist setsuwa, along with related forms of art and ritual, are interested in developing an image of the human body as a potential text of Buddhism and that, as a corollary of this, these same works elaborate an understanding of sacred writings as sentient beings. That is, the reading body and the read text (the sutra) exist along a shared material continuum. In addition, I will argue more expansively that the twinned transformations of body into textual fragment, and textual fragment into body, pressure modern scholars to think through the ramifications of medieval textuality, pushing us both to recognize the physicality of the interaction between body and text and to "re-mark again the performative possibilities of writing itself."[5]

THE FINAL AGE OF THE DHARMA

Why should practices of reading and writing—in Buddhism generally and in medieval Japan specifically—be associated so strongly with images of decay and decomposition? According to various sutras and Chinese commentaries, three separate ages follow the nirvana of any buddha who manifests as a human being in this world. In the first age, the age of the "true dharma" (Jp: *shōbō*), people are able to understand and practice the Buddhist teachings, thereby gaining enlightenment. This stage lasts either five hundred or one thousand years, depending on the source cited. In the second age, of the "imitative dharma" (Jp: *zōbō*), people are able to understand and practice the teachings only partially, and enlightenment is much rarer. This age also lasts either five hundred or one thousand years. In the "final age of the dharma" (Jp: *mappō*), which lasts some ten thousand years, both understanding and practice become increasingly corroded so as to make enlightenment virtually impossible. Fortunately, this decline from the true dharma to the final age of the dharma is cyclical, not linear, and just as the process reaches its nadir a new buddha appears in the world to start the wheel of the dharma turning once again.

The sheer temporal length of this cyclical pattern means that, generally speaking, in Buddhist cosmology it will be incredibly rare for any being to live in the age of the true dharma, even rarer for that being to be possessed of a human body and sufficient mental faculties to understand the teachings, and rarer still for that being to be blessed with geographical proximity to the Buddha, to be physically present as he is delivering the teachings. Buddhist literature has any number of stock metaphors for describing this rarity. A particularly oft-used one suggests that it is more common for a blind (or, sometimes, one-eyed) turtle to happen to bump into a piece of driftwood floating on the surface of a great ocean.[6] Timing is everything, particularly because, as we saw in chapter 1, the written teachings are themselves subject to the ravages of time, becoming increasingly obscured and unavailable in the muddied and evil age of *mappō*. It is with awareness of this temporal cycle that sutras fret about people who will cut, paste, abridge, rearrange, and burn them. Even in the absence of such violent editors, sutras claim categorically that they will fade and pass away with the flow of time.

Because of discrepancies in the purported lengths of the first two dharma periods and uncertainty about the exact year of the Buddha's passage into nirvana, Japanese authors cited different dates for the onset of *mappō*, the two most common being 552 C.E. and 1052 C.E. The earlier of these coincides with the date given in the *Nihon Shoki* (*Chronicles of Japan*, 720) as marking Buddhism's official introduction to Japan via a Korean envoy. This envoy presented the court with scriptures, sculptures, and an exhortation from the Paekche king enjoining the Japanese emperor to embrace the new faith. Though, as Michele Marra points out, Japanese in the ninth century "seemed unable to accept" the notion that they were already living in the final age, by the tenth century popular perceptions had begun to shift and a true "*mappō* consciousness" began to bloom.[7]

Mappō provides the temporal reality in which *jātaka* tales of self-sacrifice set themselves. In addition, *mappō* is the time period in which Myōe—who at thirteen tried to feed himself to wild beasts and at sixteen sought to donate some of his flesh to a leper—felt himself to be living. And *mappō* furnishes the temporal backdrop for virtually all setsuwa literature, with the possible exception of the two earliest collections. *A Wondrous Record of Immediate Karmic Retribution* (compiled ca. 823) mentions *mappō* only once, in a passage that may be a later interpolation, while Minamoto no Tamenori in *The Three Jewels* (984) warns the imperial princess, his intended reader, "It has been 1,933 years since the Buddha Śākyamuni retired from the world and, though we may be in the age of imitative dharma, the remaining years of it are few. Being born into a human body and meeting with the Buddha's teachings is even more difficult than dangling a string from the heavens and threading a needle that is bobbing deep in the sea below" (SNKBT 31: 4). Tamenori places himself and his reader in those last few moments of golden light before darkness falls. Though writing during the age of imitative dharma, his consciousness is already one of imminent decline. All later setsuwa collections simply assume *mappō* as an undeniable fact and refer frequently to their temporal location in this degenerate and polluted age. This temporal setting informs the desperate actions in which some setsuwa protagonists engage, and it highlights once again the mediating role that setsuwa play in attempting to ease the transference of meaning from the pages of sutras to the minds of believers, both of which are growing increasingly opaque.

Setsuwa literature attends to this temporal setting by shifting attention to the human body and elaborating on that body's dissolution according to two methods: first, via the natural decomposition of the body following death, and, second, through willful acts of dismemberment, like Myōe's. In its typical state the human body ages, sickens, dies, and decomposes. As we will see in the examples that follow, Buddhist literature generally, and setsuwa particularly, qualify the body as a temporary "meeting place of ills"[8] and, moreover, views the body as a container of impurity. Meditation on this impurity forms the first of the motifs this chapter will explore. While death and rebirth is, for most of us, inevitable, Buddhism also provides a way to reinscribe the body, preempting the natural process of decay through a willful act of self-sacrifice, most powerfully enacted through dismemberment. This reinscription of the human frame alters the body both externally and internally, re-marking it as a container of the dharma (Jp: *hōki*).

THE SPECTACLE OF IMPURITY

The contemplation of rotting corpses has long been part of Buddhist monastic training. Known in Japanese as *fujōkan* (literally "the spectacle of impurity"),[9] this meditative practice involves a Buddhist aspirant visiting a charnel ground in order to contemplate the degradation of the human body from the time that it is freshly dead until such time as the disjointed bones, bleached and shining in the sun, are all that remain. If he has other duties, the monk may simply visit the charnel ground at regular intervals to ensure that he is witness to each of the nine identified stages of degradation (Jp: *kusō*), or, in extreme cases, he may actually overnight for a time by the open grave. As most bodies in Japan were (and still are) cremated, the charnel grounds used for this practice would have been used by the lowest of the social classes. As such, they would have included the bodies of criminals, for whom the spectacle of their putrefaction was meant to be a symbolic punishment,[10] and perhaps others who could not be identified, did not have any remaining family to care for them after death, or whose families simply found cremation too expensive.

Toward the end of his all-night sermon, the priestly narrator of the late-twelfth-century setsuwa collection *A Collection of Treasures* describes various Buddhist objects of contemplation, ending his brief survey by commenting on the human body. He notes that "both one's own body and the bodies of others are impure . . . like a painted pitcher filled with shit and all sorts of other filth" (SNKBT 40: 301). He reminds his listeners of two famous Chinese beauties, both of whom, scapegoated as imperial seductresses during the political upheavals of the Spring and Autumn Period (770–446 B.C.E.), ended their lives abandoned in the open fields. Having jumped suddenly from the here and now of "your own body" to ancient China, the narration slows considerably to dwell on the dissolution of these beauties, as "their bodies changed, their white skin bruised and addled, their red lips turned black and a horde of maggots streamed from their mouths. . . . The stench spread wide . . . , dogs chewed off their arms and drug them away, birds plucked out their eyes and flew with them to the horizons, [the remains] desiccated on a bed of tangled grasses until only the bones were left" (SNKBT 40: 302). The description delights ghoulishly in the desecration and scattering of the corpses, as beasts drag portions of them to all points of the compass, and even the smell of them wafts away on the wind. Clearly, for the purposes of *fujōkan* meditation, it is not enough that the body die; it must also be shown to come wildly unstrung. Having conjured such a powerful vision and backed it up by quoting brief passages from authoritative sources,[11] the priest concludes by remarking that contemplating this spectacle of impurity has the paradoxical power to cleanse the beholder, transforming evil into good, sin into merit, and sexual lust into desire for the Buddhist path.

In another rendering of the *fujōkan* spectacle, *A Wondrous Record of Immediate Karmic Retribution* 3:16 describes some of the punitive aspects, as well as ultimately the curative possibilities, of having one's body subjected to a Buddhist gaze. This setsuwa features a dead woman from the Kaga district of Echizen province who is identified as Yokoe no omi Naritojime. Famed as a beauty in her youth, she was accustomed to keeping sexual company with a wide variety of men and, in an effort to keep her breasts erotically appealing to her lovers, she often refused to provide milk to her young children. On the night of the twenty-third day of the Twelfth Month of 770, the Dharma Master Jakurin experienced a dream in which he was confronted with the following vision of Yokoe: "I was walking along the road in front of [prince and Buddhist paragon] Shōtoku Taishi's palace at Ikaruga in Yamato province, heading east. The path was like a mirror, about 1 *chō* [110 meters] wide. It was straight as a plumb line with an overgrown patch on one side. When I stopped and peered into the grove of trees, I saw a large, bloated woman crouching down there naked. Both of her breasts were swollen, each as big as a mounded earthen oven, with pus oozing from each nipple. Wrapping her arms around her knees, she looked down at her breasts and moaned in great pain" (NKBZ 10: 288–89).

Jakurin asks her who she is and she identifies herself, going on to list her particular sins. She confesses, "When I was yet a young woman, I was licentious and lewd, abandoning my children so that I could have sex with many men. For days on end my children were hungry for my milk. . . . Due to the sin of allowing them to go hungry in my last incarnation, I am now punished with these painful, swollen breasts" (NKBZ 10: 289). Recalling the dream after waking, the priest searches out her children and determines that if they show their forgiveness by copying out sutras in her name, their mother will be relieved of her pain. Once Jakurin informs them of the situation, her now-adult children complete the copies and their mother is forgiven, appearing in a later dream to thank Jakurin for helping alleviate her suffering.

Like the vast majority of tales included by Kyōkai in his *A Wondrous Record of Immediate Karmic Retribution,* this setsuwa clearly details the punishment of sin. Certain elements, such as the focus on visual probing, the punitive marking of the body so that it can be read as a ledger of sin, and the examination of the external physical self as a way of uncovering the specifics of one's internally hidden sins, are familiar tropes in Kyōkai's many stories concerning hell and punishment. The road, for example, looks "like a mirror," recalling the fantastic crystalline mirror that reflects sinners' deeds in the court of judgment, and the woman goes through a process of painful self-examination just as she would in hell (here, gazing specifically at her own breasts), thereby coming to recognize and confess her sins, the crucial first step in expiating them and lessening her suffering.

This setsuwa does not take place in hell, however, but in the dream of a male cleric who finds himself confronted with the vision of a naked woman, a woman who was formerly quite beautiful and seductive but who is now in the process of rotting, her filth oozing out of her body as he watches. In presenting the body of the dead woman for visual (and especially male clerical) examination, the setsuwa changes from a simple tale of karmic retribution and begins to interweave a number of themes central to the *fujōkan* narrative, focusing especially on the figure of a male cleric gazing on the now-putrid body of a once-beautiful woman.

Also of note is the practice described here of copying sutras for the express purpose of lessening the suffering of a dead person. The *surikuyō* ritual in which a hand-copied text was dedicated to a dead person in order either to relieve their corporeal sufferings in hell or to bring about their physical transformation from one mode of existence to another (for instance, from an animal back to a human incarnation) became increasingly popular in Japan during the Heian period (794–1185).[12] The ritual centers on the belief that a textual dedication has the power to bring about physical transformation, another dimension of performative writing that this chapter and the next will consider in some detail.

SEXUAL AROUSAL AND RELIGIOUS AWAKENING

While the praxis of *fujōkan* contemplation in a charnel ground appears to have been limited to monastics, as a motif in setsuwa narratives, *fujōkan* is treated much more expansively and may refer not only to the graveyard meditations of a Buddhist cleric but also to the forceful awakening of a layperson who, upon encountering the sight of a putrid body, is moved to take up the Buddhist path. In his setsuwa collection *A Collection of Spiritual Awakenings,* which focuses exclusively on accounts of religious apprehension (Jp: *hosshin*), Kamo no Chōmei includes the rather popular story of a man, identified as the scholar Ōe no Sadamoto, who leaves his wife for another woman.[13] His new lover soon sickens and dies, but Ōe remains so attached to her that he finds himself unable to dispose of her body and instead gazes at it lovingly for several days. As her flesh rots his religious awareness grows, and eventually he is moved to take up the Buddhist path. To test his new faith he decides to visit his former wife's house and beg food from her. She is shocked to see him, remarking, "When you treated me so cruelly, I expected you to fall in the world [but did not expect to see it with my own eyes]" (SNKS 98), and she turns her back on him. Feeling no anger or resentment at her words, the man rejoices in the realization that his faith is firm.

Writing not quite a decade later, Keisei (1189–1268) includes a somewhat similar setsuwa of erotic pursuit and sudden (re)awakening in the third volume of his *A Companion in Solitude.* Tale 3:9 relates the story of a certain monk who grew attracted to a lady-in-waiting at the court.[14] Having pursued her relentlessly, he finally succeeds in getting her to agree to meet him one evening. He arrives full of anticipation, only to have her preach to him from behind her screens about the impermanence and filth of the human body. In a blazonry of human anatomy she treats the body piece by piece, saying, "This body is a thing of malodorous filth, something without comparison. The inside of the skull is brimming with fluids and fleshy tissues. Underneath the skin muscle and bone are woven together. Through it all runs the blood, and it brims with pus, not something that a person should [desire] to come close to at all" (SNKBT 40: 441).

Lest he think her sermon just a clever way to rebuff his amorous attentions, the woman pulls the lantern near and draws back the screens—both shocking moves in themselves—allowing the priest to see her clearly for the first time.[15] Her hair is rumpled and tangled, her face and feet a bluish-yellow, her robes filthy and spattered here and there with drops of blood, and her whole body gives off a horrific odor. She explains that in order to further her own Buddhist understanding she has quit her daily toilette and has been using the contemplation of her own body as a *fujōkan*-like meditation. She invites the priest to join her in this. The priest, for his part, is overwhelmed with shock and shame. He thanks her for being "a true friend" in faith (Jp: *imijiki tomo*) and, shedding copious tears at having been so forcefully brought back to the Buddhist path, he departs posthaste (SNKBT 40: 442).

In monastic practice, contemplation of the human body after death is one of the five major contemplations, and its express purpose is to rid the practitioner of sexual desire. The meditation was designed especially to help younger clerics who had not yet mastered their erotic impulses. *Fujōkan* thus aimed at quashing not just desire in general, but explicitly the heterosexual desire of male clerics. As Hirota Tetsumichi has noticed, however, in contrast to monastic practice, the "theme of stopping pre-existing carnal passions, when handled in setsuwa, [seems to] make those passions stronger and stronger" rather than weaker, due to the tales' titillating use of graphic detail.[16] The naked woman in the grove, for example, shifts her posture in an attempt to obscure the priest's view of her exposed body. She is ultimately unsuccessful, however, as the cleric continues to stare at her, and he, and we along with him, takes in every detail of her swollen breasts. Similarly, the aroused priest in the *Companion in Solitude* story is allowed first into his beloved's chambers, then into her speaking presence, and next behind her screens of state, and ultimately he is invited (to peer) into her robes in a climactic move that parodies scenes of courtly sexual conquest common to popular romances of the time.[17]

It is important to make a strong distinction between *fujōkan* as practiced by monks and *fujōkan* as described in literature. Unlike the monastic meditations on which they are based, setsuwa about bodily disintegration are not immediately interested in "exposing" desire as a deadly trap and rendering female sexual charms "powerless," which Elizabeth Wilson points out was the original objective of the monastic contemplation.[18] While *fujōkan* as a meditative practice may have been prescribed to monks who were hounded by unwanted sexual desires, *fujōkan* as a theme in setsuwa serves to arouse the audiences' sexual appetites and curiosity—particularly the appetites of those attracted to women and the curiosity of those interested in monastic sexuality.[19]

The gendered bias of *fujōkan* setsuwa is crystal clear, and it remained a core component of impurity tales even after the setsuwa genre began to give way to later, less didactic medieval forms. An *otogizōshi* (companion tale) from the late Muromachi period (1336–92), for example, relates the intertwined stories of the titular "three monks" religious awakenings, and the first two stories are of immediate interest here. Opening the narrative, the first monk explains that one night he stumbled upon the body of his wife who had been stabbed to death and robbed of her clothing and her hair. The sight of the woman's desecrated corpse spurred him immediately to take up the Buddhist path. Hearing this story, the second monk is astonished and quickly explains that earlier in his life he had been a merciless thief. He himself had stabbed the young woman and stolen her robes, returning later, at his wife's urging, to cut off her hair as well to sell at the market for wig making. The shock of seeing his wife's greedy pleasure so shortly after having been the instrument of the other lady's pain and desecration caused the thief to renounce his ways and become a monk.

Each of the *fujōkan* narratives examined, whether setsuwa or companion tale, features a gendered division in which men are the spectators and women's bodies the spectacle. In addition, the driving force in many *fujōkan* stories is the males' erotic desire for the unveiling and subsequent sexual availability of the female body. The prevalence of such gendered dynamics of erotic attraction has led at least one scholar to argue that setsuwa on the subject of *fujōkan* "explain a connection between [hetero]sexual desire and the awakening of faith" and further to posit that the eruption of sexual desire itself may have been seen by medieval Buddhists as a potential point for the achievement of spiritual realization.[20]

On the one hand, in *fujōkan* setsuwa sexual desire is almost always the province of male voyeurs while the potential for female desire is foreclosed upon. In the cases mentioned above, for instance, the woman is either already dead and her experience of her body reduced to one of pure suffering, or the woman has chosen to emphasize disgust at her body's impurities over any sense of enjoyment in its erotic possibilities. On the other hand, while the practice of *fujōkan* meditation was aimed at monastics (and particularly men), the circulation of setsuwa on the theme of *fujōkan* had a much wider audience (in the case of *A Companion in Solitude, The Three Jewels,* and perhaps *One Hundred Sessions of Sermons,* female laity) whose attentions were focused as much on the reactions of male monastic bodies as on the putrefaction of female lay ones. The question of audience thus complicates the notion of a male-monastic-voyeur/female-laity-object dichotomy, and points instead to medieval society's intense concern with clerical capacities to feel and act on sexual arousal, as well as to curtail and control it. In short, setsuwa on the theme of *fujōkan* meditation reveal as much about the laity's visual probing of monastic bodies as they do about monastic viewings of lay bodies.

THE DECORATED VESSEL

Whether their protagonists are monastics or laity, whether they struggle to maintain their vows against the allure of lust or leverage their disappointment in erotic pursuits into a new (or renewed) religious commitment, *fujōkan* narratives all share a common view of the human body as a container, a "painted pitcher" in the words of *A Collection of Treasures*. In the discussion above I have concentrated on the ways in which this motif arouses desire and establishes the female body as an object of critical gaze, but I have remained circumspect about precisely what it is that gaze perceives in the pivotal moment of insight that transforms erotic desire into religious fervor, that moment in which the viewer suddenly begins to read the body in a fundamentally different way. In the final portion of this discussion on *fujōkan* I return more precisely to the question of writing. Here I argue that the motif of bodily impurity invites its readers to envision a total inversion of visual object in which the decorated vessel of the human body, which contains all manner of impurity, turns radically inside out to reveal its seeming opposite: the living heart of the sutras. Thus I argue that, while setsuwa shift the dynamics of *fujōkan* from monastic contemplation to lay-oriented narrative, this repositioning is part and parcel of their attempt to, as Phelan puts it, "[re]enact the affective force of the performance event," here understanding the performance event to be the radical unstringing of the human body, a performance that is viewable both from the galleries of monastic meditation and from the commoners' pit of sermon oratory.

Mujū Ichien, in his thirteenth-century *Collection of Sand and Pebbles,* provides a vital clue to unpacking *fujōkan* in the following tetralemma. Citing the writings of an unidentified ancient scholar, he creates a four-part typology of beings who maintain the bodhisattva precepts, that is, the vows to assist others along the path to enlightenment. The tetralemma pairs and repairs the conceptual opposites of inside/outside and pure/impure. The first grouping consists of those who "are externally pure but internally stained . . . breaking the precepts at will while yet adorning themselves" with monastic robes (NKBZ 52: 545). Mujū laments particularly that these wayward priests accept donations from the faithful. The second grouping presents the inverse situation: "internally clean but externally stained, they hide their merit and do not accept the offerings of believers though internally they maintain ethical standards. They are superior." Here he references primarily Buddhist hermits who, because of the rigors of their mountain asceticism, may be mistaken for beggars. The third group is pure both inside and out, "the true ideal of the teachings," while the final group is "stained both inside and out. Following only their own wishes they do not qualify as Buddhist practitioners" (NKBZ 52: 546).

In describing the first group further (externally adorned but internally impure), Mujū focuses his criticism on those who engage in "false preaching" (Jp: *jamyō seppō*)—that is, those who preach solely for the purpose of collecting donations—and he calls them thieves who steal from their parishioners (NKBZ 52: 547).[21] The salient point here is that, for Mujū, the paradigmatic sin that accounts for internal impurity stems from an abuse of the sutras, using one's specialized knowledge of them for the sake of turning a profit rather than for the sake of furthering religious awareness. Mujū's "decorated vessels" are no alluring, erotic beauties; they are, rather, corrupt monks who wear priestly robes and present themselves as having knowledge of the scriptures for the sole purpose of fleecing believers out of their resources.

We can see the tetralemmic concern with inside/outside and pure/impure at work in many setsuwa on the topic of bodily putrefaction. As cited above, *A Collection of Treasures* draws repeated attention to the white skin (which becomes bruised with stagnant blood) and the red lips (which soon spill maggots). Another example marks again, even more adamantly, the importance that female skin and monastic robes, those thin wrappers of flesh, play in demarcating the boundary between clean and polluted, internal reality and external appearance. In his *Collection of Spiritual Awakenings,* Kamo no Chōmei (1155–1216) includes the story of the priest Genpin, who was widely respected by high and low alike. Among his followers was a councilor of state (Jp: *dainagon*) whose house he was in the habit of visiting. When Genpin's visits abruptly cease the councilor calls on him, thinking him ill. Dropping his voice to a near whisper, the monk confesses that he was avoiding the layman's home because he had chanced to see the man's wife and conceived a deep lust for her. Surprised and saddened, the councilor goes home and explains the situation to his wife. In a shocking departure from court decorum, she agrees to let the priest directly into her inner chambers. Some days later he appears "properly dressed in his monastic robes" (SNKS 180) and spends about two hours simply staring at her from several feet away. He departs without a word, leaving the master of the house to assume that the monk had been visualizing the physical decomposition (Jp: *fujō*) of his wife as a way of curing himself of lust.

Chōmei's commentary on the tale is illuminating. He begins by describing the monastic contemplation and then observes that "the human body is but a string puppet of bones and flesh *[hone shishi no ayatsuri]*. . . . The six viscera and the five organs coil inside, no different from poisonous snakes. It is moist with blood, its joints held together with sinew. Only a single thin layer of skin conceals its many impurities. Powdered and perfumed, no one recognizes it for what it really is. . . . It is like a 'painted vessel filled with shit and filth,' a corpse wrapped in brocade. Though you bathe yourself in the waters of a huge sea, you cannot get clean; though you burn expensive incense, the stench will not disperse" (SNKS 181–82). Clearly Chōmei's writing is, as Phelan phrases it, "solicitous of affect . . . pointing both to itself and to the 'scene' that motivates it."[22] He seeks to horrify and shock—comparing lustful people to bugs and the physical objects of their desires to piles of feces (SNKS 182)—while commending the enlightened for recognizing that all bodies, their own included, are nothing but a temporary amalgamation of flesh and bone, a transient biological unity ever subject to fragmentation and decay. He compares the body to a marionette whose strings may be cut, rendering it lifeless.

So much for the writing *of* the setsuwa; now for the brief glimpse of writing that appears, albeit indirectly, *in* the *setsuwa*. The priest's whispered description of the symptoms of the illness plaguing him is crucial. He confesses to his patron, the woman's husband, "Ever since glimpsing your wife, my memory is shot *[mono oboezu]*, my mind scattered *[kokoro madohi]*, and my breast swollen *[mune futagarite]*" (SNKS 180). In other words, he experiences his lust as both a corporeal and a mental disturbance that prohibits his access to memory, as if his feelings of arousal have jammed his chest cavity *(mune)* and literally blocked off the passage to his mind *(kokoro)*, which at the time was conceived of as existing within the ribcage and comprising the locale of memory. Though he does not specify what he is unable to remember, we can perhaps speculate that he is speaking here of a declining ability to recall the sutras.

I will discuss the mind as the organ of memory at much greater length in the following chapter. For the moment, let me simply cite one final setsuwa in which sutra text and lustful passion compete in a more obvious manner for sovereignty over the mind-memory complex. Writing a century and a half before Kamo no Chōmei, Chingen details the story of the monk Riman in his collection *Miracles of the Lotus Sutra*. (The story also appears in *Tales from Times Now Past* 13:9). As a youth Riman impressed his teacher with two things: his struggles to master lust and his fervent practice of *Lotus Sutra* recitation. Sympathizing with his disciple's struggles to suppress sexual desire, Riman's master provides him with a potent medicine that allows Riman to keep from breaking the precepts against carnal relations with women. Thereafter Riman engages in continual recitation of the *Lotus,* chanting it even while caring for the sick and while ferrying travelers across the nearby river in a boat. One night, in a dream, Riman sees his corpse "abandoned in an open field. One hundred thousand dogs gathered there, tore apart [his] dead body, and ate it, gulping it down" (NST 7: 527). When he wonders dispassionately why there are so many dogs, a voice in the sky tells him that these are not actually dogs but members of the assembly that gathered to hear the Buddha's sermons at the Jetavana monastery in ancient India. They have taken on canine form and eaten Riman's body in order to symbolically establish a karmic link to him because of his perfect retention of the *Lotus Sutra*.

There are several points of interest in this tale. First, Riman's name suggests his defining characteristic. His monastic name literally means "full *[man]* of doctrine *[ri]*," and it indicates that everything about Riman is geared toward containing—perfectly and exclusively—the sacred teachings. The second syllable *(man)* is used in other semantic compounds to refer to the high tide or the full moon, indicating that Riman is filled to capacity with the liquid luminosity of the sutra. (One might recall here the symptoms given in the last setsuwa, whose protagonist felt his chest to be swollen with something quite different: a carnal desire that, importantly, blocked his memory.) Finally, it is interesting that Riman's master does not give him the typical, expected cure for lust—meditation on a corpse—but has him drink medicine instead, perhaps providing the impetus for the dream in which the traditional cure, delayed, comes back into play in his oracular vision. After awaking from the dream, Riman takes up sutra recitation with still greater energy and begins claiming, also habitually, that he will be reborn in paradise through the power of the *Lotus* and that, as a sign of this, he will pass away on the same day as the historical Buddha's nirvana, the fifteenth day of the Second Month. Fittingly, he dies on the designated date, having just recited the lines from the *Lotus Sutra* that read, "He is called a keeper of the precepts, a performer of ascetic practices. Thus he shall quickly attain to the unexcelled buddha path."[23]

Fujōkan stories, then, are about moving between categories in the tetralemma that organizes precept holders into a hierarchy that ranges from those who are unworthy even to be called aspirants on the path (those who are both externally impure and internally stained) to those who emulate the bodhisattva ideal (being both pleasing to look upon and internally pure). Setsuwa about *fujōkan* focus on the central axis of the taxonomy, where a practitioner, by trading the prospect of external appeal for repugnant appearance, has the opportunity to simultaneously reconfigure the contents of his physical frame, inside of which is lodged memory. What *fujōkan* stories point to is a discord between internal and external, and in these stories we begin to see how the human body can be reinvented, not as a falsely alluring painted container of blood and pus, but instead as a repository of memorized sutra text. What is necessary to make this transition happen is a shock to the senses that culminates in a symbolically hyperbolic dissolution of living body into fragmented corpse. When the lessons of the visual shock are taken to heart, the body recoheres minus its cargo of lust.

FROM DECOMPOSITION TO DISMEMBERMENT

As we have seen, setsuwa of physical decomposition typically begin with the gaze settled on the body of another being and feature protagonists who view the dissolution of that corpse as a way to strengthen their own resolve for spiritual pursuits, the paradigmatic representative of which is the reading and recitation of sutra texts. Stories of personal self-sacrifice, like Myōe's, have similar goals but commence from a very different point of view. Rather than gazing outward at the naturally dissolving body of another and cultivating an awareness of how external beauty fades, self-sacrifice setsuwa feature devotees whose faith is quite solid, whose practice advanced, and whose contemplative gaze is firmly trained inward.

Again, whereas *fujōkan* tales focus on the willfully lustful body as a container of shit and pus, self-sacrifice setsuwa center on the visual image of the willingly dismembered body as a jeweled vessel ready to serve as a container for the sutra teachings. Protagonists in this latter type of tale sacrifice their own body to create an external sign, marking the intensity and single-mindedness of their spiritual aspiration. In the course of the narrative the protagonists move, often very quickly, from a neutral position in Mujū's tetralemma (remarked neither for their appearance nor for their practice), first to a state of external ugliness (dismemberment or scarring) that paradoxically indicates an internal state of perfected capacity for one of the six perfections of the bodhisattva (discussed below), and finally to the "true ideal" of purity both internal and external.

Buddhist sutras, among them the *Lotus Sutra* and the *Greater Heart Sutra,* identify six perfections (Sk: *pāramitā*) that a bodhisattva must practice and master. By progressing through these six stages of moral perfection, the bodhisattva moves ever closer to buddhahood. The first virtue to be mastered is that of charity (Sk: *dāna*), which in turn can be divided into three varieties. In its most fundamental sense, charity means providing beings with the material goods necessary to meet their basic needs, giving things like food, shelter, and clothing. But the perfection of charity also extends to more abstract levels that attend to mental and emotional needs as well, and which aim to free people from fear and instill a sense of calm and peace. This sort of charity practice might involve providing companionship and aid during times of grief, anxiety, or illness. (Incidentally, this is the type of charity that Riman was engaged in: hospice care for the sick and ferrying travelers to the other side of a river.) Finally, at its most profound, the perfection of charity involves the gift of the dharma, that is, the act of explaining the sutras or giving the teachings to another being.

The type of perfection of charity setsuwa that I will focus on in this section has to do with this final category of giving. Ohnuma Reiko, in discussing a similar body of literature in classical Indian sources (*jātaka* and *avadāna*), has appropriated the Sanskrit term *dehadāna,* literally "gifts of the body," to designate this particular subset of giving in which there is a "complete identification" between "giver and gift."[24] A related concept of corporeal giving was a familiar trope in medieval Japanese setsuwa, where it was most often referred to as "throwing away the body" (Jp: *shashin* or *mi wo suteru*). How is it, though, that in the Japanese context the "gift of the dharma" becomes coterminous with a "gift of the body?" A closer look at some setsuwa will help explain.

GIFTS OF THE BODY

Because it begins with a series of setsuwa on the six perfections, Minamoto no Tamenori's 984 collection *The Three Jewels* provides a particularly rich source for setsuwa on themes of self-sacrifice. Each of the stories in the opening sequence focuses on an emblematic episode in one of the Buddha's earlier lives during which he progressed along the bodhisattva path, providing physical evidence that he had mastered one of the six perfections of the Buddhist teachings: the perfection of charity, discipline, forbearance, effort, meditation, and wisdom. These stories also shed light on some of the ways in which medieval Japanese Buddhists adopted and subtly reworked plot lines and motifs whose origins lay in the *jātaka* and *avadāna* of classical India.

We can see the mechanics by which the body dissolves and is reconstituted around a textual fragment in the story of King Śibi, which comprises the bulk of Tamenori's first setsuwa. King Śibi, a former incarnation of the Buddha, takes a vow of total charity. Two deities (Indra and his assistant, both borrowed from the Hindu pantheon) seek to test his resolve by transforming into a hawk and a dove. The hungry hawk chases the dove into the king's chamber, where it finds shelter underneath his robe. When the hawk, speaking, demands the return of its quarry, the king slices some flesh from his thigh and offers it instead. The hawk accepts the switch but requires that the king provide the dove's exact weight in flesh. A scale is provided and the king places on it the meat from both his thighs. When the scale does not balance against the weight of the dove, he adds the flesh of his arms, back, and chest. The scale still does not draw even and, "when the king attempted to place his entire body on the scales, his sinews snapped, his strength faltered, and he collapsed in a heap" on the floor (SNKBT 31: 12). As in *fujōkan* scenes, the king's body is radically unstrung, his threadlike sinews snapped, his body turned almost entirely inside out. He does not give his body as a single whole, but rather as a set of accumulating fragments.

Though his physical strength is sapped, he has one resource left: the power of his vow to save all beings. Drawing on the strength of this commitment, and on his fierce determination not to renege on it, he grabs onto the chains from which the weighing pans are suspended and heaves what remains of himself into the scales. Despite his physical state, "his mind was resolved and he regretted nothing" (SNKBT 31: 12). Just then the ground shakes, flowers rain from the sky, waves crash on the seas, and blossoms burst forth from dead trees, all great harbingers of the appearance of an enlightened being in the world. The hawk and dove resume their true forms, confirm that the king is indeed a bodhisattva, and predict that he will soon attain buddhahood. As a visual sign confirming this, they pour medicine over the king's body, restoring him to his former state, and they praise him for "fulfilling the *pāramitā* of charity unto the point of death" (SNKBT 31: 13).

In the crucial moment when the resources of the flesh have been utterly exhausted, what sustains the king is his vow. The vow provides the electrical jolt that allows the king to go beyond what his body is physically capable of. What, then, is the source of this vow's power? What are its particular words and whence does it spring? In Tamenori's rendering there is a headnote that precedes the setsuwa about King Śibi. Unlike the king's story, which may be located in time and space (classical India), the headnote's setting is atemporal and without location: a metacommentary explaining the contemplation of the bodhisattva who was King Śibi and who would become Buddha. This metacommentary notes that the bodhisattva, seeking to perfect the virtue of charity over a number of lifetimes, "contemplated the thought, 'If I do not train myself to give away things, then I will ever be incarnated in an impoverished and painful condition. Thus I resolve to pursue the path of buddhahood by cultivating the power to help others'" (SNKBT 31: 10). He then vows to give anyone anything they ask for, thinking, "Bestowing lands and castles, wives and children is easier to bear than getting rid of grasses and trees. Giving away head and eyes, arms and legs is even simpler than throwing away rocks and earth" (SNKBT 31: 10).

His statement is certainly hyperbolic, but the point is that lands and castles, wives and children, and even one's own body are ultimately sources of suffering, and one should be glad to throw them off in the pursuit of liberation, particularly when the goal is to share that liberation with all beings (including, presumably, the abandoned wives and children!). Importantly, the vow comprises a rough paraphrase of the opening lines of the "Devadatta" chapter of the *Lotus Sutra,* in which the Buddha, delivering a sermon to an assembly of every variety of sentient beings, recounts his past lives. He says, "In times past, throughout incalculable kalpas I sought the *Lotus Sutra,* in all those kalpas being neither negligent nor impatient. I ever appeared as a king of a realm who vowed . . . to fulfill the six pāramitās. I strove to confer gifts, in my mind never begrudging elephants, horses, the seven jewels, realms, walled cities, wives, children, slaves, servants, head, eyes, marrow, brain, flesh, muscle, arms or legs, not even begrudging bodily life itself."[25] Though the king's vow here obtains to the perfection of all six *pāramitās* the only one specifically mentioned is that of charity—his endeavor to "confer gifts"—so that this one virtue metonymically represents the sum total of all the virtues.

Tamenori's setsuwa of King Śibi thus turns on an intertextual allusion to the *Lotus Sutra.* King Śibi's vow consists of an indirect citation of a scriptural passage that in itself concerns a vow to sacrifice the body in the pursuit of that scripture, so that attention pulses back and forth between text and flesh. The intertextual allusion accomplishes three things. First, it provides scriptural authority attesting to the efficacy and appropriateness of the king's actions. Second, it subtly introduces the importance of the written scriptures into the frame of the narrative. While the overarching goal of *pāramitā* practice is nirvana, the intertext provides an additional, intermediate objective: access to the scriptures, and especially the *Lotus Sutra.* And third, the allusion provides an interpretive framework for understanding King Śibi's actions. He whittles away his extremities—first legs and arms, then chest and back flesh—gradually moving closer and closer to the core of his physical being. His sacrifice of flesh ultimately reveals that the life force that lies in his innermost depths is his commitment to a piece of sutra: five lines of one chapter of one sutra, a tiny fragment that transports him beyond attachment to the body, allows him to accomplish his deepest aspiration, and provides the kernel around which his body is then reconstructed. Through perfecting the virtue of charity, the king has emptied his body and mind of any impurity—he has no corporeal coherence and attests that his heart is free of regret. The perfection of charity requires the total gift of the body, which simultaneously constitutes physical evidence of a bone-deep belief in the Buddhist teachings and remakes the body into a Buddhist object and a container of text.

Tale 1:3 of *The Three Jewels* relates a similar story, this time pertaining to the perfection of forbearance, the virtue of withstanding inflicted pain without growing angry. As in the previous instance, Tamenori prefaces the tale with the thoughts of a bodhisattva who, seeming to speak from beyond time and space, utters a vow that duplicates language from the sutras. In this case the vow ends, "Though beaten with staves and slashed with swords [I shall recall that] this body is like foam on the water's surface" (SNKBT 31: 17), which alludes to the story of a bodhisattva from the twentieth chapter of the *Lotus Sutra* whose practice consisted of verbally acknowledging everyone he met as a future buddha. In response, people beat him with staves and poles (T 9.262.50c29). The vow also echoes what is perhaps the *Vimalakīrti Sutra's* most famous metaphor for the human body, comparing its evanescence to that of foam on the water.[26]

Tamenori follows this opening citation with a setsuwa featuring the ascetic Ksānti (Jp: Ninniku shōnin), who is practicing austerities in the woods near a king's palace. The king decides to go on a pleasure outing with his many women in attendance and, when he falls asleep, they disperse into the forest to gather flowers. Spying Ksānti, they gather around him and he preaches to them, inciting in them the desire for renunciation and the aspiration for enlightenment. On waking, the king finds himself alone and, assuming that someone has made off with his women, he draws his sword and goes in pursuit. Finding Ksānti with the women around him, the king accuses the ascetic, saying, "You have not yet separated your mind from this realm of desire. How is it that you should trust your mind when you look at my women?" (SNKBT 31: 19). Ksānti replies that his core practice is the perfection of forbearance. Predictably, the king begins to test the ascetic's resolve by chopping him limb from limb.[27]

The king severs the ascetic's arms, legs, ears, and nose before his rage finally cools. Ksānti, miraculously still able to talk, addresses the king, saying, "Why do you not cut me apart some more? Even if you were to chop and pulverize me like mustard seed or [grind] me into dust, I would in no way grow angry or resentful for even a moment. . . . King, today with an angry heart you took my body and cut it into seven pieces making seven wounds; even so, I vow that, should I become a buddha in the future, with a merciful heart I will deliver you over, leading you on the path of the seven enlightened states and severing you from the seven illusions."[28] The sage equates the pieces of his severed body with pieces of the Buddhist teachings, so that the spectacle of his scattered flesh becomes at once a symbol and a site of Buddhist lessons concerning forbearance and nonattachment.

This inverse relationship between a body that is hacked to pieces and a virtue that coalesces into perfection is well attested in both sutra and setsuwa literature. For instance, book one of *The Three Jewels* and book five of *Tales from Times Now Past* are filled with similar stories in which the destruction of the physical self triggers in some way the production in writing, or at least the citation in performance, of a scriptural fragment.[29] Similarly, in a section detailing the moral obligations and duties of a disciple of the Buddha, the *Brahma Net Sutra* states that a true child of the Buddha "should accept, keep, read, and recite the Mahāyāna sutras and the precepts. He should flay his skin for paper, draw his blood for ink, use his marrow for water, and sliver his bones for a stylus to copy them in writing, whether on bark, paper, cloth, or bamboo. He should use the seven gems, priceless incense, flowers, and all other manner of precious substances to create cases and covers to protect the scrolls of the sutras and the precepts" and to show his reverence for them (T 24.1484.1009a20–24). Additionally, the *Nirvana Sutra* has several scenes, which I discuss at greater length below, describing self-sacrifice as the legible deed of a bodhisattva, indicating that the destruction of the body (usually through cutting) marks the flesh as a palimpsest of Buddhist writing.

Arguing on the evidence of Indian tales, Ohnuma Reiko points out that a core characteristic of *dehadāna* stories is the absolute conflation of gift with giver that stems from the vow to give away anything, up to and including one's own life. This observation definitely holds true as well in the case of Japanese narratives, which are adapted from Indian source material, but it does not get all the way to the heart of the matter, for, at least in the Japanese tales, it is not actually the body that is so needed. For instance, hawks and demons may make cursory gestures to hunger and request the devotee's flesh to fulfill that need, but the underlying lack is not one of physical nourishment but of mental affliction: greed in the case of the hawk, anger and jealousy in the case of the king. No amount of food or killing is going to meet those demands because they stem from spiritual ignorance that can only be dissolved through the application of Buddhist wisdom. According to Buddhist teachings, the antidote to greed is generosity—thus Śibi gives everything of his body with no holding back—and the antidote to anger is forbearance—thus Kṣānti allows himself to be hacked to bits while exhibiting only patience and, significantly, he vows to become a buddha who will instruct the king and help him overcome his anger and jealousy. Ultimately, then, like Myōe and King Śibi, Kṣānti's violent physical desecration marks him as a vessel of the dharma (Jp: *hōki*), a shift in status that he indicates in his vow of buddhahood.

LETTER FROM MOUNT MINOBU

Motifs of self-sacrifice were incredibly well known in medieval Japan, appearing in artwork, setsuwa literature, sermons, and a variety of other media. The words of the rather fiery monk Nichiren (1222–82), who was known for his roadside sermons and who started his own school of Buddhism in 1253, give a sense of how pervasive these stories were. In his "Letter from Mount Minobu" ("Minobusan gosho"), composed for one of his followers, Nichiren offers what is quite likely the most extensive Japanese-language compendium of self-sacrifice and dismemberment tales. Coincidentally, the name of the mountain could be rendered as "overcoming *[nobu]* the body *[mi]*," so that Nichiren situates himself in a landscape whose name suggests physical privation that hones spiritual awareness, a locale from which he casts a summative, retrospective gaze onto his life and teachings.

Nichiren begins his survey with the story of Gyōbō Bonji, writing, "Long ago, when Śākyamuni was Gyōbō Bonji, he peeled off his skin and used it for paper, extracted the liquid from his marrow and used it for water, cut off his flesh and used it as an inkstone, broke up his bones and used them as brushes, all in order to meet the buddha Kāśyapa and receive the verse, 'He who practices in accordance with the dharma / and does not practice what is not the dharma / both in this life and in the next / shall be at peace.'"[30] Gyōbō Bonji literally de-constructs his body, creating from its disconnected components the various implements required for writing: paper, inkstone, water (to liquefy the ink), stylus, and brush.[31] Here the body is turned completely inside out, as skin becomes the bottommost layer and that innermost liquid, marrow, is compounded with pulverized muscle and painted atop the epidermis. Nichiren's letter continues with a long list of similar tales, most of which he references parenthetically, suggesting that his addressee knew the tales well. Among those he mentions are two from *The Three Jewels* (concerning King Śibi and the ascetic Ksānti) discussed above.

As with Tamenori's treatment in *The Three Jewels,* Nichiren prefaces these tales of self-sacrifice with a scriptural reference. In his case he begins the letter by mentioning that he has been chanting the *Lotus Sutra* continually, day and night, in his hut atop the mountain, and he claims that his life on the mountain, characterized by isolation and a deeply questing religious practice, "is no different from that of the Buddha when he was searching for the dharma."[32] Nichiren thus situates himself as the protagonist in a tale of bodily sacrifice and uses the rhetorical structure of those tales to suggest that he, like those former incarnations of the Buddha, has realized the sutra with his own body via a direct exchange of flesh for text.[33]

HAIR FOR PAPER, BLOOD FOR INK

Actually dismembering oneself (as Myōe did) or claiming that one was a living embodiment of scripture (as Nichiren did) remained extravagant gestures that were not often emulated in medieval Japan.[34] Instead, popular practice seized on the images and promises of "gifts of the body" in two much less painful ways. The first involved using nonliving tissue (hair or blood) to provide materials for copying out sutras, the goal of which was to establish a spiritual connection between the donor and the sutra by literally making part of the donor a part of the sutra. *Shashin* motifs also found their way into popular practice via a second venue that entailed "throwing away" the body in a less immediately violent fashion, essentially through a practice of slow starvation in the mountains.

Whereas for religious leaders the intention behind dismemberment practices was, presumably, to prove the sincerity and intensity of one's devotion and to approximate in one's own body the body of the historical Buddha, for laypeople metaphorical acts of dismemberment were more about creating a sense of karmic connection (Jp: *kechien*) that could be leveraged in order to relieve the suffering of already-dead loved ones or, alternately, to ward off the potential for such suffering in one's own future incarnations. However, the basic idea of an equation between physical body and written scripture remains, regardless of the differences between clerical and lay intentions informing acts of actual or metaphorical dismemberment.

In 1136, for instance, Fujiwara no Munetada, mourning his beloved wife, had a small chapel constructed near the cemetery on Mount Kōya in which he "enshrined a group of votive sutra transcriptions that he and his children had copied on decorated paper that contained strands of his recently deceased wife's hair,"[35] a practice also mentioned in *A Companion in Solitude* 2:4, in which a bereaved husband offers his wife's hair in exchange for a sutra copied in her name. Around the same time, Fujiwara no Yorinaga (1112–56) copied a sutra in blood that had been donated by his friend Fujiwara no Atsuto. A century later, Hōjō no Tokimune (1251–84) transcribed two sutras using his own blood, while "survivors of the Jōkyū Rebellion of 1221 who fled to Kōzanji outside Kyoto copied sutras, one of which was in blood, for their dead compatriots."[36] Willa Tanabe, in her book on the practice of *Lotus Sutra* transcription in Japan, notes that the frequency of this "personalization" of sutra copies by using bodily elements, and especially blood, "increased in the Kamakura period (1185–1333), when it may have been fueled by the warrior spirit."[37] More important than warrior spirit, I suspect, was the increasingly literal interpretation of traditional Buddhist metaphor, a trend that transcended social class, with monks, warriors, and aristocrats alike participating in religiously inspired dismemberment practices.

RECLUSION

While gifts of the body could be literal, violent, and sudden, generally these stories of near-instantaneous transformation were associated with previous incarnations of the Buddha. More often in medieval Japanese practice, the gift of the body was understood in a broader sense, and the term "throwing away the body" (Jp: *shashin* or *mi wo suteru*) was commonly used to describe reclusion in the mountains. It is as an heir of this tradition that Nichiren places the privations of his secluded life on a par with more spectacular acts of dismemberment.

Keisei, for example, includes in *A Companion in Solitude* two stories that touch on this theme. The first concerns the monk Nyogen (active in the early 1100s), who began his career with aspirations of becoming a great monastic scholar. Realizing that he would never match the academic accomplishments of some of his peers, he decided instead to gain a reputation for undergoing severe ascetic discipline. Leaving the scholastic center at the Tōdaiji in Nara, he "shut himself up in the mountains near Kumano and, grinding his flesh and breaking his bones," underwent austerities.[38] Once more, he realizes that others are outstripping him, performing feats "five or six times more difficult" (363), and he moves again, this time to a mountainous area in Harima, where he abandons the pursuit of worldly renown and takes up the exclusive practice of *Lotus Sutra* recitation.

A second story, also set in the mountains of Harima, features a monk who takes up a life of reclusion and eats only the tiniest portion of food every day. After three years he posts a broadsheet in a nearby village, inviting anyone interested to come visually confirm his act of "abandoning both mind and life [kokoro to inochi wo sute]" (385), and he directs them to a crag high on the mountain. When they arrive they find his corpse facing west with its palms steepled in calm repose. In his comment on the story, Keisei characterizes the monk's death in reclusion as a gift of the body, first referring to the Lotus Sutra, which he says "praises no offering above that of burning the digits of one's hands or feet in homage to the Buddha," and then suggesting that similar passages are to be found in the Brahma Net Sutra. Chapter seven of the Lotus details the acts of the bodhisattva Medicine King, which do include burning a finger as an offering, and the Brahma Net Sutra similarly speaks of vow keepers as beings who have "taken their skin for paper and their blood for ink" (T 24.1484.1009a21).

Similarly, Kamo no Chōmei, in A Collection of Spiritual Awakenings 6:13, writes of two ladies-in-waiting who left service at the imperial court to take up reclusion in the mountains.[39] The setsuwa begins with a male sage (Jp: hijiri) who is wandering the peaks near the capital in search of a secluded place where he can engage in solitary practice. He stumbles upon two small huts and catches a glimpse through the window of a woman's face, blackened and sunken in on itself. Though she stonewalls him at first, on hearing that he, too, intends to "throw away his body in the mountain forest" (SNKS 286), she finally responds to his questions, saying that she and one other have been living there for some forty years, taking turns going into a nearby village to beg for food. He leaves her in peace and returns some days later with hempen robes and a store of provisions, but he finds the huts empty and surmises that the two women have fled deeper into the mountains. In his lengthy response to the story Chōmei links the women to "King Śibi, who exchanged himself for a dove, and Prince Mahāsattva, who threw his body to tigers. Undertaking difficult and painful acts, they attained buddhahood [literally, they attained the body of a buddha]" (SNKS 290).

Reclusion in the mountains, though still qualified as a gift of the body, has somewhat different nuances than the bodhisattvic act of spectacular dismemberment. First, while hermits' acts of privation may inspire others to religious awakening, they do not take any grand vows to return in future incarnations as bodhisattvas. Rather, like the copiers of sutras mentioned above, they seem more interested in attaining rebirth in the Pure Land, where they will be free of all afflictions. Second, the process of bodily disintegration is much lengthier, taking years or even decades rather than occurring in the course of several minutes. On a physical level the end result is the same—the woman's face "sinks in" on itself in slow decay just as King Śibi's body collapses in a sudden heap, both suggesting the utter undoing of the flesh—but the process is much more time-consuming. Finally, practitioners of reclusion typically hide their corporeal degradation from others' eyes until the last moment rather than making of it a spectacular and sudden display. This slow decay of the flesh, the observation of which is aimed more at self-cultivation than at the demonstration of virtuous perfection, suggest a continuum of practice that links awareness of bodily decomposition and the commission of bodily sacrifice as described in setsuwa.[40] The remainder of this chapter will examine how the praxis of observing decay, whether after death or in reclusion, invokes the trope of dismemberment and does so precisely by zeroing in on the body's reconfiguration from a container of impurity to a container of dharma.

COMPOSING DECOMPOSITION

Though a number of setsuwa deal with the *fujōkan* theme, few of these stories are composed from the first-person perspective. Medieval Japanese literature provides two notable exceptions to this general trend. The first, and better known, is a series of nine poems (Jp: *kusō no shi*) attributed to the Shingon patriarch Kūkai (774–835, posthumously awarded the name Kōbō Daishi) and included in the *Seireishū,* a collection of his writing compiled after his death by his disciple Shinzei (800–860). The second exception is Keisei's *A Companion in Solitude.* Of the thirty-two setsuwa Keisei records, five deal with the theme of *fujōkan,* and one of these stories reveals that Keisei's own spiritual awakening was spurred by his sight of a murder victim's corpse. In the following pages I will explore what these two more personal encounters with putrefaction reveal about the urge to compose on the theme of decomposition and the way such compositions can reach beyond themselves to include narratives of bodily sacrifice. Ultimately I argue that *fujōkan* compositions use extensive intertextual allusions to gesture toward a delicate knitting together of text and body inside the contemplative mind.

Although the ten-volume set of Kūkai's writings was initially compiled in the mid-ninth century, the last three volumes of the collection, in which the poems on *fujōkan* appear, were lost for a time. The scholar-monk Saisen (1025–1115) reconstructed the final volumes based on sources that he uncovered in his research. Thus, there is some debate in modern scholarship as to whether the nine poems on decomposition were composed by Kūkai or by someone else.[41] No such uncertainty existed for medieval monks like Keisei, who quotes from the poem sequence in his own writings.

Tale 1:20 in *A Companion in Solitude,* which immediately precedes the story of Keisei's own awakening, concerns a husband and wife who are experiencing marital difficulties. The wife assumes that her husband has found a more attractive lover and suggests that he leave her. He admits that he has long been wishing to dissolve their union, but for reasons that are very different from those she supposes. He explains that when resting from his labors one day in an open meadow, he happened across a skull. Since then he has been unable to shake the image and the accompanying thought that all life ends in death, and he says that "even when [he] reach[es] out to touch [her] face" in affection, he is reminded of the skeleton that lies just beneath her flesh (SNKBT 40: 408). In the end, he does leave her to take up religious practice and seek rebirth in the Pure Land, promising that once he has achieved his aim he will come back to lead her there, too, as a sign of his love. In commenting on the story, Keisei expresses his admiration for one who, "though illiterate" *(fumi ni mo kuraki),* could see in a skeleton the same messages about impermanence and faith that we can read in "Kōbō Daishi's 'White maggots squirm in the openings of her flesh / and blue flies buzz inside her mouth. / Searching now for the beauty of old: / on the one hand sadness, on the other shame.'"[42] The quotation is a translation (from Chinese to Japanese) of the final stanza of Kūkai's third poem, which concerns the discoloration of the rotting corpse.

NINE VIEWS OF A CORPSE

Known as the *kusō no shi* (poems of the nine views), the *Seireishū* poems describe each of the nine stages of a body's putrefaction after death: the fresh corpse, swelling, discoloration, oozing filth, coming apart, fleshless bones, white bones loosely held together, disjointed white bones, and becoming ash.[43] Through the course of these nine poems, Kūkai (if he is indeed their author) utilizes many of the classical Buddhist metaphors for the human body that appear, for instance, in the *Vimalakīrti Sutra,* and in that sense his poems incorporate a number of unreferenced textual allusions. In his first poem, for instance, he writes, "Like a mayfly born in the morning and dying in the evening / in a moment we, too, collapse in death. / Like a cloud dragged across the skies our bodies, full of desire, also pass away. / As a ringed fire soon dies out, so with our body, edifice of passions. . . . / Life spans, however long or short, are all as the mist" (NKBT 71: 461).

In this striking list of metaphors for the human body, Kūkai borrows two from the *Vimalakīrti Sutra:* the comparison of the body to a cloud and to a flame. In poem number six, written on the contemplation of fleshless bones, Kūkai draws on further imagery from the *Vimalakīrti Sutra* when he compares the human body to "butterflies or floating clouds: our lives are as short as a flash of lightning," utilizing two (clouds and lightning) of the sutra's ten most famous metaphors (NKBT 71: 465). Kūkai's practice of scattering such literary allusions throughout his poems reminds his readers that his compositions, like the disjointed bones and fragmented flesh that is their subject, are but pieces of a larger whole. Though streamlined and elegant in their classical Chinese regulated five-character verse form, the poems are not sealed texts, entirely self-contained and self-referential. Rather, they consistently and insistently point to something beyond themselves, primarily the sutras. Kūkai thus presents both his poems, and the fragmented bodies that are their subject matter, as transient phenomena that nevertheless contain the abiding truths of Buddhism, truths that can be unearthed, like jewels, from the ground of the composition.

THE GIFT OF BEING SEEN

The poems also indirectly reference a scene from the very beginning of the *Nirvana Sutra.* Having learned that the Buddha is about to die, a great crowd begins to congregate around the teak trees in whose shade their teacher rests. Following the traditional hierarchy, the monks arrive first, followed by nuns, male laity, female lay believers, and then all manner of nonhuman beings, including demons, goddesses, dragonlike *naga,* and birdlike *garuda.* The narrative pauses to describe each group as it arrives. Beginning with the arrival of the male laity, most of the descriptions follow the same pattern, listing first the group's various virtuous practices and cataloging their many offerings (such as fragrant wood to be used in the pending cremation). The group then circumambulates the Buddha en masse, expresses their grief, and is seated to await his final words.

While the narrative gives scant attention to the laywomen's offerings (simply noting that they brought twice as much as the men), it dwells at length on their virtuous practices, which should very quickly begin to sound familiar. The sutra notes that the women "contemplate their own flesh, [regarding it] as four poisonous snakes. This body is ever nibbled at by innumerable types of insect, and the rotten stink of it carries wide. It is hateful, like the carcass of a mongrel. It is unclean, its nine orifices [eyes, ears, nostrils, mouth, anus, and urethra] ever running" (T 12.374.367a28-b1). The passage speaks of how the body is "ever pecked at and devoured" by all manner of canines and carrion-eating birds and concludes that one "should throw away" the body (367b9, b13). Clearly this passage shares a great deal of imagery with literature describing the male monastic praxis of *fujōkan*. Kūkai's second, third, and fourth poems, for instance, speak of wild animals fighting over the carcass, of insects eating the flesh and birds pecking at the remains, while the fourth poem quotes the sutra almost word for word, describing "the juices [that] run from the nine orifices" (NKBT 71: 463).

Whereas accounts of monastic practice tend to associate the viewing of female bodies primarily with the attempt to overcome carnal passion, very little of that language surfaces in the sutra, and I would argue that its sublimation here reveals that the women's praxis is of a different order, even though the contemplative object on view is the same. When the women regard their flesh as "four poisonous snakes," the reference is to the four elements that constitute the human body: earth, air, fire, and water. In other words, although the body appears to have an observable, intrinsic existence and to be identifiable with an individual human being, in fact it can be broken into its elements and shown to have no abiding existence. In this sense, the women's contemplation of their own bodies becomes a way of reaching analytical understanding of the core Buddhist tenets of emptiness (Sk: *śūnya;* Jp: *kū*) and no-self (Sk: *anātman;* Jp: *muga*).

Although these devout women could keep this vision to themselves—as, indeed, do the two former ladies-in-waiting discovered by the male sage in *A Collection of Spiritual Awakenings* 6:13—instead they choose to help "countless hundreds of thousands of beings cross over" to the other shore of nirvana by appearing in female form (367a27-28). It is for this act of selfless giving that the sutra qualifies the laywomen as "protectors and holders of the true dharma" (a27), identifies them as "true bodhisattvas" (b20), notes that they "adorn" themselves "with the perfection of virtue" (b22), and suggests that as enlightened beings they will "turn the wheel of the dharma in a future age" (b21). What we see here, then, is a group of people who are in the process of actively transforming themselves into containers of the dharma. Particularly because this description takes place in the context of gift giving, we should read the women's act of making themselves visually available to others as a gift that signals their perfection of charity. Their act is a "gift of the body" on a par with more violent and immediately sacrificial offerings.

Kūkai makes these connections between "gifts of the body," his poetic compositions, and the *Nirvana Sutra* much more explicit in the ninth poem of his series, which we can now read as an experiential gloss on the *Nirvana Sutra* passage. His final contemplation, on the aspect of the body becoming ash, reads in its entirety:

> Mountains and rivers last longer than ten thousand ages
> While human life is shorter than a hundred years.
> Even bones ultimately crumble away
> And coffins turn to dust.
>
> The spirit has no place to return.
> Why should it guard the tomb?
> The name on the grave marker is faint
> And the mounded earth barely covers the remains.
>
> Over days and months the bones become white dust
> Which in the end blows to the mountains on a black wind.
> Only the treasure of the three vehicles remains.[44]
> Not practicing, one suffers the eight torments.[45]
>
> What are the six sense organs now?[46]
> The four elements are simply empty names.[47]
> In winter the moss covers the mound in green
> And in summer the grasses grow thickly from its earth.
>
> In my bag there are provisions.
> Under the pines my head blues with stubble.
> In fitting with the pale sky and floating clouds above
> The pines moan in the evening breeze:
>
> All things are impermanent.   (NKBT 71: 467–69)

The poem's vision of transience is complete and all encompassing. The body, down to its very bones, has crumbled to dust and blown away. The name on the grave marker has faded. Even the clouds in the sky above scud off for the horizon. Amidst all this flux, only the Buddhist teachings, the three vehicles, persist: just as the flesh rots, revealing the white bones, as those bones, too, pass out of existence, turning to ash and blown away by the wind, they reveal the truth of impermanence. Through his penetrating vision, the poem's author has peeled back the dusty layers of human existence, revealing the abiding treasure hidden beneath the flesh.

As is common with *fujōkan*-related compositions, the poet concludes his piece with a fragment, a brief allusion to another text and another story, by appending part of a Buddhist scriptural verse, a sort of postscript that is at once both a part of the poem as well as an interpretive frame for it. The graveyard pines, sighing in the evening breeze, give voice to a portion, perhaps the most important portion, of the Buddhist teachings: "All things are impermanent" (Jp: *shogyō mujō.*) This is one of the most oft-repeated phrases of medieval Japanese Buddhism and appears in the *Nirvana Sutra* as one line in a *gāthā,* the full length of which reads: "All things are impermanent; / this is the law of birth and extinction. / When birth and death itself has been extinguished, / That tranquil extinction brings bliss" (T 12.374.450a16, 451a1). On the printed page, this fragmentary last line even looks like a fragment; it calls attention to itself as a four-character phrase following nine poems' worth of strictly regular five-character units.

By including this brief citation as part of his poem, Kūkai provides a hint, a contextual clue that demands his readers' own intellectual input in order to reach completion. Kūkai's poems are not so much a closed text as they are a prompt for a perpetually unfinished performance that takes human memory as its stage by inciting the need to access what Michael Riffaterre calls an "intertext."[48] Rather than existing on the written page, the intertext, as Riffaterre understands it, exists only in memory, and as such it may be slightly different for each individual who encounters the written text that prompts it. In this sense, intertext consists of a loose and ever-expanding net of associations that a reader makes in the process of assimilating a text.

THE HIMALAYA YOUTH

Although certainly linked to the content of the poems through its message of transience, this phrase—"all things are impermanent"—is surely not the only such passage that the poet, with his clearly voluminous knowledge of sutras and commentaries, had available to him. The fragmentary verse, and in particular this *part* of that verse, also belongs to a larger narrative (or intertext) of self-sacrificial dismemberment, a narrative that is related in the *Nirvana Sutra.* About one-third of the way through the sutra, we find the Buddha and his disciple Kāśyapa engaged in a lengthy dialogue about the value of the teachings that the Buddha is currently delivering from his deathbed. Praising them, Kāśyapa vows, "I shall now peel off my skin for paper, remove my blood for ink, use my marrow for water, and crush my bones to make a brush to write out a copy of this *Great Nirvana Sutra*" (T 12:374.449a19–21).

The Buddha responds with a tale describing one of his past lives in which he lived deep in the Himalayas and performed literally what Kāśyapa is suggesting metaphorically.

In this past life the Buddha was a youthful ascetic[49] living in one of those dark periods in which there was no enlightened being in the world and in which the Mahāyāna sutras had passed out of circulation, their written texts utterly decayed. Nevertheless, he searches for the teachings doggedly, and his efforts attract the attention of godlike beings (Sk: *deva*), one of whom decides to test him by reciting half a verse of scripture, which he has retained in memory from the teachings of previous buddhas. The deva transforms himself into the likeness of a flesh-eating demon, transports himself to the mountains within earshot of the boy, and recites, "All things are impermanent; / this is the law of birth and extinction." That is, the demon produces two lines of the verse, one line of which later appears at the end of Kūkai's poems on the corpse.

Hearing these verses, the youth thinks to himself, "This half of a verse opens understanding in my mind, like a half moon that begins to gently open the petals of a lotus" (T 12.374.450b4). Excited, he lifts the hank of tangled hair that blocks his eyes and sees the demon standing there. Surprised, the youth wonders how such an ugly creature could have been the source of such a beautiful verse. Seeing no one else, however, he asks the demon, "Where did you attain this half of a wish-fulfilling jewel?" (b15). The demon replies that he is too hungry to answer, having worn himself out searching far and wide for food to no avail. The youth then proposes an exchange that will quell both of their hungers: "You expound to me completely the remainder of the verse and I will give you my body as an offering. . . . This is like a person who gives an earthenware vessel and receives in return a vessel of the seven jewels. I will throw away my soft flesh and gain an adamantine body" (c11–12, c18–19). The demon utters the second half of the verse and the youth copies it onto nearby rocks and trees before climbing a tree and throwing himself at the demon's feet, where he expects to be devoured. At the last moment the demon keeps the youth from hitting the ground, transforms back into his deva appearance, calls the youth a bodhisattva, and prophesizes that the young man will become a buddha in the future.

This sutra passage brings into play a number of motifs from both decomposition (Jp: *fujōkan*) and self-sacrificial (Jp: *shashin*) tales, fusing them into a single narrative. First, as with the sutra-copying practice mentioned earlier in this chapter, the youth is confident in the power of Buddhist scripture to bring about physical transformation and so is not concerned about his body's impending destruction. Second, this passage echoes the language of *fujōkan* narratives in that the youth imagines and describes his death, deriding his "soft" body and using this image to reinforce his commitment to spiritual awakening. Finally, the young man speaks of his body specifically as a "vessel" and assumes that his act of self-sacrifice will remake him into a jeweled dharma vessel that will contain, at least at the outset, one small portion of the sutras, namely, the four-line *gāthā* for which he has offered his body in a direct text-for-flesh exchange.

The language of textual production and fleshly consumption dominates the narrative. The demon's far-ranging search for soft flesh to eat parallels the youth's intensive search for the written scriptures early on in the tale. And this sense of a physical-scriptural correspondence becomes obvious when the youth suggests that the offering of his whole body, soon to be torn apart in consumption, is a fair trade for the reunion of a currently fragmented, partial text.[50] By concluding his nine-poem sequence with this telegraphic citation of the *Nirvana Sutra*, Kūkai again suggests a material continuum of sutra text and human flesh. The four words "all things are impermanent," while they no doubt describe the reality of the human body, also massively expand the compass of the poem to include the abiding dharma. Just as the abandoned corpse fades away, leaving only the three vehicles, Kūkai's poem fades out, leaving only the words of scripture.

MURDER AND AWAKENING

Before concluding with a more theoretical consideration of the literary techniques of citation and fragmentation at work here, I would first like to consider one final setsuwa. Concluding a series of *fujōkan* narratives, Keisei describes his own personal corpse-inspired awakening in setsuwa 1:21 of *A Companion in Solitude*. While yet a boy Keisei happened to see the dead body of a young woman of about nineteen years that had been abandoned in a riverside meadow near his house. According to neighborhood rumor the girl had been the clandestine lover of a local married man whose wife had become jealous of his philandering. The girl had died under suspicious circumstances, and her body was left to rot. The incident caused quite a stir, and people crowded around "thick as a stand of young bamboo" to see the victim's corpse, which, Keisei recalls, was "not even like a normal human body at all, more like a segment of a big tree—no arms, no legs! It was dirty, filthy beyond description. Even if one were to pour the waters of a great ocean over oneself, still one would not feel clean. It was hard to even glance at it, totally unbearable. At a time like this, who could possibly slide a door open or line up two pillows next to one another?" (SNKBT 40: 410). That is, who could possibly entertain lustful thoughts?

Keisei follows his harrowing description of bodily dismemberment with a series of brief textual citations as he begins to knit his vision of the disjointed body into the fabric of a larger text. He writes, "Wind-blown and sun-bleached, her skin ripped open and her sinews melted apart, soiling the clean grasses and the air with her stench, surely no one wants to couple or exchange words with her now" (SNKBT 40: 411). But then, in a way, he begins to do just that. Rather than turning away in disgust, he continues to face her, pairing her body with a series of quotations from writings attributed to the great Indian Buddhist philosopher Nāgārjuna (ca. 150–250?), the Chinese founder of the Tiantai school Zhiyi (538–97), and the Japanese scholar-monk Genshin (942–1017), all of whom composed texts dealing with the contemplative praxis of *fujōkan*.

Keisei's narrative shuttles back and forth between the spectacle of the woman's body and the textual citations that he increasingly uses to describe it. Eventually the citations take over and Keisei's writing becomes a pastiche of other texts such that his reading of her dismembered body and his cento of citations merge. He explains that in weaving together this story of his own personal experience with the words from Buddhist masters, he hopes to teach his readers how to see the body (now, both the woman's corpse and their own flesh) in the proper light. He worries that, "ignorant of the body's true nature," people will continue to pile up sin upon sin, and he wants his readers instead to "straighten out their minds" (SNKBT 42). The specter of the fragment permeates Keisei's narrative: time and again he focuses on the fact that the woman's body has been desecrated and dismembered, all of his many textual citations are telegraphic and partial, and he even points out the insufficient nature of his own gesture in attempting to gather together these various bits and pieces into a single coherent narrative. Keisei insists on incompletion and, in that insistence, challenges his audience to come up with the missing parts, to complete the performance of citation.

WRITING DISAPPEARANCE

In conclusion, I return to Peggy Phelan's notion of a kind of writing that seeks not so much to capture events or record facts but, rather, primarily to reenact the emotive power of the scene that motivates it. I think that *fujōkan* and *shashin* stories, particularly when they stem from personal experience, seize on the signifying power of the fragment to communicate deeply felt spiritual truths about the transience of the human body. In recent years a number of authors have written on the topic of the fragment. Derrida, for instance, begins his essay "The Law of Genre" *with* a fragment—"No mixing of genres" *(Ne pas mêler les genres)*[51]—and goes on to argue that citations (by which he means to conjure both the use of quotations and allusions in literary texts as well as the summons to a legal preceding) will constantly undermine this law. The "law of the law of genre," he argues, is thus "a principle of contamination, a law of impurity," as the citation inevitably crosses textual bounds, becoming "an internal pocket larger than the whole."[52] According to Derrida's argument, the fragment of citation (the "internal pocket") will ultimately overpower the "whole" of the text that employs it, inaugurating a sudden turning inside out.

Drawing on these observations, Michael Riffaterre explains how this sudden threat of expansion works in medieval European texts, arguing in concert with Derrida that no text is purely self-referential or closed. He maintains that "the written text" (by which he means *any* written text) is "but a bag of tricks, a limited system of incomplete and deficient visual symbols that aid readers in the rapid recovery of vastly more extensive remembered representations."[53] In other words, he argues that the "principal mechanism of the written text" is not to be found anywhere on the written page itself, but rather inside the human skull, in memory.[54] For Riffaterre, intertextuality is "the key to the text's significance. The intertext may be as written as the text, but being elsewhere, outside the text, the relationship between the two is memorial. . . . The relevant area [of memory] is literally selected, carved out from the rest by that analogy, homology, or plain identity if the text actually quotes from or alludes to the intertext."[55] The intertext not only dwarfs the text itself, but, more importantly, serves to "put the burden of interpretation on what we know already, rather than on what the text tells us."[56] In short, the literary citation serves in ways reminiscent of the legal citation: it summons the recipient, demanding his or her participation, soliciting input.

The fragmentary reference ending Kūkai's ninth poem on putrefaction is one such citation, calling forth a much larger intertext—the stories of the Himalaya youth and of the *Nirvana Sutra* as a whole—which the poet thus summons up from the depths of his readers' memories. Similarly, the pastiche of citations that comprises nearly half of Keisei's memory of his personal experience suggests the degree to which he felt it necessary to filter the vision of that woman's body through a net of intertext. In both of these cases the text does not end at the edge of the written page but rather extends into the mind, where it actively searches for completion. Caught up in the performance of citation, the reader is thus led in the direction of a certain kind of interpretation wherein the intertext encourages the understanding that the disintegration and dismemberment of the human body is precisely the Buddhist teaching of impermanence manifesting in observable, irrefutable form. In *fujōkan* and *shashin* tales, the human body provides not only a *source* of subject matter but a *model* of composition, calling attention to and celebrating the body's transience, pointing to its fissures and orifices as those openings through which the flesh can literally be turned inside out, shedding its impurities and transforming into an embodied citation of sacred text.

FOUR

Textual Transubstantiation and the Place of Memory

NARRATIVES OF BODILY DECOMPOSITION and sacrifice are not the only kind of performative writing in the Buddhist tradition. Their focus on disappearance and disintegration into textual fragment is balanced against other religious writings and art forms that feature the performative reintegration of textual fragment into body. In chapter 1 I have already discussed the literary mechanisms through which sutras take on the characteristics of a symbiotic life form, and in chapter 2 I explored the performance venue of setsuwa collections, which are often figured as food or medicine, that is, as substances to be ingested by the human body and that then perform the work of sustenance or healing. Additionally, the previous chapter turned to a consideration of setsuwa's mechanics of textual citation, examining the ways in which the quotation of sutra fragments becomes entwined with visions of the decaying body.

Building on these earlier discussions, this chapter will focus on the various ways in which setsuwa collections elaborate an understanding of sutras as living substances capable of affecting the memorial and physical processes of the human body and, ultimately, of incorporating themselves into human form. More specifically, this chapter concentrates on the significant overlap between descriptions of medieval practices of chanting, memorizing, and copying sutras. I argue that medieval Japanese Buddhism treats the body, the mind, and the page as metaphorically intertwined locations for the inscription of sacred Buddhist text. In addition to material from setsuwa collections, this chapter will consider visual art forms (statuary and various types of decorative sutras) in order to get at the material reality of sutra scrolls in the medieval period, exploring how visual clues echo and provide descriptive language for memorial practices, how artwork can function as mute preaching and sutras as a kind of embodied art.

SCULPTING SOUND

Kūya (903–72) was, if not quite the earliest, at least one of the best-known Buddhist *hijiri,* a sort of wandering holy man who was as much associated with the ascetic rigors of immersion in nature and travel as with the ritual and doctrine of temple life. Following in the footsteps of Gyōki (668–749)—who was among the first clerics to defy the legal code restricting monks and nuns to their cloisters, leaving his monastic center to travel widely and preach to commoner audiences—Kūya spent much of his life outside the temple precincts, wandering from province to province and teaching the basics of Buddhism to whatever audiences he could gather. One of the particular practices that Kūya concentrated on was *nenbutsu* recitation, the repeated incantation of the phrase "Namu Amida butsu," meaning "I take refuge in the buddha Amida" (Sk: Amitāyus), who was believed to maintain a Pure Land in the west where those who had expressed faith in him would go after death and where they would be able to progress along the Buddhist path without the pains and distractions of everyday human life such as hunger, sickness, and desire. As *A Collection of Spiritual Awakenings* notes, Kūya was often called Ichi no Hijiri (the holy man of the marketplace) or Amida Hijiri (the holy man of the Amidist *nenbutsu*) (SNKS 298).

The statue of Kūya housed at Rokuharamitsuji, a temple he founded just on the outskirts of the Heian capital, shows a rather compact and intense man in the simple robes and straw sandals of a traveling *hijiri*. In his left hand he holds a wooden walking staff topped with a branching spike of deer antler. The staff itself bulges in a spiral pattern, narrower at the bottom and then gradually growing thicker near Kūya's hand, as if to suggest that he is drawing power and vitality out of the earth and concentrating it in the trunk of his body. In his right hand he holds a T-shaped instrument with which he strikes a flat metal bell that hangs, suspended from his shoulders, just in front of his lower torso, thus making the statue not simply a visual experience but inviting an aural one as well. His feet are firmly planted on the ground, left foot forward and right foot back, with both soles flat. Though a noted wanderer, Kūya here is not walking so much as he is bracing himself. The stance is one of power, and the entire statue seems to thrust upward, funneling its energies through Kūya's abdomen and rising beneath a chest that is partially bare, its muscles clearly tensed with exertion. His upper chest pushes forward, his eyes are all but closed, his head is tipped back slightly, and his lips are parted, releasing a stream of six tiny buddhas, each of whom rests on his own lotus petal. The statue was carved in the early Kamakura period, probably in the mid-thirteenth century, by a sculptor named Kōshō, fourth son of the famous artist Unkei (d. 1223) and member of the Kei school of Buddhist sculpture, which was famed for the vitality and physicality of its images.

The statue suggests a great deal about how medieval Buddhists conceptualized the relationship between text, writing, and voice and the degree to which these the dynamics between these three were believed to mediate themselves through and express themselves in terms of the physical body. I should note at the outset that, in assuming the plastic arts intentionally embody elements of religious belief and doctrine and that they may also be related to the act of sermonizing, I am taking the ideas of particular scholars quite seriously. Miriam Gill, for example, maintains that medieval Christian art, such as wall paintings, can now be (and was at the time) understood as examples of *"muta predication* or 'silent preaching,'" such that "meditating on a religious image was presented as 'synonymous with reading and hearing God's word.'"[1] Likewise, Jeffrey Hamburger describes devotional imagery as "oracular demonstrations" that "provide a simulacrum for the divine."[2] Finally, Carolyn Walker Bynum has argued that paintings and other kinds of religious artwork "are themselves theological statements."[3] In the discussion that follows I will be considering the statue of Kūya not simply as a piece of art, as the imaginative depiction of a historical holy man, or as a biography in sculpture, though the statue is clearly all of these things. I argue that the statue should also be understood as a multidimensional statement of theology and that, like setsuwa, it can be read for clues concerning medieval Buddhist conceptions of corporeality and textuality.

In the statue of Kūya the vocal element is perhaps the most immediately arresting, itself quite a feat considering that it is, after all, a primarily visual art form. As we approach the statue, the first elements to cross our visual plane are the percussive instrument and the iconic representation of incantatory breath as buddha body. Our eyes must navigate through and between the maze of these visually suggested sounds before they come to rest on the body itself. Kūya chants the *nenbutsu* to the accompaniment of a ringing bell. His lungs swell with air, his diaphragm tightens, and his vocal chords engage as his breath passes over them and out his mouth, his lips forming the sounds *na-mu-a-mi-da-bu-tsu*. The sound of the voice is an incantation, summoning the presence

Figure 1. Statue of the holy man Kūya (903–972), carved by Kōshō (fl. ca. 1198–1208). Photo courtesy of Rokuharamitsuji, Kyoto, and reprinted here by permission of that temple.

and the attention of Amida, who in this statue is seen to be literally, physically present in the very sound of the incantation itself, as if the airstream of the voice had carried this buddha from the chest cavity into the mouth, finally delivering him into the world beyond as embodied sound.

There is a constant exchange between those of us who attempt to cast our vision onto the image of Kūya and the close-eyed Kūya who exchanges that visual force, transforming it into an embodied incantation that pushes back out toward us. There is not a neat one-to-one correlation, however, between the voice and the corporeal forms of Amida. There are, after all, seven syllables in the Japanese incantation—na-mu-a-mi-da-bu-tsu—but only six buddha figures. The correlation, therefore, is not between body and sound so much as it is between body and writing. In written form the incantation requires only six characters, each of which is represented here as an individual buddha. In other words, it is not a sound or a voice that Kūya pushes out of himself, but a piece of embodied writing.

VOICE, WRITING, RELIC

The idea that an actual piece of writing could be housed within the human body, could permeate that body, could actually be the force animating that body, and could also incorporate into a divine body is an idea that lies at the core of Mahāyāna Buddhism. This complex doctrine of the body's entanglement with textuality forms the backbone of the "Preachers of Dharma" chapter of the *Lotus Sutra*. As discussed in chapter 1, "Preachers of Dharma" encourages the Buddhist faithful to "look with veneration on a roll of this scripture," of which the chapter is itself a part, "as if it were the Buddha himself."[4] Further, the chapter maintains that "if a good man or good woman shall receive and keep, read and recite, explain or copy in writing a single phrase" of the sutra, "that person is to be looked up to and exalted by all the worlds, showered with offerings fit for a Thus Come One," and is to be understood as a great bodhisattva who "is preaching the *[Lotus Sutra]* with breadth and discrimination."[5] Following these observations, the historical Buddha, who is preaching the text that (he knows) will later be written down as the *Lotus Sutra,* issues the following mandate: "Wherever it may be preached, or read, or recited, or written, or whatever place a roll of this scripture may occupy, in all those places one is to erect a stupa of the seven jewels, building it high and wide and with impressive decoration. There is no need even to lodge a śarīra [relic] in it. What is the reason? Within it there is already a whole body of the Thus Come One."[6]

Here the *Lotus Sutra* proposes four interrelated points. First, the written

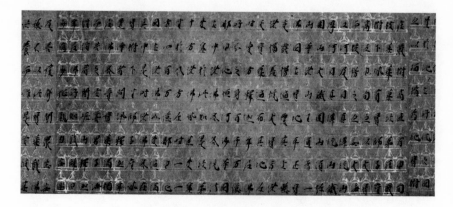

Figure 2. Copy of the *Lotus Sutra* with each character enclosed in a jeweled stupa *(ichiji hōtōkyō)*. Calligraphy attributed to Fujiwara no Sadanobu (d. 1156), twelfth century. Togakushi Jinja, Nagano Prefecture. Photo courtesy of Nara National Museum, reprinted here by permission of Togakushi Jinja.

words of the sutra contain the Buddha's voice in a way that is analogous to the placement of corporeal remains in a stupa. Both sites enshrine presence and provide a locale around which ritual activity may be organized. Second, the written words of the sutra are not simply a subcategory of relic. Rather, they supersede all other types of relic, for two reasons. In terms of scale, the sutra contains an entire body of the Buddha, whereas other types of relic typically consist of bodily pieces (hair, teeth, bones). That is, the sutra contains the words of the Buddha that are the basis of his enlightenment and therefore of his claim to be a buddha incarnate. In terms of efficacy, the sutra remains a living substance, capable of interacting with and activating those with whom it comes into contact, allowing them to become enlightened as they ingest its teachings. By contrast, bodily relics, as many have noted, are paradoxical objects, at once serving as a locale of presence and as a reminder of absence. Third, because it is the birthplace of future buddhas, any place that the entire *Lotus Sutra* exists constitutes a holy site, on a par with the site of a buddha's birth, enlightenment, first sermon, and passage into nirvana. Finally, this logic can be extended to the human body, which, once someone has memorized the words of the sutra, becomes a container (skin and flesh) of a container (the mind) of the words of the sutra.

As the following discussion will demonstrate, Japanese setsuwa literature on the topic of faulty memory explicitly posits this final extension in logic when it describes the act of memory as a type of writing. In fact, entire genres of sutra copying developed around the belief in a sacred text-body com-

Figure 3. Copy of the *Golden Light Sutra* in which the characters are arranged to form the shape of a stupa *(Konkōmyō saishōōkyō hōtō mandara)*. Twelfth century. Daichōjuin sutra repository at Chūsonji, Iwate Prefecture. Photo courtesy of Nara National Museum, reprinted here by permission of Chūsonji.

pound, as with the *ichiji hōtōkyō* (one-character jeweled stupa sutra), in which a miniature stupa is drawn around each written character in the text, and the *hōtō mandara* (jeweled stupa mandala), in which the written characters of the sutra are rearranged to form the architectural profile of a stupa.[7] Based on earlier, continental forms, both versions of the jeweled stupa sutras became increasingly popular in Japan during the medieval period. I contend that sutra-copying techniques like these provided a vocabulary for medieval setsuwa compilers to describe the process of sutra memorization, envisioning the memory as a kind of written text.

Throughout this chapter I will return to a discussion of devotional artwork, a discussion that will be more fully informed by a consideration of intervening material drawn from setsuwa collections. For the time being, however, it is enough to assert that medieval Japanese Buddhist practice is behaving in a completely orthodox manner when it conflates body, voice, and writing into a complex nexus of worship, devotion, sacred presence, and religious experience. In other words, the Kūya statue is not some bizarre localization or misreading of general Buddhist conceptions, but is in fact a wholly orthodox illustration of core Mahāyāna Buddhist beliefs as expressed, for instance, in the *Lotus Sutra*.

WRITING AND MEMORY

In my exploration of this nexus of body, voice, and writing, I follow Mary Carruthers's assertion that writing and memory are simply two different ways of storing a text, two different holding places, both of which are temporary and subject to damage and decay, while the work itself is understood to be abiding, eternal, everlasting, and, in a religious context, sacred.[8] Carruthers argues, for instance, that "books are themselves memorial cues and aids, and memory is most like a book, a written page or a wax tablet upon which something is written."[9] Medieval Japanese practices of reading and recitation involved pronouncing the words of the text aloud, using the voice, the mouth, and the breath, and not simply the eyes. The voice represents the activation of either the memorial or the externally written text (or both). Throughout this chapter, then, I will be using the word *text* to indicate a recognizable unit of religious teachings as copied down on paper (written), carved into the mind/heart (remembered), or produced through breath and sound either when looking at an externally written text (read) or when called forth from memory (recited). Though the "work" is believed to have a permanent, abiding presence somewhere out there, it may be localized and physicalized as "text" in the here and now in ways that are generally governed by a dominant metaphor of writing and the written character.[10]

FAULTY MEMORY

This notion of the memory as yet another place, aside from the page or scroll, to write or store a text is supported by the motif, common in medieval setsuwa collections, of a devout person who is unable to remember all the words to a sutra despite great efforts and incredible concentration. He may have successfully memorized nine-tenths or more of the text but still be completely unable to master the final portion. *Miracles of the Lotus Sutra* 78, for instance, tells the story of the priest Kakunen (dates uncertain, but thought to have lived in the Ōhara area and been active at the nearby Mount Hiei temple complex just north of the Heian capital). Despite being mentally and spiritually prepared for the practice of sutra memorization—having "a heart that was pure, steady, and gentle"—and despite many years of regularly reciting the *Lotus Sutra,* Kakunen ultimately found himself unable to memorize a mere three lines of what is a fairly substantial written text (NST 7:545). The *Lotus Sutra* is 69,384 characters in the 406 C.E. translation into classical Chinese overseen by the Indo-Iranian monk Kumārajīva (ca. 344–413), which is the Chinese translation most commonly used in Japan. Throughout the medieval period, sutra-copying practices generally relied on a standard of seventeen characters per line. To put things into perspective then, Kakunen found himself unable to remember a mere fifty-one characters (three lines' worth), representing less than one-tenth of one percent of the total sutra.

The particular wording of the *Miracles of the Lotus Sutra* setsuwa concerning Kakunen provides some insights into one of the ways in which medieval Buddhists understood the complex relationships between writing, voice, memory, and body. Describing Kakunen's predicament, the setsuwa explains, "Whenever he recited that particular sutra [the *Lotus Sutra*], there were three lines of the written text that, again and again, he was unable to recite. Every time he reached that point he would completely forget those three lines of writing and, though he piled up dark recitation upon dark recitation, time and again he was unable to bring [those three lines] into the light" (NST 7: 545).

This passage makes use of a number of very particular terms that crop up consistently in setsuwa about faulty memory. The term that I have translated as "recite" (Jp: *jusuru*) indicates the devotional act of chanting a sutra aloud and suggests that the chanter is doing so from memory, without looking at the physical, external object of the written text. This suggestion is made binding later in the passage as the compiler insists that Kakunen is engaging in "dark recitations" (Jp: *anju*),[11] recitations that rely entirely on the memory and that consist of vocalizations of the written text as recorded in the "dark" recesses of the human mind, the *kokoro* of the earlier quote. Probably with half- or fully closed eyes, and at least with an inward-trained gaze, Kakunen is thus reading aloud from a sutra that he sees written in his mind, mentally envisioning each character as it moves from darkness into light and back again into darkness. This smooth movement of light over the scrolls of his mind is consistently interrupted when three lines of written text refuse visualization, resist being brought "into the light."

The visualization technique indicated here bears a certain similarity to a particular form of sutra copying that, though expensive, was relatively common during the medieval period, namely the *konshi kinji kyō* (literally "dark blue paper gold character sutra"), which, as the name suggests, involved using a form of liquefied gold to write sutras on scrolls of indigo-dyed paper. Willa Jane Tanabe notes that the paper was "beaten with mallets to produce a sheen, and then glazed.... The resulting depth of color suggested lapis lazuli, which, along with gold and silver, was one of the seven precious jewels or treasures mentioned in the *Lotus Sutra* and other scriptures."[12] In other words, part of the reason for the navy and gold decoration scheme has to do precisely with this notion, stemming from the *Lotus Sutra,* that the sutra text should be enshrined in a jeweled stupa. Additionally, part of the reason for doing the calligraphy in gold was that one of the marks of a buddha's body is golden skin. The specialized form of calligraphy thus served as a visual reminder of the *Lotus Sutra*'s claim that the sutra itself contained the physical body of the Buddha. Additionally, the coloring, meant to represent precious jewels like lapis lazuli and gold, also symbolized the treasure of the contents themselves. The teachings of the Buddha, recorded in written form in the sutras, number among the "three treasures" (Jp: *sanbō*) of Buddhism.

The metaphors of light and dark used in the *Miracles of the Lotus Sutra* tale reflect the artistic tradition of gold-on-blue sutra copying, with the individual characters of the memorial sutra momentarily shining gold in the mind's eye before dropping back into the indigo field, the darkness of the memory. For Kakunen, not being able to recall the three lines is equivalent to a dark spot on the scroll, an error or omission, a place where the expected characters were either never written or were damaged beyond the point of legibility.

THE SUTRA INSIDE

However small a portion of the whole these three lines may represent, not being able to remember them causes Kakunen to suffer strong emotions of "grief and anxiety," and he implores the bodhisattva Fugen (Sk: Samantabhadra) for divine assistance (NST 7: 545). Fugen is a natural choice as a close attendant to the historical Buddha, whose words Kakunen is attempting to remember, and as a deity particularly charged with overseeing doctrinal law and spiritual practice. Fugen grants Kakunen a dream in which an old man reveals the root cause of Kakunen's situation, saying, "You have karmic debts from a past life

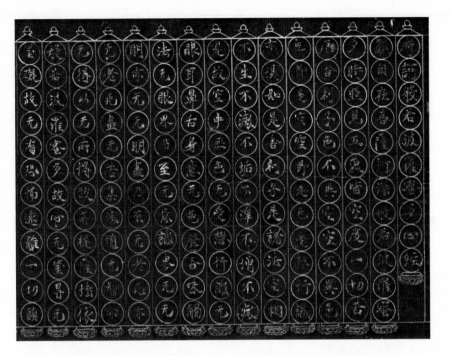

Figure 4. Copy of the *Heart Sutra (Hannya shingyō)* in which the characters are in gold ink against a dark blue background *(konshi kinji Hannya shingyō)*. Part of the *Heike Nōkyō*, 1164. Itsukushima Jinja, Hiroshima Prefecture. Photo courtesy of Nara National Museum, reprinted here by permission of Itsukushima Jinja.

that are bringing about consequences in this life, and thus you completely forget these three lines of written text. In a past life you were incarnated as a bookworm and lived inside of the *Lotus Sutra*, where you ingested and destroyed three lines. But, since you lived inside the sutra, you were able to achieve a human body in this incarnation and you recite the *Lotus Sutra*. Since you ate the written text, you are unable to recite those three lines from memory" (NST 7: 545). Remembering this dream upon waking, Kakunen is suddenly able to recall the three lines without any difficulty, and he continues to recite his now-complete memorial sutra for the rest of his life, never again missing even a single character.

The Kakunen tale also appears in *Tales from Times Now Past* 14:13, a collection that postdates *Miracles of the Lotus Sutra* by approximately eighty years.[13] As with the earlier version, the *Tales from Times Now Past* text refers to the practice of recitation, using the compound verb *dokuju*. *Doku* indicates the act of reading while looking at a written text, whereas *ju* indicates recitation strictly from memory. The suggestion is that Kakunen engages in both of these activities, using the process of repeated reading to inscribe his memory. In addition to the light-dark imagery, *Tales from Times Now Past* also employs a visual metaphor for forgetting, using the term *kaku*, "to be hidden," as behind a door or gate, or "to go missing." The *Tales from Times Now Past* text thereby reinforces the idea that Kakunen visually searches his memorial text in much the same way that he would visually search a written one.

Miracles of the Lotus Sutra contains several other, related setsuwa, one of which speaks more precisely to the process of repeated reading. The account relays the story of the priest Ezō, who was devoted exclusively to the *Lotus Sutra*. "He single-heartedly read the *Lotus* until he was able to recite it from memory easily, bringing it into the light. But every time he got to the 'priest gāthā' in the 'Expedient Means' chapter, he would err and forget two characters. Though he practiced constantly for years, he was completely unable to retain these two characters, always forgetting them utterly. When he was looking at the sutra he was able to make them out clearly, but as soon as he left the text and tried to recite, he would immediately be unable to remember them. Coming to this point [in his recitation], he would grieve over the weight of his sins and pray to gain insight" (NST 7: 526).

Like the tale examined earlier, this setsuwa relies on a metaphorical language of light and darkness. Though when Ezō looks at the written sutra all the characters are plain to see, when he attempts to pull them out of the darkness of his memory, he is consistently stymied by the absence of two characters. Checking his memorial text against the physical artifact of the written text, he is clearly able to recognize his error, but when he turns that vision back to the internal text, the writing is still incomplete. He concludes, then, that there is a deeper problem, one that is probably tied up with the weight of his sins from a past life.

In a move that is familiar from the story of Kakunen, Ezō sequesters himself and prays, this time to the merciful bodhisattva Kannon (Sk: Avalokiteśvara). Kannon grants him a dream in which an old man appears and reveals to him the following: "In your former life when you read and recited the *Lotus Sutra,* you read while facing a fire. Sparks from the flames crackled out and burned two characters in the sutra. You did not repair the sutra by rewriting the characters. That is why in this life, though you read the sutra, you utterly forget the two characters" (NST 7: 526). The old man then tells Ezō that the sutra in question—the one that was actually singed—still exists in the real world, that is, the world outside Ezō's memory. He reveals its location and suggests that the priest find and repair the sutra. As soon as Ezō awakens—and before he repairs the sutra written on paper—he is able to recall the missing characters with no difficulty, indicating that his memorial text has already been repaired. Still, he follows the old man's suggestion, finding and fixing the calligraphy version that he had damaged earlier.

Again, this setsuwa is repeated in the *Tales from Times Now Past* collection, though with slightly more elaboration. In the *Tales from Times Now Past* version, the dream occurs "just at daybreak," at which time the two characters, which had been lost "in darkness," are miraculously restored to Ezō's memory (SNKBT 35: 311). The literary convention that conflates the dawning of a revelatory dream with the dawning of day perhaps carries extra weight here. Daybreak—or, more precisely, the moment of the appearance of the morning star in the lightening sky—was the exact time of day that the historical Buddha gained enlightenment and, as a symptom of that, was able to recall all of his past lives. The story of Ezō's restored memory therefore ties into an entire system of Buddhist symbolism in which memory, signaled with symbols of light overcoming or punctuating dark, is linked both to the specific practices of sutra copying and to the processes of enlightenment, illumined understanding, and self-knowledge. By knowing himself (his former incarnation), Ezō's ability to know the text is also restored.

A Wondrous Record of Immediate Karmic Retribution also contains a similar story suggesting that Japanese Buddhism envisioned the memory as a written page from at least the ninth century. In this story a priest of the Tajihi family finds himself unable to recite accurately from memory, always forgetting one character of the *Lotus Sutra*. He asks for clarification and is told in a dream that, in his last life, his reading lamp burned a hole in the sutra and he never bothered to repair it. He is instructed to go find the text and fix it, at which point he is immediately able to recite the sutra in its entirety (NKBZ 10: 70–73). Both the Ezō and Tajihi stories employ a parallelism in which the action of conducting written repairs on a paper sutra serves either as a precursor to, or a condition and rehearsal of, the divine restoration of their own personal memorial text. The damaging flame, which earlier allowed the men to read, is replaced with a divine clarity, which allows the men to remember.

PAST LIFE, PRESENT MEMORY

These setsuwa can easily be read as tales of karmic retribution. In each instance, regardless of which collection they appear in, the setsuwa specifically mention the role of past sins in creating the present situation. Priests who damaged the *Lotus Sutra* in a past life, either out of negligence or necessity—What else is a book worm to eat?—are punished in this life by being unable to memorize precisely that portion of the sutra that they once destroyed. Taken together, however, these setsuwa suggest a concern with something more than simply the illustration of sin and retribution. They are also commentaries on medieval perceptions of textuality as lived, personal experience. In other words, these setsuwa suggest a general medieval Buddhist understanding of sutras as texts that can and do embody themselves in one's memory, written in the mind exactly as one has personally encountered them. There are, for example, many other setsuwa in which the priest is not to blame (at least not in any direct or immediate sense) for his faulty memory. Before developing a more detailed commentary on the relationship between body, text, voice, and memory as understood in the context of medieval Buddhism, I would first like to introduce a handful of these setsuwa, so as to separate out the sin-and-punishment narrative and focus more selectively on the depiction of embodied textuality.

Because of its exclusive concern with the *Lotus, Miracles of the Lotus Sutra* is particularly rich in setsuwa dealing with faulty memories and their miraculous restoration. Though no doubt greatly influenced by the ideas of Chingen, the text's compiler, the motif is not entirely the province of a single compilation, nor does it reflect only the idiosyncrasies of a single editor. *Tales from Times Now Past,* for instance, repeats each of the *Miracles of the Lotus Sutra* setsuwa I will examine below, generally with some degree of elaboration. Tale 77 from *Miracles of the Lotus Sutra* tells the story of the priest Gyōhan. A devotee of the *Lotus Sutra,* Gyōhan has been able to remember the entire text except for the "Medicine King" chapter (Jp: *Yakuōbon*). The setsuwa describes the situation as follows: "He was by nature a tranquil person. He had set his heart on the pursuit of the Buddhist law and he read and recited the *Lotus Sutra* with great care, able to make his way through the entire text by memory without impediment. But, when he came to the 'Medicine King' chapter, he always had difficulty with the dark recitation. Though he practiced for many years, he was never able to recite it" (NST 7: 545).

Seeking to remedy the situation, Gyōhan turns first to the state of his memory organ, the mind (Jp: *kokoro*), reconfirming his mastery of tranquil concentration. When this does not solve the problem he begins cultivating a "repentant heart" (also *kokoro;* NST 7: 545). Praying for clarity, he receives a dream in which an old man, in the appearance of a Shintō god, tells him that karma from a past life is keeping him from being able to recite the sutra in its entirety. In his former life Gyōhan had been incarnated as a black horse owned by a *Lotus Sutra* devotee. In the course of his years of service, Gyōhan the horse had managed to hear all the sections of the sutra except the "Medicine King" chapter. Though an animal in his previous life, Gyōhan has been reborn not only as a human but, even more providentially, as a *Lotus* devotee "through the force of hearing the sutra," that is, simply through the sound of the sutra that had imprinted itself on his equine memory and affected the form of his physical reincarnation (NST 7: 545). After explaining this, the old man makes Gyōhan a rather interesting promise: " 'If you read well in your present life, in the next incarnation you will, without restraint, move through this sutra with clarity and will reach great enlightenment.' Knowing his karma, Gyōhan opened his ignorant and unenlightened heart, believed in the *Lotus Sutra* deeply, and read the sutra day and night without halting" (NST 7: 545).

The basic plot and most of the language of this setsuwa come as no surprise. As before, the setsuwa insists on a distinction between "reading" (Jp: *doku*) the sutra—an action that involves sitting before a written text and running one's eyes across the paper as one enunciates the words—and "reciting" the sutra from memory (Jp: *ju, anju, fuju*). The setsuwa also employs familiar metaphors of light and dark, speaking of "dark recitations" (Jp: *anju*) and promising "clarity" of understanding. The heart-mind, as the memory organ, is also of importance here, the compiler being careful to point out that Gyōhan is a "tranquil" person, one who is by definition able to concentrate and set his heart on the accomplishment of a goal.[14] His faulty memory, then, does not stem from a lack of mental preparation and must have its causes elsewhere. Finally, the relationship between "reading" and "reciting" is, if anything, made more evident in this setsuwa than in the ones examined previously. In his dream Gyōhan is instructed to "read"—*not* to "recite"—the sutra. In distinction from other setsuwa in which the memory is miraculously restored, Gyōhan will have to exert his own, very human powers in order to complete his memorial text. Sitting with an "opened" heart in front of an equally open sutra scroll, Gyōhan can now proceed to transcribe in full the sutra that he holds in his hands, transforming it into a sutra that he will hold in his mind. He is told that this is the work of a lifetime.

RECITATION AS MOVEMENT THROUGH SPACE

In addition to the familiar and more explicit metaphors of clarity and obscurity, this setsuwa also includes a second layer of imagery that hints at another way of conceptualizing the act of memorization as physical movement, as tracing the body through space.[15] The setsuwa describes Gyōhan's usual facility at being able to "move through" recitations without "impediment," using a word (Jp: *gai, samatageru*) that suggests stumbling over rocky ground. When he "arrives at" or "comes to" the "Medicine King" chapter, he is forced to a complete stop, unable to find a way to pass through. The old man promises Gyōhan that if he dedicates himself in this life to the formal writing of his memory through the act of repeated reading, in his next life he will be able to pass through his recitations "without restraint" and will "reach a clarity of understanding." This second layer of imagery is important because it suggests that, at least for Chingen, there is an understanding of textual interactions (writing, reading, memorizing, and reciting) as ocular or oral acts that are also embodied and spatial, based on the notion of a body's movement through textual terrain.

Miracles of the Lotus Sutra 80, concerning the priest Myōren, repeats most of the plot and imagery from the Gyōhan story.[16] Like Gyōhan, Myōren begins with "reading while facing the written" sutra, a practice that gives birth to the desire to memorize the text in its entirety. Chingen again describes recitation in terms of freedom of movement, noting that, as a result of his readings, Myōren "enjoyed reciting through" the text and "desired to make it through the entire sutra" on his own, without forgetting a single line and "without encountering impediments" (NST 7: 545). Myōren's wish speaks of a desire for mental clarity and spiritual focus, the ability to set aside the distractions of worldly passions that might otherwise clutter his mind and make his memorial text impassable in the way that rocks and stones clutter a road and make it bumpy and unnavigable.

Suspecting the intrusion of past karma on the present situation, Myōren prays to know the root cause of his faulty memory and is led on a bit of a wild goose chase. He first consults the deities at Inari Grand Shrine, near modern Osaka, where he is referred to the temple at Hase near the old capital at Nara. He sequesters himself for a time before he is told to move on to Mount Mitake, southeast on the mountainous Kii Peninsula, where the process repeats itself, sending him first to seclusion at nearby Mount Kumano and then to the Sumiyoshi Shrine, back near Osaka, before he finally finds his answer at Mount Daisen in Hahaki, far to the south. At Daisen a deity comes to him in a dream and reveals that in his last life Myōren was a cow belonging to a man from Mimasaka. His owner once left him in the enclosure between the priests' quarters at a temple while he paid a visit to the main hall. While stuck in that space, Myōren the cow overheard a monk reciting the *Lotus Sutra* and thus was exposed to the first seven scrolls' worth before his master reappeared and led him away just as dawn was breaking. Awakened from his dream, Myōren vows to continue pursuing the path toward buddhahood.

Myōren's peripatetic and, until the end, unsuccessful search for access to memories of his past lives emulates and reproduces his memorial movement that probes for ways to move past the mental blockade that impedes him from passing smoothly from the seventh to the eighth scroll of the sutra. The physical process of traveling through space to a certain place, shutting himself up there, and being pried out again by divine intervention serves as a physical rehearsal for the unblocking of Myōren's memorial text. In the end, as with Gyōhan, his dream opens up a clear understanding of his past life, a memory that unlocks his ability to memorize the remainder of the sutra through a lengthy process of repeated reading, during which he will continually need to check his memorial text against that of the sutra he holds in his hands.

Miracles of the Lotus Sutra and *Tales from Times Now Past* contain two other setsuwa of faulty memory. In tale 89 of *Miracles of the Lotus Sutra* the priest Kairen is informed in a dream that he is unable to memorize the last three chapters of the *Lotus Sutra* because, as a grasshopper in his last life, he heard a monk chanting the sutra but was crushed to death—by the monk no less!—before the recitation was finished. Like Myōren, Kairen had traveled considerable distances, sequestering himself at several different places, before he was finally granted knowledge of his past incarnation. Both the *Miracles of the Lotus Sutra* and the *Tales from Times Now Past* versions of this tale include the regular metaphors of light and dark, but only *Miracles* picks up the motif of movement, transforming it into a metaphor for memory.[17] Finally, *Miracles of the Lotus Sutra* 93 and *Tales from Times Now Past* 14:17 relate the story of the priest Tenjō, who is determined to memorize the chapters that have been giving him trouble. "Though resting neither day nor night, reciting each single verse thirty thousand times," Tenjō is still unable to fill in the blank spaces of his memorial sutra.[18] Tenjō is ultimately informed in a dream that in his last life he was a snake who sat, coiled in the rafters of a mountain stable, as a traveling monk spent the night below chanting the *Lotus Sutra*. Originally intent on attacking the priest, the snake was calmed by the chanting and ended up listening attentively. Unfortunately for the snake, dawn broke and the monk left before finishing his recitation. Because of this karmic connection, Tenjō was able to be reborn as a monk, though the incomplete, serpentine text still exists in his memory, refusing (until now) to be written over.

EMBODIED MEMORY

In the final analysis, setsuwa on the motif of faulty memory are concerned with more than a rehearsal of sin and retribution. While communicating a specific understanding of both the nature of textuality and the functioning of memory, they also comment on the crucial role of the body and its senses in performing textual acts such as writing, reading, remembering, and reciting. Medieval Japanese Buddhist culture was a memorial culture in which writing on paper was "only one way among several to remember a 'text.'"[19] To reiterate for the sake of clarity, by "text" I mean a recognizable unit of religious teachings that may be copied down on paper (handwritten), carved into the mind/heart (remembered), or produced through breath and sound (read, recited, chanted). Writing is any act "that encodes information in order to stimulate the memory to store or retrieve information."[20] In this expanded definition, the particular practices of copying out a sutra, for example in the gold-on-blue technique discussed earlier, is writing. Vocalizing or repeating a phrase over and over again so as to carve it deeply into the memory is writing. Visualizing the lightening and darkening characters of a memorized sutra in order to recite it properly therefore involves reading, correcting, and perfecting a memorial text that functions as writing. Passively listening to a chanted text, allowing it to enter into one's mind unimpeded, initiates an act of transcription that may require a second lifetime, and a miraculous dream, to reach full legibility.

These activities leave marks. The cow that overheard the sutra recitation, for example, may die and be reincarnated into the form of a monk, but the cow's experiences with sacred text do not pass away. They remain written in the monk's memory: the text of the sutra that the cow experienced is the *same* text that is lodged in the monk's memory, marked and remarkable for its gaps and imperfections. It is only by accessing information about his own past, by remembering (or being made to remember) the exact place and condition in which he originally encountered the text, that the monk is able to clear the way for further progress. The sutra inside, created through an amalgamation of sensory experience and textual encounters, is an embodied one in the sense that it is surrounded by and housed in the body, creating physically legible symptoms, such as the contortions of grief and anxiety, and forcing bodily action, such as the need to wander from place to place in search of revelation.

TEXT AND TEXTILE

The restoration of memory through a revelatory dream that stitches together past life and present memory and thus restores a damaged sutra suggests the textile nature of the written word in Buddhist textual culture and the way the sound of the chanted sutras wends its way through a variety of material forms, including the written page and the human body. According to one traditional etymological understanding, the Sanskrit word *sūtra* denotes the vertical "warp thread" through which other materials could be interwoven to create a fabric. From there, the semantic range of the word extends to indicate the essential teachings that might be gathered together into a memorized discourse or, later, an external text inscribed on leaves or bark. To borrow a phrase from colloquial English, the sutras represent the basic thread of the Buddha's argument, and the term *sutra* may be etymologically related to modern English's "sew" and "suture," both of which refer to pulling together and binding into place a material (such as cloth or skin) that may have been ripped or injured, or which may simply need to be joined in order to be useful. Chinese-language translations and transliterations of the term *sutra* maintain this connection to the notion of textile, with the most common Chinese translation (Ch: *jing*) also suggesting the warp of a fabric as indicated by the inclusion of the component character for "thread."[21] This is more than mere wordplay, and medieval Japanese setsuwa take seriously the idea of the sutra as a warp thread through which the believing body could be woven into a durable fabric by means of a repeated shuttling of the chanting voice.

One Hundred Sessions of Sermons, for instance, contains a setsuwa that makes explicit the connection between written text and threaded textile, both of which come into intimate contact with bodies human and divine. The sermon delivered by the Ajari Kōunbō[22] on the eighth day of the Third Month of 1110 concerns the tenth chapter of the *Lotus Sutra,* "Preachers of Dharma." As discussed above, this section of the *Lotus Sutra* maintains that material copies of the sutras contain within them the entire body of the Buddha. This chapter of the sutra also returns repeatedly to the topic of the Buddha's robes, stating metaphorically that these robes are woven of the perfection of forbearance (T 9.262.31c26). Speaking to the assembly, Buddha asserts, "You should know that, after the extinction of the Thus Come One, anyone who is able to write, keep, read, recite, make offerings to, or expound [this sutra] to another shall be covered with the robes of the Thus Come One" (31b22–23). In other words, any being who is capable of storing or replicating the words of the sutra will be protected by the Buddha and should be honored in the same way that one honors a buddha. The robe serves as the external sign of this status.

In glossing this chapter from the *Lotus Sutra* in his sermon, Kōunbō singles out this image of the Buddha's robes as "the heart" (Jp: *kokoro*) of the "Preachers of Dharma" (HZ 100), and he outlines the miraculous powers of robes that belonged to various holy men. A typical instance describes their ability to heal: "When these robes were worn by those who were ill, their sickness went away completely" (HZ 100). The sermon goes on to describe the Buddha's robes as "woven of the threads of the six pāramitā[23] and the fibers of the ten thousand practices"[24] and suggests that any who hear the teachings and take joy in them will experience "the eradication of the ills of evil and passion" (HZ 100). After a series of setsuwa on this theme, Kōunbō concludes his sermon by commending his audience for undertaking the ritual of sutra copying, remarking, "Surely no one can doubt that the power of offering copied sutras . . . completely eradicates sin" (HZ 102). In the course of his sermon, then, Kōunbō draws a parallel between the robes of holy men and the fabric of the sutra scrolls, both of which evince miraculous abilities to ease suffering and erase sin. But how exactly does the robe become commensurate with the scroll?

One of Kōunbō's stories, the one he spends the most time on, has to do with Kūya, the "holy man of the marketplace" discussed at the start of this chapter. The story was an incredibly popular one for at least two hundred years, appearing parenthetically in *A Collection of Treasures* (ca. 1180) and at full length in *A Collection of Spiritual Awakenings* (1214–15) and two other setsuwa collections.[25] According to the story, Kūya is headed into the capital on business early one summer morning when he happens to notice a person shivering uncontrollably by the side of the road. Though he does not recognize the man, he is concerned for his welfare and stops to inquire after his health, asking him how he can be so cold on such a hot day. The man addresses Kūya by name, quickly identifies himself as the deity of the Matsuo Shrine, and explains, "On my body I wear the robe of the *Heart* [Jp: *Hannya no koromo*], because people have come to my shrine and offered readings [of that sutra]. But I do not have the robe of the *Lotus* [Jp: *Hokke no koromo*], and so the storm of deluded reasoning blows violently and the frost of evil passion grows thick, making me unbearably cold" (HZ 101). Typical offerings to Shintō deities include material goods (fruit and flowers, for instance) as well as entertainment (song, dance, poetry, etc.), and it was not uncommon to read the *Heart Sutra* in front of a shrine as just such an offering. In this instance, the Matsuo deity claims that receiving a reading of the *Heart Sutra* is equivalent to receiving an offering of a single layer of clothing, and that this single layer is insufficient.

The deity then asks Kūya to chant the *Lotus* for him, but the holy man does him one better. He responds, "Since it will be some time before I am able to come offer a reading at your shrine, it would be better for me to offer you this short-sleeved underrobe. Though it is dirty and rimed with sweat, I have worn it waking, sleeping, standing, and sitting these last forty years while reading the *Lotus Sutra* day and night to the point of permeation [Jp: *Hokkekyō wo yoru hiru yomishimete*]" (HZ 101). In his response Kūya stresses the constancy of his robe wearing (forty years, whether asleep or awake) and links this constant "habit" (the pun is appropriate here) with his regular practice of constantly reading the *Lotus*. He indicates that just as the robe has become shiny with grime from rubbing against his body, it has also become suffused with the sound and the power of his sutra readings. He offers this doubly saturated robe as literal protection against the metaphorical chill of delusion and passion. The deity accepts the robe with great joy and vows to serve as Kūya's guardian deity.

Other versions of the Kūya narrative repeat the story almost verbatim, as in *A Collection of Spiritual Awakenings,* and they gloss the story in a similar fashion. *A Collection of Treasures,* for instance, explains the Kūya setsuwa by remarking, "The more than sixty-nine thousand characters of the *Lotus Sutra* all become golden buddhas that stream forth from the chanting tongue [Jp: *dokuju no shita*] and shine upon the devotee's head, cleansing him completely of the sins and obstructions that lead to endless rebirth. . . . When Kūya read [the *Lotus Sutra*] by the Ōmiya stream, the great deity of Matsuo was relieved of his suffering on cold nights. Surely we should have no doubt that [sutra chanting] will sustain us in lives to come" (SNKBT 40: 323–24).

In summoning the vision of tiny golden buddhas streaming from the chanter's mouth, this brief commentary on the story calls to mind the image of Kūya housed at Rokuharamitsuji (which it predates by several decades), and it suggests that medieval Buddhism understood written character, voiced sutra, and buddha body to comprise different modes of a single synesthetic whole.[26] Thus the robe seems to soak up the efficacy of the sound of the sutra almost as it would soak up the smell of incense, and it is wrapped around the body of the believer the way a layer of thick silk brocade was wrapped around a sutra scroll to prevent wear and tear. The robe, like the scroll, is a piece of fabric that is permeated, in this case not with ink but with the sound of the reading voice. Both sutra and robe, then, represent the sounds of the Buddhist teachings rendered in tactile form, so that they can now be picked up and held or worn against the skin in a sensually comforting and reassuring way.

In these various versions of the Kūya story, we see that sutra chanting was credited with the power to bring about benefits both immediate and long-term, relieving suffering from illness or cold, cleansing one of sin, or supplying the provisions to sustain one on the long path to buddhahood. Other setsuwa suggest that creating copies of the sutras, whether on paper or through oral recitation, was also a means of gaining physical and visual access to the divine body of the Buddha. *Miracles of the Lotus Sutra* 118 makes this correlation between written word, voice, and buddha body clear when it tells the story of a certain woman, the first daughter of Fujiwara no Kanetaka.[27] The setsuwa begins by noting that she read the *Lotus* ceaselessly in her devotions and that, "by carrying out these practices herself, she piled up large numbers of sutra copies" (NST 7: 563). Again drawing on the metaphor of textile, the setsuwa suggests the fervor of her devotions by qualifying them specifically as "fragrant practices" (Jp: *kunju*), indicating that she engages in sutra reading with enough regularity that the aroma of incense, burned as an offering to the Buddha during her daily practices, has come to permeate her robes. In addition, the setsuwa makes no clear distinction between the act of reading the sutras aloud and that of copying them on paper. The oral readings result in the "piling up of a large number" of sutras, as if each vocal repetition resulted in the completion of another written copy.

As the story continues, the daughter of Kanetaka suddenly falls ill, grows cold, and dies, only to revive after the passage of one night. Having recovered her senses, she tells her gathered relatives that she traveled through fields and over mountains, arriving at a large temple complex. She recalls the architectural layout of the place in some detail and mentions the throngs of priests, bodhisattvas, and wise men walking about the courtyard. After some time spent looking on in awe, she is finally approached by an old priest who speaks to her, saying:

> "How has this good woman come to this temple? Good woman, this is the land into which you will be born in your future life, but as of now the number of your *Lotus Sutras* is not yet sufficient. How is it you were born in this land when you should have many years and months yet? For now, you should return quickly whence you came." When I looked into one of the halls, I saw thousands of sutras piled up there. Asking the priest about them, he told me, "These are the *Lotus Sutra*. Good woman, these are the sutras that you have read over the years. . . . " When I looked in the lecture hall, I saw a great golden-colored Buddha there shining and illuminating [the room]. Holding the hem of his priestly robes, he hid his face but spoke to me in the beautiful tones of the *kalavinka* bird, saying, "Good woman, since you have read the *Lotus Sutra*, I show you my body and allow you to hear my voice. Go back to your home and keep this sutra well. . . . Later, I will not hide my face from you and I will allow you to see my whole body." (NST 7: 563)

Escorted back to the human realm by two young boys, the daughter of Kanetaka resumes her devotions with increased fervor.

In this story the woman's recited sutras gain her visual access to the Buddha's body; each recitation allows her to see more and more of that body until ultimately nothing shall be hidden from her sight.[28] Textuality thus ties the body of the believer to the embodied object of her devotion. Reading the sutras aloud, the voiced text permeates her robes and writes itself so deeply in her body that the laws of karma and transmigration are momentarily set aside, allowing her to see first her own body's future surroundings, then the warehoused copies of text that will bring her there, and finally the very body of the Buddha himself, who promises full visual access to his bare face in the future, as if her recitations both weave and unweave the very cloth that covers him.

As can be seen from setsuwa such as these, sutra copying in medieval Japan, whether accomplished vocally or chirographically, was not just an exercise in mastery, of stringing together the correct syllables in a beautiful voice or of brushing ink on paper in ornate calligraphy. It was, rather, an act of embodied devotion in which each element was charged with life and energy, in which the paper one held in one's fingers could be understood to metaphorically represent the cloth of the Buddha's robes and in which the calligraphy of one's own hand or the breath of one's mouth was believed to compose the body of the Buddha himself. This suggests in turn that we need to consider the act of writing, and in particular writing done in religious contexts such as this, not just as an act of documentation but as an embodied devotion, in the sense that writing moves well beyond the edge of the page, illuminating the dark recesses of the mind and rubbing up against the surface of the body as a tactile and sensual presence.

SUTRA HERMITS

This discussion of the textile nature of sutras helps shed light on more sensational stories about sutras serving as a kind of life force that not only permeates the robes but pushes deeper into the human corpus, abiding there as a symbiont that lengthens human life and may even keep portions of the body miraculously cohered for a time after death. In terms of extended life, Buddhist ideas about the efficacy of reading and reciting sutras meld with native Japanese folklore concerning mountain hermits, resulting in a number of setsuwa about a type of being known as the "sutra-keeping hermit" (Jp: *jikyō sennin*) or the "chanting hermit" (Jp: *dokuju sennin*). One of the most popular of these setsuwa concerns the wandering ascetic Giei, whose story appears in the eleventh-century *Miracles of the Lotus Sutra,* the twelfth-century *Tales from Times Now Past,* and the thirteenth-century *A Collection of Spiritual Awakenings.*[29]

According to these three versions of the setsuwa, Giei sets out from the syncretic religious complex at Kumano to engage in austerities in the mountains. After wandering for several days he finds himself lost and without access to food or water. In the late afternoon he stumbles across a solitary hut that, though small, is beautifully adorned with a flowering garden. Giei catches a glimpse of an equally handsome young man, whom he judges to be about twenty years old. Not wishing to disturb the youth, Giei watches and listens as the young hermit finishes his recitation of the *Lotus Sutra*. As soon as he is done the hermit calls out to Giei, and the two engage in a lengthy conversation in which the hermit's contributions consist almost exclusively of quotations from the sutra. For instance, when the hermit claims to be more than one hundred years old, Giei accuses him of lying, to which the hermit responds with a quote from the *Lotus Sutra* to the effect that those who hear the sutra shall be healed of sickness and shall not age. The hermit provides Giei with food and lodging for the night, and the following morning directs him to a nearby village. When he reaches the village Giei tells his story, and all those who hear it develop a deeper faith.

All of the versions of the tale focus on the beauty and clarity of the young hermit's voice. In *A Collection of Spiritual Awakenings* it is "mysterious, beyond the ability of words to capture even in metaphor" (SNKS 164). *Miracles of the Lotus Sutra* does venture a metaphor, describing it as "deeply resonant, like the harmonious melding of two stringed instruments" (NST 7: 518). And *Tales from Times Now Past* states that the hermit's chanting "was infinitely refined, as if his very flesh was dyed with it" (Jp: *mi ni somu ga gotoshi;* NKBT 24: 206). These metaphors suggest that the hermit's voice weaves together the words and phrases of the sutra with the physical stuff of his flesh, setting up a beautiful resonance between the two and joining them in a life-regenerating harmony. The voice is the key agent in linking flesh to text because it is the voice that circulates the words of the sutra along with the breath, through the lungs, over the vocal cords, out the mouth, and back into the ears in a life-giving cycle of renewal in which the hermit's body becomes a visible and audible citation of sutra text. The cycle cannot be continued indefinitely, however, and eventually even the bodies of these sutra-infused hermits will die and begin to decay, leaving only bones.

CHANTING SKULLS

What happens when a body that has been utterly suffused with sutra text dies? In what ways does the sutra remain miraculously legible in the bones? In the following section I will examine a series of setsuwa on the motif of the chanting skull in order to illustrate and explore more fully this link between sutras and the miraculous suturing of the human body with sacred text. *A Wondrous Record of Immediate Karmic Retribution* 3:1, for instance, contains the two earliest Japanese stories on the motif of chanting skulls.[30] According to this setsuwa collection, the monk Eigō traveled to the remote village of Kumano in Ki province in order to teach fishermen there the truths of Buddhism. He wins the people over and achieves their respect, earning the moniker "The Bodhisattva of the South" and drawing attention from further afield (NKBZ 10: 248). One day an unnamed *dhyāna* (meditation) master comes to study under Eigō, bringing with him a special copy of the *Lotus Sutra* that was "written out in miniature characters, shrinking the total number of scrolls down to just one which he carried" as he learned to recite it from memory (NKBZ 10: 248). Like the priests in the faulty memory setsuwa, this monk has been carrying around a physical copy of the sutra that he has been slowly transcribing into his memory through a devotional process of meditation, during which he calms and focuses his mind, allowing for attentive reading and recitation.

Eventually the *dhyāna* master decides to part from Eigō and move deeper into the mountains. Significantly, he leaves his small sutra behind, suggesting that the composition of his memorial text has been successfully completed. About two years later, the villagers head into the mountains to cut wood for making a boat. While camped in the forest they "heard the sound of someone reciting the *Lotus Sutra*. The days passed and the months went by and still the sound did not stop . . . continuing as before without pause" (NKBZ 10: 249). The villagers assume a pious ascetic is in the vicinity and want to offer him some food to create a karmic connection with him, but they are unable to find him. When they return six months later, they still hear the voice chanting without rest. This time they tell Eigō, who heads into the mountains to listen for himself. "Searching around, he found a corpse. Its two feet tied with a hemp rope, it was hanging over a cliff, where it had been thrown to its death" (NKBZ 10: 249). Relying on an examination of various objects, such as a metal water pitcher the master always carried, Eigō identifies the corpse as that of the *dhyāna* master. No foul play is indicated here: in the syncretic religious practices of medieval Buddhism, rituals involving extreme ascetic acts were often undertaken, particularly in a deep mountain setting. One of those practices involved hanging oneself by the feet over a cliff or sharp incline and reciting sacred phrases, such as the text of a sutra, in that position.[31]

His curiosity apparently satisfied, Eigō leaves the mountains without disturbing the body. The villagers return to the spot three years later and report to Eigō once again that they can still hear the voice chanting. This time he re-solves to take more decisive action. "Returning yet again, Eigō gathered the bones together, looking closely at the skull. Though it had been three years, the tongue had not rotted but was still alive. Truly we know from this the mys-terious powers of the Great Vehicle [the Mahāyāna teachings] and the great merit the monk piled up through his recitations of the sutra. . . . He threw away his body and his bones bleached white in the sun, but still his tongue did not fester in the skull" (NKBZ 10: 249). *A Wondrous Record of Immedi-ate Karmic Retribution* reinforces this miraculous vision by appending a fur-ther story about a *dhyāna* master in the Yoshino district, another mountain-ous area known as a center of syncretic religious practice. Going from peak to peak reciting the sutras, the ascetic suddenly hears a voice somewhere ahead of him on the path and it, too, is reciting the same sutras, namely the *Lotus Sutra* and the *Diamond Sutra*. "Stopping to listen, he pushed aside the un-derbrush and found there a skull. It had been there for quite some time and was bleached in the sun, but the tongue had not rotted and was still alive. The *dhyāna* master picked the skull up and enshrined it in a purified place. . . . He lived together with it, reading the sutras and practicing the rituals six times a day. As the *dhyāna* master read through the *Lotus Sutra,* the skull read along with him. Looking at the skull's tongue, he could see it flapping and moving!"[32]

Both of these linked setsuwa are almost obsessively interested in the act of visually probing the postmortem human body. In the Eigō story, the gaze be-comes more intimate and more penetrating with each successive return. At first the body remains invisible, as the villagers cannot find the chanter. Next the priest discovers the corpse—or at least the corpse's bound feet—and confirms its identity, leaving the rest of the body quite literally hanging by a thread. On his final return the priest gathers the now-scattered bones and peers into the skull, where he sees a still-red, fleshy tongue moving with the sounds of the sutra.

As the exclamation "Truly we know!" inherently suggests, the bleached bones may belong to the *dhyāna* master, but the textured tongue belongs to the sutra, visually representing the degree to which the sutra had permeated the monk's body, to the extent that the sutra can still hold part of that body (mandible, cranium, tongue) stitched together even after death. In the sec-ond story, the one that takes place in Yoshino, the *dhyāna* master may "read" the sutras in order to memorize them, but he is equally interested in and in-spired by reading the chanting skull, perhaps as visible evidence that his own spiritual goals are indeed attainable. The skull is a spectacle, showing that sutras can be written on and in the body, that ingested sutras transform the body, and that the sutras are, in fact, what holds the body of the devout practitioner together, threading through the skull even after death.

Turning to the *Miracles of the Lotus Sutra* collection in order to consider some final elaborations of the chanting skull motif, we find the story of the priest Ichiei.[33] A devoted *Lotus* reciter, Ichiei is on pilgrimage to Kumano when he finds himself camped in the woods one evening:

> In the deep of the night came the voice of someone reciting the *Lotus Sutra*. The voice was extremely refined, and listening carved it into the marrow of his bones. He thought that there must be someone else spending the night nearby. When [the voice] finished reciting the first scroll, it paid homage to the Three Treasures and confessed a great number of sins. Just as it had finished reciting the entire sutra, the sky grew bright with the coming dawn. In the bright light of morning [Ichiei could see] the skull of a dead body. Its trunk was still linked and had not become at all scattered, though green moss covered the body, showing that many years and months had passed. Looking at the skull, there was a tongue inside its mouth. It was red and fresh, not at all damaged. (NST 7: 519)

Here we see the reiteration in an even more forceful manner of many familiar details. First, the setsuwa emphasizes the notion of embodied writing. Both men, living and (mostly) dead, house sutras that have been written into the recesses of their memory and are able to recite them at will. Ichiei undergoes a further transcriptive experience as the skull's refined voice writes the words to the sutra into his body once again, "carving" them into the "marrow of his bones." The specific character used here (Jp: *mei, shirusu*) suggests both the act of carving a person's name on a memorial marker and that of carving something into the heart, so as not to forget it—a kind of deep writing in which the human body is always implicated. In addition, the setsuwa insists on spectacle and visual confirmation, placing the red tongue on a contrasting field of green moss to make it stand out all the more. Finally, the body is still "linked," each of the bones still stitched together into a recognizable whole, "not at all scattered." Except for this fact of miraculous articulation, the scene calls to mind the final poem of the *kusō no shi* (discussed in the previous chapter), which mentions both a name carved faintly on a tombstone and the coiling of moss around the burial mound. The fact of continual sutra recitation provides the core distinction between the utterly impure and unstrung corpse of the poem and the peaceful, still-articulated body of the corpse Ichiei finds. It is the power of the sutra, its harmonious union with the flesh accomplished through the musical shuttle of the voice, that holds the body sutured together.

Thus far the setsuwa has remained on familiar ground. Rather than the story ending here, however, the setsuwa continues to elaborate on the situation. Having found the skull and visually confirmed the miraculous presence of a living tongue, Ichiei questions the skull, asking why such an obviously devoted practitioner should still be stuck in this human realm rather than having achieved rebirth someplace more propitious. The skull, its tongue stilled during the daylight hours, answers Ichiei in spirit form, informing him that his name is Enzen, that he once lived on Mount Hiei, and that he had made "a vow to complete sixty thousand continuous readings of the *Lotus Sutra*" (NST 7: 519). At the time of his death he had only finished reciting about half of them. Now, however, he is almost done and expects to be reborn shortly in the Tuṣita Heaven of the buddha of the future, Maitreya. Ichiei moves on but returns later to find the body completely gone. Shedding copious tears, he concludes that Enzen has finally achieved the rebirth for which he had so ardently hoped.

There are many other setsuwa concerned with the discovery of chanting skulls. *Miracles of the Lotus Sutra* 22 and *Tales from Times Now Past* 13:10 describe the skull of the monk Shunchō, which, in an early effort at criminal reform, continues to recite the *Lotus Sutra* from its position just outside the local prison walls until eventually a wandering ascetic picks it up and deposits it deep in the mountains. *Miracles of the Lotus Sutra* 64 and *Tales from Times Now Past* 13:10 relate the story of the priest Kōshin, who passes away and is buried but whose voice continues to recite the *Lotus Sutra,* as vowed, from inside the grave.[34] *Tales from Times Now Past* 13:12 also provides some interesting overlap between meditation on the decay of a human body (Jp: *fujōkan*) and the chanting skull motif. In this setsuwa a certain monk goes deep into the mountains to gather flowers for the altar. Darkness falls while he is gone, and he is forced to spend the night in the open. Late at night he hears a faint voice reciting the *Lotus Sutra*. At daybreak he decides to find the chanter and spends a great deal of time searching a steep, mossy area. Suddenly a rock seems to jump up and move away from him, resolving itself into the shape of a nun. When he questions her she explains that all these years she has chanted the *Lotus,* never hindered by even a single sexual impulse. Seeing him, however, she is once again impeded by lustful thoughts and made to take on female shape again. She heads deeper into the mountains to start her devotions anew. The setsuwa ends by noting how sinful women are by nature and how many obstructions they have to overcome.

Taken together, these setsuwa perform an interesting twist on the Buddhist doctrine of "no self" (Jp: *muga*), which comprises one of the most central Mahāyāna teachings. Properly speaking, the doctrine of *muga* denies the existence of an abiding self, pointing to the persistence of karma rather than the persistence of a body. If that is the case, however, who is the Enzen who achieves rebirth in Maitreya's land? Who is the Kōshin who recites from the grave? The point of these setsuwa, I believe, is that sutras permeate the body at the level of life force, fundamentally affecting biological processes and transforming the body from a purely sensual mechanism into a citation of Buddhist text. It is not that *no* body survives or that *no* self survives; it is rather that body and self survive *only insofar as* they incorporate, are composed of, and actively perform the citation of Buddhist textuality writ large.

SUTRAS INCARNATE

Setsuwa that feature the salvific incorporation of sutras further buttress this idea of the corporeal possibilities of sacred textuality, as sutras do more than reincarnate themselves in the memory of devotees or manifest symbiotically in the postmortem skulls of saints. In the setsuwa that I will examine next, sutras also incorporate themselves externally, as fully fleshed beings in this and other realms of incarnation, in order to save devotees from pain or embarrassment, rescue them from imminent danger, or attest the efficacy of a practitioner's devotions. In other words, setsuwa present sutras as a kind of text that works to conflate writing done on paper with writing done through the voice and recorded in the body such that at its most miraculous the text is able to come to life, literally incorporating itself, and speak in dialogue with the human.

Medieval setsuwa compilers were fascinated with the idea that the written words of the sutras could take on three-dimensional human form. Tale 2:19 from *A Wondrous Record of Immediate Karmic Retribution* tells the story of a certain devoted lay practitioner who regularly recited the *Heart Sutra* and who was also involved in the practice of making handwritten copies of various religious texts.[35] The setsuwa notes that "the sound of her voice as she recited the *Heart Sutra* was complexly beautiful and, for that reason, clergy and laity alike" often asked permission to listen to her as she chanted the sutras during her daily practice (SNKBZ 10: 179). One night, unexpectedly and without pain, the woman dies in her sleep and is taken to the court of King Emma, who typically reviews a person's good and evil karmic acts and determines the mode of their suffering in hell. He has not summoned her to examine her soul, however, but to ask her if he may listen and judge for himself the beauty of her chanting voice. She stays for three days before he decides to return her to the human realm, where her death apparently has not been noticed.

On her way back to the human realm she glimpses "three men at the gate, each wearing a yellow robe. Greeting her with great happiness, they spoke, saying 'We have met you only once before. Since we have not seen you for some time now, we were longing to see you again. How wondrous to meet you just now! Go back—return with good speed. We will meet you without fail in three days' time at Nara's east market'" (SNKBZ 10: 179). At this juncture the woman does not yet know exactly who the men are, but, as promised, she goes to the market three days later and looks for them. Having waited all day to no avail, she is about to return home when a man walks by with sutras for sale. Ever pious, she expresses interest in buying them. Opening the sutras to inspect them, the woman realizes that they are the two scrolls of the *Brahma Net Sutra* and one scroll of the *Heart Sutra* that she had copied out on yellow paper long ago and had intended to have formally dedicated, but which were stolen from her before the ceremony. She purchases the sutras and organizes the appropriate rituals, firm in the knowledge that "the three men whom she had promised to meet were the three sutra scrolls" she encountered at the market (SNKBZ 10: 179). After the ceremony, the woman returns to her practices with increased devotion.

This setsuwa, which is repeated in *Tales from Times Now Past* 14:31, continues the metaphorical association of textuality and textile noted earlier in this chapter. Aside from the number of scrolls, the crucial link that allows the pious woman to recognize the three sutras as the three men she had met at the border of King Emma's court is color: the yellow of their robes matches the color of the paper on which she had earlier written the sutras.[36] While the yellow robes clothe the bodies of the three men, the yellow fibers of paper provide a surface on which the individual characters of the sutras can be composed. If the cloth is identified with the paper, then the bodies of the three men—bodies that she had seen, greeted, spoken with, and promised to meet again—are the written characters of the sutras incarnate.[37]

Aside from providing visual confirmation of the efficacy of a believer's devotions, incorporated sutras also function in more actively salvific ways and may even save a person from torture in hell. *One Hundred Sessions of Sermons* and *Miracles of the Lotus Sutra* are particularly rich in setsuwa on the motif of textual incorporation, most likely because the former was produced in conjunction with a sutra-copying ritual and the latter aimed specifically to highlight miracles associated with the text of the *Lotus Sutra*. The *One Hundred Sessions* sermon delivered by the Ajari Kōunbō on the eighteenth day of the

Second Month of 1110 concerns a wicked man known only as the Unbelieving Man (Jp: *fushin no otoko*). The man's attempts to keep the teachings of Buddhism from penetrating his body are as humorous as they are literal. Whenever he hears the Buddha's name he rushes to "wash out his ears," and whenever he finds himself inadvertently thinking of the Buddhist teachings, he immediately "rinses out his mouth" (HZ 85), as if thoughts and sounds of Buddhism were something that he could physically scrub off with water.

Oddly enough, one day he acts completely out of character and pays a meditation master to copy out a single character of a sutra, likely in connection with some sort of fund-raising (Jp: *kanjin*) campaign. As Janet Goodwin notes, the rhetoric of these campaigns often spoke of the merit and efficacy of providing even the most miniscule amount of support,[38] and the Unbelieving Man's support is about as miniscule as possible: he pours out the water to wet the inkstone and then watches as the alms collector writes out a single character on his behalf. Appalled by his momentary lapse, he rushes off to rinse out his mouth and suddenly falls down dead. Appearing in hell, he is chased to the court of King Emma by demons hoisting iron staffs. Just as he is about to be condemned to the deepest hell, however,

a buddha, emanating light, appeared out of the sky, riding on a cloud, saying, "This man has merit. Entrust him to me." King Emma said, "He has nothing of the sort! He should be driven into hell." With which the buddha argued, saying, "He has poured water to wet an inkstone for the writing of a single character of the 'Expedient Means' chapter of the *Lotus Sutra*. I am the very first buddha-character of the very first line" [Jp: *sono saishō no kudari no hate no hotoke moji nari*]. Hearing this, King Emma descended from his throne and bowed, saying, "Return immediately to the human world and engage in various acts of merit there." (HZ 86)

In this case a single character of the sutra embodies as a buddha and comes to the legal, moral, and miraculous defense of the Unbelieving Man. The story was a fairly well-known one, appearing in continental collections as well as in the Japanese *A Collection of Treasures,* in which case the unknown compiler prefaces the story by stating, "Going to the marketplace and gathering paper [for the purpose of creating sutra copies], one escapes the tortures of hell, and [pouring out] the water for wetting the inkstone, one douses the flames of hell, . . . engaging in any one of the five varieties of sutra devotion [Jp: *goshu hōshi no gyō*] becomes the cause of one's eventual attainment of buddhahood" (SNKBT 40: 322).

Working with similarly hyperbolic rhetoric, Kyōshakubō, another preacher involved with the *One Hundred Sessions of Sermons* event, also focuses his sermon on the idea of textual incorporation. He opens his oration by claiming that one receives karmic benefit from even the slightest contact with a sutra, whether a portion of one line brushes the ear in passing or an unbeliever intones a short phrase of it even in jest (HZ 133). He goes on to tell the story of a man named Sonko, who is approached by a *Lotus* devotee who recites the sutra as a way of begging for food. Sonko mocks the man and chases him off, causing him to drop the copy of the *Lotus Sutra* that he had worn around his neck. Sonko picks up the mendicant's sutra and shoves it in a corner of his house. Many years later Sonko dies and goes to hell, where he sees "many demons in the service of King Emma. They had the heads of cattle or horses, with glaring eyes and snaggled teeth. Among these there was one who seemed to regard me with pity and, unlike the others, he gently drew nearer" (HZ 134).

This uncharacteristically kind demon advises Sonko to remind King Emma that, in mocking the mendicant, he had actually recited the title of the *Lotus Sutra*. When taken before the court Sonko uses this defense and is granted immediate release, with the stern warning that he should reform his ways once he returns to the land of the living. On his way out of hell Sonko happens to meet the kindly demon again and expresses his thanks, to which the demon replies, "Don't you remember? . . . You took the sutra bag the monk had dropped, and even now it is safely enshrined in your house. Though battered by the wind and rain over the years, one scroll of that sutra remains. I am the [portion of the] sutra contained in that one scroll" (HZ 135).

Both of these setsuwa, and the many others like them,[39] have at their crux the idea of a scriptural fragment that comes into contact with the sinner through the agency of a monk or mendicant, and that transforms itself into either a buddha or (much less often) a kindly demon. In order to effect a miraculous salvation, the text becomes flesh and intercedes vocally on behalf of the sinner. The motif of the text made flesh signifies on the level of performance, scripting for the audience the way in which they are to conceive of their interactions with the orating priest seated before them. The *One Hundred Sessions of Sermons* orators, themselves given to quoting scriptural fragments from sutras, create through the structure of their sermons a critical awareness in their audience members that, like Sonko and the Unbelieving Man, they practice the law imperfectly, in fits and starts, and, unless they allow the words and sounds of the sacred text to permeate their minds and bodies, they connect with the scriptures only indirectly. In contrast to the listening audience, the priest, marked by his black robes and shaved head and serving in his function as a mouthpiece of the Buddhist teachings, stands in as a local manifestation or incorporation of the texts from which he cites. Like the manifestations in the setsuwa, the priest, too, offers guidance, assistance, and salvation. The text, both literally and figuratively, has become a body that speaks and a body that, through speaking, saves.

To cite one final instance of this motif, *Miracles of the Lotus Sutra* 110 relates the following story regarding an unnamed official from Higo province.[40] Leaving his home while it is still pitch-dark one morning, the man wanders all day and finds himself lost and alone in the deep mountains just as the sun is setting. He spots a small hut standing by itself in the middle of a field, and when he approaches to ask for a night's lodging he is met by a beautiful woman in gorgeous robes. Suspecting that she is a man-eating demon, he immediately jumps on his horse and gallops away, but she gives chase, along the way changing back into her demonic form.

About to be overtaken by the demon, the man's horse stumbles and the man falls headlong into a deep hole. The demon eats the horse, bones and all, and threatens to come in after him when a voice—not the man's—answers the demon from deep in the hole, telling her to go away. She is immediately agitated and eventually departs, leaving the man in fear that he has unwittingly lodged himself in the lair of an even fouler beast. The voice, however, comforts him, saying,

"I am not a being of the human race, nor am I a demon, deity, or some other such thing. I am the first character of the *Lotus Sutra*, the character *myō*.[41] Long ago, there was a wandering ascetic. Atop the western ridge here he raised a stupa, interred a *Lotus Sutra* inside it, and made a vow, saying, 'May the *Lotus Sutra* remain in this barren plain and rescue all beings from danger.' Many months and years have passed since, the stupa has fallen and rotted away, and, as for the *Miraculous Lotus Sutra,* it has been battered by the winds, blown and scattered across the land. Only the character *myō* still remains here to provide deliverance. As you are no doubt well aware, many evil flesh-eating demons gather in this vicinity. Abiding in this place, I have delivered many beings from their danger, perhaps seventy thousand or more." When dawn brightened the next day, a young boy appeared out of the hole in the ground and guided the official away. (NST 7: 560)

Other setsuwa tell of miners trapped in a collapsed shaft who are given food and water by young boys, corporeal manifestations of their families' fevered devotions that feature sutra recitations dedicated to the missing men's safety and well-being.[42] Other tales relate stories of daughters being saved from natural disasters such as earthquakes by a chorus of chanting monks (incorporations of a worried mother's sutra recitations) that miraculously appears in the garden, luring the would-be victim from her house moments before its collapse.[43] Finally, a spate of setsuwa features a faithful monk faced with torture or death who recites the sutras and is saved from his suffering when a Buddhist statue, literally brought to life by the power of the sutra, intervenes on his behalf.[44]

ONE CHARACTER, ONE BUDDHA

As with many of the other examples of embodied textuality I have examined in this chapter, this transformation of text—often of one single character of a text—into fleshed being has its parallel in a certain sutra-copying method: the *ichiji ichibutsukyō*, literally "one-character, one-buddha sutra." As the name suggests, this method of production features alternating vertical lines of written characters and tiny buddha figures such that each individual character is paired with a miniature representation of a buddha, thus suggesting—indeed, insisting upon—the identification of written character with buddha body. In a related form of sutra copying, *rendaikyō* (lotus throne sutra), the alternating lines are merged and each written character sits atop a lotus blossom, substituting written character for buddha body and visually suggesting that the character is nothing more and nothing less than the physical body of a buddha. Thus each written character of a sutra is a body that devotees produce, rehearse, and perform with their own bodies when they read, memorize, and chant the texts of Buddhism.

The stories of setsuwa compilers capture this chirographic tradition in narrative form, as in a passage from *One Hundred Sessions of Sermons*. In this story a young boy copies and begins to read the *Lotus Sutra*, completing one copy every night. On the night he completes his one-hundredth reading, he dreams that "feathers grew out of my left and right sides and, feeling as if I wanted to fly, I examined them with some trepidation, only to see that the written characters [Jp: *moji*] of the *Lotus Sutra* were growing into wings" (HZ 93). He flies on these wings to the Pure Land, and the moment that his feet touch ground his wings disperse, this time into thousands of tiny golden buddhas, each one representing a written character from the *Lotus* that he has been learning to read.

Writing in a similar vein, Kamo no Chōmei in *A Collection of Spiritual Awakenings* concludes a story about the efficacy of sutra recitation by stating that, though the Buddha has passed into nirvana, he has left the *Lotus Sutra* "as a physical proxy" (Jp: *kono kyō shōjin ni kawarite*), which continues to teach and instruct all beings (SNKS 303). Likewise, Mujū Ichien draws a parallel between Buddhist statuary and sutra scrolls when he writes in *A Collection of Sand and Pebbles*, "Statues of clay and wood spring forth from the great wisdom [of the buddhas], and sutra scrolls of paper and ink issue forth from the dharma realm. Truly, statues are carved as temporary manifestations of Buddhist wisdom, and written characters make manifest the entirety of the dharma realm" (NKBZ 52: 219). As manifestations of the buddhas' wisdom and of the dharma of the teachings—that is, as manifestations of the very things that make a buddha a buddha—these material objects of wood and clay, paper and ink have spiritual potency. Worshipping Buddhist statuary, Mujū continues, results in the accrual of merit, and "facing the sutra scrolls," whether to make offerings to them or to read them, "inevitably expunges sin" (NKBZ 52: 219). In treating sutra scrolls and statues together, Mujū points out that in the medieval mind these material art forms were believed to possess a life force and a humanoid form. Statues and sutra scrolls functioned as locales of presence that could be activated through the power of worship and vocalization and could positively affect the physical conditions and the material reality in which their believers lived. For those who believed in the sermons and teachings of medieval Buddhism, sutras and statues were Buddhist bodies held in a sort of stasis until activated by the force of belief and devotional praxis.

THE HEIKE-DEDICATED SUTRAS
AND THE PUZZLE OF EMBODIMENT

In conclusion, I would like to turn to a consideration of one last piece of medieval Japanese Buddhist artwork in order to stress again the mutual permeability of sutra and body and the way that the praxis of devotional reading weaves sacred writing and human flesh together into a single organism. The *Heike Nōkyō* is a heavily decorated hand-copied sutra set that the powerful warrior and politician Taira no Kiyomori (1118–81) dedicated to the Itsukushima Shrine in the Ninth Month of 1164. The set consists of thirty-three scrolls, and the texts included reflect standard medieval practices of sutra recitation. The twenty-eight scrolls of the *Lotus Sutra* comprise the bulk of the set. The *Lotus* is accompanied by four other sutras, each in one scroll: the *Sutra of Immeasurable Meanings* and the *Sutra of Meditation on the Bodhisattva Universal Virtue* (Sk: Samantabhadra; Jp: Fugen)—with which devotees typically bookended the *Lotus Sutra,* chanting the former as a prefatory text and the latter as a conclusory one—and the *Sutra of Meditation on the Buddha Amitāyus* (Jp: Amida) and the *Heart Sutra,* both popular texts for recitation in their own right. The remaining thirty-third scroll is a short petition (Jp: *ganmon*) composed by Kiyomori in which he offers the entire set to the deity at Itsukushima, with the request that the deity protect the clan and allow it to continue its political ascendancy.

The thirty-three-volume set is a particularly exquisite representative of the incredible artistry and expense that could go into the creation of such dedicated sutras. In order to show their loyalty to and support for the man who was one of the most powerful military and political figures of his day, Kiyomori's collaborators spared no expense. The paper and calligraphy are of the finest quality, the axles around which the paper was wound are tipped with cut crystal or shaped metal, the protective covers are intricately brocaded, and the frontispiece for each chapter is exquisitely decorated, often with copious amounts of gold foil and silver dust.

The frontispiece for the scroll containing the twenty-third chapter of the *Lotus Sutra,* entitled "The Former Affairs of the Bodhisattva Medicine King," is no exception and has particular bearing on our discussion as it illustrates the interpenetration of writing and body, pointing to that interpenetration as both the message and the hope of Buddhism. The frontispiece pictures a noblewoman with flowing hair and full court robes in the lower right-hand corner. On her lap she holds an open sutra scroll that is almost visibly indistinguishable from the fabric of her robes. She is looking up, over her shoulder, to the corner diagonally opposite, where a golden buddha sits atop purple clouds, a traditional symbol of the "welcoming procession" (Jp: *raigō*) in which the buddha Amida comes to the believer at the moment of her death in order to lead her to the Pure Land, sometimes referred to as the world-sphere Comfortable.

The artwork links the two bodies, of the buddha and the woman, through a series of visual cues both subtle and obvious. The buddha casts forth from his forehead three rays of golden light, which bisect the painting diagonally and fall on the woman's face and upper torso. These gold lines underscore the visual reciprocity of the scene, as the woman returns the buddha's iconic light with a hopeful gaze. Around these strong diagonals are wrapped the gentle undulation of a sandy brownish line that stretches from the buddha to the woman and suggests the rippling surface of a muddy pond, from which several lotus flowers can be seen growing. Finally, scattered throughout the frame of the illustration are also a handful of written characters, some lightly

Figure 5. Frontispiece to "The Former Affairs of the Bodhisattva Medicine King" chapter of the *Lotus Sutra (Heike nōkyō Yakuōbon mikaeshi)*. Part of the *Heike Nōkyō*, 1164. Itsukushima Jinja, Hiroshima Prefecture. Photo courtesy of Nara National Museum, reprinted here by permission of Itsukushima Jinja.

disguised in the "reed hand" (Jp: *ashide*) technique: above the woman's head, the kana *moshi* (if); in a diagonal chain falling from the tip of her right sleeve, the kana *arite* (there is); below her knees, the kana *kono* (this); level with her shoulders, the Chinese characters *kokoni myōjū* (when this life is over); on the edge of the golden shore, the character *sunawachi* (straightaway); below the Buddha's left knee and among the lotus petals beneath him, the mixed kanji-kana phrase *anraku sekai* (the world-sphere Comfortable); and finally, atop the lotus blossom that rests beside the buddha at the top of the painting, the single character *mumaru* (to be born).[45]

Collectively, these chirographic fragments form a rough paraphrase of a passage that appears in the written text of the chapter that the frontispiece is illustrating. This chapter of the *Lotus Sutra* opens with the Buddha Śākyamuni addressing a large assembly of beings with the story of one of his previous incarnations in which he, as a buddha named Pure and Bright Excellence of Sun and Moon, preached the *Lotus Sutra* to an assembly that included the bodhisattva Seen with Joy by All Living Beings. Just before entering ultimate nirvana, Pure and Bright Excellence entrusts the sutra and any relics that may be gleaned from his soon-to-be-cremated body to the bodhisattva. Stepping back into the narrative present, the Buddha then identifies Seen with Joy as a previous incarnation of the bodhisattva Medicine King, who is currently listening to the sermon.

Concluding the story within a story and speaking now to the assembly at large, the Buddha praises the *Lotus Sutra* at length, ascribing any number of blessings to those who are able to accept, keep, read, recite, copy, or explain even a portion of it in those latter days after his own nirvana. In one of these promises he claims, "After the extinction of the Thus Come One, within the last five hundred years, *if there is* a woman who hears *this* scriptural canon and practices it as preached, *at the end of this life* she shall go *straightaway to the world-sphere Comfortable,* to the dwelling place of the buddha Amida, where he is surrounded by a multitude of great bodhisattvas, there to be re*born* on a jeweled throne among lotus blossoms."[46] Certain words and phrases from this passage (in italics), which medieval readers would have encountered in classical Chinese, show up as words and phrases in the frontispiece, where they have been translated into Japanese and arranged into Japanese word order.

For the fragmentary words and phrases to cohere into a single, meaningful sentiment, however, one must read certain of the pictorial images *as words*. That is, the image of the court lady has to be read as "woman," the golden buddha figure as "the buddha Amida," the sutra in her lap as "scriptural canon," and the lotus pedestal floating on the pond as "a jeweled throne among lotus blossoms." Reading these pictorial details as writing yields the sentence, "If there is a woman who hears this scriptural canon, when this life is over, she will be immediately reborn on a jeweled throne amidst lotus blossoms surrounding the buddha Amida." One could push this analysis a step further and read the image of the handheld sutra as a visual approximation of the words *from* the sutra that refer to the auditory power *of* the sutra. In fact, a close inspection of the scroll that the woman is holding reveals it to be a roll containing precisely this chapter of the *Lotus Sutra* that, in the temporal frame of the painting, the woman has clearly just been reading before she was pleasantly interrupted by the beams of light shining from the buddha to illumine her face. Reaching out from inside her sleeve, her finger marks her exact spot in the text: "If there is a woman who has heard this chapter on the former affairs of the bodhisattva Medicine King and who is able to accept and keep it, she will quit her female body and never again receive [that form]. If, after the Thus Come One's extinction . . . " (T 9.262.54b28–29).

There are three salient points to be gleaned here. First, the woman's finger points directly to the words "Thus Come One" (Jp: *nyorai*) in the passage. In other words, what we see in the frontispiece is her vision of those two characters of the text that have taken on corporeal form as a shining, golden buddha who appears before her eyes as a salvific force in her world. Second, the golden buddha has appeared in response to her reading practice. Her act of reading the sutra, of accepting it and keeping it in close faith, allows her to meet the conditions stipulated in the sutra for rebirth in the Pure Land. In a moment of sensual fusion, her reading voice touches her ears just as the illuminated buddha springs into being, summoned forth by the sound of her devotions. Finally, the last phrase that she reads bleeds into the first phrase that she *is*. That is, according to the logic of the frontispiece, the woman reading this chapter of the sutra is the woman who appears in the very next sentence of this chapter of the sutra. It is an individualization of sutra text that takes place at the speed of light and that results in the melding of human body and sacred writing. That one finger, holding her place in the text, vaults her into the world of the sutra and she becomes part and parcel of its fabric. Through the process of devotional reading the woman incorporates herself into the sutra and her body becomes a written and spoken character. Her body is a portion of the text in which she believes, and the text in which she believes fluctuates seamlessly between corporeal and chirographic forms.

In the end, setsuwa and religious artwork should be read as theological statements on the nature of textuality. As Willa Jane Tanabe has pointed out, since the introduction of Buddhism to Japan in the sixth century, the sutra has been "regarded as an object of worship as much as a document of discourse."[47] I would extend her statement to argue that sacred writing, whether done on paper or on the human heart and mind, is as much a form of worship as it is a technology of discourse, as much an act of the present moment as it is an artifact of the past, as much a performance endeavor as it is a recorded document. Setsuwa make no substantial distinction between texts produced chirographically and texts produced orally. Both have the ability to take on corporeal form and intervene on behalf of the believer. Both are methods for transforming the human body, permeating it with Buddhist textuality, and preparing it as a site for the manifestation of Buddhist presence. Both the voice that emanates from one's mouth when one chants the sutras, and the patterns of ink traced by one's hand when one copies the sutra calligraphically on paper, contain the presence and the body of the Buddha. As such, the religious acts of sutra copying and recitation may be most profitably understood as what Robert H. Sharf has called "socially sanctioned and ritually structured meditations on the puzzle of embodiment."[48]

Conclusion
On Circumambulatory Reading

I BEGAN THIS BOOK with the figure of Myōe (1173–1232), the monk who cut off his own ear, believing wholeheartedly in the material connection between the sacred words he read from the sutras' pages and the physical matter of his own body. To mark one was to mark the other. And I ended the last chapter with the complementary image of the sutra-reading noblewoman (painted in 1164), whose figure provides a metacommentary on the ways in which medieval Japanese Buddhists conceived of the text-flesh continuum. The reading voice allows reality to pulse between the word *(buddha)* and the thing (Buddha). One-eared Myōe, the noblewoman with her finger in the scroll, and the many others figures I have examined in the intervening chapters tell us that Buddhism takes language very seriously. Language is not an abstract concept, not an idea that is floating, unanchored, and amorphous— somewhere "out there"— but is a physical substance that trickles into our ears like medicine, chisels itself into our minds, fuses with our life force. We hold it in the tips of our fingers; we wear it like a robe on the skin; we roll it over our red and flashing tongues. As human beings, language is who we are when we are at our best; it is what keeps us alive, how we connect to the divine.

To return to the issue of Buddhist textual culture, then, at the outset I proposed three inter-related vectors for approaching the question of how Buddhist language works in the material realm of written pages and human bodies. The first of these vectors has to do with ontology: where does text exist?

The second has do to with sociology: how can we understand text not (only) as a material "thing," but (also) as a material "event"? And the third concerns history: what do Buddhist books look like? When, where, how, why, by and for whom were they created?

Chapters 1 and 2 focused on the first question, of ontology. Exploring the "mode of existence" of sutras and setsuwa, I pointed to the ways in which these generic forms move beyond the edge of the page. In the case of sutras, there is a crucial distinction to be made between "text" and "work." Simply speaking, the text is the thing we can hold in our hands. Perhaps this is a scroll, stained yellow with insecticide, hand-printed with neat columns of Chinese characters, covered with a stiff silk wrapper, and bound with a cord. Perhaps it is a recent English translation by Burton Watson or Leon Hurvitz, cut into pages and bound up one side, with highlighting and marginalia courtesy of previous readers. According to the sutras, we can court some truly horrendous karma by destroying many, most, or even all of these texts, and still we will not have destroyed the "work." The sutras will continue to exist in the universe, safely sealed away in the memories of bodhisattvas, still penetrable to the eyes of buddhas, simply awaiting an opportunity to be reborn into the world as language. Though they work in a different way, setsuwa likewise claim to exceed the limits of the written page, acting on the human body as food, medicine, or sound, pulling readers along like a forceful preacher or a matchmaker. As specific kinds of language, sutras and setsuwa permeate their reader-listeners, altering their internal landscapes, fusing with their lifeblood, shaping their lived reality.

Chapters 3 and 4 move to the sociological question. Focusing on setsuwa that describe the reading, chanting, memorizing, carrying, copying, and expounding of sutras, I sketch the contours of a medieval Japanese Buddhist textual culture. In this culture written sutras are most certainly things (most often, handwritten scrolls), but they are also *events*. Sutras make themselves legible in the rotting of a corpse. You can taste them in your sour breath, see them in wrinkles and bruises, touch them in your sagging skin. Carve away at yourself long enough, past muscle and sinew, and you may find their words are what stand between you and death. Sutra texts advocate for you in hell, they meet you in the market, they save you from monsters, and they dance on the tip of your tongue, each one of their written characters a shining golden buddha streaming forth from the mouth in a beam of light. Setsuwa literature attests to the various methods, practices, and meditations that establish a material continuum between flesh and text such that the human body can be seen to dissolve into fragments of sacred writing, and sacred writing can be understood to incorporate miraculously into human forms.

Having thus explored the ways in which Buddhist language, as communicated through the written page, works on human bodies, I now want to turn the question around in order to concentrate on the third vector, that of book history. This concluding chapter thinks through how Buddhist language, as manipulated by human bodies, materializes as physical forms in this world. I should note that each of the preceding chapters has posited a cycle of textual production and reproduction in which sacred text circulates through the human body, transforming and rewriting that body before being reborn into the world. This cycle typically follows a set pattern that begins with accepting and keeping a sutra, and continues with the acts of reading, reciting, and expounding for others, before coming full circle with the writing of another copy of the sutra text. Of all these ways of engaging with a sutra, reading is the crucial gesture, because this action moves the sutra from the page to the mind, allowing the sensual union of flesh and writing, and inaugurating the generative cycle by which a devotee might reproduce a text.

In conclusion, then, I want to take up precisely this cycle of textual production, relating it to given technologies of sutra devotion and, in particular, of sutra reading that developed on the continent and found use and elaboration in medieval Japan and beyond. Thus, these final notes will follow the trajectory suggested by the last chapter, turning to a closer consideration of the material aspects of Buddhist textuality and focusing on "the potential of abstract ideas to shape the material world."[1]

THE SPACE OF READING

Book historians typically outline three potential correlations between reading practice and material form. The scroll form, they argue, mandates "linear" reading, reading that must begin at the start of a document and carry through, unbroken, to the end. This somewhat confining technique may be contrasted to the increased freedom of "spatial" or "radial" practices, in which the reader, freed either by the turning of a page (as with the bound book, or codex) or by formatting (such as a newspaper headline or hyperlink) finds him- or herself able to move at will between multiple texts or between distinct parts of the same text.[2] But is it not possible to imagine other models of reading, alternative spatializations of textual engagement? In this conclusion I carry forward the concerns of earlier chapters, refocusing them on an exploration of technologies that developed in East Asia for the purpose of reading Mahāyāna Buddhist sutras. While I make extended reference to cultural and technological trends on the continent (primarily China), my main focus is on their adaptation in medieval Japan. I argue that although "linear" might describe some aspects and some instances of reading, specific technologies such as the revolving sutra library, the scroll, and the DVD optical disk suggest a recurrent Mahāyāna notion of reading as a spatialized ritual activity linked to circumambulation.

Certainly Mahāyāna supports other modes of reading praxis: there are long and well-developed traditions of vocalized reading (recitation singly or in groups)[3] and analytical reading (for the purpose of discerning doctrine, composing commentaries, or furnishing material for sermons). Reading for these purposes tends to be "linear," following the grammatical (or at least the aural) flow of the text from beginning to end, or "radial," combining reading of a primary text with consultation of various commentaries and other reference materials.[4] Additionally, perhaps due in part to the sheer size of the Mahāyāna canon and the massive length of some of its texts, over the centuries various schools and spiritual leaders have articulated a variety of techniques for compressed, emblematic, or representative reading. As categories of speech, *dhārani* and mantra, for instance, are both regarded as potent verbal formulas that condense large amounts of scripture into short, easily memorized phrases. In the most extreme case, the enormous corpus of *Perfection of Wisdom* sutras may be compressed into the single syllable *a*.[5]

Thus, in addition to "linear," "spatial," and "radial" practices of reading, Mahāyāna culture articulates other modes of textual engagement, one of which might be called "circumambulatory reading." Circumambulatory reading is a specific manifestation of pervasive Buddhist notions that "reading" need not necessarily involve a word-for-word parsing of meaning, but may occur (either partially or completely) on acoustic and/or mimetic levels. The various practices and material forms that I am referring to under the rubric of "circumambulatory reading" represent one particular subset within a wider taxonomy of Buddhist reading practice. Calling attention to recurrent metaphors of circling, encircling, turning, and revolving clarifies the spatial and embodied logic of various ritual acts (such as the spinning of text around an axis) and material preferences (such as for sutra libraries, scrolls, and DVDs).

TURNING THE WHEEL

The philosophical underpinnings of Buddhist cosmology build off a preexisting foundation of Indic ideas. One of the most basic is the concept of time as a repeating cycle in which phenomenal existence continually begins, flourishes, declines, falls apart utterly, and begins again. Buddhism takes this temporal pattern and asserts that a new cycle starts when a being (a buddha) attains enlightenment at the very nadir of decline and consents to preach publicly the dharma to which he has been awakened. Sutras provide any number of metaphors for this revelatory act of preaching, comparing it to blowing a conch, raining moisture, beating a drum, raising a banner, lighting a lamp, or providing others with a feast of fragrant food or sweet nectar.[6] Many of these metaphors materialize as paratextual elements in Asian practices of sutra reading. Tibetan prayer flags flapping in the breeze constitute raised banners, percussive instruments used throughout Asia to keep time during sutra chanting provide the beating drums, and the propensity for wandering ascetics in Japan to construct baths and institute practices of ritual bathing suggest the importance of gentle, soaking moisture.[7] All of these technologies, of course, are embedded in their own ritual subtraditions and imbued with their own logics. But it is the Sanskrit phrase *"dharma cakra pravartana"* and its Sino-Japanese calque *"tenbōrin"* that sutras employ most often to describe the teaching of the law, and it is this metaphor of "turning the wheel" that Buddhist technologies of reading preferentially literalize in their material forms.

The short phrase crystallizes many of the most essential ideas of Mahāyāna Buddhism. *Dharma* (Jp: *hō, bō*) speaks to the Law, the Buddhist teachings (sermons and sutras) that express as precisely as possible in language the true nature of reality, itself another meaning of the multivalent term *dharma.*[8] *Cakra* (Jp: *rin*), taken in the popular Japanese context,[9] refers to the wheel of a cart or a carriage and is a metonym for the "one vehicle" (Sk: *ekayāna;* Jp: *ichijō*) of the Mahāyāna (Jp: *daijō,* literally "Great Vehicle") teachings, that is, the assertion that all beings, regardless of the time, place, or circumstances of their birth, eventually will become fully enlightened buddhas. *Pravartana* (Jp: *ten*) means "rolling forward" or "setting in motion," and its Sanskrit root *–vrt* is related to the Latin *–vert* and English *–ward,* suggesting both the turning of a wheel and a turning toward enlightenment. Taken together, the phrase provides one of the international symbols for Buddhism, the eight-spoked wheel.

The wheel as a Buddhist symbol of preaching or teaching is thus firmly established. But how does it also become a productive metaphor for reading? As discussed in chapter 1, sutras employ any number of metafictional techniques that work to overcome spatial and temporal bounds and incorporate their reader-listeners as characters in the text. In the context of the reading moment, the distinction between the Buddha who is speaking in the sutras and the reader who is enunciating the Buddha's spoken words blurs. When reading in ritually appropriate ways, and with the proper preparation (mastery of the text, clearing and centering of the mind, etc.), the reader's voice speaks the words of the Buddha, and the reading voice becomes indistinguishable from the preaching voice.[10] Reading provides a way to ritually reperform preaching.

CIRCUMAMBULATING THE SUTRAS

The basic metaphor of circular movement through space provides an abstract notional template that manifests as several distinct technologies and concrete techniques for reading sutras. Perhaps the most obvious example of repetitive, ritualized circular movement in Buddhism is the simple act of circumambulation. As discussed previously, Mahāyāna texts equate the written and spoken words of sutras with bodily relics of the Buddha, such as might be established in a stupa. Most famously, the *Lotus Sutra,* referring to itself, stipulates, "Wherever [this sutra] may be preached, or read, or recited, or written, or whatever place a roll of this scripture may occupy, in all those places one is to erect a stupa of the seven jewels, building it high and wide and with impressive decoration. There is no need even to lodge a [relic] in it. What is the reason? Within it there is already a whole body of the Thus Come One."[11] Thus the *Lotus* argues that the sutra scroll is like a stupa, is in fact a stupa of the highest order, because it contains the entire physical makeup of the Buddha. The logical supposition would be that, stemming from this claim that sutras function as stupas, we should see requests that believers interact with sutra scrolls in the same ways that they interact with stupas. In other words, we should see reading as an instance of circumambulation.

Though it is a much less common request, at times sutras *do* specifically ask that in addition to reading, reciting, copying, and expounding upon them, their devotees also circumambulate them. In language that nearly echoes that of the *Lotus Sutra,* the *Diamond Sutra* states, "Any place this sutra exists . . . is just like a stupa, and all beings should venerate it, make offerings, and circumambulate it, scattering flowers and burning incense at that place" (T 8.235.750c20–23). In a more extensive episode toward the very end of the *Flower Ornament Sutra,* the pilgrim Sudhana, who has been traveling his entire life in search of the Buddhist teachings, finally arrives before Maitreya, who immediately eulogizes Sudhana's many virtues, chief among them the persistence of his determination for enlightenment. Sudhana responds by circumambulating Maitreya in a worshipful act of respect that signals Sudhana's recognition that the bodhisattva embodies the dharma teachings for which he has been searching. Maitreya then grants Sudhana a vision in which he sees Maitreya "perambulating around the sutra scrolls, chanting them and making written copies of them for hundreds of thousands of years" (T 10.279.435c17). In this short passage the entire spatial arrangement of the *Flower Ornament Sutra* suddenly changes. After traveling due south for decades, Sudhana quickly falls into orbit around Maitreya, who just as quickly reveals that he himself is in constant orbit around the sutras.

This interlude suggests that, like planets revolving around a sun, devotees use circumambulation to call attention to and honor the gravity of the object that they circle, whether that object is a living being, a relic, or a sutra scroll. Both Sudhana's circumambulation of Maitreya and Maitreya's movement around the sutras gesture toward the sutras as a fount of energy that has the power to entrain the body and mind, and it is significant that Maitreya's movement around the sutras parallels other devotional acts of cyclic textual production: chanting and copying. What is important to understand is that in circumambulation the circled center is not static but rather responds in kind to the movements of the devotee. Just as Sudhana's perambulation of Maitreya sets Maitreya in motion, Maitreya's perambulation of the sutras sets the sutras turning. Bernard Faure touches gently, though interestingly, on a similar idea of circumambulation as a kind of gravitational pull when he writes concerning Buddhist statuary, "The notions of aniconic center and iconic periphery explain the importance of circumambulation that leads the practitioner from periphery to center, from bottom to top, from the senses to the spirit, from multiplicity to oneness."[12] In other words, like icons, sutras are "ritually animated" and, unless literally profaned, return the devotional energies of their devotees with an equal intensity.[13] That is why in setsuwa and other miracle literature sutras can do things like take on anthropomorphic form.

DŌGEN AND ZEN TURNS OF SPEECH

The concept of circumambulation as reading was not limited to the continent but had currency in medieval Japan as well. The Zen master Dōgen (1200–1253), for instance, often puns humorously on this idea of "turning" the dharma, and his essay "Reading Sutras" (Jp: "Kankin") is a typical example of his work. The essay, which began as a lecture delivered to an assembly of his followers in 1241, echoes the language of textual devotion found in sutras. Dōgen mentions an array of potential activities—contemplating, reading, reciting, writing, accepting, and keeping sutras—and then, as in the *Diamond Sutra* and the *Lotus Sutra,* he points to the importance of the place where sutras exist. He maintains, "The reality of hearing, keeping, accepting, and expounding sutras and so on exists in our ears, eyes, tongues, and noses, in our organs of mental and physical perception, in the places we go and those where we listen and speak" (DZZ 268). In other words, for Dōgen sutras exist both in an architectural locale (a lecture, meditation, or sutra-reading hall) and in a bodily one. He points to the continuity of sutra reading, arguing that once someone has become a true "holder of the sutras" (Jp: *jikyōsha*), "from kalpa to kalpa the hands never let go of the sutras, and from dawn to dusk there is no time they are not being contemplated" (DZZ 269). In this respect he points to an understanding of sutra reading as "practice and experience" (Jp: *shūshō;* DZZ 268), a notion that, in its understanding of reading as an embodied act, bears superficial similarities to his contemporary Nichiren's (1222–82) idea of "reading with this very body," discussed in chapter 3.

Dōgen continues the essay, outlining four instances in which sutra reading is appropriate: when a patron requests it, when it is part of a standing obligation (as, for instance, on the Emperor's birthday), when an individual monk wishes to consult the sutras, or when a fellow monk dies. He spends the bulk of the essay on the first instance, the patron's request, and it is here that his treatment of reading as circumambulation comes to the fore. He cites three very similar stories. In the first an old woman asks master Shinsai (778–897?) of the Kannon-in temple compound to recite the entire canon, and he complies by descending from his meditation seat and circumambulating it. Dōgen comments that Shinsai's reading consists of him going around the seat, the seat going around him, him going around himself, and the seat going around itself (DZZ 270). In the second story an old woman asks master Shinshō (dates unknown) to recite the entire canon. His response is the same: he descends from his meditation seat and circumambulates it once. In the third story a government official asks master Tōzan Gohon (807–69) to recite the entire canon. The master descends his meditation chair and leads the official in a single circumambulation of it.

As in the passage from the *Flower Ornament Sutra* that details the meeting of Sudhana and Maitreya, Dōgen points to circumambulation as a technique associated with reading. Rather than encircle a stupa or a sutra scroll, however, Dōgen's masters move around their meditation cushions, thus pointing to that seat as a locale where the sutras exist. This is fitting given that Zen emphasizes seated meditation as a method for realizing the teachings of the sutras in "practice and experience," and it further recognizes that a master is someone whose body and mind is a stupa-like, living container of the dharma. Elsewhere in the essay Dōgen asserts that the in-breath and the out-breath of *samādhi* meditation constitutes a continual recitation, not just of one sutra, but of myriad millions of sutra scrolls (DZZ 269), as if the meditative breath enacts a continual unrolling and rerolling of sacred text. In the essay Dōgen criticizes the idea of sutra reading done simply for the purpose of piling up merit, without any concomitant attempt to gain an experiential understanding of what is being read, but we can also see that he is talking about meditation as a kind of reading.

The essay pivots on the crucial idea of "turning": turning the sutras' meaning over and over in one's mind, the slow turn of breath coming in and going out, the turning of the sutra scrolls in one's hand, taking a turn around the meditation cushion. Dōgen maps all of these activities onto the same ritual space. All of these various approaches intimate that the movement of the body through space is a physical enactment of reading, and they suggest that the process of turning and turning again results in a fine attenuation of sutra text and the embodied heart-mind.

REVOLVING SUTRA LIBRARIES

The spatial logic of circumambulation also informs the workings of other Buddhist technologies of sutra reading, one of the most complex of which is the revolving sutra library (Jp: tenrinzō or, more commonly, rinzō). In Buddhist architecture temples consist of multiple buildings, each with its own purpose. These may include a main hall with devotional icons, a lecture hall, a sutra hall or library, a kitchen, a bell tower, and so forth. The revolving sutra library (when a temple has one) is housed within the sutra hall and is, properly speaking, a building within a building. Placed at the center of the hall, the revolving library typically is constructed as an eight-sided pavilion, inside of which are housed copies of the entire Chinese Buddhist canon, with the scrolls (Jp: kansubon) or concertina booklets (Jp: orihon) sliding into narrow drawers, the ends of which may be carved or painted with images of buddhas. The entire apparatus connects to a central wooden pillar, or "axle" (Jp: jiku), which rests in a mortar base. Small handles protrude from each of the eight corners, and these may be grasped, allowing a devotee to turn the entire library in a clockwise direction. One revolution is said to accrue the same amount of merit as one reading of the entire canon.[14]

Chinese tradition has long asserted that Fu Xi (497–569), more popularly known as Fu Daishi, invented the revolving sutra library with his two sons in the early sixth century, and statues of the three are often installed just in front of the structure. Japanese sources from the medieval period to the present day also typically recognize Fu as the inventor of the technology, though this is difficult to corroborate. Fu's earliest biographers do not associate him with

Figure 6. Revolving sutra library from the mid-Tokugawa period (1600–1868). The library contains a Ming era (1368–1644) Chinese version of the Buddhist canon. Image courtesy of Seiryōji, Kyoto, and reprinted here by permission of that temple.

the invention, and it is possible that the technology developed first in northern India.[15] Some Chinese sources, notably the scholar-official Liu Dong writing in 1635, suggest that the idea of rotating sutra texts came from India,[16] though this may refer to the practice of continually rotating representative portions of a sutra (as with the so-called "prayer wheel," which rotates not prayers but a metonymic sutra phrase) and did not necessarily extend to the much more labor-intensive and architecturally demanding practice of rotating an entire copy of the canon.

Even if we cannot decisively credit Fu with the creation of the revolving sutra library, the device finds its longest and best-attested history in China, where it is first mentioned in an inscription dating to 823. According to L. C. Goodrich, the inscription describes the various virtuous acts of one Chinese Buddhist who hand-copied the entire canon, at that time consisting of 5,327 rolls, which were installed in a revolving sutra repository in the year 809. The first architectural sketches appear in the *Yingzao Fashi,* "the official standard for building construction, published and enforced by the Song sovereign in 1103."[17] The earliest records of revolving sutra libraries in India (in the eleventh century) thus seem to postdate references to the technology in China by at least two centuries, and it seems probable that this is one aspect of Buddhist material culture that traveled from China to India rather than the other way around.

Though clearly very expensive to manufacture, revolving sutra libraries were constructed at a number of locations in both China and Japan. In addition to the example from 823 cited above, another was constructed in 836 at the Nanchansi in Suzhou, and the Japanese pilgrim Ennin (794–864) saw one at Mount Wutai in 840 during his visit to Tang China.[18] The techniques for constructing revolving sutra libraries were not introduced to Japan until several centuries later, during the Kamakura period (1185–1333), from the Southern Song (1127–1279). Some of the oldest surviving libraries may be found at Onjōji in Yamaguchi (fourteenth century), Zuiōji in Ehime (1390–94), and Ankokuji in Gifu (1408).[19] Revolving sutra libraries continued to be constructed through the mid-1400s in China and at least as late as the 1600s in Japan.

IMAGINING SUTRA REVOLUTION

As with circumambulation in general, the revolving sutra library functions by literalizing the metaphor for reading and preaching as "turning the wheel of the dharma." Earlier researchers mistook the library's purpose, believing that monks who were engaged in the work of translating the sutras from Sanskrit to Chinese developed the revolving library as a way to save space and time, making all of the sutras easily accessible to a seated circle of their peers.[20] As Guo Qinghua notes, however, the device "was not a convenience to enable monks to search the sutra[s], but a physical metaphor . . . based on the belief that to revolve a cabinet containing a full set of sutra[s] had the same merit as to have read all the volumes."[21]

A story from Liu Dong's 1635 *Dijing Jingwulüe,* a survey of sights in the environs of the imperial capital, contains most of the salient elements and suggests the potential for the technology to excite the popular imagination. Concerning the revolving library at Longfusi, Liu writes, "People may read the canon or make donations. If one's virtue or gift is equal to one *tsang* [one of the three "baskets" of Buddhist teachings], it is sufficient to make one turn of the wheel."[22] In other words, one may either read the sutras aloud and amass virtue in that manner, or one may make a donation of cash or other material goods as a gift. If either of these contributions amounts to "one basket" of the Buddhist teachings, then one is allowed to grasp the handle of the library and revolve it once. The "basket" refers to the "three baskets" (Sk: *tripitaka;* Jp: *sanzō*) of the Buddhist canon, whose texts are typically classified as belonging to one of three categories (or "baskets"): the sutras, which are thought to record the sermons of the Buddha; the *vinaya,* or compendia of monastic codes of behavior; and the *abhidharma,* or higher teachings.

All three of these methods of acquiring merit—reading the canon, making a donation, and rotating the library—involve the reader in turning the wheel of the dharma. While the reader acquires merit in performing these actions, each requires varying resources of literacy, education, and leisure time, or at least the financial well-being to purchase these and effect their result (a reading of the entire canon) by mechanical means. Liu's story continues, however, by referencing a popular legend about "a poor girl who was not able to read the canon, and was likewise unable to make a donation, was ashamed and contrite, and therefore placed one cash on the revolving mechanism. It then turned without ceasing, which made everyone in the temple surprised. They then tried to stop it, but the wheel went *ya ya* just like the start of the roll of a drum."[23] This story underscores the mechanization of merit that the revolving library makes so visible. It further points to the potential of circumambulatory reading as a merit-producing mimetic activity. Additionally, the tale attests not to the value of the girl's coin but the ardor of her intentions, and it suggests that what truly "turns" the sutras is the power of the awakened heart.

In the case of Japan, the Noh play "Rinzō" (The Revolving Sutra Library), composed in the early 1500s by Kanze Nagatoshi (1488–1541) and still performed occasionally today, offers an intriguing glimpse into the place that the revolving sutra library held in that country's late medieval imagination. A playwright in the third generation from Zeami, Nagatoshi is known for penning plays that stretched the performative norms of Noh. "Rinzō" is no exception and is one of the few plays in the repertoire to make use of a prop, in this case a lightweight eight-sided structure of cloth and bamboo meant to suggest the revolving library. His play is also unusual in the rather large number of characters that appear onstage.

Briefly, the play follows the movements of three monks from Dazaifu Tenmangū. Dazaifu, located in the northwestern corner of Kyūshū, served as the southern outpost of the Japanese imperial court during the Nara (710–84) and Heian (794–1185) periods and was an important locale for diplomatic and cultural relations with the continent. The Tenmangū Shrine located there is a subsidiary of the main Tenmangū Shrine at Kitano, on the northern side of the imperial capital far to the east. At the play's opening the three monks (one priest and his two attendants) speak of their desire to travel to the capital, and especially to worship at the revolving sutra library housed at the Kitano shrine, where they will be able to make offerings to all of the works in the canon throughout the course of a single night.[24]

Their travel progresses smoothly and quickly, and they arrive at Kitano late one evening, whereupon they express their joy that revolving sutra libraries have found their way to Japan from "the great Tang, in order to save beings in this final age. It is said that one can make an offering at the revolving library and establish a karmic connection just by touching it with one's hand" (YSG 51). Gazing at the building that houses the library, they express their thanks to its inventor, Fu Daishi, and his two sons, who they suppose reside now in a Pure Land of unsurpassed joy. The three monks are greeted by an old man who claims that he is actually a manifestation of the god Agni, an Indic fire deity adopted by Buddhism as a protector of the dharma. He opens the door to the revolving library and invites the monks to worship, noting the deep karmic connection they must have to the device's creators, who, "though laymen," are at least partially responsible for the transmission of the dharma to Japan (YSG 51). The old man then mysteriously fades from sight, leaving the monks to worship before the canon.

The monks begin chanting the sutras as a musical offering. As if responding to the clarity and resonance of their voices, the haze begins to clear, leaving the moon to shine like a "mirror in a cloudless night sky" (YSG 52). The lead monk notes several miraculous signs—a mysterious fragrance, strains of heavenly music, purple clouds, and a rain of flowers—all harbingers of a visit from the Pure Land. At this point the door of Agni's miniature shrine (Jp: zushi) opens to the west,[25] the direction in which the Pure Land lies. Fu Daishi and his two sons appear onstage and Fu instructs his sons to present an entire copy of the canon to the priests. Meanwhile, Fu kneels and bows before the priests, half-speaking and half-miming the lines, " 'If you would chant these sutras, how excellent, how excellent that would be!' And he joins their night concert with dancing" (YSG 52). While the monks chant and Fu dances to the music of their offering, the old man reappears, now in his true form as the fire god Agni. He invites the monks to stand and turn the revolving library.

As the monks turn the library Fu and Agni dance briefly in tandem before Fu and his sons rise into the sky, returning to the Pure Land on thrones of lapis lazuli decorated with the seven precious jewels.

The play turns on two climactic moments, the first of which occurs just before the old man disappears. In a beautifully poetic passage he puns repeatedly on the place-name Kitano Tenmangū, literally "north field shrine of the saturated heavens." Speaking to the monks as he dances mimetically, he says, "Though the paths of the teachings are many, there is but one enlightenment: the moon in the breast. May it never cloud over! Everything in the three worlds arises from the human heart [Jp: *sangai yui* (or *tada*) *isshin*]. This place is the shrine of the north. The North Star does not wander, and all of the stars that saturate the heavens revolve around it. I open the revolving library and invite you to worship quietly" (YSG 51). Through its poetic imagery, his speech, accompanied by the intricate pattern of dance, weaves together the natural scenery of a starry night sky with the monks' heartfelt desire to touch and turn the sutra library, indicating that the strength and constancy of their single-minded (Jp: *isshin*) religious longing has somehow helped bring about the appearance of this sutra library in the phenomenal world (Jp: *sangai*). The idea of the North Star remaining as the unwobbling pivot in a sky of spinning light, and the identification of the North Star with Kitano, also suggests that the monks have arrived at the centermost point of the Buddhist cosmos, the axis around which all else revolves.[26]

The conclusion of the play echoes and amplifies these images of brilliant revolution. With Fu already dancing and the monks already chanting, Agni suddenly reappears "before their eyes and, facing the holy men, he speaks as he draws near. 'Now turn the merit of your circumambulatory chanting [Jp: *gyōdō*] toward me and establish the karmic connection.' He beckons the holy men, 'Place your hands, as you have long desired, on the revolving library.' Together they push it around. Round and round, the brilliance of the sun and moon! The clarity and freshness of the unclouded law!" (YSG 52). The passage comes together like a set of giant gears that lock into one another and begin turning as the monks, who have been circling the library and the sutras as they chant, now take hold of the library and turn it. The wheeling stars, the circumambulating monks, and the revolving sutras all pivot around the single axis of the sutra library.

In the world of the play the melding of the two devotional acts of chanting and circumambulation releases a wave of light, illuminating the night sky as if it were midday. This sudden flash calls to mind the light miracles that precede the Buddha's sermons (the beacon he emits from between his brows as a sign that he is about to begin preaching, as at the start of the *Lotus*),[27] and, in fact, the monks' turning of this wheel of the dharma seems to refresh the teachings, bringing them renewed brilliance. In effect, this turning of the sutra library equates, at least locally, to the Buddha's turning of the dharma in his sermons and represents a more widespread desire on the part of Japanese devotees to turn back time, a refusal to accept the notion that by the time Buddhism reached Japan the religion was, by most accounts, already in the age of its decline.[28] In this sense, circumambulatory reading is about renewal, about starting the clock over again, and about the power of religious devotion to effect the rebirth of sacred text as a force powerfully present in the here and now.

THE SCROLL

As with circumambulation and the revolving sutra library, the Buddhist scroll takes the spatial efficacy of circular movement as its chief operating principle. Scholars of book history and theoreticians of the textual condition, material culture, and reading practice, however, typically consider the scroll a site of "linear reading."[29] In some senses this is an accurate description. Unlike hypertext, which encourages its readers to jump at will between an array of web pages, and unlike the bound codex, which allows a reader to open to any page at any time, the scroll is a single long, continuous sheet that must be unwound, linearly, from beginning to end, and then rewound, rather than simply closed, when one is done reading. Many scholars have pointed out how cumbersome this is, and historians of the Western book have often assumed that this lack of ease was one of the major reasons that the codex replaced the scroll so quickly in most of Europe and the Mediterranean, where it almost completely superseded the scroll between the second and fourth centuries C.E.[30]

It would certainly have been possible for Buddhist East Asia to adopt the codex, or a codex-like form (folded, fastened along one edge, and provided with a stiff protective cover), as the preferred material format for sutras, and at least three factors would lead one to expect precisely this development. First, the Indian precedent for the material form of written text was palm leaf that was written on, pressed between two sturdier boards, and bound with a string to form a single text. This could have had a profound effect on the material form of Chinese Buddhist texts for, as John Kieschnick argues, "At first, modeled as it was on the Indian palm-leaf manuscripts from which Chinese Buddhist translations derived, the booklet was seen as a distinctly Buddhist format for a text. In other words, the early owner of a Buddhist text could feel that Buddhist books were something entirely different from other, common books [i.e., the typical Chinese scroll of fabric or paper], not only in their un-usual language, literary style, and sacred content, but even in the way they looked, the way one held them, and the way one turned the pages."[31]

That this material form did hold a certain appeal because of its foreignness and authenticity can be gauged from the Japanese pilgrim Ennin's journal en-try for the seventeenth day of the Fifth Month of 840, during his visit to Mount Wutai. Making the rounds of the various temples and subtemples and view-ing their treasures, Ennin notes that one building boasted the skull of a long-dead Indian monk, bones of the Buddha contained in a bottle of precious stone, and three copies of the *Lotus Sutra:* one in miniature characters, one in gold characters, and one in the Indian format (Jp: *bonkō*).[32] Thus, early gen-erations of Chinese and Japanese Buddhists were familiar with paged texts and bound booklets and associated those forms specifically with sacred Bud-dhist text, even including them in relic hordes, but neither Chinese nor Japa-nese Buddhism moved quickly to adopt or to adapt that technology.

Second, on the whole, Buddhism proves to have been remarkably eager to create and perfect new technological forms for text. Of all the world's many textual cultures, it is Buddhism that provides the world's "earliest extant ex-ample of a complete book on paper," a copy of the *Sutra of Parables* written in China in 256 C.E.[33] Chinese Buddhism also gives us the first extant printed text in the world (before 751), the earliest example of a woodcut illustration in a printed book (868), and the earliest hand-colored print (947).[34] Japanese Buddhism was also engaged in these types of material advances, at times on a scale rare in the preindustrial world. For instance, an imperial directive in the year 764 ordered the creation of one million miniature stupas (Jp: *hyaku-mantō*), each of which was stuffed with a selection of incantations (Jp: *darani*) that appear at the end of the *Unflawed Pure Light Great Dhāraṇī Sutra* (T. 1024), which were mass-printed either by woodblock or copper-plate.[35] In other words, East Asian Buddhist textual culture was not a con-servative undertaking that resisted change and clung to old forms out of sheer habit, but was rather a remarkably active force for innovation and change, and for several centuries served as the primary driving force behind technologi-cal improvements in East Asian textual culture.

Third, Buddhist East Asia possessed the necessary resources, both material and financial, to have adopted and produced a codex format from quite an early age. Chinese inventors had produced a durable form of fine, absorbent paper by 105 C.E. They had also perfected the making of glue for binding and the concoction of boiled tree bark for a paper-borne insecticide. Long-last-ing handwritten codices were thus possible from the second century, and Buddhists in China were capable of producing printed codices by at least 835 C.E., and possibly as much as a century earlier, with carved woodblocks. Furthermore, in addition to sutra copying done by temples and clans, the Chinese and Japanese imperial governments patronized Buddhist textual production actively, establishing governmental bureaus expressly charged with creating copies and translations of Buddhist texts. In China an imperial decree promulgated in 581 mandated that "all Buddhist works be copied for deposit in the temples and large cities, with a specially prepared copy to be kept in the imperial library," resulting in the transcription of more than 130,000 scrolls' worth of material.[36] A quarter century later, in 606, a second emperor created a special governmental office for the translation of Buddhist works. Textual projects remained a central concern, often showcasing the authority and wisdom of imperial rule, and during the Song dynasty Buddhist texts again benefited from imperial mandate, resulting in several runs of the complete canon.

Likewise, in Japan an official bureau of sutra copying (Jp: *shakyōshi, shakyōjo*) was established by imperial decree in 728 C.E. to oversee the production of thousands of scrolls that were then distributed across the country. The workshop manufactured sutras according to a standardized format, with a norm of seventeen characters per line, and work was highly specialized, divided among calligraphers, proofreaders, frontispiece artists, metal polishers, and so on. Even after the scriptorium was closed, with the moving of the capital from Nara to Heian in the 780s, the imperial family and leading aristocratic clans continued to sponsor sutra-copying projects, an activity that reached its greatest volume in the eleventh and twelfth centuries.

East Asian Buddhism thus had a precedent for a codex-like form and also possessed the technologies, skill, material resources, and financial wherewithal to produce such a form on a mass scale. Nevertheless, in both China and Japan the rolled scroll persisted as a major material format for Buddhist text for a surprisingly long time. As Tsuen-Hsuin Tsien points out, "Much Buddhist literature . . . retained the form of rolls" as late as the twelfth century in China, and Peter Kornicki notes that in Japan the scroll "did not go into decline until the Tokugawa period [1600–1868]," showing particular resiliency as a chosen form for religious texts and some literary classics.[37]

This is not to say that the scroll remained the only, or even always the dominant, form for Buddhist scripture. Codex-like booklets dating to the year 899 have been found in Dunhuang, whose caves are filled with sutras, and folded concertina booklets (Jp: *orihon*)—essentially a rolled scroll that has been folded, accordion-like, every several lines—became increasingly popular in China and Japan starting in the ninth century, particularly for longer texts such as the *Greater Heart Sutra*, which comprises six hundred volumes. A special ceremony to recite this lengthy sutra is still performed in Japan today, as it has been since at least the medieval period. In this ceremony the chapters of the sutra (invariably in concertina form for this purpose) are divided among a team of monks, all of whom simultaneously "read" their allotted portions by holding the concertina booklets aloft, one at a time, and enunciating some portion of the text therein while releasing the front cover and allowing the folded pages to cascade, like a Slinky, from their upraised left hand into their lowered right palm. The ceremony is called a *tendokue*, literally a "ritual" *(e)* of "reading" *(doku)* by "turning" *(ten)*. Even in the case of sutra recitation from concertina booklets, then, we see—at least on the level of the naming of the ritual *(tendoku)* and the emblematic, mimetic action it entails (the dramatic unfurling of the sutra text)—an attempt to reconcile the booklet form with a ritual preference for a textual format that allows for the "turning" of the sutra text.

SPATIAL EFFICACY

If Buddhist East Asia had the technical prowess to create handwritten codices by the second century, and if codices are truly more convenient to use than scrolls, then why did Buddhists continue to produce scrolls for approximately another millennia? Stephen Teiser begins to unravel the conundrum when he notes that the "history of the Chinese book followed no single, invariant line of development." He argues instead that extant textual examples show copies of the same sutra in the same geographical area around the same time appearing in a variety of formats, and that this textual variety reflects "the wide range of settings" in which a given text might conceivably be used.[38] Teiser surmises that miniature copies might have been used as handy pocket guides while larger booklets may have seen service as reference volumes. In other words, the form fits the function.

While other forms may have been more durable, more portable, or more convenient to reference, my research into medieval Japanese literature suggests that it was the scroll that was considered the most miraculous. To put it slightly differently, of all the available textual forms, the scroll proved to be the material type ideally suited for the production of miracles. For instance, *emakimono* (picture scrolls depicting historical, fictional, or miraculous events) from medieval Japan consistently show their protagonists reading aloud from sutra scrolls or seated beside reading desks on which are piled stacks of rolled sutras.[39] Similarly, when Japanese setsuwa specify a material form for the su-

Figure 7. An illustration of the descent of Amida and his twenty-five attendants to welcome a devotee to rebirth in the Pure Land *(Amida nijūgo bosatsu raigōzu)*. The practitioner has passed away in the most propitious manner, seated upright with hands clasped before his reading desk on which rest the eight scrolls of the *Lotus Sutra*. Kamakura era, thirteenth or fourteenth century. Chion'in, Kyoto. Photo courtesy of Chion'in and reprinted here by permission of that temple.

tras, it is always the rolled scroll.[40] Several setsuwa, for example, refer to a sutra scroll that miraculously rewinds itself once the reader is done intoning it.[41] Another *setsuwa* describes the long, cylindrical form of a sutra that turned itself into a snake to save a devotee's life.[42] Similarly, setsuwa that feature anthropomorphized sutras often stress that the silk clothing wrapped around the human manifestation is reminiscent of the silk brocade cover of the scroll, pointing to the visual similarity of the long, thin scrolls and the shape of the erect human form.[43] I would argue that in these tales it is as much the shape of the scroll as the words contained therein that accounts for their ability to function in miraculous ways.

All of this evidence suggests that, inconvenience aside, the scroll as a material form for Buddhist text maintained a certain resilience. There are three possible reasons for this, two of which are very practical and one of which has to do with the spatial efficacy of the scroll as a material form that supports ritual circumambulation. One practical reason that the scroll may have endured is that, especially during the Song dynasty (960–1279 C.E.), print runs of the Buddhist canon were a state-sponsored activity. After the state adopted a standard format—a scroll on yellow paper treated with insecticide and printed with fourteen characters per line—the Song editions typically maintained this form, which became a visible mark of the canons' authority as officially approved editions. Other countries that received copies of the Song canon—Korea in 991, Annam in 1010, Khitan in 1019, and Tangut in 1035—tended to reproduce many of its formal qualities in their own subsequent productions. In Buddhist cultures such as Japan, whose first copies of the Song canon arrived with Chōnen (938–1016) in the late 980s and again through Jōjin (1011–81) in the 1070s, the scroll may simply have been what Buddhist texts looked and felt like to the vast majority of Buddhists who would never have seen the flat strips of the Indian-style book.

A second practical reason that the scroll persisted in Buddhist East Asia when it faded so much more quickly in most of Europe and the Mediterranean is that scrolls in East Asia are simply much easier to read. Silk and especially paper provide a much more durable writing surface than fragile papyrus and can be extended to any length by stitching or gluing, and they are much more affordable and flexible than vellum. In addition, the scroll format is simply better suited to vertically composed languages like Chinese and Japanese, both of which classically were written in top-to-bottom columns that read from right to left. Holding the unread portion of the still-wound scroll in the left hand, one can take the leading edge in the right hand and open a portion of text with the hands held at a natural angle, as if one were reading a newspaper. It is possible to read along smoothly, winding up with the right hand and unwinding with the left, all the way to the end of the text. This arrangement makes reading considerably easier than is the case with horizontal print, in which case one either has to read block by block (like scrolling through microfiche) or with the hands held at an unnatural angle, with one hand up by the forehead and the other down around the sternum (like an actor reading aloud a proclamation).

Perhaps the driving factor in the scroll's persistence as *a* form (if not the *only* form) for Buddhist sutras, however, has to do with ideological concerns about ritual efficacy and the proper space of reading. As the preceding discussion has argued, there is something particularly powerful about the act of "turning" Buddhist scripture, an act whose ritual and spatial properties I have theorized here as "circumambulatory reading." The metaphor that equates enunciating the Buddhist teachings with "turning the wheel of the dharma" provides the notional template, of which certain technologies (such as the revolving sutra library and the persistence of the scroll) are the material traces and for which specific tropes (as with Dōgen's punning) are the linguistic residue. While other textual forms, such as the concertina booklet, may have approximated this function through mimesis (the dramatic unfurling of scripture) or naming *(tendokue),* scrolls come closest to materializing it. I suggest, then, that the scroll persists because it possesses, inherent in its material form, something that the codex and the folded booklet do not, namely a certain spatial efficacy that, in the demand for rolling and unrolling, allows the reader to mimetically perform the act of "turning the wheel of the dharma." Given the prevalence of circumambulation and its linkage to practices of reading in the Mahāyāna Buddhist tradition, and in light of the incredible inventiveness and complexity of devices like the revolving sutra library, it is not too far-fetched to suggest that one reason for the scroll's tenure through the medieval period and even into the early modern era lies precisely in this ability to perform, at the material level, spatial movements that echo long-standing traditions of reverence, worship, and enunciation.

Terminology is instructive here. Scrolls are constructed through the combination of a number of discrete components. The bulk of a scroll is, of course, the wound paper, silk, hemp, or other fabric (Jp: *honshi*) on which the text is brushed or the illustrations painted. To the leading edge of this may be glued a section of stiffer material (Jp: *hyōshi*), either heavier paper or, in fancier productions, silk brocade. A layer of paper or cloth (Jp: *mikaeshi*) may be pasted to the internal side of the *hyōshi,* and this may contain further information about the author, title, or place of composition, or it may be decorated with a frontispiece illustration. The external side of the *hyōshi* generally bears a small label (Jp: *daisen*) in the upper left-hand corner, listing the name of the work or some other identifying information. The leading edge of the *hyōshi* is often protected by a slender rod of metal or wood (Jp: *hassō*) to which is attached a string (Jp: *himo*), which, when the scroll is wound shut, can be wrapped around the cylinder and used to secure it closed. To keep the string from slipping loose, the end may either be knotted or decorated with a small bead, the name of which (Jp: *tsuyu,* literally "dewdrop") invokes a classic Buddhist metaphor for transience.

The most crucial component of the scroll, however, is the central rod (Jp:

jiku, literally "axle") around which the text is rolled, the pivot around which everything else turns. The idea of the axle that lies at the center of the scroll clearly evokes other technologies of reading—circumambulation and the revolving sutra library—and it functions according to the same spatial logic. The scroll concretizes and materializes the metaphor of "turning the wheel of the dharma," as is attested persistently at the linguistic level. Japanese grammar requires that nouns be enumerated through the use of special counters: three "sheets" of paper, one "cylinder" of pen, and so forth. One may choose to count scrolls by any of three terms, speaking, for instance, of the eighty "rolls" (Jp: *kan*) of the *Flower Garland Sutra,* the eight "wheels" (Jp: *rin*) of the *Lotus Sutra,* or the single "axle" (Jp: *jiku*) of the *Heart Sutra.* Each counting word seizes on the circling movement of rolling and unrolling the scroll as the crucial mimetic act. This turning ritually reenacts that moment when the historical Buddha gave the teachings, providing a technological and mechanical means for making that moment and those teachings present, manifest in the here and now of reading.

Certainly having to reroll a scroll may be inconvenient, but in the context of ritual reading, might not have devotees used the duration of that "interruption" to consider the rarity of coming across an intact copy of the scripture, the wonder of being possessed of a human mind capable of reading it, and the joy of hearing the Buddha's words issuing from one's own mouth? Or, perhaps, a devotee might visualize, if only for a few minutes, that wondrous realm to which the power of his reading will transport him and the pains that his reading might alleviate in others.[44] Given the spatial efficacy and the attendant miraculous possibilities of the scroll as a material form, the difficulty of reference and the inconvenience of rewinding seem minor sacrifices indeed.

DIGITAL DREAMS

Even in the contemporary period we find continuing evidence of Buddhists working to adapt and fine-tune new technologies to similar ends, privileging the circumambulatory aspects of reading.[45] Recent efforts include the creation of digital videos of spinning prayer wheels that can be loaded to one's desktop as a screensaver, animated images of prayer wheels that a user can click and drag right to left (clockwise as seen from above, the proper direction of circumambulation), and banners reading "Om Mani Padme Hum," which can be set to scroll continuously using JavaScript. There have been projects to fill prayer wheels (real or virtual) with this phrase stored on microfilm and DVD optical disk, with Jidgal Dagchen Sakya endorsing the optical disk project by noting, "The new Sakya Monastery prayer wheels" use the technology "to put more mantras inside a prayer wheel than any other prayer wheel ever created. . . . Mindfully turning a prayer wheel with 1.3 trillion mantras produces the same merit and benefits as having recited 1.3 million mantras," which he estimates would take approximately forty-two thousand years.[46]

Other sites encourage devotees to load copies of a mantra on disk drives or hard drives (but *not* flash drives), which spin the mantra in the same manner as a prayer wheel, but much faster, "somewhere between 3600 and 7200 rpm, with a typical rate of 5400 rpm."[47] While experiments with computer-assisted revolution may have begun in Japan,[48] the concept has been taken up most actively by Tibetan Buddhists, especially practitioners in the West, who typically cite the Dalai Lama as approving and encouraging these developments.[49] While web authors celebrate the technical potential, however, they also remind users to be mindful: "It wouldn't hurt to think of the mantra from time to time while it's spinning around on your disk drive."[50]

James O'Donnell, in discussing the development of the written word in the Western world from the age of papyrus to contemporary developments in cyberspace, reminds us of a crucial point when he argues that cutting-edge technologies typically embody old wishes in new forms. The modern version of completely searchable digital text represents, he argues, the latest technological innovation supporting a desire that stretches back at least to the library at Alexandria, which comprised the greatest and most searchable body of written knowledge in its time. In a poignant phrase that resonates deeply with my discussion here, he notes, "What has changed is not the dream, but the sense of technical possibilities."[51] Technologies of reading concretize and provide three-dimensional, material evidence of how a given culture structures its most deeply held desires, its most abiding "dreams" of text. In many of its technologies of reading—circumambulation, revolving sutra libraries, scrolls, and now screen savers and hard disks—Buddhism provides tangible evidence of an abiding drive to yoke centripetal movement to contemplative readiness in a powerful circling that has the potency to renew the cycle of the dharma and turn the wheel of the teachings spinning again.

NOTES

1. This passage appears in the *Kōzanji Myōe shōnin gyōjō*, an account of Myōe's deeds focusing on his time at Kōzanji, in the mountains at the edge of the Heian capital. This translation is adapted slightly from George Tanabe, *Myōe the Dream-keeper: Fantasy and Knowledge in Early Kamakura Buddhism*, 60.

2. For more on this dream, see Nomura Takumi, "Myōe no shashingyō to kotoba," 30 ff. For an English-language study of Myōe and his dreams, see Tanabe, *Myōe the Dreamkeeper*.

3. "The Phrase *sa prthivīpradeśaś caityabhūto bhavet* in the *Vajracchedikā*: Notes on the Cult of the Book in Mahāyāna" in Gregory Schopen, *Figments and Fragments of Mahāyāna Buddhism in India: More Collected Papers*, 25–62. I discuss Schopen's theory in more detail in chapter 1. The basic argument, simplified here for the sake of brevity, is that Mahāyāna distinguished itself by establishing cultic centers organized around written sutras that were recited, worshipped, and circumambulated. For later qualifications to his original argument, see Schopen's "On Sending Monks Back to Their Books: Cult and Conservatism in Early Mahāyāna Buddhism," in the same volume, and his entry on "Mahāyāna" in Robert Buswell, Jr., *Encyclopedia of Buddhism*, especially his comment that the "cult of the book" was not an "attempt by the 'new' [Mahāyāna] movement to substitute one similar cult (the cult of the book) for another similar cult (the cult of relics)" but was likely meant instead "to shift the religious focus . . . to doctrine, to send monks, nuns, and even laymen quite literally back to their books" (497).

4. Konta Yōzō, Nagatomo Chiyoji, and Maeda Ai are leading scholars. For summative accounts of the state of the field in Japan, see Peter Kornicki and Henry D. Smith II. There is a vast secondary literature in Japanese dealing with issues of calligraphy and the illustration, circulation, and dedication of manuscripts from which I draw freely, and gratefully, in this study. Nevertheless, far more needs to be done, and in a more interdisciplinary manner, before the "history of the book" in pre-Tokugawa Japan becomes clear.

5. For studies of Japan see Peter Kornicki, Henry D. Smith II, and Mary Elizabeth Berry. Research on Chinese print culture has been much more active. See Cynthia Brokaw, Kai-Wing Chow, Susan Cherniack, John H. Winkleman, and Tsien Tsuen-Hsuin. Tsien is one of the few scholars working consistently before the twelfth century.

6. Henri-Jean Martin, Lucien Febvre, Roger Chartier, G. Thomas Tanselle, Robert Darnton, and Elizabeth Eisenstein have been among the most active in developing this field.

7. For instance, Roger Chartier wrote in 1995, "More than ever, perhaps, one of the critical tasks of the great libraries is to collect, to protect, to inventory (for example, in the form of collective national catalogues, the first step toward retrospective national bibliographies), and, finally, to make accessible the kinds of books that have been those of men and women who have read since the first centuries of the Christian era, the kinds of books that are still our own. Only by preserving the understanding of our culture of the codex may we wholeheartedly realize the 'extravagant happiness' promised by the screen" (*Forms and Meanings: Texts, Performances, and Audiences from Codex to Computer,* 24). Chartier's linkage of the national bibliography with the history of the book is typical, the field of book history having developed more or less directly out of the Annales school and the Bibliothèque de France project. The connection between book history and the development of a national vernacular may be operative in East Asia as well. For further discussion, see the conclusion of this book and Victor H. Mair, "Buddhism and the Rise of the Written Vernacular in East Asia: The Making of National Languages."

8. Jerome McGann is the leading proponent of this type of textual scholarship, which he terms "the textual condition." See also D. C. Greetham and, for a separate development of the "sociology of text," D. F. McKenzie.

9. Jerome McGann, *The Textual Condition,* 21.

10. The key texts here are by F. W. Bateson, René Wellek and Austin Warren, James McLaverty, and Peter Shillingsburg.

11. James McLaverty, "The Mode of Existence of Literary Works of Art: The Case of the Dunciad Variorum," 82.

12. Silk screens, lithographs, and woodblock prints offer interesting challenges to this admittedly simplified schema.

13. For models of how to accomplish this, I am indebted to studies of medieval

Christendom, such as Mary Carruthers's work on memory, Jody Enders's on theater and rhetoric, Bruce Holsinger's on the desire for polyphony, and Martin Irvine's on textual culture. I have also been encouraged by Charles Hallisey's characterizations of Buddhism as both a "translocal tradition" and a "transcultural phenomenon" in "Roads Taken and Not Taken in the Study of Theravāda Buddhism" (51).

14. The phrase is Chartier's. He argues that the shift from monastic learning to the urban school "changed everything," including "the method of reading, which ceased to be participation in the mystery of the Sacred Word, and became a regulated and hierarchized decoding of the letter *(littera),* the sense *(sensus),* and the doctrine *(sententia)*" (*Forms and Meanings,* 16–17).

15. In framing the text as negotiated meaning rather than as artifact, scholarship of the textual condition resonates strongly with anthropological and performance studies approaches to language as "a species of situated human communication" (Richard Bauman, *Verbal Art as Performance,* 8), exemplified by people like Clifford Geertz, Richard Bauman, and Victor Turner in anthropology and Richard Schechner, Elizabeth Fine, Diana Taylor, and Peggy Phelan in performance studies. My concern here is not with "performative" language (as defined by J. L. Austin and pursued by thinkers like Jacques Derrida and Judith Butler), though I do recognize and elucidate the rhetorical power of various tropes, metaphors, and figures in later chapters. Rather, my concern is with language (sutras and setsuwa, specifically) as used in a performance context (preaching).

16. Or, to invoke another metaphor, the concentrated mind (Jp: *isshin*) is analogous to a clean, blank writing surface, and the voice, as it intones the sutras, acts like a writing instrument, transcribing the words from the scroll onto the ledger of memory.

17. David Scott Kastan, *Shakespeare and the Book,* 117–18.

18. The phrase appears in the introduction to his *Inscription and Erasure: Literature and Written Culture from the Eleventh to the Eighteenth Century,* ix.

19. For treatments of setsuwa as folklore or oral literature, see Komine Kazuaki, Komatsu Kazuhiko, Kawada Junzō, Nishimura Satoshi, and Yamashita Kin'ichi. For the place of setsuwa in Japanese national literature see Konishi Jin'ichi. For its use as raw material for histories of people, places, and practices, see Rajyashree Pandey, *Writing and Renunciation in Medieval Japan: The Works of the Poet-Priest Kamo no Chōmei;* Laurel Rasplica Rodd, "Nichiren and Setsuwa"; Frederic Kotas "The Craft of Dying in Late Heian Japan"; and the work of Fukuda Akira, Furuhashi Nobuyoshi, Gokoji Tsutomu, Kikuchi Hiroki, Murakami Manabu, and Saeki Shin'ichi. For setsuwa and popular religious culture, see Hirota Tetsumichi, Nakai Katsumi, Satō Kenzō, and Shiba Kayono.

20. See Kyoko Motomichi-Nakamura, Edward Kamens, Yoshiko K. Dykstra, Marian Ury, and Robert Morrell.

21. For the impact of these continental forms on Japanese tales, see Yoshiko K. Dykstra, "The Japanese Setsuwa and the Indian Avadāna"; Robert Campany,

Strange Writing: Anomaly Accounts in Early Medieval China; and Donald Gjertson, *Miraculous Retribution: A Study and Translation of Tang Lin's Ming Pao Chi.*

22. Martin Irvine, *The Making of Textual Culture: 'Grammatica' and Literary Theory,* 15. For textual communities see Brian Stock, *The Implications of Literacy: Written Language and Models of Interpretation in the Eleventh and Twelfth Centuries.*

23. "Chanting and Liturgy," in Robert Buswell, Jr., *Encyclopedia of Buddhism,* 137.

24. For discussions of Buddhist liturgy, see Nagai Yoshinori, Fukuda Akira, and Satō Michiko. For excellent studies of sutra chanting as an aesthetic pursuit linked to "skilled preaching" (Jp: *nōsetsu*), see Shiba Kayono and Shimizu Masumi.

25. For the most part, preachers seem to have preferred to extemporize rather than to read from prepared notes. Dōgen's essays, some of which were delivered as spoken teachings to an assembly of his students, are one exception to this trend. In addition, whereas most recorded setsuwa are rough sketches or kernels of stories, the twelfth-century Japanese collection *Notes Taken While Listening to One Hundred Sessions of Sermons (Hyakuza Hōdan Kikigakishō)* is unusual in that it contains several examples of what seem to be entire sermons, transcribed more or less as delivered. For more on this collection, see chapter 2.

26. Occasionally, one sees the term *setsuwa* used in a very wide folkloric sense to indicate a common narrative that is broadly attested in numerous variant forms: for instance, the "Cinderella setsuwa" or the "Urashima Tarō setsuwa." For early analyses of setsuwa as a folkloric genre, see Saitō Kiyoe, Matsumura Takeo, Kawaguchi Hisao, Fujita Tokutarō, Kazamaki Keijirō, Katayose Masayoshi, Kunisaki Fumimaro, Nishio Kōichi, and Suzuki Tōzō. For a discussion of the origin and range of the term *setsuwa* in Japanese scholarship, see Komine Kazuaki, *Setsuwa no mori: chūsei no tengu kara Isoppu made,* 298–302; Hisamatsu Sen'ichi, *Shinpan Nihon bungakushi,* vol. 3, 195–96; and D. E. Mills, *A Collection of Tales from Uji: A Study and Translation of Uji Shūi Monogatari,* 1–4.

27. As translated by Stephen Miller and Patrick Donnelly, *The Wind from Vulture Peak: Origins of Buddhist Poetry in the Japanese Court Tradition.* The poem appears in the twelfth-century *Senzaishū* imperial poetry anthology. SNKBT 10: poem #1250.

28. For more on *yuya nenbutsu* and the role of *hijiri* in constructing public baths, see Nakao Takashi, *Chūsei no kanjin hijiri to shari shinkō,* 4 ff. Building baths was one of the activities in which *hijiri,* wandering Buddhist monks who commonly coordinated public works projects, often engaged. See Janet Goodwin, *Alms and Vagabonds: Buddhist Temples and Popular Patronage in Medieval Japan.*

29. See Goodwin, *Alms and Vagabonds,* 107–41, and John Kieschnick, *The Impact of Buddhism on Chinese Material Culture,* 199–219, for more on Buddhist bridge building. As Goodwin notes, explaining the popularity of these projects, "Efforts aimed simultaneously to save people's souls and to improve their welfare must have been more powerful in spreading Buddhism than those directed only toward the soul or toward the purse" (*Alms and Vagabonds,* 141).

30. Konishi Jin'ichi, *A History of Japanese Literature*, vol. 3, *The High Middle Ages*, 126.

31. Campany, *Strange Writing*, 3.

32. Ibid., 323. To an extent, even triply foreign, as Robert Buswell, Jr., reminds us, given that the first Japanese encounter with Buddhism came through a Korean envoy. See his *Currents and Countercurrents: Korean Influences on East Asian Buddhist Traditions*.

33. Alan Cole, *Text as Father: Paternal Seductions in Early Mahāyāna Buddhist Literature*, 9.

34. The phrase is Robert Morrell's, in *Sand and Pebbles (Shasekishū): The Tales of Mujū Ichien, A Voice for Pluralism in Kamakura Buddhism*.

35. Here I am invoking William LaFleur's suggestion that, for the purposes of literary and cultural studies, periods should be bounded not by politics and governmental developments, but rather by ideas and concepts, a "basic intellectual and religious *shape*" (emphasis in original) (*The Karma of Words: Buddhism and the Literary Arts in Medieval Japan*, 9).

36. Pandey, *Writing and Renunciation in Medieval Japan*, 1.

37. See Kuroda Toshio and Taira Masayuki. For two representative studies of medieval practices that span Heian and Kamakura and suggest that later praxes elaborated on earlier models, see Brian Ruppert on relic worship and Robert H. Sharf and Elizabeth Horton Sharf on icon veneration.

38. For more on the use of *jātaka* and *avadāna* in teaching the dharma in India, see Joel Tatelman, *The Glorious Deeds of Pūrna: A Translation and Study of the* Pūrnāvadāna, 4, and John Strong, *The Legend of King Aśoka*, 22; for their use in China, see Victor Mair, "Buddhism and the Rise of the Written Vernacular in East Asia," 713.

39. The phrase comes from Walt Whitman's poem "Out of the Cradle Endlessly Rocking" but aptly captures the classical Japanese metaphor offered by Kūkai (774–835), founder of the Japanese Shingon school and a foundational theoretician of word and text. In one of his essays positing the interpenetration of writing, sound, gesture, and absolute reality, he writes, "The mantras are the woof, the sacred mudras are the warp, and the *samādhi* is the shuttle; they weave the brocade of the ocean-like assembly [i.e., mandala] greatly admired by sentient beings" (as cited in Fabio Rambelli, *Buddhist Materiality: A Cultural History of Objects in Japanese Buddhism*, 118).

1. THE ONTOLOGY OF SUTRAS

1. Leon Hurvitz, *Scripture of the Lotus Blossom of the Fine Dharma (The Lotus Sutra), Translated from the Chinese of Kumārajīva*, 332; T 9.262.61a15–16. I refer to sutras by their shortest common name in English (e.g., the *Lotus Sutra*). Notes provide references to the *Taishō* canon, giving accession number, page, register, and lines. Thus T 9.262.61a15–16 refers to the fifteenth and sixteenth lines of the first

(a) register of page 61 of *Taishō* text number 262 (the *Lotus Sutra*), which can be found in volume 9.

2. Hurvitz, *Scripture of the Lotus Blossom*, 332; T 9.262.61a16–17.

3. Hurvitz, *Scripture of the Lotus Blossom*, 333, with minor changes; T 9.262 .61b4–5. Here and throughout this chapter I have standardized the terminology of sutra devotion (e.g., "forgets" and not Hurvitz's "suffers from the loss from memory"). I note these instances of standardization, along with slight alterations in phrasing, punctuation, and word order, as "minor changes" and explain more substantive changes in the footnotes. In cases where multiple alterations would have been necessary, either for accuracy or to preserve the standard vocabulary I develop in this chapter, I translate the passage myself, providing citations for alternate English translations that the reader may wish to consult for comparison.

4. Hurvitz, *Scripture of the Lotus Blossom*, 333–34; T 9.262.61a23–24.

5. See, respectively, Donald Lopez, "Inscribing the Bodhisattva's Speech: On the *Heart Sutra*'s Mantra"; Alan Cole, *Text as Father: Paternal Seductions in Early Mahāyāna Buddhism;* and David McMahan, "Orality, Writing, and Authority in South Asian Buddhism: Visionary Literature and the Struggle for Legitimacy in the Mahāyāna."

6. I borrow the term "mainstream Buddhism" from Jan Nattier, who argues that there was a "gradual emergence of the bodhisattva path [Mahāyāna], and of the literature associated with it, within the Mainstream Buddhism community" (*A Few Good Men: The Boddhisattva Path according to* The Inquiry of Ugra [Ugra-pariprcchā], 102).

7. Kenneth Chen, *Buddhism in China: A Historical Survey,* 12. One noteworthy exception to this trend is Gregory Schopen's entry on "Mahāyāna" in *Encyclopedia of Buddhism,* ed. Robert Buswell, Jr., 492–99. Schopen discusses at length our changing picture of early Indian Mahāyāna and notes, "The Mahāyāna may well have been either a collection of marginalized ascetic groups living in the forest, or groups of cantankerous and malcontent conservatives embedded in mainstream, socially engaged monasteries, all of whom continued pouring out pamphlets espousing their views and values, pamphlets that we now know as Mahāyāna sutras. We simply do not know" (494–95).

8. See Hirakawa Akira, "The Rise of Mahāyāna Buddhism and Its Relationship to the Worship of Stupas."

9. Paul Harrison, "Searching for the Origins of the Mahāyāna: What Are We Looking For?" 62. Sasaki Shizuka and Jan Nattier offer similar assessments of the monastic origins of the Mahāyāna and its slow emergence from within mainstream Indian Buddhist traditions. See also Jonathan Silk, "What, If Anything, Is Mahāyāna Buddhism? Problems of Definitions and Classifications."

10. "The Phrase *sa prthivīpradeśaś caityabhūto bhavet* in the *Vajracchedikā:* Notes on the Cult of the Book in Mahāyāna," in Gregory Schopen, *Figments and Fragments of Mahāyāna Buddhism in India: More Collected Papers,* 25–62.

11. Gregory Schopen, "The Mahāyāna and the Middle Period in Indian Buddhism: Through a Chinese Looking-Glass," 5.

12. Nattier, *A Few Good Men,* 185.

13. Here I pursue a suggestion made by Charles Hallisey, that Buddhist scholars should try shifting their point of intellectual focus, to "expect meaning to be produced in local circumstances rather than in the origins of the tradition," thus valuing the wide variety of Buddhist vernaculars and "creat[ing] a space for the study of the full range of Buddhist literature" ("Roads Taken and Not Taken in the Study of Theravāda Buddhism," 50).

14. This question was originally posed by F. W. Bateson in "Modern Bibliography and the Literary Artifact." James McLaverty rephrases the question and takes it up at length in "The Mode of Existence of Literary Works of Art: The Case of the Dunciad Variorum," 82 ff. See also Fabio Rambelli, "Materiality and Performativity of Sacred Texts," in *Buddhist Materiality: A Cultural History of Objects in Japanese Buddhism,* 88–128.

15. Illustrated versions of the *Heart Sutra* (known in Japanese as *esetsu Shinkyō*) ✓ began to appear during the Tokugawa period (1600–1868). A monk named Zenpachi, who was trained at Chūsonji in Hiraizumi, is credited with creating the first of these sometime between 1670 and 1690 for the purpose of teaching illiterate farmers in the mountainous areas of modern-day Iwate Prefecture. The rebus-like arrangement was used locally for some time before achieving wider popularity when it was published in Tachibana Nankei's (1753–1805) *Tōyūki* (*A Record of Travels in the East*) in 1797.

16. Thomas Cleary, *The Flower Ornament Scripture: A Translation of* The Avatamsaka Sutra, 1.

17. Pamela Waugh, *Metafiction: The Theory and Practice of Self-Conscious Fiction,* 2.

18. See Donald Lopez, "Authority and Orality in the Mahāyāna." Lopez describes the authors of Mahāyāna sutras as "usurp[ing]," "appropria[ting]," and "fictional[izing]" (25) pre-Mahāyānic narratives in order to create a legitimizing "conceit of orality" (21). For a list of the many aspects of doctrine that these techniques of appropriation threatened to overturn or revise, see 22–23.

19. Richard Gombrich ("How the Mahāyāna Began") and David McMahan ("Orality, Writing, and Authority in South Asian Buddhism") both suggest revelation as a potential source of Mahāyāna scripture. For "wily authors," see Cole, *Text as Father,* 1–23.

20. For an example of how the mechanism of entrustment can work smoothly, see the *Sutra of Meditation on the Buddha Amitāyus* (Jp: Amida). In this sutra, the Buddha, accompanied by Ānanda, appears before Queen Vaidehī, who has been imprisoned by her son. The sutra opens with a description of the setting and circumstances and, just before the sermon proper begins, Buddha says, "Ānanda, you must receive and keep the Buddha's words and widely proclaim them to the mul-

titude of beings" (Inagaki Hisao and Harold Stewart, *The Three Pure Land Sutras*, 78–79; T 12.365.341c18). When the sermon is over, Buddha and Ānanda fly through the air back to Vulture Peak, where Ānanda "fully expounds" the teaching for the assembly, who all rejoice to have heard the Buddha's words as spoken by Ānanda and ratified by Buddha (T 12.365.346b19–20). On "Thus have I heard," see Jonathan Silk "A Note on the Opening Formula of Buddhist Sūtras."

21. For another example of multiple entrustments, see the *Vimalakīrti Sutra*, in which one chapter is entrusted to the buddha Maitreya, with the bulk of the text (under two different names) entrusted to Ānanda.

22. T 12.374.377c24–26. For an alternate translation, see Yamamoto Kosho, *The Mahāyāna Mahāparinirvāna Sutra: A Complete Translation from the Classical Chinese Language in Three Volumes*, 54.

23. T 12.374.379b14–16. For an alternate translation, see Yamamoto, *The Mahāyāna Mahāparinirvāna Sutra*, 60.

24. T 12.374.428b8–12. For an alternate translation, see Yamamoto, *The Mahāyāna Mahāparinirvāna Sutra*, 263.

25. T 12.374.602a8–9. For an alternate translation, see Yamamoto, *The Mahāyāna Mahāparinirvāna Sutra*, 993.

26. Schopen (*Figments and Fragments of Mahāyāna Buddhism in India*, 26–32), and Nagao Gajin (*Yuimakyō wo yomu*, 25 ff.) offer early explorations of the ways in which Mahāyāna sutras simulate oral contexts as a literary trope. See also McMahan, "Orality, Writing, and Authority in South Asian Buddhism," 265, and, for a more forceful argument, Cole, *Text as Father*, 327.

27. Inagaki and Stewart, *The Three Pure Land Sutras*, 70, with minor changes; T 12.360.279a11–12.

28. Hurvitz, *Scripture of the Lotus Blossom*, 191–92; T 9.262.34a22–b2.

29. Burton Watson, *The Vimalakīrti Sutra*, 143; T 14.475.557a10–11. Rather than "wiping out," the term *danzen* indicates cutting, as in scraping down wooden blocks onto which sutras have been carved, thus effectively erasing them.

30. Yamamoto, *The Mahāyāna Mahāparinirvāna Sutra*, 239–40, with minor changes; T 12.374.421c26–422a3.

31. The *Nirvana Sutra* also describes an event in the distant past when Māra burned all the Mahāyāna scriptures in a great bonfire, and it accuses Brahmins of snatching charred fragments from the fire and inserting them into their own sacred texts (T 12.374.474a8–14).

32. Watson, *The Vimalakīrti Sutra*, 139, with minor changes; T 14.475.556b20–22. For a translation from the Tibetan, see Robert Thurman, *The Holy Teaching of Vimalakīrti: A Mahāyāna Scripture*, 98.

33. T 9.278.624a14–15. For an alternate translation, see Luis Gomez, "The Whole Universe as a Sutra," 112. Cleary, *The Flower Ornament Scripture* (1102–3), also translates a similar passage from a different Chinese version, T 279.10 .272c–273a1.

34. T 9.278.624a6–7.

35. For a critique of the slippery nature of the term "text," see D. C. Greetham, *Textual Scholarship: An Introduction,* 1 ff.

36. One should note that Buddhism considers portions of the "work" to be ineffable. See, for instance, José Ignacio Cabezón, *Buddhism and Language: A Study of Indo-Tibetan Scholasticism,* 78. Though I will be restricting my remarks here to the case of sutras, these general observations about the dual ontological modality of sacred text may open up interesting avenues for considering similar phenomena regarding Buddhist icons, which are at once specific material instantiations (a carving made of wood, for instance) and an embodiment of a cosmological being (Amida, for example). See Robert and Elizabeth Sharf, *Living Images: Japanese Buddhist Icons in Context,* and Rambelli, *Buddhist Materiality.*

37. Shillingsburg terms this a "document." For reasons that will become clear, I prefer the term "container," which is more sensitive to the metaphors and mechanics of Mahāyāna Buddhist textual culture.

38. Hurvitz, *Scripture of the Lotus Blossom,* 144–47; T 9.262.25a12–c6.

39. Buddhist cosmology maintains that the universe moves through repeating cycles of growth and decay called *kalpas.* The length of a *kalpa* might be likened to the amount of time it would take to move a mountain-sized pile of tiny mustard seeds, one seed at a time, to a place billions of miles distant.

40. The *Lotus Sutra* contains a similar story in its opening pages; see Hurvitz, *Scripture of the Lotus Blossom,* 14–15; T 9.262.4a24–b18. For an in-depth discussion of this scene, see Cole, *Text as Father,* 75–81.

41. The *Lotus Sutra* contains other hints that some of its versions are greatly more expanded than our own. In another of his former incarnations, Śākyamuni hears a voice in the sky that expounds to him "twenty thousand myriads of millions of gāthās" of the *Lotus Sutra,* as it had been preached by the buddha King of Imposing Sound (Hurvitz, *Scripture of the Lotus Blossom,* 281; T 9.262.51a3–5). Monks in medieval China and Japan were aware of this discrepancy and formulated a variety of theories, according to which multiple versions of a sutra might exist: a smaller one, transmitted in speech and then in writing to the inhabitants of this world, and one or more "expansive versions," which may or may not be stored elsewhere but are nevertheless not available to beings in this realm of existence. For more on this topic, see Rambelli, *Buddhist Materiality,* 115–17, and Ryūichi Abe, *The Weaving of Mantra: Kūkai and the Construction of Esoteric Buddhist Discourse,* 275 ff. As Abe notes, these versions are not distinct from one another, but are rather "mutually inclusive levels of the same sutra" (276).

42. T 12.374.529c1–3. For an alternate English translation, see Yamamoto, *The Mahāyāna Mahāparinirvāna Sutra,* 681.

43. T 12.374.540a18–19. For an alternate English translation, see Yamamoto, *The Mahāyāna Mahāparinirvāna Sutra,* 726.

44. The *Flower Ornament Sutra* abounds with visions of this sort in which count-

less buddhas or bodhisattvas, all sharing the same name, speak the same sutras in perfect unison to a multitude of different beings in widely disparate times and spaces.

45. See, for instance, the *Flower Ornament Sutra* (T 10.279.209b26) or the *Sutra of Immeasurable Life* (T 12.360.273a28).

46. Hurvitz, *Scripture of the Lotus Blossom,* 76, with minor changes; T 9.262 .15b10–12.

47. For a lively discussion of this phenomenon, see Cole, *Text as Father,* 124–30.

48. T 8.235.749b24–25. Compare Edward Conze's translation from the Sanskrit: "from [this sutra] has issued the utmost, right and perfect enlightenment of the Tathāgatas, Arhats, Fully Enlightened Ones, and from it have issued the Buddhas" (*Buddhist Wisdom Books, Containing* The Diamond Sutra *and* The Heart Sutra, 40).

49. René Wellek and Austin Warren, *Theory of Literature,* 138–39 and 144.

50. McLaverty, "The Mode of Existence of Literary Works of Art," 105.

51. Greetham, *Textual Scholarship,* 343.

52. Hurvitz, *Scripture of the Lotus Blossom,* 178; T 9.262.31b26–29.

53. Schopen, *Figments and Fragments of Mahāyāna Buddhism in India,* 25–62. As discussed earlier in this chapter, Schopen's thesis linking book culture to the *origins* of the Mahāyāna is an overstatement, and we should be wary of placing too much emphasis on it. Suffice it to say that something interesting, suggestive, and potentially fecund was happening in the structure and symbolism of Mahāyāna sutra literature as it developed in the early centuries of the Common Era on the Indian subcontinent, and that these possibilities—however they were or were not taken up in actual practice in India—provided rich ground for literary, ritualistic, and iconographic elaboration in medieval Japan.

54. Harrison, "Searching for the Origins of the Mahāyāna," 51.

55. While the *Lotus Sutra* anchors writing at the end of the sequence, its sequential location in the other sutras is much more volatile, with Pure Land sutras generally omitting the acts of writing or copying altogether. Additionally, all of the sutras mentioned here also include other forms of recommended textual engagement, though these are mentioned with less persistence and regularity. These other acts include understanding, contemplating, penetrating the meaning of, and practicing in accordance with the teachings, and also circumambulating, worshipping, revering, and making offerings to the sutra scroll.

56. As Stephen Teiser notes, many sources outline not five but ten methods of sutra devotion: "One of the Yogācāra treatises translated by Hsüan-tsang (602–64) states: 'Within this Great Vehicle there are ten methods. One is to write and copy. Two is to make offerings. Three is to give to others. Four is to listen attentively with a concentrated mind when others intone and read. Five is to unroll scriptures and read them oneself. Six is to receive and uphold. Seven is to explain properly the meaning of the text to others. Eight is to chant and intone. Nine is to think it over.

Ten is to cultivate the practice'" (*The Scripture on the Ten Kings and the Making of Purgatory in Medieval Chinese Buddhism*, 141). Although Japanese Buddhists did reference many of these other activities, throughout the medieval period popular literature like setsuwa typically referenced only five varieties of sutra devotion (Jp: *goshu hōshi*), which is, indeed, the term used in the setsuwa collection *A Collection of Treasures* (ca. 1180).

57. T 8.235.750b4–6. Compare Edward Conze's translation from the Sanskrit: "It is not difficult for me to accept and believe this discourse on Dharma when it is being taught. But those beings who will be in a future period, in the last time, in the last epoch, in the last 500 years, at the time of the collapse of the good doctrine, and who, O Lord, will take up this discourse on Dharma, bear it in mind, recite it, study it, illuminate it in full detail for others, these will be most wonderfully blest" (*Buddhist Wisdom Books*, 53).

58. T 8.235.750b11. Compare Edward Conze's rendering of the Sanskrit, "Most wonderfully blest will be those beings who, on hearing this Sutra, will not tremble, nor be frightened, or terrified" (*Buddhist Wisdom Books*, 53).

59. Hurvitz, *Scripture of the Lotus Blossom*, 29; T 9.262.7a9.

60. Watson, *The Vimalakīrti Sutra*, 120, with minor changes; T 14.475.553b5.

61. Cleary, *The Flower Ornament Scripture*, 1099; T 10.279.308c6–7.

62. Many sutras combine the character for "listen" with the character for "accept" to form a compound (Jp: *bunju*, meaning "receptive listening") that captures the sense of emotional preparation and spiritual confidence I have been discussing.

63. Hurvitz, *Scripture of the Lotus Blossom*, 180, rendering the last phrase literally (compared to Hurvitz's "and obey it without violation"); T 9.262.31c29–32a2.

64. Hurvitz, *Scripture of the Lotus Blossom*, 72, with minor changes; T 9.262.14c27–29.

65. This phrase appears, for instance, in the *Nirvana Sutra* (T 12.374.411a8) and several times in the *Lotus Sutra* (for example, Hurvitz, *Scripture of the Lotus Blossom*, 76; T 9.262.15b9). For lengthier discussions of sutras and the economy of gift giving, see Cole, *Text as Father*, 304–11.

66. For a discussion of this compound term (Ch: *shou chi*) with respect to a particular person (the monk Tao-chen) and a particular sutra (*The Scripture on the Ten Kings*), see Teiser, *The Scripture on the Ten Kings*, 138–51. Teiser notes the breadth of the semantic range but does not connect "accepting and keeping" in that particular instance to the act of memorization. For a discussion of the multivalence of the equivalent Sanskrit term *(dhāreti)*, see Natalie Gummer, "Articulating Potency: A Study of the *Suvarna(pra)bhāsottamasūtra*," 138 ff. For a useful parsing of "holding" as a multivalent term in medieval Japan, see Kikuchi Hiroki, "Jikkyōsha no genkei to chūseiteki tenkai," 1363–66.

67. Sutras also use the term *juji* to indicate upholding (accepting and keeping to) monastic vows. In this case the semantic range is much narrower and more eas-

ily defined because both the object being upheld (the rules) and the kind of person doing the upholding (a monk or nun) are much more stable than is the case with "upholding" a sutra.

68. Cleary, *The Flower Ornament Scripture,* 910, with minor changes; T 10.279 .243a8.

69. Cleary, *The Flower Ornament Scripture,* 818, with minor changes; T 10.279 .213b5.

70. Cleary, *The Flower Ornament Scripture,* 854 and 855, with minor changes; T 10.279.226c29 and 227a11.

71. T 10.279.345c24–25. For an alternate translation, see Cleary, *The Flower Ornament Scripture,* 1216.

72. T 10.279.373c22. For an alternate translation, see Cleary, *The Flower Ornament Scripture,* 1301.

73. T 12.374.472b28. For an alternate translation, see Yamamoto, *The Mahāyāna Mahāparinirvāna Sutra,* 444. The *Flower Ornament Sutra* and the *Lotus Sutra* also employ the term in the same way. At times the *Lotus Sutra* also indicates this kind of perfect memory by using the phrase *shikkai juji* (Jp), indicating the act of "completely accepting and holding all" of a sutra.

74. T 8.235.752b17–18. Compare Edward Conze from the Sanskrit: "Those who by my form did see me, / And those who followed me by voice / Wrong the efforts they engaged in, / Me those people will not see" (*Buddhist Wisdom Books,* 63).

75. T 8.235.752b28–29. Compare Conze: "As stars, a fault of vision, as a lamp, / A mock show, dew drops, or a bubble, / A dream, a lightning flash, or cloud, / So should one view what is conditioned" (*Buddhist Wisdom Books,* 68).

76. Cleary, *The Flower Ornament Scripture,* 318, with minor changes; T 10.279 .70c5.

77. Watson, *The Vimalakīrti Sutra,* 135, with minor changes; T 14.475 .555c22–23.

78. Watson, *The Vimalakīrti Sutra,* 145, with minor changes; T 14.475.557b7–9.

79. For more on *dhāranī* as the "grasp" of memory, see Paul Copp, "Notes on the Term 'Dhāranī' in Medieval Chinese Buddhist Thought," in which he suggests that "Future studies of [the] term [Jp: *juji;* Ch: *shouchi;* English "accept and hold"] might explore the extent to which the 'receiving and keeping' or 'upholding' (two of its common translations) of a text implies something more like its *absorption* within the person of the Buddhist in a way that echoes the 'grasp' of spiritual ideals displayed in the *Dhāranī* of the bodhisattva" (506).

80. Inagaki and Stewart, *The Three Pure Land Sutras,* 17, with several changes; T 12.360.268c3–4. Inagaki and Stewart compress a number of important terms in the passage, which ends "should not acquire eloquence and wisdom in upholding sutras and reciting and expounding them."

81. Hurvitz, *Scripture of the Lotus Blossom,* 15, with minor changes; T 12.262 .4b12–13.

82. T 12.374.548b9–10. For an alternate translation, see Yamamoto, *The Mahāyāna Mahāparinirvāna Sutra,* 763.

83. T 12.374.537b11–15. For an alternate translation, see Yamamoto, *The Mahāyāna Mahāparinirvāna Sutra,* 715.

84. Hurvitz, *Scripture of the Lotus Blossom,* 174, with minor changes; T 9.262 .30c9–12.

85. Hurvitz, *Scripture of the Lotus Blossom,* 204; T 9.262.36b17.

86. See, for instance, Hurvitz, *Scripture of the Lotus Blossom,* 216 (T 9.262 .38b18–19), which suggests that, even in an evil age, there are people who "when they have listened, shall be able to keep [or hold]; when they have kept shall be able to recite; when they have recited, shall be able to preach; and when they have preached, shall be able to write or cause others to write." There is some indication that Chinese translations of the sutras give more weight to the act of writing than do the Sanskrit texts on which they are based. Natalie Gummer notes, for instance, that Chinese translations of some passages from the *Sutra of Golden Radiance* (Jp: *Konkōmyōkyō,* T 663) explicitly extend merit to those who write or copy the sutras, whereas in the Sanskrit written sutras simply appear and the merit is to be gained through activities such as reading, reciting, and expounding. See her *Articulating Potency,* 199–202.

87. The *Nirvana Sutra* makes this claim (T 12.374.390a26). The *Flower Ornament Sutra* suggests that bodhisattvas are also "vessels of purity" (T 10.279.138a7–20).

88. Watson, *The Vimalakīrti Sutra,* 125, with minor changes; T 14.475.554a16, 23–24.

89. T 12.274.545b21 and 601c4. For an alternate translation, see Yamamoto, *The Mahāyāna Mahāparinirvāna Sutra,* 748 and 995. See also line 602a7 for a third usage of this same metaphor to describe Ānanda's capacious memory.

90. T 12.374.560c10–11. For an alternate translation, see Yamamoto, *The Mahāyāna Mahāparinirvāna Sutra,* 818. This passage counteracts the previous statement (T 12.374.419b3) that *icchantika* are "not dharma vessels" and therefore have no hope of aspiring to enlightenment.

91. Watson, *The Vimalakīrti Sutra,* 43–44; T 14.475.540c26–28.

92. T 9.262.35b17–18, 20. For an alternate translation, see Hurvitz, *Scripture of the Lotus Blossom,* 199–200.

93. Hurvitz, *Scripture of the Lotus Blossom,* 200–201; T 9.262.35c7.

94. T 12.374.399c2–3. For an alternate translation, see Yamamoto, *The Mahāyāna Mahāparinirvāna Sutra,* 145.

95. Hurvitz, *Scripture of the Lotus Blossom,* 288; T 9.262.52a22–27.

96. T 12.374.399b3. For an alternate translation, see Yamamoto, *The Mahāyāna Mahāparinirvāna Sutra,* 144.

97. The usual vow invokes the word *goji* (Jp), variously translated as above. For example, in the *Flower Ornament Sutra* a multitude of buddhas, all sharing the same name, vow to "protect and keep this teaching, so that all bodhisattvas of the future

who have not heard it will be able to hear it" (Cleary, *The Flower Ornament Scripture*, 413, with minor changes; T 10.279.92a15–16).

98. T 12.374.370a18, 25. For an alternate translation, see Yamamoto, *The Mahāyāna Mahāparinirvāna Sutra*, 22.

99. Hurvitz, *Scripture of the Lotus Blossom*, 202 and 291; T 12.262.36a7–10, 52c11–12.

100. *A Wondrous Record of Immediate Karmic Retribution* 2:31 and *Tales from Times Now Past* 12:2 tell of a young girl born with a club fist. When she finally opens it at age seven, she is found to have been clenching a relic in answer to her parents' long-forgotten vow to build a pagoda around just such an object. *A Wondrous Record of Immediate Karmic Retribution* 3:18 and *Tales from Times Now Past* 14:26 relate the fate of a scripture copyist who has sex with a female pilgrim in the sutra hall and dies immediately afterward. *Uji Shūi Monogatari (A Gleaning of Tales from Uji)* 6 concerns a *hijiri* who claims to have "cut off the root of desire" (his penis). On closer inspection he is found to have merely bound it tightly and, when it is released, it rises in a towering erection "tap tapping against his belly" (NKBT 27: 62). *A Wondrous Record of Immediate Karmic Retribution* 3:19, *The Three Jewels* 2:4, and *Miracles of the Lotus Sutra* 98 concern the "Lump Nun" of Higo Province, who was born with a miraculous ability to memorize sutras, a skill that at least partially offsets her equally miraculous lack of a vagina.

2. LOCATING *SETSUWA* IN PERFORMANCE

1. Satō Akio, *Hyakuza hōdan kikigakishō*, 136.

2. For a general discussion of the popularity of Buddhist religious services in the medieval period, see Konishi Jin'ichi, *A History of Japanese Literature*, vol. 3, *The High Middle Ages*, 117–36 and 314–49. Gomi Fumihiko, Gorai Shigeru, Hirota Tetsumichi, Komine Kazuaki, Ikegami Jun'ichi, and Murogi Mitarō variously explore the "place" (Jp: *ba*) of sermonizing in medieval Japan as an epistemological concept, as an architectural locale, as a performance, and as an effect of orality. Margaret Childs examines the overlap between sensuality and sermon rhetoric in her "Kyōgen Kigo: Love Stories as Buddhist Sermons."

3. As one indication, journals publishing setsuwa scholarship include *Kokubungaku kaishaku to kanshō* (National literature: interpretation and appreciation), *Kokugo kokubun* (National language, national literature), and *Kokubungaku tōsa* (National literature survey). The modern academic tendency to see literature in terms of the development of cultural and national distinctiveness is a product of the intersection of eighteenth- and nineteenth-century Japanese nativist (Jp: *kokugaku*) philosophy and the creation of a modern academic system in the nineteenth and twentieth centuries. See Peter Nosco, H. D. Harootunian, and Yoda Tomiko.

4. Joel Tatelman, *The Glorious Deeds of Pūrṇa: A Translation and Study of the Pūrṇāvadāna*, 33.

5. John Strong, *The Legend of King Aśoka*, 22.

6. Tatelman, *The Glorious Deeds of Pūrṇa*, 8. For an analysis of the underlying structure and philosophy of *jātaka*, see Hikata Ryūshō.

7. On the cosmological aspects of *zhi guai*, see Robert Campany, *Strange Writing: Anomaly Accounts in Early Medieval China*.

8. I follow Donald Gjertson in seeing Chinese "anomaly accounts" (also translated "strange tales") as an important mediating genre between Indian "karmic biographies" and Japanese "explanatory tales." See also Itō Chikako, and Yoshiko Dykstra, "The Japanese *Setsuwa* and the Indian *Avadāna*."

9. As far as I am aware, there is no comprehensive overview of setsuwa in any Western language. Konishi Jin'ichi's discussion of setsuwa vis-à-vis the classical genres of *waka* (Japanese poetry) and *monogatari* (prosimetric narratives, that is, prose narratives organized around poetic interludes) is perhaps the best survey and may be found in *A History of Japanese Literature*, vol. 2, *The Early Middle Ages*. For topical treatments, see Lorinda Kiyama; Thomas Howell, Jr.; R. Keller Kimbrough, *Preachers, Poets, Women, and the Way: Izumi Shikibu and the Buddhist Literature of Medieval Japan*, 28–51; and Michelle Li, *Ambiguous Bodies: Reading the Grotesque in Japanese Setsuwa Tales*, 14–51. In Japanese, see the works of Komine Kazuaki, Kojima Takayuki, Iwamoto Yutaka, Masuda Katsumi, Uematsu Shigeru, Honda Giken, and Nishio Kōichi. *Setsuwa no gensetsu*, edited by Honda et al., is an excellent critical introduction to setsuwa, its mediate location between oral and written traditions, and its relations to other medieval genres.

10. Kojima Takayuki, "*Kankyo no Tomo* Kaisetsu," SNKBT 40: 543.

11. Heijōkyō (modern-day Nara) was the capital of Japan from 710 until 784. The capital was moved, perhaps in part to weaken the influence that the powerful monasteries had on imperial politics. For more on Kyōkai, see Fukushima Kōichi; Hashikawa Tadashi; Takase Shōgon, *Nihon genpō zen'aku ryōiki*, 19–23; and Kyoko Motomichi-Nakamura, *Miraculous Stories from the Japanese Buddhist Tradition: The* Nihon Ryōiki *of the Monk Kyōkai*, 3–14.

12. Motomichi-Nakamura also provides a complete translation of the collection into English, and Gjertson gives a translation of the *Ming Pao Chi*. Kyōkai was also familiar with the *Panjo Yenji*, compiled by Meng Hsien-chung in 718. See also Konishi Jin'ichi, *A History of Japanese Literature*, vol. 1, *The Archaic and Ancient Ages*, 425–27. On the textual history of the *Nihon Genpō Zen'aku Ryōiki*, see Amemiya Shōji, Itabashi Tomoyuki, Koizumi Michi, and Ikeda Kikan. For Chinese sources, see Tokushi Yūshō, Yagi Tsuyoshi, and Donald Gjertson.

13. The restrictions were defied by a handful of wandering monks and nuns, the earliest of whom was Gyōki (668–749). Nemoto Seiji's *Nara jidai no sōryo to shakai* provides an excellent history of the tradition of self-ordained monks and nuns (Jp: *shidosō*), who at times were beaten with canes, stripped of their robes, and exiled for their attentions to the physical and spiritual needs of the lower social classes. Following the eighth century, the state lost the battle to restrain self-

ordained monks and nuns, and restrictions gradually loosened. Ryūichi Abe discusses the impact that the state regulations had on "severely limit[ing] direct contact between the ordained and the masses" (79) in *The Weaving of Mantra: Kūkai and the Construction of Esoteric Buddhist Discourse,* 76–83.

14. For more on Minamoto no Tamenori see Okada Mareo. For textual history, including sources and structure, see Mizuta Norihisa, Yasuda Naomichi, Mori Masato, Kasuga Kazuo, Izumoji Osamu, and Nakagawa Chūjin.

15. The idea of creating a setsuwa collection for the purpose of introducing an upper-class and recently tonsured woman to the Buddhist path seems to have been a relatively common one. The *Kohon setsuwashū* (*A Collection of Setsuwa from Old Books,* probably created by 1180, but unknown outside the family until 1949) and *A Companion in Solitude* (1222), of which more below, also perform this function. For a lengthier introduction to *The Three Jewels,* including its manuscripts and its historical context, see Edward Kamens's *The Three Jewels: A Study and Translation of Minamoto Tamenori's* Sanbōe. Kamens also provides a translation of the collection into English.

16. For more on the textual history, authorship, and historical context of *Miracles of the Lotus Sutra,* see Akashi Mitsumaro, Kagamishima Hiroyuki, Kurobe Michiyoshi, Uematsu Shigeru, and Yamane Kenkichi.

17. For a lengthier introduction to and a full translation of *Miracles of the Lotus Sutra,* see Yoshiko Dykstra, *Miraculous Tales of the Lotus Sutra from Ancient Japan:* The Dainihonkoku Hokekyō Kenki *of Priest Chingen.*

18. Other extant twelfth-century setsuwa collections include *Gōdanshō* (*Notes of Conversations with Ōe no Masafusa,* 1111, which includes one section on Buddhism), *Konjaku Monogatari* (*Tales from Times Now Past,* by 1120?), *Uchigikishū* (*A Collection Written While Listening,* ca. 1111–34, author unknown), the *Kohon Setsuwashū* (*A Collection of Setsuwa from Old Books,* by 1180?), the *Hōbutsushū* (*A Collection of Treasures,* ca. 1180?), the *Senjūshō* (*Collected Notes on Selected Tales,* ca. 1183–99?, author unknown), and the *Uji Shūi Monogatari* (*A Gleaning of Tales from Uji,* 1190–1242, author unknown). Future archival research may well reveal more texts from this general time period.

19. "*Za*" indicates a single "seated" session. Although extended sermonizing events like this one often featured two daily sessions, internal evidence from the collection indicates there was only one daily gathering.

20. Because of its fairly recent rediscovery, scholarship on *One Hundred Sessions of Sermons* is not as plentiful as it is for other collections. Yamagishi and Satō's studies are foundational. See Mori Masato and Kikuya Ryōichi for more on the oral and performance contexts of the *Hyakuza* sermonizing event.

21. Marian Ury, *Tales of Times Now Past: Sixty-Two Stories from a Medieval Japanese Collection,* 1. W. Michael Kelsey theorizes that the internal organization of each volume follows conventions of poetic linking in his "*Konjaku Monogatarishū:* Toward an Understanding of Its Literary Qualities."

22. For more on the textual history, sources, and authorship of *Tales from Times Now Past*, see Matsuo Hiroshi, Andō Naotarō, Yamane Kenkichi, Robert Brower, Ikegami Jun'ichi, Komine Kazuaki, and Katayose Masayoshi.

23. See his discussion of the collection in SNKBT 40: 516–18.

24. See Koizumi Hiroshi, *Hōbutsushū: chūsei koshahon sanshu* and *Koshōhon Hōbutsushū*, reprised by Yamada Shōzen in SNKBT 40: 530–35. For further information on the authorship and textual history of this collection, see Tachibana Sumitaka, Chiba Shōgen, Uryū Tōshō, and Atsumi Kaoru.

25. On *A Collection of Spiritual Awakenings*, see the scholarly survey by Hayashi Masahiko et al. For more on Kamo no Chōmei and his authorial activities, see Yamada Shōzen and Furuhashi Tsuneo, "*Hosshinshū* shiron: Kamo no Chōmei bannen no chosaku to shinkyō." Takao Minoru, Iwata Taijō, Kifuji Saizō, and Morishita Yōji provide discussions of the text's structure and its changes over time. For information on cultural and historical contexts, including the relation between the collection and public preaching, see Takao Minoru; Imamura Mieko; and Furuhashi Tsuneo, "Kamo no Chōmei, *Hosshinshū* ni okeru 'hosshin' to 'ōjō.'"

26. For further discussion of the authorship, historical context, and textual history of *A Companion in Solitude*, see Hashimoto Shinkichi, Nagai Yoshinori, Kobayashi Yasuharu, Hirabayashi Moritoku, and Harada Kōzō.

27. According to tradition, women are faced with five obstructions that are inherent to their gender. The five obstructions, or "five obstacles" (Jp: *goshō*), have to do with the impossibility of achieving rebirth directly from a female form into any of five higher physical forms, including that of a buddha. Technically speaking, a woman must first experience the human, male form before she can gain entry to any of these five, higher paths.

28. For an English translation of the former and a summary of the latter, see Robert Morrell, *Sand and Pebbles (Shasekishū): The Tales of Mujū Ichien, A Voice for Pluralism in Kamakura Buddhism*, 146–47 and 188.

29. Konishi Jin'ichi, *A History of Japanese Literature*, vol. 3, 316. See also Sekiyama Kazuo, *Sekkyō no rekishi: bukkyō to wagei*.

30. See Morrell, *Sand and Pebbles (Shasekishū)*, 42–44.

31. For a more in-depth discussion of the cultural context, textual history, and authorship of *A Collection of Sand and Pebbles*, see Andō Naotarō, *Setsuwa to haikai no kenkyū*, 131–209; Kobayashi Tadao; Kumahara Masao; Robert Morrell; Sakurai Yoshirō; and Watanabe Tsuyana.

32. Komatsu Kazuhiko, "Setsuwa no keisei to hensen," 34.

33. Komine Kazuaki, *Setsuwa no mori: chūsei no tengu kara Isoppu made*, 309.

34. Komine Kazuaki, "Setsuwa no ronri: hanashi no shōjin to isō," 40.

35. Komatsu Kazuhiko, "Setsuwa no keisei to hensen," 30; Satō Akira, "Enzuru shutai: *Uji shūi monogatari* no hyōgen kikō," 46.

36. Komine Kazuaki, *Chūsei setsuwa no sekai wo yomu*, 38.

37. See chapters 46 and 47, "Beneath the Oak" and "Trefoil Knots," for the full

narrative. Edward Seidensticker, *The Tale of Genji,* 799–871. Komine also employs the sexual conquest metaphor in his *Setsuwa no mori,* 146 and 310.

38. Paul Zumthor, *Speaking of the Middle Ages,* 22.

39. Ibid., 41–44.

40. Ibid., 81.

41. Sarah Kay, "Analytical Survey 3: The New Philology," 304.

42. The idea of ruminating on a religious text or incantation is also a recurrent image in medieval Christian writings. Scholar and Benedictine priest Jean Leclercq has written of the link between "aural memory" and the "mastication of divine words" in medieval Christian practice. Similarly, he has described the "deep impregnation with the words of Scripture" in which such rumination results (*The Love of Learning and the Desire for God: A Study of Monastic Culture,* esp. 72–75). Some contemporary Japanese efforts to increase sutra-reading activity among the laity have likewise seized on the metaphor of reading as chewing, as in Kamada Shōken's *Okyō wo tabeyō (1): Dokyō wa shisha no tame dewanai* (On eating sutras: reading the sutras isn't for the deceased).

43. Vimalakīrti services were often held at temples that took as their chief devotional object an image of the Yakushi buddha, the buddha of medicine. See Matsuno Junji, *Bukkyō gyōji to sono shisō.*

44. Leon Hurvitz, *Scripture of the Lotus Blossom of the Fine Dharma (The Lotus Sutra), Translated from the Chinese of Kumārajīva,* 101.

45. SNKBT 3: 106, poem 2789.

46. NKBZ 52:20. Mujū repeats this figuration of his text as a marital go-between in his concluding remarks (615).

47. See the sermons from the third and eighth days of the Third Month (Satō, *Hyakuza hōdan kikigakishō,* 94 and 102).

48. SNKS 133–36. To conclude the story, the huntsman-novice goes to a nearby mountain temple and, from there, to a west-facing cliff by the edge of the sea. Refusing any food, he shouts a greeting to Amida and then sits to wait for his answer. When a group of monks goes to check on him some days later, they find him still seated there, a blue lotus flower growing from the corpse's tongue. For other versions of this story, see *Tales from Times Now Past* 19: 14 and the final volume of *A Collection of Treasures,* 343–45.

49. It was customary at the time to give leftover food offerings to beggars after the service's completion.

50. All of the setsuwa in section 6 of *A Collection of Sand and Pebbles* treat the topic of preaching (NKBZ 52: 313–50). For more on the use of setsuwa in medieval preaching, see Kawaguchi Hisao.

51. As described by Gokoji Tsutomu, drawing on material from the courtier diaries *Gyokuyōki* and *Meigetsuki,* in his "Setsuwa bungaku ni arawareta Agui-ryū: Chōken to Seikaku wo chūshin ni," 136. For more on the Agui school, see Shimizu

Yūshō and Lorinda Kiyama, as well as Nagai Yoshinori and Kiyomizu Yūsei's edited volume *Agui shōdōshū.*

52. From this point on I will summarize the less formal version of events, which is what Shinjō does, providing occasional comments about which sections of the liturgy may be entrusted to other celebrants, if present.

53. *Hōsokushū,* 495.

54. Ibid., 497.

3. DECOMPOSING BODIES, COMPOSING TEXTS

1. Peggy Phelan, *Mourning Sex: Performing Public Memories,* 11–12.

2. Peggy Phelan, *Unmarked: the Politics of Performance,* 148.

3. Caroline Walker Bynum makes a similar argument regarding medieval Christianity in *Fragmentation and Redemption: Essays on Gender and the Human Body in Medieval Religion:* "The twelfth and thirteenth centuries in western Europe saw renewed debate over dozens of theological matters . . . in which the relationship of part to whole is crucial, and a new emphasis on miracles . . . in which bodies are the mediators between earth and heaven. It was a period in which the overcoming of partition and putrefaction—either through reunion of parts into a whole or through assertion of part *as part* to *be* the whole—was the image of paradise" (13).

4. For *kyōgen kigo,* see Nagai Giken, "Kyōgen kigo ni tsuite"; Margaret Childs, "Kyōgen Kigo: Love Stories as Buddhist Sermons"; Michele Marra, *The Aesthetics of Discontent: Politics and Reclusion in Medieval Japanese Literature;* and William LaFleur, *The Karma of Words: Buddhism and the Literary Arts in Medieval Japan.* For *waka soku darani,* see Yamada Shōzen, "Waka soku darani kan no tenkai"; and R. Keller Kimbrough, "Reading the Miraculous Power of Japanese Poetry: Spells, Truth Acts, and a Medieval Buddhist Poetics of the Supernatural." For *sokushin jōbutsu,* see Yoshito Hakeda, *Kūkai: Major Works, Translated, With an Account of His Life and a Study of His Thought;* and Abe Ryūichi *The Weaving of Mantra: Kūkai and the Construction of Esoteric Buddhist Discourse.* For *hongaku shisō,* see Jacqueline Stone, *Original Enlightenment and the Transformation of Medieval Buddhism.*

5. Peggy Phelan, *Unmarked,* 148.

6. The metaphor appears, for instance, in the *Lotus Sutra* (T 9.262.60b1) and the *Nirvana Sutra* (T 12.374.498c26).

7. Michele Marra, "The Development of Mappō Thought in Japan, Parts I & II," 39.

8. As in the *Vimalakīrti Sutra,* T 14.475.539b14.

9. *Discourses on the Greater Wisdom Sutra* (Sk: *Mahāprajñāpāramitaśāstra;* Jp: *Daichidoron*)—translated into Chinese by Kumārajīva in 402–5 and attributed to Nāgārjuna (ca. 150–250?)—and the Chinese Tendai patriarch Zhiyi's (538–97)

Great Calming and Contemplation (Ch: *Mohe zhiguan;* Jp: *Makashikan*), ca. 594, were the two key textual vectors through which *fujōkan*, as a literary theme and a spiritual praxis, entered Japanese culture. Japanese sources typically reference either one or both of these texts.

10. See Amino Yoshihiko et al., *Chūsei no tsumi to batsu.*

11. He cites Zhiyi's (538–97) *Great Calming and Contemplation* (Ch: *Mohe zhiguan;* Jp: *Makashikan*) and Genshin's (942–1017) hugely influential *Essentials for Rebirth in the Pure Land* (Jp: *Ōjō yōshū*) before eventually quoting a passage from the *Diamond Sutra* to the effect that "Who seeks me in visible form / or searches for me in sound / travels a false path / and will not be able to see the Thus Come One" (T 8.235.752a17–18).

12. Yoshiko K. Dykstra, *Miraculous Tales of the Lotus Sutra from Ancient Japan: The Dainihonkoku Hokekyō Kenki of Priest Chingen,* 3. Setsuwa on the theme of *surikuyō* are fairly common. For an instance of *surikuyō* in which a copy of the *Lotus Sutra* transforms an ex-monk from the form of a snake, affecting his rebirth in Amida's Western Paradise, see *Miracles of the Lotus Sutra* 7. In a rather typical case, *A Wondrous Record of Immediate Karmic Retribution* 3:9, a man's dead wife begs him to copy sutras on her behalf to lessen her suffering in hell. See also *A Companion in Solitude* 2:6, in which a deceased woman's hair is offered to defray the costs of copying a sutra.

13. The tale also appears one hundred years earlier in *Tales from Times Now Past* of ca. 1120 (tale 19:2), as well as in the thirteenth-century collection *Uji Shūi Monogatari (A Gleaning of Tales from Uji)* 4:7.

14. In classical Japanese court society, women of rank were usually seen only by other women or by related males who had not yet achieved sexual maturity. Men therefore frequently became attracted to women based on attributes other than their physical appearance, such as their ability to compose poetry or play an instrument, their scent or fragrance, or their calligraphy.

15. For a similar scene from classical Japanese literature, see chapter 25 of *The Tale of Genji,* in which Genji finally succeeds in allowing his adoptive daughter's suitor to see her face by sneaking lightning bugs into her room, their gentle glow suddenly lighting up her face. Genji has planned the surprise, thinking: "Now he [the suitor] would see, and be genuinely excited. Genji would not have gone to such trouble if she had in fact been his daughter. It all seems rather perverse of him" (Seidensticker, *The Tale of Genji,* 432). Chapter 30 of the same *monogatari* describes one of Genji's son's early sexual encounters as he suddenly thrusts his hand behind the woman's screens, grabbing the hem of her robe (484).

16. Hirota Tetsumichi, *Chūsei bukkyō setsuwa no kenkyū,* 128–29. For more on the titillation of confessional detail and the fear that specificity might lead to new sin, see Allen Frantzen's work on Middle English penitents in *Before the Closet: Same-Sex Love from* Beowulf *to* Angels in America.

17. See the discussion of *kaimami* in chapter 2.

18. Elizabeth Wilson, "The Female Body as a Source of Horror and Insight in Post-Ashokan Indian Buddhism," 93.

19. For an extended study of the ambivalently sexual bodies of orators in the Christian tradition, see Claire Waters, *Angels and Earthly Creatures: Preaching, Performance and Gender in the Later Middle Ages*.

20. Fujimoto Akira, "Aiyoku to fujōkan: *Hosshinshū* to *Kankyo no Tomo* no hikaku," 14. See Margaret Childs on love stories as Buddhist sermons. Classical and medieval Buddhist rites of confession also provided fodder for early modern satirists such as Ihara Saikaku (1642–93), who incorporated highly detailed spoofs of "love confession" (Jp: *iro zange*) into erotic prose narratives. For example, in a clear satire of classical tales of visits to mountain-dwelling sages (Jp: *hijiri*), Saikaku's *A Woman Who Loved Love* (Jp: *Kōshoku Ichidai Onna*, whose title could be rendered more playfully as *A One-Woman Love Machine*) features a group of young men who make a pilgrimage into the mountains to find a reclusive older woman. They beseech her to enlighten them on the topic of sex, a desire that she indulges to the fullest with a "confession" of her young and lustful ways. For more on Saikaku's adaptations of setsuwa, see Gotō Kōzen and Munemasa Iso'o.

21. These false preachers earn Mujū's scorn throughout *A Collection of Sand and Pebbles*, and he devotes much of book six to calling out their faults. Interestingly, "false preaching" (Jp: *jamyō seppō*) may have been a term of Mujū's own coining; the more standard phrase would have been "impure preaching" (Jp: *fujō seppō*). See Nakamura Hajime, *Kōsetsu bukkyōgo daijiten*, "fujō seppō" (1442) and "jamyō seppō" (748).

22. Phelan, *Mourning Sex*, 11–12.

23. Hurvitz, *Scripture of the Lotus Blossom of the Fine Dharma (The Lotus Sūtra), Translated from the Chinese of Kumārajīva*, 193; T 9.262.34b17–18.

24. Ohnuma Reiko, "Dehadāna: The 'Gift of the Body' in Indian Buddhist Narrative Literature," 309. See also John Strong, "The Transforming Gift: An Analysis of Devotional Acts of Offering in Buddhist 'Avadāna' Literature."

25. Hurvitz, *Scripture of the Lotus Blossom*, 195, with minor changes; T 9.262 .34b25–29.

26. The *Vimalakīrti Sutra* compares the body to a cluster of foam, a bubble, a flame, the leaf of a plantain, a phantom, a dream, a shadow, an echo, a drifting cloud, and lightning (T 14.475.539b15–21). Kamo no Chōmei, author of *A Collection of Spiritual Awakenings*, opens the most famous of his works, *An Account of My Hut (Hōjōki)*, with the image of foam gathering and dispersing on the surface of flowing water, a metaphor that he uses to describe humans and their habitations.

27. Here we see the motifs of *fujōkan* (decomposition) and *shashin* (bodily self-sacrifice) working toward the same ends. What the king has done in the Ksānti tale essentially is to accelerate the process of bodily decay. The whole episode stems from sexual jealousy and, in this case, the setsuwa simply divides the painted beauty and the desecrated corpse into two bodies (the pleasure women in the grove and the

hacked-apart sage) that exist side by side, rather than presenting them as before-and-after versions of the same being.

28. SNKBT 31: 20. The seven enlightened states are discretion in selecting proper doctrines, right effort, joy in practicing the proper doctrines, cheerfulness and physical relaxation, rejection of attachment to objects, concentration, and tranquility. The seven illusions are two kinds of craving or desire, anger, pride, ignorance, possession of false views, and doubt.

29. In a variation on the motif, a disciple may offer to serve as the physical proxy for his ill teacher, combining the trope of self-sacrifice with the natural process of decay found in *fujōkan* narratives. In this case the setsuwa ends with a confirmation of a different sort. Rather than identifying the willing sacrifice as a bodhisattva soon to become a buddha, he is identified as a "dharma vessel." See *A Collection of Spiritual Awakenings* 6:1 and *Tales from Times Now Past* 19:24.

30. "Minobusan gosho," *Shōwa teihon Nichiren shōnin ibun*, 2: 1916. Nichiren takes the story from *Discourses on the Greater Wisdom Sutra* (Sk: *Mahāprajñā-pāramitā śāstra;* Jp: *Daichidoron*).

31. The *Brahma Net Sutra* and the *Nirvana Sutra* contain similar passages, but, given Nichiren's reference to Kāśyapa, it is probably the *Nirvana Sutra* that he has in mind here.

32. "Minobusan gosho," 2: 1916. For a full English translation, see Laurel Rasplica Rodd, *Nichiren: Selected Writings,* 158 ff. On Nichiren and his concept of reading with the body, see Ruben Habito, "Bodily Reading of the *Lotus Sutra:* Understanding Nichiren's Buddhism."

33. For letters in which Nichiren makes this claim specific, see Rodd, *Nichiren,* 123 and 109.

34. At least, these acts were not emulated with much success. Setsuwa collections contain a number of stories about people who vowed to "give their body"—for instance, through drowning or self-immolation—but whose resolve faltered at the last moment. See *A Collection of Sand and Pebbles* 4:7 and 4:8 for two typical examples.

35. Nishiguchi Junko, "Death and Burial of Women of the Heian High Aristocracy," 420. See also entries in the courtier's diary *Chūyūki,* which references similar transcriptions on the following dates: 1130.6.34, 1136.7.15, and 1137.7.20.

36. Willa Jane Tanabe, *Paintings of the Lotus Sutra,* 56 ff. See also John Kieschnick, "Blood Writing in Chinese Buddhism."

37. Tanabe, *Paintings of the Lotus Sutra,* 56.

38. SNKBT 40: 363. See also *A Collection of Spiritual Awakenings* 4:9, which uses "grinding the heart and liver" as a metaphor for devotional sincerity (SNKS 189). Hymn 59 in Shinran's (1173–1262) *Shōzōmatsu wasan* likewise makes use of this trope as a metaphor for devotion: "The benevolence of the [Buddha's] great compassion, / even if we must crush our bodies it should be returned in gratitude. / The benevolence of masters and teachers, / even if we must break our bones, should be returned in gratitude" (59).

39. Mujū Ichien, compiler of *A Collection of Sand and Pebbles,* includes a much-truncated version of this story in section three of his *Zōtanshū (A Collection of Casual Digressions).*

40. Katherine Ulrich has noticed a similar link in Vedic practice and South Asian literature. She argues that "dismemberment is often a response to fragmentation and can serve as a means—for those both inside and outside the tradition—of moving between different registers: the corporeal, social, textual, theological, and ritual" ("Divided Bodies: Corporeal and Metaphorical Dismemberment and Fragmentation in South Asian Religions," 3).

41. On the poems' authorship, see Nakamura Tanio, "Kusōshi emaki no seiritsu." On *fujōkan* motifs in art and poetry, see Kanda Fusae, "Behind the Sensationalism: Images of a Decaying Corpse in Japanese Buddhist Art."

42. SNKBT 40: 409. Kōbō Daishi is Kūkai's posthumous title. In translating to Japanese Keisei has made some minor changes, none of which affect the sense of the verse.

43. This is but one of several similar systems of appellation for the nine stages. For more see Sakai Shirō, "Kōbō Daishi kusōkan ni tsuite"; and Fusae, "Behind the Sensationalism."

44. The three vehicles (Sk: *śrāvaka*) are the three ways of reaching enlightenment, namely by hearing the Buddha's teachings directly, by studying and reaching understanding on one's own, and by relying on assistance from advanced beings such as bodhisattvas.

45. The eight torments are birth, old age, sickness, death, separation from what we love, meeting with what we hate, unattained ends, and all the ills of the five *skandhas* (form, emotion, image, memory, and thought).

46. The six sense organs are the eyes, ears, nose, tongue, skin, and consciousness.

47. The four elements are the aforementioned earth, water, fire, and air.

48. Michael Riffaterre, "The Mind's Eye: Memory and Textuality," 33.

49. The specific term (Jp: *dōji*) typically refers to a child who has entered the temple and may be responsible for some menial duties but who has not yet taken the tonsure. By extension the term can also indicate either a monk who is particularly youthful in appearance or simply a boy.

50. Minamoto no Tamenori also includes this past-life story of the Buddha in the first volume of *The Three Jewels,* following the section on the perfection of virtues. As in the sutra, the boy begs the demon to complete the verse, saying, "Having heard half of this verse feels to me like seeing only half the moon or gaining only half a jewel. . . . I beg you: tell me the rest, all the way to the end" (SNKBT 31: 40). At the demon's prompting the boy explains his reasoning as follows: "Eventually, this body will surely die without my having been able to accomplish even a single act of merit. Today, for the purpose of the law, I will cast off this dirty, filthy body, knowing that I will become a buddha, attaining a pure and wonderful body.

It is like throwing away an earthenware vessel in exchange for a vessel made of jewels" (SNKBT 31: 42).

51. Jacques Derrida, "The Law of Genre," as translated by Stephen Barker in *The Act of Literature*, 223. The French could also be read as a command: "Do not mix genres!"

52. Ibid., 227–28.

53. Riffaterre, "The Mind's Eye," 30.

54. Ibid.

55. Ibid., 33.

56. Ibid., 36.

4. TEXTUAL TRANSUBSTANTIATION AND THE PLACE OF MEMORY

1. Miriam Gill, "Preaching and Image: Sermons and Wall Paintings in Later Medieval England," 155.

2. Jeffrey Hamburger, "The Visual and the Visionary: The Image in Late Medieval Monastic Traditions," 166, 162.

3. Caroline Walker Bynum, *Fragmentation and Redemption: Essays on Gender and the Human Body in Medieval Religion*, 80. Like Gill and Hamburger, Walker Bynum is concerned with medieval European Christianity. Several of the essays in Robert and Elizabeth Sharf's *Living Images: Japanese Buddhist Icons in Context* make similar arguments with respect to Buddhist icons in Japan.

4. Leon Hurvitz, *Scripture of the Lotus Blossom of the Fine Dharma (The Lotus Sūtra), Translated from the Chinese of Kumārajīva*, 174; T 9.262.30c11.

5. Hurvitz, *Scripture of the Lotus Blossom*, 175; T 9.262.30c17–18, 20–23.

6. Hurvitz, *Scripture of the Lotus Blossom*, 178; T 9.262.31b26–29.

7. See Willa Jane Tanabe, *Paintings of the Lotus Sutra*. Max Loehr provides evidence that sutra texts melded with Buddhist architecture in other ways. He cites the example of eighty-four thousand small scrolls commissioned in 975 to be given in offering to a certain stupa in China. When the stupa collapsed in 1924, "it was found that there was a hole in each of the bricks used to build the [stupa], and that a sutra was inserted in each hole," the stupa having been designed to make use of eighty-four thousand bricks, the precise number of relic grains said to have come from the historical Buddha's body (Max Loehr, *Chinese Landscape Woodcuts from an Imperial Commentary to the Tenth-Century Printed Edition of the Buddhist Canon*, 9).

8. See Mary Carruthers, *The Book of Memory: A Study of Medieval Culture*, esp. 8–10.

9. Ibid., 16.

10. For more on "work" versus "text," see chapter 1. The Himalaya Boy (Jp: Sessen Dōji) setsuwa discussed in the previous chapter illustrates this point quite

well. When Sessen Dōji hears a demon recite a sutra fragment he repeats the words over and over, "carving them deeply into his heart." The metaphor of "carving" refers to a technology of writing, such as incising words into wooden blocks or clay tablets (SNKBT 31: 43). For the text of the Sessen Dōji story, see *The Three Jewels* 1:10, *Nirvana Sutra* (T 12:449b–51b), and Zhiyi's *Great Calming and Contemplation* (Ch: *Mohe zhiguan;* Jp: *Makashikan;* T 46: 272a).

11. To highlight the metaphorical system at work I am translating very literally. The term *anju,* for instance, might be rendered "recitation from memory," but this loses the sense of "darkness" *(an).* Similarly, the term *meiryō* could be translated "to understand *[ryō]* clearly or with illumination *[mei]*." For a useful discussion of the trope of darkness in sutra recitation practice in medieval Japan, and an overview of sutra recitation as an activity particularly suited to nighttime, see Kikuchi Hiroki, "Jikyōsha no genkei to chūseiteki tenkai," 1366–70 and 1379–80.

12. *Paintings of the Lotus Sutra,* 79. This discussion benefits from Michael Camille's interest in the "text and what it can tell us about how books as objects could become sites of subjectivity [and] self-embodiment" in medieval European culture ("The Book as Flesh and Fetish in Richard de Bury's *Philobiblion,*" 38). On medieval Biblical editions composed on purple paper with gold ink, see Martin Irvine, *The Making of Textual Culture: 'Grammatica' and Literary Theory,* 14–15 and 470 n. 44.

13. *Shūi Ōjōden (A Gleaning of Tales of Rebirth in the Pure Land)* 1:13, compiled approximately sixty years after the *Hokke Genki,* also contains a much-truncated version of the story (NST 6: 300).

14. Generally I translate the Japanese word *kokoro* as "mind," with the understanding that the mind is embodied. Gyōhan's story reminds us of the full semantic range, using *kokoro* to indicate the locale of both memory and faith, a breadth of meaning that I have tried to capture, just at this instance, as "heart-mind."

15. While the *Tales from Times Now Past* version of this setsuwa (SNKBT 35: 314–15) contains the familiar imagery of clarity and obscurity, it includes no metaphors of movement. *Miracles of the Lotus Sutra* may reflect the idiosyncratic ideas of its compiler Chingen, who often uses these metaphors in his stories related to memory. In this, he is likely expanding on the language in sutras that refers to the memory of a bodhisattva as "without impediment" (*Flower Ornament Sutra,* T 10.279.226c29 and 227a11, for example).

16. This setsuwa also has its corollary in the *Tales from Times Now Past* collection (tale 14:18).

17. For the *Miracles of the Lotus Sutra* text, see NST 7: 552–53. For the *Tales from Times Now Past* text, see SNKBT 35: 315–16.

18. NST 7: 554. For the *Tales from Times Now Past* text, see SNKBT 35: 317–19.

19. Mary Carruthers, *The Book of Memory,* 8.

20. Ibid., 32.

21. See the entry for *kyō* (sutra) in Nakamura Hajime's *Kōsetsu bukkyōgo daijiten*, 234 a–d, and the *Oxford English Dictionary* entries for "sew" and "sutra."

22. *Ajari* (esoteric master) is a title used in the Shingon and Tendai sects of Buddhism.

23. For a discussion of the *pāramitā* (perfections), see the previous chapter. The six perfections are charity, discipline, forbearance, effort, meditation, and wisdom.

24. That is, all meritorious actions that bring joy, reduce suffering, and assist others along the Buddhist path.

25. The two other collections are *Kojidan* (*Conversations about Ancient Matters*, 1212–15), tale 3:92, and a later work by Mujū Ichien, *Zōtanshū* (*A Collection of Casual Digressions*, 1305) 9:4. For a similar narrative, this time an exchange between Saichō (767–822) and the deity of the Yahata Shrine, see *The Three Jewels* 3:3 (984), *Miracles of the Lotus Sutra* 3 (1040–44), *Tales from Times Now Past* 11:10 (ca. 1120), and *Kokon Chomonjū* (*A Collection of Old and New Tales Heard*, 1254) 39.

26. On the relation between voice, written word, and Buddha body, see Abe Ryūichi's *The Weaving of Mantra: Kūkai and the Construction of Esoteric Buddhist Discourse*, and Collette Cox, *Disputed Dharmas: Early Buddhist Theories on Existence*.

27. This story is repeated in *Tales from Times Now Past* 13:36.

28. For variations on this motif, see the sermons from the Third Month, third day and twenty-sixth day, in *One Hundred Sessions of Sermons* (HZ 92–94 and 113–16) and *Miracles of the Lotus Sutra* 12.

29. *Miracles of the Lotus Sutra* 11 (NST 43: 518–19), *Tales from Times Now Past* 13:1 (NKBT 24: 206–8), and *A Collection of Spiritual Awakenings* 4:1 (SNKS 164–68). For similar stories, see *A Collection of Spiritual Awakenings* 3:12 (SNKS 160–63) and the *One Hundred Sessions* sermon for the first day of the Third Month of 1110 (HZ 87–89).

30. *Tales from Times Now Past* 12:31 repeats and elaborates slightly on the story of Eigō. See SNKBT 35: 159–61. Aside from appearances in setsuwa collections, the chanting skull motif is a common element in hagiographies of high priests (Jp: *kōsōden*). For a list of examples, see NKBZ 10: 248.

31. These practices are not strictly the province of Buddhist priests per se but belong also to Shugendō, a variety of spiritual practice sometimes translated as "mountain worship" or "mountain asceticism." A great deal of what is now labeled "Shugendō" and separated from "Buddhism" proper was common to Tendai and Shingon Buddhist practice throughout the medieval period. See Carmen Blacker, *The Catalpa Bow: A Study of Shamanistic Practices in Japan;* Miyake Hitoshi's *Shugendō: Essays on the Structure of Japanese Folk Religion;* and Gorai Shigeru's entries on Shugendō his six-volume *Shūkyō minzoku shūsei*.

32. NKBZ 10: 249. Though the term used in this passage is "to read" (Jp: *doku*) and not "to recite" (Jp: *ju*), in this instance the compiler clearly intends some overlap in what the two terms denote. Though the *dhyāna* master may be making reference to an externally written text, clearly the skull is not.

33. This story also appears in *Tales from Times Now Past* 13:11 (compiled ca. 1120) and *Kokon Chomonjū (A Collection of Old and New Tales Heard)* 15 (compiled in 1254).

34. Similar setsuwa can be found in *Tales from Times Now Past* 7:14, 12:38, 13:10, 13:29, and 13:30; *Miracles of the Lotus Sutra* 39, 41, 56, and 63; *Shūi Ōjōden (A Gleaning of Tales of Rebirth in the Pure Land)* 1:6; and *Kokon Chomonjū (A Collection of Old and New Tales Heard)* 2.

35. The woman is a "lay believer" (Jp: *ubai;* Sk: *upāsikā*), meaning that she upholds the five basic precepts of cloistered life but maintains her lay status and does not live in a formal religious setting. The five precepts include injunctions against killing, lustful behavior, theft, lying, and the consumption of alcoholic beverages.

36. At the time sutra copyists often used a textual preservative that discouraged bookworms and silverfish and that left the paper dyed yellow. See Peter Kornicki, *The Book in Japan: A Cultural History from the Beginnings to the Nineteenth Century.*

37. This conflation of clothing with paper may make more sense when one remembers that sutras were written on long scrolls of paper that were rolled up, with the words inside. A layer of stiffer silk brocade on the outside was tied in place with a string. The arrangement may have been visually reminiscent of the kimono that more well-to-do folk wound around their bodies and secured with a sash.

38. Janet Goodwin, *Alms and Vagabonds: Buddhist Temples and Popular Patronage in Medieval Japan.*

39. For similar examples, see *A Wondrous Record of Immediate Karmic Retribution* 1:19 and 1:30; *The Three Jewels* 2:9; *Miracles of the Lotus Sutra* 32, 70, and 97; *Tales from Times Now Past* 13:6 and 14:28; and the *One Hundred Sessions* sermon from the twenty-eighth day of the Second Month.

40. This same story appears with slight variations in *Tales from Times Now Past* 12:28 and *Shūi Ōjōden (A Gleaning of Tales of Rebirth in the Pure Land)* 2:21.

41. *Myō,* the first character in the full title of the *Lotus Sutra* (Jp: *Myōhō Rengekyō*), means "mysterious" or "miraculous."

42. See *A Wondrous Record of Immediate Karmic Retribution* 3:13; *The Three Jewels* 2:17; *Miracles of the Lotus Sutra* 40 and 108; and *Tales from Times Now Past* 14:9.

43. See *A Wondrous Record of Immediate Karmic Retribution* 2:20; *The Three Jewels* 2:12 and 2:15; and *Tales from Times Now Past* 14:30.

44. See *Miracles of the Lotus Sutra* 57, 71, 72, 85, 114, and 115; also *Tales from Times Now Past* 17:41 and 17:40.

45. I am indebted to Julia Meech-Pekarik's work on the "reed hand" technique and its use in this and other artworks. See her "Disguised Scripts and Hidden Poems in an Illustrated Heian Sutra: Ashide and Uta-e in the *Heike Nōgyō.*"

46. Hurvitz, *Scripture of the Lotus Blossom,* 300, with minor changes; T 9.262 .54c1–3.

47. Tanabe, *Paintings of the Lotus Sutra,* xvii.

48. Sharf and Sharf, *Living Images,* 16.

CONCLUSION

1. John Kieschnick, *The Impact of Buddhism on Chinese Material Culture*, 157. D. C. Greetham and James McLaverty make similar arguments, to the effect that "the ontology of the literary work is as much in its physical form as in its language" (D. C. Greetham, *Textual Scholarship: An Introduction*, 343). To rephrase slightly, this conclusion will argue that the efficacy of the Buddhist sutra lies not only in the language of its message, but also in its physical forms and their attendant practices of reading.

2. For more extended definitions of linear, spatial, and radial reading, see Jerome McGann, *The Textual Condition*, 106–16.

3. Recitation praxis is one of the most active fields of Buddhist studies in Japan today. See Shiba Kanoyo, *Dokyōdō no kenkyū*, and Shimizu Masumi, *Dokyō no sekai: nōdoku no tanjō*.

4. See, for instance, Thomas Hare's discussion of the Japanese monk Kūkai's (774–835) reading practices, which might well be described as extensively "radial" in nature ("Reading Writing and Cooking: Kūkai's Interpretive Strategies").

5. For a useful parsing of the term *dhāraṇī*, its etymology, and its semantic range, see Paul Copp, "Notes on the Term 'Dhāraṇī' in Medieval Chinese Buddhist Thought." For the recitation of the massive *Perfection of Wisdom* sutra corpus through the single Sanskrit syllable *a*, see Edward Conze, *Perfect Wisdom: The Short Prajñāpāramitā Texts*, 201. On the difficulty of distinguishing between mantra and *dhāraṇī*, see Robert Sharf, *Coming to Terms with Chinese Buddhism: A Reading of the Treasure Store Treatise*, 337, n. 3.

6. For example, at the start of the *Lotus Sutra* the Buddha emits a ray of light from between his brows. Manjuśrī reads the portent as follows: "Good men, I surmise that the Buddha, the World-Honored One, now wishes to preach the great Dharma, to precipitate the great Dharma-rain, to blow the great Dharma-conch, to beat the great Dharma-drum, to set forth the great Dharma-doctrine" (Leon Hurvitz, *Scripture of the Lotus Blossom of the Fine Dharma [The Lotus Sūtra], Translated from the Chinese of Kumārajīva*, 12; T 9.262.3c12–14). For dharma preaching as fragrant food and sweet nectar, see chapter 11 of the *Vimalakīrti Sutra* (T 14.475.553b13–554c26). For the dharma as a banner and a lamp, see the *Nirvana Sutra* (T 12.374.586b17 and b19, respectively).

7. Nakao Takashi describes a popular proselytizing practice utilized by the monk Chōgen (1121–1206). Called *"yuya nenbutsu"* (literally, "bathhouse invocations of Amida"), the practice involved chanting while bathing, experiencing the warming and cleansing process as a "drenching" of oneself in sacred sound "the way one pours [hot water] over one's body" (*Chūsei no kanjin hijiri to shari shinkō*, 4). See also Abe Yasurō, "Yuya no kōgō: Kōmyō Kōgō yusegyō no monogatari wo megurite." Many setsuwa attest to the importance of bathing as a way of preparing for

Buddhist activities. See *The Three Jewels* 2:5, *A Wondrous Record of Immediate Karmic Retribution* 2:11, *A Companion in Solitude* 1:10, and *The Three Jewels* 3:4. On ritual bathing in Sanskrit, Chinese, Tibetan, and Khotanese versions of the *Sutra of Golden Radiance* (Jp: *Konkōmyōkyō*; T 663), see Natalie Gummer, "Articulating Potency: A Study of the *Suvarna(pra)bhāsotthamasūtra*," 231–98.

8. See Ryūichi Abe, *The Weaving of Mantra: Kūkai and the Construction of Esoteric Buddhist Discourse*, and Fabio Rambelli, *Buddhist Materiality: A Cultural History of Objects in Japanese Buddhism*, 77–78.

9. In the Sanskrit context, *cakra* refers to a wheel-shaped weapon that is the hallmark of a world ruler (Sk: *cakravartin*). Though the *cakra* as a spiritual weapon does appear in medieval Japan in the form of a ritual implement in certain esoteric schools and practices, it is much more common in the wider cultural sphere to see it glossed instead as a cart wheel. Buddhist visual arts, such as textile patterns woven into robes or illustrated frontispieces to sutras, often contain images of a single cart wheel, and Buddhist-inflected Japanese poetry employs extended puns in which "mounting" (Jp: *nori*) a wheeled cart is a metaphor for accepting the Buddhist "law" (Jp: *nori*).

10. We can see this idea at work in setsuwa about sutra reciters emitting rays of light from their mouths as they chant, an occurrence that calls to mind the tendency for buddhas to produce beams of light from their forehead as a preface to or substitute for verbal preaching. See *A Wondrous Record of Immediate Karmic Retribution* 1:14, *The Three Jewels* 2:7, and *Tales from Times Now Past* 11:4 and 14:32.

11. Hurvitz, *Scripture of the Lotus Blossom*, 178; T 9.262.31b26–29.

12. Bernard Faure, "The Buddhist Icon and the Modern Gaze," 809.

13. Ibid., 770. Faure reminds us that "profaning the icons of a temple" can be a literal as well as an aesthetic act, "literally bringing them from inside the temple to outside, in broad daylight, in front of the temple *[pro fanum]*" (775).

14. My discussion here paraphrases and updates an earlier survey by L. Carrington Goodrich, "The Revolving Book-Case in China."

15. Gregory Schopen makes the latter assertion in his very brief "A Note on the 'Technology of Prayer' and a Reference to a 'Revolving Bookcase' in an Eleventh-Century Indian Inscription," in *Figments and Fragments of Mahāyāna Buddhism in India: More Collected Papers*, 345–49.

16. Cited in Goodrich, "The Revolving Book-Case in China," 145.

17. Guo Qinghua, "The Architecture of Joinery: The Form and Construction of Rotating Sutra-Case Cabinets," 96.

18. In his journal entry for 5.23.840 Ennin describes the following scene: "The grotto wall is hard and has a yellow tinge, and there is a high tower where the mouth of the grotto would be.... Up in the tower at the grotto entrance is a revolving repository *[tenrinzō]* made as a hexagon" (Edwin Reischauer, *Ennin's Diary: The Record of a Pilgrimage to China in Search of the Law*, 247). This six-sided shape is a departure from the more typical octagon.

19. A dozen or more further examples exist, including at Tōshōgū in Nikkō, Hasedera in Kamakura, Seiryōji in the Saga district of northern Kyoto, Chion'in in eastern Kyoto, Nishihonganji in central Kyoto, and Shitennōji in Osaka.

20. Goodrich makes this mistake ("The Revolving Book-Case in China," 157), as do Herbert Giles and Franz M. Feldhaus (quoted in ibid., 130). These men were likely misled by surface similarities between the revolving sutra library and the book wheel, that "emblematic object of learned readership in the Renaissance ... which permitted the opening of several books at a time, and thus the extraction and comparison of passages taken as essential" (Roger Chartier, *Forms and Meanings: Texts, Performances, and Audiences from Codex to Computer,* 95).

21. Guo, "The Architecture of Joinery," 103–5.

22. Quoted in Goodrich, "The Revolving Book-Case in China," 145.

23. Quoted in ibid.

24. Buddhism combined with the worship of native deities (Jp: *kami*) in a variety of ways to form syncretic religious practices, and it is not unusual to see hybrid temple-shrine compounds. Tenmangū shrines were established to honor Tenman Tenjin, the posthumous name given to the courtier Sugawara no Michizane (845–903), recognized as a deity of scholarship and literature. The revolving sutra repository installed at the Kitano Tenmangū Shrine was moved to its current locale (Zuiōji) in 1871.

25. The Nihon Meicho Zenshū Kankōkai edition, on which I base my translation, has the doors of the miniature shrine opening "in the four directions" rather than "in a westerly direction." Typically shrines of this type open on only one side, and, given the preponderance of imagery associated with the western Pure Land in the passage, I have assumed that the character "four" is a typo that should read "west."

26. This assertion echoes sentiments uttered earlier in the play that identify Japan as at the cutting edge of Buddhism's slow movement eastward (YSG 51) and maintain that, though these are latter days, "the path of the law yet remains in the east" (YSG 50). Such figural claims establish Japan as a place situated in Buddhist time rather than as a nation contesting itself against other nations. This structure situates the Japanese isles as the eastern edge, and the event horizon, of a fundamentally Buddhist world.

27. "At that time the Buddha emitted a glow from the tuft of white hair between his brows that illuminated eighteen thousand worlds to the east, omitting none of them" (Hurvitz, *Scripture of the Lotus Blossom,* 4; T 12.262.2b17–18).

28. By most accounts Buddhism entered the stage of decline (Jp: *mappō*) in 552 C.E., ironically the very same year traditionally given as marking Buddhism's introduction to Japan. By other accounts, *mappō* began in 1052. For a lengthier discussion of Buddhist temporal cycles, see chapter 3.

29. See McGann, *The Textual Condition,* 101–28, and James O'Donnell, *Avatars of the Word: From Papyrus to Cyberspace,* 50–63.

30. See David Diringer, *The Book Before Printing: Ancient, Medieval and Ori-*

ental, 113–69; Greetham, *Textual Scholarship;* and O'Donnell, *Avatars of the Word*, 50–63. One notable exception to the codex's ascendancy is the use of the scroll in some Jewish religious contexts, as required by the Talmud. Recently some scholars of Western book history have begun to suggest that the codex gained ground over the scroll rather more slowly than was first thought. See Chartier, *Forms and Meanings*, 18–23.

31. Kieschnick, *The Impact of Buddhism on Chinese Material Culture*, 180.

32. Reischauer, *Ennin's Diary*, 235.

33. Tsuen-Hsuin Tsien, *Written on Bamboo and Silk: The Beginnings of Chinese Books and Inscriptions*, 86.

34. See Kieschnick, *The Impact of Buddhism on Chinese Material Culture*, 164–85.

35. See Mimi Hall Yiengpruksawan, "One Millionth of a Buddha: The Hyakumantō Darani in the Scheide Library," and Brian Hickman, "A Note on the Hyakumantō Dharani."

36. Tsien, *Written on Bamboo and Silk*, 18.

37. Peter Kornicki, *The Book in Japan: A Cultural History from the Beginnings to the Nineteenth Century*, 42. See also Denis Twitchett, *Printing and Publishing in Medieval China*, 68, and Kieschnick, *The Impact of Buddhism on Chinese Material Culture*, 180–81.

38. Stephen Teiser, *The Scripture on the Ten Kings and the Making of Purgatory in Medieval Chinese Buddhism*, 152.

39. Enomoto Ei'ichi has observed a similar trend ("Kyōten no tendoku ni tsuite," 48).

40. As with the word *volume*, which speakers of modern English continue to use to count books even though they are no longer, properly speaking, "rolls" (Latin: *volumen*), the Chinese counter *juan* (Jp: *kan*) was first used specifically for rolled texts and later continued to be used even when texts appeared in different material forms. Thus, simply because a medieval tale uses the word *scroll* does not necessarily mean that the text in question was, in fact, still in the scroll form. In my experience, however, whenever setsuwa provide further details about the material form of a miracle-producing text, that text is always clearly a rolled scroll. Robert Campany's and Donald Gjertson's work on the Chinese miracle tale suggests that this is likely also the case in that body of literature.

41. See *Miracles of the Lotus Sutra* 11, NST 7: 518; *Tales from Times Now Past* 13:1, NKBT 24: 206; and *A Collection of Spiritual Awakenings* 4:1, SNKS 165.

42. *Miracles of the Lotus Sutra* 113, NST 7: 561–62.

43. *A Wondrous Record of Immediate Karmic Retribution* 2:19, NKBZ 10: 179.

44. A treatise on reading the sutras *(Dokyō yōjin)*, attributed to Genshin (942–1017) but likely of later origin, suggests these as appropriate thoughts to cultivate when pausing between scrolls or chapters of the *Lotus Sutra*.

45. I would like to thank Natalie Gummer for drawing my attention to digital

prayer wheels ("Buddhist Books and Texts: Ritual Uses of Books") and for her generosity in sharing the sources I reference here (personal correspondence, September 6, 2008). All websites listed below were accessed on September 8, 2008.

46. See "The Power of a 'Modern' Prayer Wheels" *[sic]* at www.snowlionpub.com/pages/N68_6.html.

47. See "Digital Prayer Wheels" at www.dharma-haven.org/tibetan/digital-wheels.htm.

48. The authors of the Dharma Haven site note that "the first *mani* wheel we found that could be displayed on a Web page . . . came from a Japanese web site" (www.dharma-haven.org/tibetan/digital-wheels.htm).

49. The Dharma Haven site makes this assertion, as do the authors of websites dealing with the Mani Microfilm project ("Microfilm for Stupas and Prayer Wheels" at www.fpmt.org/resources/mani.asp#top) and the Energy Infuser project ("Energy Infusion and Prayer Wheel" at www.prayer-wheel.com).

50. This comment is attributed to Deb Platt, as cited on www.dharma-haven.org/tibetan/digital-wheels.htm.

51. O'Donnell, *Avatars of the Word,* 32.

GLOSSARY

AGUI (Jp) 安居院. Founded by the father-and-son team of Chōgen (1126–1203) and Seikaku (1167–1235), this temple lent its name to the liturgical school founded by the two men.

AJARI (Jp) 阿闍梨. Esoteric master. A title used in the Tendai and Shingon schools.

ANĀTMAN (Sk). See *muga.*

ANJU (Jp) 暗誦. Literally, "dark recitation." Refers to the practice of reciting a sutra completely from memory.

ARHAT (Sk). A human being who, over the course of many lifetimes, has attained a buddha-like state of enlightenment. To become an *arhat* is the ultimate goal of Theravada Buddhist practice.

AVADĀNA (Sk). Karmic biography. A genre of Sanskrit literature that seeks to link karmic deeds from past lives with the present-day world of the story.

BODHI (Sk). Awakening. Can refer either to the process of gradually awakening to the true reality of things, or to the culmination of that process. Jp: *bodai.*

BODHISATTVA (Sk). An enlightened being who, rather than entering into extinction (Sk: *nirvana*), chooses to remain active in the world with the ultimate goal of bringing about universal liberation from suffering. Jp: *bosatsu* 菩薩.

BRAHMIN (Sk). A member of the highest, priestly caste of the four social classes in Hinduism.

BUTSUJI (Jp) 仏事.   Buddhist service. A term used in Agui school literature. Refers to a less formal type of preaching situation in which the presiding priest performs whatever parts of the liturgy that are called for, does not sit on a high platform, and is not accompanied by a retinue.

CAKRA (Sk).   Wheel. In Indian contexts, the *cakra,* a type of weapon that precedes the monarch into battle and subdues foes in all directions, is one of the possessions of the universal monarch (Sk: *cakravartin*). As a four-, six-, or eight-spoked wheel, the *cakra* is also a symbol of Buddhism, calling to mind the Four Noble Truths, the six paths of existence, or the Noble Eightfold Path. See also *dharma cakra pravartana.*

DĀNA (Sk).   Giving. The first of the "six perfections" (see *pāramitā*) of the bodhisattva, *dāna* is the supreme virtue of generosity, particularly generosity that helps support monks and nuns.

DANNA (Jp) 旦那.   Patron, donor. Refers to the person at whose instigation a preaching event is organized: for instance, a lay believer who sponsors a service in order to dedicate a sutra that she or he has copied.

DEHADĀNA (Sk).   Gift of the body. A type of giving (Sk: *dāna*) in which the giver gives all or part of his or her body.

DHĀRANĪ (Sk).   The grasp of memory. Literally, to "grasp," "hold," or "maintain." *Dhāranī* are sometimes called "spells" or "incantations," and they consist of a series of Sanskrit syllables that generally do not make full grammatical sense. When they appear in translated sutras, *dhāranī* are transliterated, in part because their meaning is unclear, in part because their sound is thought to contain power. Jp: *darani* 陀羅尼.

DHARMA (Sk).   Although it has a wide semantic range, in its most general usage, the term refers to the "law," the eternal principles (such as transience) governing all conditioned existence. To the extent that Buddhism attempts to make these laws visible, *dharma* is also used as a synonym for the Buddhist teachings. Jp: *hō* 法.

DHARMA CAKRA PRAVARTANA (Sk).   Turning the wheel of the law. Most specifically, the phrase refers to the historical Buddha's first sermon following his enlightenment. By extension, it refers to preaching in general. The phrase is an extension of the pre-Buddhist notion of a universal monarch (see *cakra*). Whereas the monarch uses a wheel-weapon to subdue enemies, the Buddha uses the "wheel" of the dharma to subdue ignorance, craving, and hatred. Jp: *tenbōrin* 転法輪.

DHYĀNA (Sk).   Meditation; more precisely, the mental and spiritual state produced by meditation. Jp: *zen* 禅 (not to be confused with Zen, Jp: *Zenshū* 禅宗).

DŌJI (Jp) 童子.   In Japanese, the term refers generally to a child or youth. In

Buddhist contexts it indicates a young person who has entered the temple and may undertake menial duties but who has not yet taken the tonsure. By extension, the term can indicate a youthful-looking monk.

EKOTOBA (Jp) 絵詞.   Literally, "illustration writing." A category of Japanese text in which illustrations and written explanations run parallel to one another, or in which illustrations appear as panels surrounded left and right by writing.

ENGO (Jp) 縁語.   Literally, "related words." A classical Japanese poetic technique in which a series of semantically related words are combined to heighten the emotional effect of a poem.

FUDOKI (Jp) 風土記.   Gazetteer. Records from the Japanese provinces that contain accounts of geography, products, and descriptions of the origins of place names.

FUJŌKAN (Jp) 不浄観.   Spectacle of the unclean. A monastic meditative practice aimed at reducing carnal desire by observing all the stages of a corpse's putrefaction.

FUSHOKU (Jp) 付嘱.   To entrust. Term used in sutras to indicate the formal responsibility for remembering and transmitting a dharma teaching.

GANMON (Jp) 願文.   A formal written request presented by the chief officiant of a Buddhist service or ceremony on behalf of the patron (Jp: *danna*).

GĀTHĀ (Sk).   Sutra verse. Poetic portions of sutras that praise the Buddha or enumerate the virtues of his teachings. The term is sometimes used in a more general sense to refer to other expressions of the dharma in poetic form. Jp: *ge* 偈.

GOSHŌ (Jp) 五障.   The "five obstacles," which, in traditional Buddhist thought, stand between a woman and her physical realization of buddhahood (namely, her inability to embody five types of being, including that of the buddha).

GOSHU HŌSHI (Jp) 五種法師.   Five varieties of dharma preacher. Outlined most famously in the *Lotus Sutra,* the five categories are those who accept and keep (Jp: *juji* 受持) the sutra, those who read it (Jp: *dokyō* 読経), those who recite it (Jp: *jukyō* 誦経), those who explain it to others (Jp: *sekkyō* 説教), and those who copy it in writing (Jp: *shakyō* 写経).

HIJIRI (Jp) 聖.   Ascetic. In medieval Japan, these aspirants often espoused syncretic practices and stood apart from the officially ordained clergy. They tended to be solitary practitioners, undergoing ascetic practice in the mountains, or interacted with the general populace rather than confining their activities to temple settings.

HŌBEN (Jp) 方便.   Expedient means or skillful means. The skillful employment of a variety of stratagems by enlightened beings for the express purpose of bringing other beings to enlightenment. Examples include visits to brothels, feigned illness, and the use of half truths. Sk: *upāya*.

HŌE (Jp) 法会.　Buddhist ceremony. A term used in Agui school literature. Refers to type of formal preaching situation in which the presiding priest sits on a high platform and is accompanied by a retinue of ritual specialists, each responsible for a discrete part of the liturgy.

HŌKI (Jp) 法器.　Dharma vessel. A term used in several Mahāyāna sutras to specify someone who is mentally and spiritually prepared to receive the dharma teachings and to remember them.

HOSSHIN (Jp) 発心.　Literally, "awakened mind" or "the awakening of mind." Refers to a moment or experience of spiritual awakening. A contraction of the longer phrase, "awakening of the aspiration for enlightenment" (Jp: *hotsu bodaishin* 発菩提心). See also *bodhi*.

HŌTŌ MANDARA (Jp) 宝塔曼陀羅.　Jeweled stupa mandala. A type of sutra in which the Chinese characters of the text are arranged to form the shape of a stupa.

ICHIJI HŌTŌKYŌ (Jp) 一字宝塔経.　One-character jeweled stupa sutra. A type of sutra in which a line drawing of a miniature stupa is drawn around each Chinese character of the text.

ICHIJI ICHIBUTSUKYŌ (Jp) 一字一仏経.　One-character one-buddha sutra. A type of sutra in which there are two parallel lines of writing, such that each Chinese character (Jp: *kanji*) of the text is paired with a small line drawing of a buddha.

JĀTAKA (Sk).　Birth stories. Stories of the historical Buddha's former incarnations. Jp: *honshōtan* 本生譚.

JIKU (Jp) 軸.　Axle. The central rod around which the fabric of a scroll is wrapped.

JIKYŌSHA (Jp) 持経者.　Literally, "one who carries the sutra." A type of sutra devotee who, either literally (in the hands or in a pouch around the neck) or figuratively (in memory), carries a complete sutra on (or in) their person.

JU (Jp) 誦.　To recite. One of the types of sutra devotion described in Mahāyāna sutras (see *goshu hōshi*). Indicates vocal recitation from a memorized text, without reference to a written copy. This sense is more explicit when in combination, as with the terms *anju* 暗誦 and *fuju* 諷誦.

KAIMAMI (Jp) 垣間見.　Peeking between the fence slats, an activity related to romantic pursuit in classical Japanese literature. In the homosocial aristocratic culture of Heian (794–1185) Japan, women of rank typically did not appear in public. Interested gentlemen might sneak up to their garden fence and peek through.

KALPA (Sk).   Buddhist cosmology maintains that the universe moves through repeating cycles of growth and decay called *kalpas*. The length of a *kalpa* might be likened to the amount of time it would take to move a mountain-sized pile of tiny mustard seeds, one seed at a time, to a place billions of miles distant.

KAMI (Jp) 神.   Deity. One of the native gods or goddesses of Japan who were often, but not always, identified with natural forces. The institutionalized worship of these deities is known as Shintō 神道.

KANA (Jp) 仮名かな.   The Japanese syllabary. This system for writing Japanese has two forms, the more rounded *hiragana* ひらがな and the more linear *katakana* カタカナ. Entire works can be written in kana, but because of the large number of homophones it is more typical to combine them with Chinese characters (Jp: *kanji*), generally using kanji for nouns and the stems of adjectives and verbs, and using kana for the remainder, including the inflective endings of adjectives and verbs.

KANA HŌGO (Jp) 仮名法語.   Vernacular tract. A tract written mostly or entirely in kana with the aim of bringing the Buddhist teachings to a large popular audience.

KANJI (Jp) 漢字.   Chinese characters. In Japanese writing, kanji are used in combination with a native syllabary (Jp: *kana*).

KANJIN (Jp) 勧進.   Alms-raising campaign. A type of public campaign to raise funds or materials for Buddhist projects, such as the repair of a temple or the carving of a statue.

KANSUBON (Jp) 巻子本.   Scroll. A type of text in which writing done on a material-like paper, cloth, or silk is rolled up, often around a wooden rod (Jp: *jiku*), for storage.

KECHIEN (Jp) 結縁.   Karmic connection. The term refers to any act that forges a tie with the Buddhist faith. Acts of *kechien* include giving alms, providing materials for the construction of a temple, writing a single character of a sutra, and ritually invoking a specific deity.

KOKORO (Jp) 心.   Mind. The semantic range of this word is large, encompassing human mental and emotional functions ("heart," "mind") and also suggesting the "essence" or "kernel" of something. In medieval setsuwa literature, the *kokoro*—or *shin* in compound words such as "single-minded, whole-hearted" (Jp: *isshin*)—is the locus of memory and spiritual realization.

KOKUGAKU (Jp) 国学.   National learning. In its broadest sense *kokugaku* refers simply to the study of Japanese classical literature. In its more specific sense, *kokugaku* refers to a particular philosophical school (Nativism) that developed beginning in the Edo period (1600–1868) and whose proponents attempt to imagine the essence of Japanese native culture before it was affected by foreign imports such as Buddhism.

KONSHI KINJIKYŌ (Jp) 紺紙金字経. Literally, "indigo paper, gold character sutra." A type of handwritten sutra using gold letters on dark blue paper.

KŌSŌDEN (Jp) 高僧伝. Biographies of notable Buddhist priests. A genre consisting of stories, facts, and legends about high-ranking or influential monks.

KUNJU (Jp) 薫修. A Buddhist term referring to robes that have become permeated with the scent of incense (Jp: *kun*) burned during the wearer's devotional activities (Jp: *shu, ju*).

KUSŌ (Jp) 九相. Nine views. The nine stages of a body's putrefaction after death, including the fresh corpse, swelling, discoloration, oozing filth, coming apart, fleshless bones, white bones loosely held together, disjointed white bones, and ash.

MAHĀYĀNA (Sk). Great Vehicle. The type of Buddhism traditionally practiced throughout most of East Asia. In distinction to mainstream Buddhism— sometimes referred to as Theravada (properly, one of its schools) or, derisively, as Hīnayāna (Small Vehicle)—Mahāyāna promotes pursuance of the bodhisattva path. (See *bodhisattva*.) Jp: *Daijō* 大乗.

MANTRA (Sk). Incantation, magic formula, spell. Short combinations of syllables that generally do not translate easily or directly, mantras are thought to be powerful when chanted. There is some sense that mantras represent the "essence" or "heart" of the Buddhist teaching in which they appear.

MAPPŌ (Jp) 末法. The final age of the dharma. Buddhist cosmology maintains that all conditioned phenomena are impermanent. While all buddhas discover the same true nature of reality, any individual buddha's specific teaching of that reality will be forgotten gradually over a finite period of time. The exact timing of this loss differs between texts, but the time frame most prominent in medieval Japan held that the final age of the dharma began in 1052 C.E.

MONOGATARI (Jp) 物語. Narrative tale. One of the major genres of classical Japanese literature. These lengthy tales often involve scores of characters acting over wide geographical or temporal terrain. *Monogatari* are often heavily poetic, with prosaic interludes serving as transportation between emotional peaks as expressed in classical Japanese poetry (Jp: *waka*).

MUDRA (Sk). Hand gesture. In Buddhist statuary, mudras can indicate what the buddha or bodhisattva is doing: preaching, for instance, or witnessing the moment of his enlightenment. Jp: *shuin* 手印.

MUGA (Jp) 無我. No-self. The Buddhist teaching that all of conditioned existence, even the notion of "self" or "I," is subject to impermanence. Sk: *anātman*.

NENBUTSU (Jp) 念仏. A religious practice, common in Pure Land schools, in which a devotee invokes the buddha Amida by uttering (often repeatedly) the phrase "homage to Amida Buddha" (Jp: *namu Amida butsu*).

NIRVANA (Sk). The state of freedom from suffering and rebirth. Occasioned by the extinction of desire, nirvana is often compared to a flame that has been blown out or extinguished, leaving coolness and calm. Jp: *nehan* 涅槃.

NŌSETSU (Jp) 能説. Talented preacher. A term used in medieval documents to specify a preacher who was known for his skill at oration.

ORIHON (Jp) 折本. Folding booklet. A type of text in which writing done on material like paper, cloth, or silk is folded every several lines so that it may be stretched open or closed, like an accordion.

OTOGI ZŌSHI (Jp) 御伽草子. Companion tale. A type of short prose narrative popular throughout the late medieval and early modern periods in Japan. The stories often end with a moral or brief didactic observation.

PĀRAMITĀ (Sk). Perfection. The spiritual practices of a bodhisattva. The "six perfections" are giving (Sk: *dāna*), ethical behavior (Sk: *śīla*), forbearance (Sk: *kṣānti*), effort (Sk: *vīrya*), meditation (Sk: *dhyāna*), and wisdom (Sk: *prajña*). Jp: *haramitsu* 波羅蜜.

RAIGŌ (Jp) 来迎. Welcoming procession. The belief that the buddha Amida will appear at the moment of a devotee's death to accompany the believer to the Pure Land.

RENDAIKYŌ (Jp) 蓮台経. Lotus throne sutra. A type of sutra in which each written character sits atop a lotus petal throne.

RENGA (Jp) 連歌. Linked verse. A genre of classical Japanese poetry in which a group of poets take turns composing links of alternating patterns of 5–7-5 and 7–7 syllables per line. Rather than combining to form a narrative, each link connects to the one immediately previous in a way that is fresh and unexpected.

RITSURYŌ (Jp) 律令. Literally, "laws and ordinances." A court-based system of government active in Japan during the Nara (710–84) and early Heian (794–1185) periods that created an aristocratic hierarchy and a centralized government under the emperor. Based on Chinese models, the codes were enacted in 668 and remained in place, at least nominally, until the twelfth century.

ROKKON (Jp) 六根. Literally, "six roots." The six sense organs: the eyes, ears, mouth, nose, body, and consciousness.

SAMĀDHI (Sk). Concentration. Buddhist teachings maintain that the practice of meditation enables one to enter this calm and focused state, from which vantage point the practitioner can achieve the ability to distinguish between the real and the illusory.

SANBŌ (Jp) 三宝. The "three treasures" of Buddhism: the Buddha, his teachings (the dharma), and his followers (the sangha of practitioners).

SANGHA (Sk).   The community of Buddhist practitioners, consisting of monks, nuns, and lay believers.

SEKKYŌ (Jp) 説経.   Preaching. Literally, "explaining the sutras."

SEPPŌ (Jp) 説法.   Preaching. Literally, "explaining the dharma."

SESSEN DŌJI (Jp) 雪山童子.   The "Himalaya Youth" is a character who appears in the *Nirvana Sutra* and in numerous setsuwa. An earlier incarnation of the being who would become the historical Buddha, the youth offered to feed his body to a demon in exchange for half a verse of Buddhist teachings.

SETSUWA (Jp) 説話.   Explanatory tale. A type of narrative used in the context of sermons. Setsuwa marshal concrete details to explain or illustrate abstract points of doctrine.

SHASHIN (Jp) 捨身.   Literally, "throwing away the body." A motif of physical sacrifice (often, cutting or burning the body) that appears in numerous setsuwa. Typically the self-sacrifice is a sign of religious self-cultivation or is done in order to gain access to otherwise inaccessible portions of the Buddhist dharma.

SURI KUYŌ (Jp) 刷り供養.   A type of ritual in which a hand-copied sutra is dedicated to a dead person in order to relieve their sufferings in hell or to bring about their physical transformation from one mode of existence to another (for instance, from animal back to human).

TENDOKU (Jp) 転読.   Literally "turn-read." Particularly, to read a sutra.

UBAI (Jp) 優婆夷.   A female believer who upholds the five basic precepts of cloistered life but maintains her lay status and does not live in a formal religious setting. The five precepts are injunctions against killing, lustful behavior, theft, lying, and the consumption of alcoholic beverages. Sk: *upāsikā*.

UPĀSIKĀ (Sk).   See *ubai*.

UPĀYA (Sk).   See *hōben*.

WAKA (Jp) 和歌.   Literally, "Japanese poem." A type of single-author classical Japanese poetry composed in five phrases of 5, 7, 5, 7, and 7 syllables each for a total of 31 syllables.

YANJI (Ch) 験記.   Miracle tale. A type of classical Chinese literature.

ZENKON (Jp) 善根.   Literally, "good roots." These roots may be created by reducing greed, hatred, and ignorance, cultivating instead generosity, love, and wisdom.

ZHI GUAI (Ch) 志怪.   Strange tale, anomaly account. A genre of classical Chinese literature that compiles stories of strange or anomalous happenings.

WORKS CITED

PRIMARY SOURCES

All sutra references are to the *Taishō Shinshū Daizōkyō*. See the Note on Sutras.

"Ama." Author unknown. Shin Nihon Koten Bungaku Taikei 57. Nishio Haruo, ed. Tokyo: Iwanami Shoten, 2003.

Chūyūki. Diary of Fujiwara no Munetada (1062–1141). Tokyo Daigaku Shiryō Hensanjo hen. Tokyo: Iwanami Shoten, 1993.

Dokyō yōjin. Author unknown; attributed to Genshin (942–1017) but almost certainly a later work. *Dai Nihon Bukkyō Zensho* 24, pages 327–28. Tokyo: Bussho Kankōkai, 1913. Also in *Eshin Sōzu Zenshū* 5. Tanaka Shūji, ed., pages 497–501. Kyoto: Shibunkan Shuppan, 1984.

Genzenshū. By Seikaku (1167–1235). Nagai Yoshinori and Kiyomizu Yūsei, ed. *Agui shōdōshū: jo maki*. Tokyo: Kadokawa Shoten, 1972.

Gōdanshō. Compiled by Ōe no Masafusa (1041–1111). Shin Nihon Koten Bungaku Taikei 32. Gotō Akio, Ikegami Jun'ichi, and Yamane Taisuke, eds. Tokyo: Iwanami Shoten, 2005.

Hōbutsushū. Compiler unknown (ca. 1180). Shin Nihon Koten Bungaku Taikei 40. Koizumi Hiroshi, Yamada Shōzen, Kojima Takayuki, and Kinoshita Motoichi, eds. Tokyo: Iwanami Shoten, 2001.

"Hōjōki." By Kamo no Chōmei (1155–1216). Shinchō Nihon Koten Shūsei. Miki Sumito, ed. Tokyo: Shinchōsha, 1976.

Hokke genki. Compiled by Chingen (ca. 1040–43). Nihon Shisō Taikei 7. Inoue Mitsusada and Ōsone Shōsuke, eds. Tokyo: Iwanami Shoten, 1974.

Hōsokushū. Compiled by Shinjō (fl. ca. 1298). Nagai Yoshinori and Kiyomizu Yūsei, ed. *Agui shōdōshū: jo maki.* Tokyo: Kadokawa Shoten, 1972.

Hosshinshū. Compiled by Kamo no Chōmei (1155–1216). Shinchō Nihon Koten Shūsei. Miki Sumito, ed. Tokyo: Shinchōsha, 1976.

Hyakuza hōdan kikigakishō. Compiler unknown (ca. 1110). Satō Akio, ed. *Hyakuza Hōdan Kikigakishō,* 1963. Also Yamagishi Tokuhei, ed., *Hokke Shūhō Ippyakuza Kikigakishō,* 1976, and Kobayashi Yoshinori, ed., *Hokke Hyakuza Kikigakishō Sōsakuin,* 1975.

"Kankin." Dōgen (1200–1253). *Dōgen Zenshi Zenshū,* vol. 1. Also in Nihon Shisō Taikei 12. Ōkubu Dōshū, ed. Tokyo: Chikuma Shobō, 1969.

Kankyo no tomo. Attributed to Keisei (1189–1268). Shin Nihon Koten Bungaku Taikei 40. Koizumi Hiroshi, Yamada Shōzen, Kojima Takayuki, and Kinoshita Motoichi, eds. Tokyo: Iwanami Shoten, 2001.

Kikigakishū. Attributed to Saigyō (1118–90). Waka Bungaku Taikei 21. Kubota Jun, ed. Tokyo: Meiji Shoin, 2003.

Kohon setsuwashū. Compiler unknown (late 11th or 12th century). Shin Nihon Koten Bungaku Taikei 42. Miki Sumito, Asami Kazuhiko, Nakamura Yoshio, and Kouchi Kazuaki, eds. Tokyo: Iwanami Shoten, 2005.

Kojidan. Compiled by Minamoto no Akikane (1160–1215). Shin Nihon Koten Bungaku Taikei 41. Kawabata Yoshiaki and Araki Hiroshi, eds. Tokyo: Iwanami Shoten, 2005.

Kokinwakashū. Revised version completed ca. 914. Nihon Koten Bungaku Taikei 8. Saeki Umetomo, ed. Tokyo: Iwanami Shoten, 1958.

Kokon chomonjū. Compiled by Tachibana no Narisue (fl. ca. 1254). Shinchō Nihon Koten Shūsei. Nishio Kōichi and Kobayashi Yasuharu, eds. Tokyo: Shinchōsha, 1983.

Konjaku monogatari. Compiler unknown (ca. 1180). Nihon Koten Bungaku Taikei 22–26. Yamada Yoshio, Yamada Tadao, Yamada Hideo, and Yamada Toshio, eds. Tokyo: Iwanami Shoten, 1959–63.

Kōshoku ichidai onna. 1686. Composed by Ihara Saikaku (1642–93). Shinpen Nihon Koten Bungaku Zenshū 66. Teruoka Yasutaka and Higashi Akimasa, eds. Tokyo: Shōgakkan, 1996.

"Kusō no shi." Attributed to Kūkai (774–835) but likely of later origin. Nihon Koten Bungaku Taikei 71. Watanabe Shōkō and Miyasaka Yūshō, eds. Tokyo: Iwanami Shoten, 1965.

Man'yōshū. Completed ca. 759. Shin Nihon Koten Bungaku Taikei 1–4. Satake Akihira, Yamada Hideo, Kudō Rikio, Ōtani Masao, and Yamazaki Yoshiyuki, eds. Tokyo: Iwanami Shoten, 1999.

"Minobusan gosho." By Nichiren (1222–82). *Shōwa teihon Nichiren shōnin ibun,* vol. 2. Tokyo: Nichiren Kyōgaku Kenkyūjo, 1988.

Nihon ryōiki. Compiled by Kyōkai (fl. 780–823). Nihon Koten Bungaku Zenshū 10. Nakada Norio, ed. Tokyo: Shogakkan, 1995.

Ōjō yōshū. By Genshin (942–1017). Nihon Shisō Taikei 6. Ishida Mizumaro, ed. Tokyo: Iwanami Shoten, 1970.

"Rinzō." Written by Kanze Nagatoshi (1488–1541). Nihon Meicho Zenshū Kankōkai, ed. *Yōkyoku sanbyaku gojūbanshū,* 1928.

Sanbōe. Compiled by Minamoto no Tamenori (fl. ca. 1011). Shin Nihon Koten Bungaku Taikei 31. Mabuchi Kazuo, Koizumi Hiroshi, and Konno Tōru, eds. Tokyo: Iwanami Shoten, 1997.

Senjūshō. Compiler unknown (ca. 1183–99?), attributed to Saigyō (1118–90). Kojima Takayuki and Asami Kazuhiko, eds. Tokyo: Ōfūsha, 1985.

Senzaiwakashū. Compiled by Fujiwara no Shunzei (1114–1204). Shin Nihon Koten Bungaku Taikei 10. Katano Tatsurō and Matsuno Yōkichi, eds. Tokyo: Iwanami Shoten, 1993.

Shasekishū. Compiled by Mujū Ichien (1226–1312). Nihon Koten Bungaku Zenshū 52. Kojima Takayuki, ed. Tokyo: Shogakkan, 2001.

Shōzōmatsu wasan. By Shinran (1173–1262). Kyoto: Ryukoku University Translation Center, 1980.

Shūi ōjōden. Compiled by Miyoshi no Tameyasu (1049–1139). Nihon Shisō Taikei 7. Inoue Mitsusada and Ōsone Shōsuke, eds. Tokyo: Iwanami Shoten, 1974.

Taishō shinshū daizōkyō. Edited by Takakusu Junjirō, Watanabe Kaigyoku, and Ono Gemmyō. 100 vols. Tokyo: Taishō Issaikyō Kankōkai, 1924–34.

Uchigikishū. Compiler unknown (ca. 1111–34). Hashimoto Shinkichi, ed. Tokyo: Koten Hozonkai, 1927.

Uji shūi monogatari. Compiler unknown (ca. 1190–1242). Nihon Koten Bungaku Taikei 27. Watanabe Tsunaya and Nishio Kōichi, eds. Tokyo: Iwanami Shoten, 1960.

Zōtanshū. Compiled by Mujū Ichien (1226–1312). Yamada Shōzen and Miki Sumito, eds. Tokyo: Miyai Shoten, 1973.

SECONDARY SOURCES

Abe Ryūichi. *The Weaving of Mantra: Kūkai and the Construction of Esoteric Buddhist Discourse.* New York: Columbia University Press, 1999.

Abe Yasurō. "Yuya no kōgō: Kōmyō kōgō yusegyō no monogatari wo megurite." *Bungaku* 54:11 (1986): 76–87, and 55:1 (1987): 79–92.

Akashi Mitsumaro. "*Hokke genki* seiritsu kō." *Kyōto Joshidai Jinbun Ronsō* 8 (April 1966): 59–80.

Amemiya Shōji. "Enpōbon *Nihon ryōiki.*" *Ōtani Gakuhō* 20:2 (June 1939): 33–44.

———. "Kōyabon kei *Nihon Ryōiki* shōkō." *Ōtani Gakuhō* 16:3 (October 1935): 51–73.

———. "*Nihon ryōiki* ni tsuite." *Kokugo Kokubun* 4:5 (1934): 68–89.

Amino Yoshihiko, Kasamatsu Hiroshi, Ishii Susumi, and Katsumata Shizuo. *Chūsei no tsumi to batsu*. Tokyo: Tokyo Daigaku Shuppankai, 1998.

Andō Naotarō. "*Konjaku monogatari* maki jūshichi shutten kō." *Kokugo Kokubun* 19:1 (September 1950): 51–54.

———. *Setsuwa to haikai no kenkyū*. Tokyo: Kasama Shoin, 1979.

Andreasen, Esben. *Popular Buddhism in Japan: Shin Buddhist Religion and Culture*. Honolulu: University of Hawai'i Press, 1998.

Arai Kōjun. "Myōe shōnin no 'Jūmujin-in shari kōshiki.'" *Buzan Kyogaku Taikai Kiyō* 5 (October 1977): 76–97.

Atsumi Kaoru. "*Hōbutsushū* shoki shohon no tenkai sō." *Aichi Kenritsu Daigaku Bungakubu Ronshū (Kokubungaku Kahen)* 21 (December 1970): 76–91.

Bargen, Doris G. *A Woman's Weapon: Spirit Possession in the Tale of Genji*. Honolulu: University of Hawai'i Press, 1997.

Bateson, F. W. "Modern Bibliography and the Literary Artifact." In *English Studies Today*, 2nd ser., ed. G. A. Bonnard, pp. 67–77. Bern: Francke Verlag, 1961. Reprinted as "The New Bibliography and the 'New Criticism.'" In Bateson, *Essays in Critical Dissent*, pp. 1–15. Totowa, NJ: Rowman and Littlefield, 1971.

Bauman, Richard. *Verbal Art as Performance*. Prospect Heights, IL: Waveland Press, 1977.

Berry, Mary Elizabeth. *Japan in Print: Information and Nation in the Early Modern Period*. Berkeley: University of California Press, 2006.

Blackburn, Anne M. *Buddhist Learning and Textual Practice in Eighteenth-Century Lankan Monastic Culture*. Princeton, NJ: Princeton University Press, 2001.

Blacker, Carmen. *The Catalpa Bow: A Study of Shamanistic Practices in Japan*. London: Allen and Unwin, 1975.

Brokaw, Cynthia. *Printing and Book Culture in Late Imperial China*. Berkeley: University of California Press, 2005.

Brower, Robert H. "The *Konzyaku Monogatarisyū*: An Historical and Critical Introduction, with Annotated Translations of Seventy-Eight Tales." PhD diss., University of Michigan, 1952.

Buswell, Robert E., Jr., ed. *Currents and Countercurrents: Korean Influences on East Asian Buddhist Traditions*. Honolulu: University of Hawai'i Press, 2006.

———, ed. *Encyclopedia of Buddhism*. New York: Macmillan Reference, 2004.

Bynum, Caroline Walker. *Fragmentation and Redemption: Essays on Gender and the Human Body in Medieval Religion*. New York: Zone Books, 1992.

———. *Holy Feast and Holy Fast: The Religious Significance of Food to Medieval Women*. Berkeley: University of California Press, 1987.

Cabezón, José Ignacio. *Buddhism and Language: A Study of Indo-Tibetan Scholasticism*. Albany: State University of New York Press, 1994.

Camille, Michael. "The Book as Flesh and Fetish in Richard de Bury's *Philobiblion*." In *The Book and the Body*, ed. Dolores Warwick Frese and Katherine O'Brien O'Keefe. Notre Dame, IN: University of Notre Dame Press, 1997.

Campany, Robert Ford. "Notes on the Devotional Uses and Symbolic Functions of Sutra Texts as Depicted in Early Chinese Buddhist Miracle Tales and Hagiographies." *Journal of the International Association of Buddhist Studies* (January 1991): 28–72.

———. *Strange Writing: Anomaly Accounts in Early Medieval China.* Albany: State University of New York Press, 1996.

Carruthers, Mary. *The Book of Memory: A Study of Memory in Medieval Culture.* Cambridge: Cambridge University Press, 1990.

Chartier, Roger. *Forms and Meanings: Texts, Performances, and Audiences from Codex to Computer.* Philadelphia: University of Pennsylvania Press, 1995.

———. *Inscription and Erasure: Literature and Written Culture from the Eleventh to the Eighteenth Century.* Philadelphia: University of Pennsylvania Press, 2007.

Chen, Kenneth. *Buddhism in China: A Historical Survey.* Princeton, NJ: Princeton University Press, 1964.

Cherniack, Susan. "Book Culture and Textual Transmission in Sung China." *Harvard Journal of Asiatic Studies* 54:1 (June 1994): 5–125.

Chiba Shōgen. "*Hōbutsushū* seiritsu kō." *Kokubungaku Tōsa* 1 (December 1931).

Childs, Margaret. "Kyōgen Kigo: Love Stories as Buddhist Sermons." *Japanese Journal of Religious Studies* 12:1 (March 1985): 91–104.

Chow, Kai-Wing. *Publishing, Culture, and Power in Early Modern China.* Stanford, CA: Stanford University Press, 2004.

Cleary, Thomas, trans. *The Flower Ornament Scripture: A Translation of* The Avatamsaka Sutra. Boston: Shambhala Publications, 1993.

Cole, Alan. *Text as Father: Paternal Seductions in Early Mahāyāna Buddhist Literature.* Berkeley: University of California Press, 2005.

Conze, Edward. *Buddhist Wisdom Books, Containing* The Diamond Sutra *and* The Heart Sutra. London: George Allen and Unwin, 1966.

———, trans. *Perfect Wisdom: The Short Prajñāpāmitā Texts.* Devon, England: The Buddhist Publishing Group, 1993.

———. *The Prajñāpāmitā Literature.* London: Mouton and Company, 1960.

Copp, Paul. "Notes on the Term 'Dhāranī' in Medieval Chinese Buddhist Thought." *Bulletin of SOAS* 71:3 (2008): 493–508.

Cox, Collette. *Disputed Dharmas: Early Buddhist Theories on Existence.* Tokyo: The International Institute for Buddhist Studies, 1995.

Darnton, Robert. *Revolution in Print: The Press in France, 1775–1800.* Berkeley: University of California Press, 1989.

Derrida, Jacques. "The Law of Genre." Translated by Stephen Barker in *Acts of Literature,* ed. Derek Attridge. New York: Routledge, 1992.

"Digital Prayer Wheels." Available at www.dharma-haven.org/tibetan/digital-wheels.htm (accessed September 8, 2008).

Diringer, David. *The Book Before Printing: Ancient, Medieval and Oriental.* New York: Dover Publications, 1982. Reprint of *The Hand-Produced Book,* 1953.

Dobbins, James C. *Jōdo Shinshū: Shin Buddhism in Medieval Japan.* Honolulu: University of Hawai'i Press, 2002.

Dykstra, Yoshiko K. "The Japanese *Setsuwa* and the Indian Avadāna." *Journal of Intercultural Studies* 6 (1979): 3–19.

———. *Miraculous Tales of the Lotus Sutra from Ancient Japan:* The Dainihonkoku Hokekyō Kenki *of Priest Chingen.* Tokyo: Sanseidō Printing Company, 1983.

———. "Miraculous Tales of the Lotus Sutra: The *Dainihonkoku Hokkegenki.*" *Monumenta Nipponica* 32:2 (Summer 1977): 189–210.

Eisenstein, Elizabeth. *The Printing Press as an Agent of Change: Communications and Cultural Transformations in Early Modern Europe.* Cambridge: Cambridge University Press, 1979.

Enders, Jody. *The Medieval Theatre of Cruelty: Rhetoric, Memory, Violence.* Ithaca, NY: Cornell University Press, 1999.

———. *Rhetoric and the Origins of Medieval Drama.* Ithaca, NY: Cornell University Press, 1992.

"Energy Infusion and Prayer Wheel." Available at www.prayer-wheel.com (accessed September 8, 2008).

Enomoto Ei'ichi. "Kyōten no tendoku ni tsuite." *Tōyō Gaku Kenkyū* 27 (1992): 45–58.

Faure, Bernard. "The Buddhist Icon and the Modern Gaze." *Critical Inquiry* 24:3 (Spring 1998): 768–813.

Febvre, Lucien, and Henri-Jean Martin. *The Coming of the Book: The Impact of Printing 1450–1800,* trans. David Gerard. London: Verso, 1984.

Fine, Elizabeth C. *The Folklore Text: From Performance to Print.* Bloomington: University of Indiana Press, 1994.

Foard, James H. "Ippen Shōnin and Popular Buddhism in Kamakura Japan." PhD diss., Stanford University, 1977.

Frantzen, Allen J. *Before the Closet: Same-Sex Love from* Beowulf *to* Angels in America. Chicago: University of Chicago Press, 1998.

Fujimoto Akira. "Aiyoku to fujōkan: *Hosshinshū* to *Kankyo no Tomo* no hikaku." *Nihon Bungaku* 24:10 (October 1975): 10–20.

Fujita Tokutarō. "Setsuwa bungaku no imi." *Kokubungaku kaishaku to kanshō* 6:2 (February 1941): 1–10.

Fukuda Akira. "Setsuwa to katarimono: ji'in no sekkyō wo megutte." *Kokubungaku Kaishaku to Kanshō* 46:8 (August 1981): 107–15.

Fukushima Kōichi. "*Nihon ryōiki* ni arawareta Kyōkai no kangaekata." *Heian Bungaku* 3 (1959): 99–138.

Furuhashi Nobuyoshi. "Setsuwa no ronri: hanashi no shōnin no isō." *Kokubungaku Kaishaku to Kanshō* 46:8 (August 1981): 36–42.

Furuhashi Tsuneo. "*Hosshinshū* shiron: Kamo no Chōmei bannen no chosaku to shinkyō." *Kenkyū Kiyō (Tanki Daigakubu)* 36 (2003): 138–132 (reverse pagination).

―――. "Kamo no Chōmei, *Hosshinshū* ni okeru 'hosshin' to 'ōjō.'" *Bungaku Kenkyū* 21 (March 2007): 1–15.

Furuya Minoru. "Sōshokukyō: gokuraku ōjō he no onegai." In *Zusetsu Nihon no bukkyō* 3: *Jōdokyō,* ed. Hamashima Masaji, pp. 183–200. Tokyo: Shinchōsha, 1989.

Geertz, Clifford. *The Interpretation of Cultures: Selected Essays.* New York: Basic Books, 1973.

Gill, Miriam. "Preaching and Image: Sermons and Wall Paintings in Later Medieval England." In *Preacher, Sermon and Audience in the Middle Ages,* ed. Carolyn Muessig, pp. 155–80. Leiden: Brill, 2002.

Gjertson, Donald E. "The Early Chinese Buddhist Miracle Tale: A Preliminary Survey." *Journal of the American Oriental Society* 101:3 (July–September 1981): 287–301.

―――. *Miraculous Retribution: A Study and Translation of Tang Lin's Ming Pao Chi.* Berkeley, CA: Centers for South and Southeast Asian Studies, 1989.

Gokoji Tsutomu. "Setsuwa bungaku ni arawareta Agui-ryū: Chōken to Seikaku wo chūshin ni." *Tendai Gakuhō* 20 (November 1978): 135–38.

Gombrich, Richard. "How the Mahāyāna Began." In *The Buddhist Forum,* ed. Tadeusz Skorupski, pp. 21–30. London: SOAS, 1990.

Gomez, Luis O, trans. "The Whole Universe as a Sutra." In *Buddhism in Practice,* ed. Donald S. Lopez, Jr. Princeton, NJ: Princeton University Press, 1995.

Gomi Fumihiko. "Setsuwa no ba, katari no ba." *Bungaku* 55:2 (February 1987): 27–38.

Goodrich, L. Carrington. "The Revolving Book-Case in China." *Harvard Journal of Asiatic Studies* 7:2 (July 1942): 130–61.

Goodwin, Janet R. *Alms and Vagabonds: Buddhist Temples and Popular Patronage in Medieval Japan.* Honolulu: University of Hawai'i Press, 1994.

Gorai Shigeru. *Kōya hijiri.* Tokyo: Kadokawa Shoten, 1965.

―――. *Shūkyō minzoku shūsei.* Tokyo: Kadokawa Shoten, 1995.

Gotō Kōzen. "Saikaku to setsuwa bungaku." *Kokubungaku Kaishaku to Kanshō* 6:2 (February 1941): 109–20.

Greetham, D.C. *Textual Scholarship: An Introduction.* New York: Garland Publishing, 1994.

Gummer, Natalie. "Articulating Potency: A Study of the *Suvarna(pra)bhāsottha-masūtra.*" PhD diss., Harvard University, 2000.

―――. "Buddhist Books and Texts: Ritual Uses of Books." In *Encyclopedia of Religion,* 2nd ed., ed. Lindsay Jones, pp. 1261–65. Detroit: MacMillan Reference Books, 2005.

Guo Qinghua. "The Architecture of Joinery: The Form and Construction of Rotating Sutra-Case Cabinets." *Architectural History* 42 (1999): 96–109.

Habito, Ruben. "Bodily Reading of the *Lotus Sutra:* Understanding Nichiren's Buddhism." *Japanese Journal of Religious Studies* 26:3–4 (1999): 281–306.

Hakeda, Yoshito S. *Kūkai: Major Works, Translated, With an Account of His Life and a Study of His Thought*. New York: Columbia University Press, 1972.

Hallisey, Charles. "Roads Taken and Not Taken in the Study of Theravāda Buddhism." In *Curators of the Buddha: The Study of Buddhism under Colonialism*, ed. Donald S. Lopez, Jr, pp. 31–62. Chicago: University of Chicago Press, 1995.

Hamashima Masaji, ed. *Zusetsu Nihon no bukkyō* 3: *Jōdokyō*. Tokyo: Shinchōsha, 1989.

Hamburger, Jeffrey. "The Visual and the Visionary: The Image in Late Medieval Monastic Traditions." *Viator: Medieval and Renaissance Studies* 20 (1989): 160–82.

Harada Kōzō "*Kankyo no tomo* kikō to Keisei no sōan seikatsu." *Bukkyō Bungaku Kenkyū*. Kyoto: Hōzōkan, 1976.

Hare, Thomas. "Reading Writing and Cooking: Kūkai's Interpretive Strategies." *Journal of Asian Studies* 49:2 (May 1990): 253–73.

Harootunian, H. D. *Things Seen and Unseen: Discourse and Ideology in Tokugawa Nativism*. Chicago: University of Chicago Press, 1988.

Harrison, Elizabeth. *Encountering Amida: Jōdo Shinshū Sermons in Eighteenth Century Japan*. PhD diss., University of Chicago, 1992.

Harrison, Paul. "Searching for the Origins of the Mahāyāna: What Are We Looking For?" *The Eastern Buddhist* 28:1 (1995): 48–69.

———. "Who Gets to Ride in the Great Vehicle? Self-Image and Identity among the Followers of the Early Mahāyāna." *Journal of the International Association of Buddhist Studies* 10:1 (1987): 67–89.

Hashikawa Tadashi. "*Ryōiki* no kenkyū." *Geibun* 8:3 (1922): 187–203.

Hashimoto Shinkichi. "Keisei shōnin no jiseki." *Shigaku Zasshi* 22:7 (July 1911). Reprinted in *Denki tenseki kenkyū*. Tokyo: Iwanami Shoten, 1972.

Hayashi Masahiko, Akiu Yoshinori, and Yokoyama Jun. "*Hosshinshū* kenkyū bunken mokuroku." *Chūō Daigaku Kokubun* 50 (March 2007): 53–68.

Hickman, Brian. "A Note on the Hyakumantō Dharani." *Monumenta Nipponica* 30:1 (Spring 1975): 87–93.

Hikata Ryūshō. *Honjōkyōrui no shisōteki kenkyū*. Tokyo: Sankibō Busshorin, 1954.

———. *Jātaka gaikan*. Tokyo: Suzuki Zaidan, 1961.

Hirabayashi Moritoku. "Keisei shōnin denkō hoi." *Kokugo to Kokubungaku* 47:6 (June 1970): 35–46.

Hirakawa Akira. "The Rise of Mahāyāna Buddhism and Its Relationship to the Worship of Stupas." *Memoirs of the Research Department of the Tōyō Bunkō* 22 (1963): 57–106.

Hirota, Dennis. *No Abode: The Record of Ippen*. Honolulu: University of Hawai'i Press, 1997.

Hirota Tetsumichi. *Chūsei bukkyō setsuwa no kenkyū*, rev. ed. Tokyo: Benseisha, 1990.

Hisamatsu Sen'ichi, ed. *Shinpan Nihon bungakushi*, vol. 3. Tokyo: Shibundō, 1972.

Holsinger, Bruce. *Music, Body, and Desire in Medieval Culture: Hildegard of Bingen to Chaucer.* Stanford, CA: Stanford University Press, 2001.

Holt, John C. "Protestant Buddhism? Review of *Buddhism Transformed: Religious Change in Sri Lanka,* by Gombrich and Obeyesekere." *Religious Studies Review* 17:4 (October 1991): 307–12.

Honda Giken. "Setsuwa to wa nani ka." In *Setsuwa no Kōza* 1. Tokyo: Benseisha, 1991.

Honda Giken, Ikegami Jun'ichi, Komine Kazuaki, Mori Masato, and Abe Yasurō, eds. *Setsuwa no gensetsu: kōshō, shoshō, baitai.* Tokyo: Benseisha, 1991.

Howell, Thomas Raymond, Jr. "*Setsuwa,* Knowledge, and the Culture of Reading and Writing in Medieval Japan." PhD diss., University of Pennsylvania, 2002.

Hurvitz, Leon, trans. *Scripture of the Lotus Blossom of the Fine Dharma (The Lotus Sūtra), Translated from the Chinese of Kumārajīva.* New York: Columbia University Press, 1976.

Hyōdō Hiromi. *Katari no jōsetsu: "Heike" katari no hasshō to hyōgen.* Tokyo: Yūseidō, 1985.

———. *"Koe" no kokumin kokka: Nihon.* Tokyo: Nihon Hōsō Shuppan Kyōkai, 2000.

Ienaga Saburō. *Chūsei bukkyō shisōshi kenkyū.* Kyoto: Hōzōkan, 1955.

———, ed. *Nihon Emakimono Zenshū: Japanese Narrative Scrolls,* vol. 6, *Jigoku zōshi, gaki zōshi, yamai no sōshi.* Tokyo: Kadokawa Shoten, 1960.

Ikeda Kikan. "*Nihon ryōiki* ni itsubun wa hatashite gisaku naruka." *Kokubungaku Tōsa* (December 1931). Reprinted in *Monogatari bungaku* 2. Tokyo: Shibundō, 1968.

Ikegami Jun'ichi. *Konjaku monogatari shū no sekai: chūsei no akebono.* Tokyo: Chikuma Shoten, 1983.

———. "Kōshō no setsuwa ni okeru ba to wadai no kankei: *Gyokuyō* no kiji kara." *Gobun* 43 (June 1984): 1–9.

Imamura Mieko. "*Hosshinshū* to shōdō: Tsugarukabon 'Chūnagon Akimoto no koto' nado." *Kokugo to Kokubungaku* 75:8 (August 1998): 32–46.

Inagaki Hisao and Harold Stewart, trans. *The Three Pure Land Sutras.* Berkeley, CA: Numata Center for Buddhist Translation and Research, 2003.

Inoue Mitsusada, *Nihon kodai no kokka to bukkyō.* Tokyo: Iwanami Shoten, 1971.

Irvine, Martin. *The Making of Textual Culture: 'Grammatica' and Literary Theory, 350–1100.* Cambridge: Cambridge University Press, 1994.

Ishida Mosaku et al. *Japanese Buddhist Prints.* New York: Harry N. Abrams, 1964.

Itabashi Tomoyuki. "*Nihon ryōiki* no senjutsu nenji ni tsuite." *Kokugo to Kokubungaku* 7:2 (1930): 132–42.

———. "*Ryōiki* Enryaku yonen izen gensensetsu ni tsuite." *Bungaku* 21:11 (1953): 757–64.

Itō Chikako. *Bukkyō setsuwa no tenkai to hen'yō.* Tokyo: Nonburu, 2008.

Iwamoto Yutaka. *Bukkyō setsuwa kenkyū jōsetsu.* Kyoto: Hōzōkan, 1967.

Iwata Taijō. "*Hosshinshū* no keisei to *Hokkekyō* kanren no setsuwa." *Ōzaki Gakuhō* 137 (February 1984): 48–74.

Izumoji Osamu. "Sanbōe no hensan ishiki." *Bungaku* 43:3 (March 1975): 241–66.

Kabutogi Shōkō. *Hokke hangyō no kenkyū.* Tokyo: Daitō shuppansha, 1982.

Kagamishima Hiroyuki. "*Hokke genki* kenkyū josetsu." *Bungaku* 1: 1–2 (1936): 22–32.

Kamada Shōken. *Okyō wo tabeyō (1): Dokyō wa shisha no tame dewanai.* Tokyo: Bukkyō Ji'in Seianji Shuppanbu, 2003.

Kamakura Kyōiku Iinkai. *Kamakura kokuhō kanzuroku daigoshū: Kamakura no emaki,* 2nd ed., ed. Miura Katsuo. Yokohama: Nakagawa Insatsu Shushiki Kaisha, 1983.

———. *Kamakura kokuhō kanzuroku dainijūrokushū: Kamakura no emaki II (Muromachi jidai),* ed. Miura Katsuo. Tokyo: Shushiki Kaisha Benridō, 1984.

Kamens, Edward. *The Three Jewels: A Study and Translation of Minamoto Tamenori's* Sanbōe. Ann Arbor, MI: Center for Japanese Studies, 1988.

Kanda Fusae. "Behind the Sensationalism: Images of a Decaying Corpse in Japanese Buddhist Art." *The Art Bulletin* (March 2005): 1–52.

Kastan, David Scott. *Shakespeare and the Book.* Cambridge: Cambridge University Press, 2001.

Kasuga Kazuo. *Setsuwa no gobun: kodai setsuwabun no kenkyū.* Tokyo: Ōfusha, 1975.

Katayose Masayoshi. "Honchō setsuwa bungaku no ichi yōshiki." *Kokubungaku Kaishaku to Kanshō* 6:2 (February 1941): 11–19.

———. *Konjaku monogatari shū no kenkyū.* Tokyo: Sanseidō, 1974.

Kawada Junzō. *Kōtō denshō ron.* Tokyo: Heibonsha Raiburarii, 2001.

Kawaguchi Hisao. "Setsuwa no hassei to denpan ni tsuite." *Kokubungaku Kaishaku to Kanshō* 6:2 (February 1941): 138–46.

———. "Tonkō henbun no seikaku to waga kuni shōdō bungaku: setsuwa to sekkyōshi no keifu." *Kanazawa Daigaku Hōbungaku Ronshū, Bungaku Hen* 8 (January 1960): 1–20.

Kay, Sarah. "Analytical Survey 3: The New Philology." *New Medieval Literatures* 3: 295–326.

Kazamaki Keijirō. "Setsuwa bungaku no bungeisei." *Kokubungaku Kaishaku to Kanshō* 6:2 (February 1941): 20–27.

Keinzle, Beverly Mayne, Edith Wilks Kolnikowski, Rosemary Drage Hale, Darleen Pryds, and Anne T. Thayer, eds. *Models of Holiness in Medieval Sermons.* Lovaine-la-Neuve: Federation Internationale des Instituts d'Etudes Medievales, 1996.

Kelsey, W. Michael. "*Konjaku Monogatarishū:* Toward an Understanding of Its Literary Qualities." *Monumenta Nipponica* 30:2 (Summer 1975): 121–50.

Kieschnick, John. "Blood Writing in Chinese Buddhism." *Journal of the International Association of Buddhist Studies* 23:2 (2001): 177–94.

———. *The Impact of Buddhism on Chinese Material Culture.* Princeton, NJ: Princeton University Press, 2003.

Kifuji Saizō. "*Hosshinshū* no seiritsu." *Bungaku* 47:1 (January 1979): 110–23.

Kikuchi Hiroki. "Jikkyōsha no genkei to chūseiteki tenkai." *Shigaku Zasshi* 104:8 (August 1995): 1361–96.

Kikuya Ryōichi. "Kuchigatari no setsuwa ni tsuite: Daianji *Hyakuza hōdan kikigaki* wo chūshin toshite." *Bungaku* 19:9 (September 1951): 48–56.

Kimbrough, R. Keller. *Preachers, Poets, Women, and the Way: Izumi Shikibu and the Buddhist Literature of Medieval Japan*. Ann Arbor, MI: Center for Japanese Studies, 2008.

————. "Reading the Miraculous Power of Japanese Poetry: Spells, Truth Acts, and a Medieval Buddhist Poetics of the Supernatural." *Japanese Journal of Religious Studies* 32:1 (2005): 1–33.

Kiyama, Lorinda. "Performative Preaching: The Art and Politics of Persuasion in Medieval Japan." PhD diss., Stanford University, forthcoming.

Kobayashi Tadao. "Mujū to Rengeji." *Kaishaku* (June 1959).

————. "*Shasekishū* no hampon ni tsuite." *Kokugakuin Zasshi* (June 1959): 39–50.

Kobayashi Yasuharu. "*Kankyo no tomo* josetsu, 1–4." Waseda Daigaku Kyōiku Gakubu Gakujutsu Kenkyū 16, 17, 18, and 20 (December 1967, 1968, 1969, and 1971): 117–28, 136–46, 79–88, and 29–37.

Kobayashi Yoshinori. *Hokke hyakuza kikigakishō sōsakuin*. Tokyo: Musashino Shoin, 1975.

Koizumi Hiroshi, ed. *Hōbutsushū: chūsei koshahon sanshu*. Tokyo: Koten Bunko, 1971.

————, ed. *Koshahon Hōbutsushū*. Tokyo: Kadokawa Shoten, 1973.

Koizumi Michi. "Kōyabon *Nihon ryōiki* kō." *Kokugo Kokubun* 21:10 (1952): 11–21.

————. "*Ryōiki* no shohon wo megutte." *Kuntengo to Kunten Shiryō* 34 (December 1966): 18–38.

Kojima Takayuki. *Chūsei setsuwashū no keisei*. Tokyo: Wakakusa Shobō, 1999.

————. "*Kankyo no tomo* Kaisetsu." SNKBT 40: 542–63. Tokyo: Iwanami Shoten, 2001.

Komatsu Kazuhiko. "Setsuwa no keisei to hensen." *Kokubungaku Kaishaku to Kanshō* 46:8 (August 1981): 30–35.

Komine Kazuaki. *Chūsei setsuwa no sekai wo yomu*. Tokyo: Iwanami Shoten, 1998.

————. *Konjaku monogatari shū no keisei to kōzō*. Tokyo: Kasama Shoin, 1985.

————. *Setsuwa no koe: chūsei sekai no katari, uta, warai*. Tokyo: Shinseidō, 2000.

————. *Setsuwa no mori: chūsei no tengu kara Isoppu made*. Tokyo: Iwanami Shoten, 2001.

Konishi Jin'ichi. *A History of Japanese Literature*, vol. 1, *The Archaic and Ancient Ages*. Trans. Aileen Gatten and Nicholas Teele. Princeton, NJ: Princeton University Press, 1984.

————. *A History of Japanese Literature*, vol. 2, *The Early Middle Ages*. Trans. Aileen Gatten. Princeton, NJ: Princeton University Press, 1986.

———. *A History of Japanese Literature,* vol. 3, *The High Middle Ages.* Trans. Aileen Gatten and Mark Harbison. Princeton, NJ: Princeton University Press, 1991.

Konta Yōzō. *Edo no hon'yasan.* Tokyo: Nihon Hōsō Shuppan Kyōkai, 1977.

Kornicki, Peter. *The Book in Japan: A Cultural History from the Beginnings to the Nineteenth Century.* Leiden: Brill, 1998.

Kotas, Frederic. "The Craft of Dying in Late Heian Japan." In *Bukkyō Bungaku no Kōsō,* ed. Imanari Genshō, pp. 598–574 (reverse pagination). Tokyo: Shintensha, 1996.

Kumahara Masao. "*Shasekishū* to Kamakura." *Ihō Kanazawa Bunko* 26–28 (July–September 1947).

Kunisaki Fumimaro. "Setsuwa to setsuwa bungaku." *Kokubungaku Kaishaku to Kanshō* 6:2 (February 1941): 10–13.

Kurobe Michiyoshi. "*Konjaku monogatarishū* maki jūgo to *Hokke genki.*" *Dōhō Gakuhō* 14:15 (May 1976): 345–54.

Kuroda Toshio. *Nihon chūsei no kokka to shūkyō.* Tokyo: Iwanami Shoten, 1975.

LaFleur, William. *The Karma of Words: Buddhism and the Literary Arts in Medieval Japan.* Berkeley: University of California Press, 1983.

Leclercq, Jean. *The Love of Learning and the Desire for God: A Study of Monastic Culture,* trans. Catherine Misrahi. New York: Fordham University Press, 1982.

Li, Michelle Osterfeld. *Ambiguous Bodies: Reading the Grotesque in Japanese Setsuwa Tales.* Stanford. CA: Stanford University Press, 2009.

Littau, Karin. *Theories of Reading: Books, Bodies and Bibliomania.* Cambridge, UK: Polity Press, 2006.

Loehr, Max. *Chinese Landscape Woodcuts from an Imperial Commentary to the Tenth-Century Printed Edition of the Buddhist Canon.* Cambridge, MA: Harvard University Press, 1968.

Lopez, Donald. "Authority and Orality in the Mahāyāna." *Numen* 42 (1995): 21–47.

———. "Inscribing the Bodhisattva's Speech: On the *Heart Sutra's* Mantra." *History of Religion* 29:4 (May 1990): 351–72.

Maeda Ai. *Kindai dokusha no seiritsu.* Tokyo: Yūseidō, 1973.

———. *Text and the City: Essays on Japanese Modernity.* Durham, NC: Duke University Press, 2004.

Mair, Victor H. "Buddhism and the Rise of the Written Vernacular in East Asia: The Making of National Languages." *Journal of Asian Studies* 53:3 (August 1994): 707–51.

Marra, Michele. *The Aesthetics of Discontent: Politics and Reclusion in Medieval Japanese Literature.* Honolulu: University of Hawai'i Press, 1991.

———. "The Development of Mappō Thought in Japan, Parts I & II." *Japanese Journal of Religious Studies* 15:1 (1988): 25–54; 15:4 (1988): 287–305.

Martin, Henri-Jean, and Lucien Febvre. *The Coming of the Book: The Impact of Printing 1450–1800,* trans. David Gerard. London: Verso, 1984.

Masuda Katsumi. *Kodai setsuwa bungaku.* Tokyo: Iwanami Shoten, 1958.

Matsumura Takeo. "Setsuwa no shokan keisō." *Bungaku* 2:5 (May 1934): 128–46.

Matsuno Junji. *Bukkyō gyōji to sono shisō.* Tokyo: Ozo Shuppan, 1980.

Matsuo Hiroshi. *Konjaku Monogatari no buntai no kenkyū.* Tokyo: Meiji Shoin, 1966.

McGann, Jerome. *The Textual Condition.* Princeton, NJ: Princeton University Press, 1991.

McKenzie, D. F. *Bibliography and the Sociology of Texts: The Panizzi Lectures, 1985.* London: British Library, 1986.

McLaverty, James. "The Mode of Existence of Literary Works of Art: The Case of the Dunciad Variorum." *Studies in Bibliography* 37 (1984): 82–105.

McMahan, David. "Orality, Writing, and Authority in South Asian Buddhism: Visionary Literature and the Struggle for Legitimacy in the Mahāyāna." *History of Religions* 37: 3 (February 1998): 249–74.

Meech-Pekarik, Julia. "Disguised Scripts and Hidden Poems in an Illustrated Heian Sutra: Ashide and Uta-e in the *Heike Nōgyō*." *Archives of Asian Art* 31 (1977–78): 43–78.

"Microfilm for Stupas and Prayer Wheels." Available at www.fpmt.org/resources/mani.asp#top (accessed September 8, 2008).

Miller, Stephen D. With translations by Stephen D. Miller and Patrick Donnelly. *The Wind from Vulture Peak: Origins of Buddhist Poetry in the Japanese Court Tradition.* Forthcoming.

Mills, D. E. *A Collection of Tales from Uji: A Study and Translation of Uji Shūi Monogatari.* Cambridge: Cambridge University Press, 1970.

Minamisato Michiko. "*Ryōiki* no seiritsu jijyō." *Gobun Kenkyū* 66–67 (1989): 51–61.

Miner, Earl, Hiroko Otagiri, and Robert E. Morrell, eds. *The Princeton Companion to Classical Japanese Literature.* Princeton, NJ: Princeton University Press, 1985.

Miyake Hitoshi. *Shugendō: Essays on the Structure of Japanese Folk Religion.* Ann Arbor, MI: Center for Japanese Studies, 2001.

Miyama Susumu. *Ezetsu Nihon no bukkyō 4: Kamakura bukkyō.* Tokyo: Shinchōsha, 1988.

Mizuta Norihisa. "Toji Kanchi'in bon *Sanbō ekotoba* no kisai seishiki no seiritsu." *Kokugo Kokubun* 21:7 (August 1952): 33–41.

Mori Masato. "Setsuwa no imi to kinō: *Hyakuza hōdan kikigakishō* kō." *Kokugakuin Zasshi* 92:1 (January 1991): 236–49.

Morishita Yōji. "Rufubon *Hosshinshū* no naiteki kōzō: jidai teijigo wo tegakarini." *Kokubungakukō* 136 (December 1992): 1–13.

Morrell, Robert E. "Kamakura Accounts of Myōe Shōnin as Popular Religious Hero." *Japanese Journal of Religious Studies* 9:2–3 (June-September 1982): 171–98.

———. "Mujū Ichien's Shintō-Buddhist Syncretism: *Shasekishū* Book I." *Monumenta Nipponica* 28:4 (Winter 1973): 447–88.

————. *Sand and Pebbles (Shasekishū): The Tales of Mujū Ichien, A Voice for Pluralism in Kamakura Buddhism*. Albany: State University of New York Press, 1985.

Motomichi-Nakamura, Kyoko. *Miraculous Stories from the Japanese Buddhist Tradition: The Nihon Ryōiki of the Monk Kyōkai*. Cambridge, MA: Harvard University Press, 1973.

Muessig, Carolyn, ed. *Preacher, Sermon and Audience in the Middle Ages*. Leiden: Brill, 2002.

Munemasa Iso'o. "Saikaku to bukkyō setsuwa." *Bungaku* 34:4 (April 1966): 13–26.

Murakami Manabu. "Setsuwa Tales and Hijiri Ascetics." *Acta Asiatica* 37 (1979): 85–103.

Murogi Mitarō. *Katarimono (mai, sekkyō, ko jōruri) no kenkyū*, rev ed. Tokyo: Kazama Shobō, 1992.

Murphy, James J. *Rhetoric in the Middle Ages: A History of Rhetorical Theory from St. Augustine to the Renaissance*. Berkeley: University of California Press, 1974.

Nagai Giken. "Kyōgen kigo ni tsuite." *Nihon Bukkyō Gakkai Nenpyō* 29 (October 1963): 331–44.

Nagai Yoshinori. "*Kankyo no tomo* no sakusha, seiritsu, oyobi sozai ni tsuite." *Taishō Daigaku Kenkyū Kiyō* 40 (January 1955).

Nagai Yoshinori and Kiyomizu Yūsei, eds. *Agui shōdōshū*, vol. 1. Tokyo: Kadokawa Shoten, 1972.

Nagano Kazuo. "Bukkyō setsuwa ni okeru jujitsu to kyokō: *Nihon Ryōiki* wo sozai ni." *Kokubungaku Kenkyū* 87 (1985): 13–23.

Nagao Gajin. *Yuimakyō wo yomu*. Tokyo: Iwanami Shoten, 1986.

Nagatomo Chiyoji. *Kinsei kamigata: sakka shoshi kenkyū*. Tokyo: Tokyōdō Shuppan, 1994.

Nakagawa Chūjin. "Minamoto Tamenori no *Sanbōe*." In *Setsuwa Bungaku*, ed. Nihon Bungaku Kenkyū Shiryō Kankōkai. Tokyo: Yūseidō, 1972.

Nakai Katsumi. "Nihon Ryōiki no sekaikan: bukkokudo ni okeru kyūsai no ronri." *Kokugaku Kenkyū* 90 (1986): 1–11.

————. "Tsumibito no shinshō fūkei: shigen to shite *Nihon ryōiki*." *Waseda Daigaku Kokubun Gakkai* 92 (1987): 11–21.

Nakamura Hajime, *Kōsetsu bukkyōgo daijiten*. Tokyo: Tokyo Shoseki, 2001.

Nakamura Tanio. "Kusōshi emaki no seiritsu." In *Gaki zōshi, jigoku zōshi, yamai no sōshi, kusōshi emaki*, ed. Akiyama Ken et al. *Nihon Emaki Taisei 7*. Tokyo: Chūō Kōronsha, 1977.

Nakao Takashi. *Chūsei no kanjin hijiri to shari shinkō*. Tokyo: Furukawa Kōbunkan, 2001.

Nara Kokuritsu Hakubutsukan, ed. *Taifū hisai fukkō shi'en: Itsukushimajinja kokuhōten*. Osaka: The Yomiuri Shimbun, 2005.

Nattier, Jan. *A Few Good Men: The Bodhisattva Path according to* The Inquiry of Ugra (Ugrapariprccha). Honolulu: University of Hawai'i Press, 2003.

Nemoto Seiji. *Nara jidai no sōryo to shakai.* Tokyo: Yūzankaku Shuppan, 1999.
Nishiguchi Junko, "Death and Burial of Women of the Heian High Aristocracy." In *Engendering Faith: Women and Buddhism in Premodern Japan,* ed. Barbara Ruch. Ann Arbor, MI: Center for Japanese Studies, 2002.
Nishijima, Gudo Wafu, and Chodo Cross, ed. *Master Dōgen's Shōbōgenzō, Book 1.* Working, Surrey: Windbell Publications, 1994.
Nishimura Satoshi. "Hyakuyo kayoi setsuwa kō," *Kokugakuin Zasshi* 86:8 (August 1985): 17–28.
Nishio Kōichi. *Chūsei setsuwa bungaku ron.* Tokyo: Hanawa Shobō, 1963.
Nomura Takumi. "Myōe no shashingyō to kotoba." *Nihon Bungaku* 31:4 (April 1982): 28–35.
Nosco, Peter. *Remembering Paradise: Nativism and Nostalgia in Eighteenth-Century Japan.* Cambridge, MA: Harvard University Press, 1990.
O'Donnell, James J. *Avatars of the Word: From Papyrus to Cyberspace.* Cambridge, MA: Harvard University Press, 1998.
Ohnuma Reiko. "Dehadāna: The 'Gift of the Body' in Indian Buddhist Narrative Literature." PhD diss., University of Michigan, 1997.
Okada Mareo. "Minamoto Shitagō oyobi dō Tamenori nenpu." *Ritsumeikan Daigaku Ronsō* 8 (January 1943): 39–68; 12 (May 1948): 1–24.
———. "Minamoto Tamenori den kō." *Kokugo to Kokubungaku* 19:11 (January 1942): 25–37.
Pandey, Rajyashree. *Writing and Renunciation in Medieval Japan: The Works of the Poet-Priest Kamo no Chōmei.* Ann Arbor, MI: Center for Japanese Studies, 1998.
Payne, Richard K., ed. *Re-Visioning "Kamakura" Buddhism,* Honolulu: University of Hawai'i Press, 1998.
Phelan, Peggy. *Mourning Sex: Performing Public Memories.* New York: Routledge, 1997.
———. *Unmarked: The Politics of Performance.* New York: Routledge, 2001.
Phelan, Peggy, and Jill Lane, eds. *The Ends of Performance.* New York: New York University Press, 1998.
Pye, Michael. *Skillful Means: A Concept in Mahayana Buddhism.* London: Gerald Duckworth, 1978.
Rambelli, Fabio. *Buddhist Materiality: A Cultural History of Objects in Japanese Buddhism.* Stanford, CA: Stanford University Press, 2007.
———. *Vegetal Buddhas: Ideological Effects of Japanese Buddhist Doctrines on the Salvation of Inanimate Beings.* Kyoto: Italian School of East Asian Studies, 2001.
Reischauer, A. K. "Genshin's *Ōjō Yōshū:* Collected Essays on Birth into Paradise." *Transactions of the Asiatic Society of Japan* 7 (1930): 16–97.
Reischauer, Edwin O., trans. *Ennin's Diary: The Record of a Pilgrimage to China in Search of the Law.* New York: Ronald Press Company, 1955.
Riffaterre, Michael. "The Mind's Eye: Memory and Textuality." In *The New*

Medievalism, ed. Marina S. Brownlee, Kevin Brownlee, and Stephen G. Nichols, pp. 29–45. Baltimore, MD: Johns Hopkins University Press, 1991.

"Rinzou." Available at www.glopad.org/pj/ja/record/piece/1000137 (accessed August 21, 2008).

Rodd, Laurel Rasplica. "Nichiren and Setsuwa." *Japanese Journal of Religious Studies* 5: 2–3 (June–September 1978): 159–83.

———. *Nichiren: Selected Writings.* Honolulu: University of Hawaiʻi Press, 1980.

Ruch, Barbara, ed. *Engendering Faith: Women and Buddhism in Premodern Japan.* Ann Arbor, MI: Center for Japanese Studies, 2002.

———. "Medieval Jongleurs and the Making of a National Literature." In *Japan in the Muromachi Age,* ed. John W. Hall and Toyoda Takeshi, pp. 279–309. Berkeley: University of California Press, 1977.

Ruppert, Brian D. *Jewel in the Ashes: Buddha Relics and Power in Early Medieval Japan.* Cambridge, MA: Harvard University Press, 2000.

Saeki Shin'ichi. "Kanjin hijiri to setsuwa: arui wa 'setsuwa' to 'katari.'" In *Heike monogatari: setsuwa to katari,* ed. Mizuhara Hajime. Tokyo: Yūseidō, 1994.

Saitō Kiyoe. "Chūsei ni okeru setsuwa bungaku no geidōkan." *Bungaku* 2:5 (May 1934): 54–70.

———. "Setsuwa bungaku no honshitsu." *Kokugo to Kokubungaku* 4:4 (April 1927): 124–44.

Sakai Shirō. "Kōbō Daishi kusōkan ni tsuite." *Mikkyō Gakkaihō* 14 (1975): 1–10.

Sakurai Yoshirō. "*Shasekishū* ichimen: hōgo to shōdō no kyōkan de." *Bungaku* (April 1969): 75–90.

Sakya, Jigdal Dagchen. "The Power of a 'Modern' Prayer Wheels" *[sic].* *The Snow Lion Newsletter.* Available at www.snowlionpub.com/pages/N68_6.html (accessed September 8, 2008).

Sasaki Shizuka. "A Study of the Origin of Mahāyāna Buddhism." *Eastern Buddhist* 30:1 (1997): 79–113.

Sasaki Takashi. "Chūsei sanbungaku no kataritetachi." *Nihon Bungaku* 27:11 (November 1978): 27–36.

Satō Akio. "Chūsei bunka ni okeru bukkyō juyō no ichi keitai: *Hyakuza hōdan* oboegaki 1." *Shūkyō Bunka* (October 1951): 43–70.

———. *Hyakuza hōdan kikigakishō.* Tokyo: Nan'undo Ofusha, 1963.

Satō Akira. "Enzuru shutai: *Uji shūi monogatari* no hyōgen kikō." *Bungei Kenkyū* 119 (September 1988): 45–52.

Satō Kenzō. "Monogatari to minzoku bungei: *Nihon ryōiki* ron." *Kokugakuin Zasshi* 54:1, 156–64.

Satō Michiko, ed., *Chūsei ji'in to hōe.* Kyoto: Hōzōkan, 1994.

Schechner, Richard. *Between Theater and Anthropology.* Philadelphia: University of Pennsylvania Press, 1981.

———. *Performance Studies: An Introduction.* London: Routledge, 2002.

Schopen, Gregory. *Bones, Stones, and Buddhist Monks: Collected Papers on the Ar-*

chaeology, Epigraphy, and Texts of Monastic Buddhism in India. Honolulu: University of Hawai'i Press, 1997.

———. Figments and Fragments of Mahāyāna Buddhism in India: More Collected Papers. Honolulu: University of Hawai'i Press, 2005.

———. "The Mahāyāna and the Middle Period in Indian Buddhism: Through a Chinese Looking-Glass." The Eastern Buddhist 32:2 (2000): 1–25.

Schroeder, John W. Skillful Means: The Heart of Buddhist Compassion. Honolulu: University of Hawai'i Press, 2001.

Seidensticker, Edward G., trans. The Tale of Genji. New York: Alfred A. Knopf, 2000.

Sekiyama Kazuo. Sekkyō no rekishi: bukkyō to wagei. Tokyo: Iwanami Shoten, 1978.

Sharf, Robert H. Coming to Terms with Chinese Buddhism: A Reading of the Treasure Store Treatise. Honolulu: University of Hawai'i Press, 2002.

Sharf, Robert H., and Elizabeth Horton Sharf, eds. Living Images: Japanese Buddhist Icons in Context. Stanford, CA: Stanford University Press, 2001.

Shiba Kayono. "'Dokyōdō' kō." Bungaku 9:1 (January 1998): 124–34.

———. Dokyōdō no kenkyū. Tokyo: Fuzama Shobō, 2004.

Shillingsburg, Peter L. "Text as Matter, Concept, and Action." Studies in Bibliography 44 (1991): 31–82.

Shimizu Masumi. Dokyō no sekai: nōdoku no tanjō. Tokyo: Yoshikawa Kōbunkan, 2001.

———. "Nōdoku to nōsetsu: ongei 'dokyō' no ryōiki to tenkai." Chūsei Kayō Kenkyūkai 15 (December 1997): 22–36.

Shimizu Yūshō. "Aguiryū no shōdō ni tsuite." In Bukkyō Bungaku Kenkyū 10, pp. 107–28. Kyoto: Hōzōkan, 1971.

Shingaku Junrō. "Shinran in okeru myōgō honzon no shisō." Shinshugaku 78 (March 1988): 1–29.

Silk, Jonathan. "A Note on the Opening Formula of Buddhist Sūtras." Journal of the International Association of Buddhist Studies 12:1 (1989): 158–63.

———. "What, If Anything, Is Mahāyāna Buddhism? Problems of Definitions and Classifications." Numen 49 (2002): 76–109.

Smith, Henry D. II. "The History of the Book in Edo and Paris." In Edo and Paris: Urban Life and the State in the Early Modern Era, ed. James L. McClain, John M. Merriman, and Ugawa Kaoru. Ithaca, NY: Cornell University Press, 1994.

———. "Review: Japaneseness and the History of the Book." Monumenta Nipponica 53:4 (Winter 1998): 499–515.

Stock, Brian. The Implications of Literacy: Written Language and Models of Interpretation in the Eleventh and Twelfth Centuries. Princeton, NJ: Princeton University Press, 1983.

Stone, Jacqueline I. Original Enlightenment and the Transformation of Medieval Buddhism. Honolulu: University of Hawai'i Press, 1999.

———. "Seeking Enlightenment in the Last Age: Mappō Thought in Kamakura

Buddhism, Parts I & II." *The Eastern Buddhist* 13:1 (Spring 1985): 28–57; 13:2 (Autumn 1985): 34–64.

Strong, John. *The Legend of King Aśoka*. Princeton, NJ: Princeton University Press, 1983.

———. "The Transforming Gift: An Analysis of Devotional Acts of Offering in Buddhist 'Avadāna' Literature." *History of Religions* 18:3 (February 1979): 221–37.

Suzuki Tōzō. "Setsuwa bungaku no kenkyū to mukashi banashi." *Kokubungaku Kaishaku to Kanshō* (February 1941): 121–32.

Tachibana Nankei. *Tōyūki*. Tokyo: Shōeidō, ca. 1903.

Tachibana Sumitaka. "*Hōbutsushū* no ihon kenkyū." *Kokugo Kokubun* 2:2–4 (February-April 1932).

———. "Taira no Yasuyori den kō." *Ōtani Gakuhō* 12:1 (January 1931).

Taira Masayuki. *Nihon chūsei no shakai to bukkyō*. Tokyo: Hanawa Shobō, 1992.

Takao Minoru. "*Hosshinshū* no kisoteki shomondai wo megutte: shohon honbun no ginmi kara." *Bukkyō Bunka Kenkyūjo Kenkyū Kiyō* 17 (March 1987): 17–55.

———. "Setsuwashū toshite no *Hosshinshū*: sono sekai no kiban wo kangaeru." *Bukkyō Bunka Kenkyūjo Kenkyū Kiyō* 12 (December 1981): 1–29.

Takase Shōgon. *Nihonkoku genpō zen'aku ryōiki (Kokuyaku issaikyō 24)*. Tokyo: Daitō Shuppansha, 1936–40.

Tanabe, George J., Jr. "Chanting and Liturgy." *Encyclopedia of Buddhism*. Ed. Robert E. Buswell, Jr. New York: Macmillan Reference USA, 2004.

Tanabe, George J., Jr., and Willa Jane Tanabe, eds. *The Lotus Sutra in Japanese Culture*. Honolulu: University of Hawai'i Press, 1989.

———. *Myōe the Dreamkeeper: Fantasy and Knowledge in Early Kamakura Buddhism*. Cambridge, MA: Council on East Asian Studies, 1992.

Tanabe, Willa Jane. *Paintings of the Lotus Sutra*. New York: Weatherhill, 1988.

Tanselle, G. Thomas. *The History of Books as a Field of Study: A Paper*. Chapel Hill, NC: Hanes Foundation/Academic Affairs Library, 1981.

Tatelman, Joel. *The Glorious Deeds of Pūrna: A Translation and Study of the* Pūrnā-vadāna. Delhi: Motilal Banarsidass, 2000.

Taylor, Diana. *The Archive and the Repertoire: Performing Cultural Memory in the Americas*. Durham, NC: Duke University Press, 2003.

Teiser, Stephen F. *The Scripture on the Ten Kings and the Making of Purgatory in Medieval Chinese Buddhism*. Honolulu: University of Hawai'i Press, 1994.

Thompson, Augustine. "From Texts to Preaching: Retrieving the Medieval Sermon as Event." In *Preacher, Sermon and Audience in the Middle Ages,* ed. Carolyn Muessig, pp. 13–37. Leiden: Brill, 2002.

Thurman, Robert A. F., trans. *The Holy Teaching of Vimalakīrti: A Mahāyāna Scripture*. University Park: Pennsylvania State University Press, 1990.

Tokushi Yūshō. "*Nihon ryōiki* ni inyō seru kyōkan ni tsuite." *Bukkyō Kenkyū* 1:2 (February 1937): 51–65.

Tsien, Tsuen-Hsuin. *Written on Bamboo and Silk: The Beginnings of Chinese Books and Inscriptions.* Chicago: University of Chicago Press, 2004.

Tsuji Nobuo, ed. *Zusetsu Nihon bukkyō 5: shomin bukkyō.* Tokyo: Shinchōsha, 1990.

Turner, Victor. *The Anthropology of Performance.* New York: PAJ Publications, 1988.

Twitchett, Denis. *Printing and Publishing in Medieval China.* New York: Frederic C. Beil, 1983.

Tyler, Royall, trans. and ed. *Japanese Nō Dramas.* London: Penguin Books, 1992.

Ueda Nobuo. "*Nihon ryōiki* setsuwa to butten." *Kokugo Kokubun* 54:8 (1985): 21–43.

Uematsu Shigeru. *Kodai setsuwa bungaku.* Tokyo: Hanawa Shobō, 1964.

——. "Minwa to *Hokkekyō* to Jizō bosatsu to." *Nihon no Setsuwa* 2 (1973): 211–39.

Ulrich, Katherine Eirene. "Divided Bodies: Corporeal and Metaphorical Dismemberment and Fragmentation in South Asian Religions." PhD diss., University of Chicago, 2002.

Ury, Marian. *Tales of Times Now Past: Sixty-Two Stories from a Medieval Japanese Collection.* Ann Arbor, MI: Center for Japanese Studies, 1979.

Uryū Tōshō. "*Hōbutsushū* kenkyū bunken mokuroku." *Kaishaku* 16:7 (July 1970).

Watanabe Tsunaya. "*Shasekishū* shohon no oboegaki." *Kokugo to Kokubungaku* 28:10 (1941).

Waters, Claire M. *Angels and Earthly Creatures: Preaching, Performance and Gender in the Later Middle Ages.* Philadelphia: University of Pennsylvania Press, 2004.

Watson, Burton, trans. and ed. *The Vimalakīrti Sutra.* New York: Columbia University Press, 1997.

Waugh, Pamela. *Metafiction: The Theory and Practice of Self-Conscious Fiction.* London: Routledge, 1984.

Wellek, René, and Austin Warren. *Theory of Literature.* New York: Harcourt, Brace and Company, 1956.

Wilson, Eizabeth. *Charming Cadavers: Horrific Figurations of the Feminine in Indian Buddhist Hagiographic Literature.* Chicago: University of Chicago Press, 1996.

——. "The Female Body as a Source of Horror and Insight in Post-Ashokan Indian Buddhism." In *Religious Reflections on the Human Body,* ed. Jane Marie Law. Bloomington: Indiana University Press, 1995.

Winkleman, John H. "The Imperial Library in Southern Sung China, 1127–1279. A Study of the Organization and Operation of the Scholarly Agencies of the Central Government." *Transactions of the American Philosophical Society* 64:9 (1974): 1–61.

Yagi Tsuyoshi. "*Nihonkoku genpō zen'aku ryōiki* to *Myōhōki* ni tsuite." *Gobun* 25 (March 1965): 15–24.

Yamada Shōzen. "Futari no Chōmei: *Hōjōki* kara *Hosshinshū* he." *Kokubungaku Tōsa* 9 (March 1973): 56–64.

———. "*Hōbutsushū* kaisetsu." SNKBT 40: 507–41. Tokyo: Iwanami Shoten, 2001.

———. "Waka soku darani kan no tenkai." In *Shinbutsu shugo to shugen,* ed. Tanabe Saburōsuke, 101–8. Nihon no bukkyō 6. Tokyo: Shinchōsha, 1989.

Yamagishi Tokuhei. *Hokke shūhō ippyakuza kikigakishō.* Tokyo: Benseisha, 1976.

Yamamoto, Kosho, trans. *The Mahāyāna Mahāparinirvāna Sutra: A Complete Translation from the Classical Chinese Language in Three Volumes.* Ube City: Karinbunko, 1973–75.

Yamane Kenkichi. "*Konjaku monogatari* to *Nihon ryōiki* to no kankei." *Gobun* 23 (August 1960): 15–21.

———. "Reigentan no shūshū." *Nihon no Setsuwa* 3 (1973): 106–15.

Yamashita Kin'ichi. "Katarareru setsuwa to kakarareta setsuwa: kirō setsuden wo chūshin ni." *Kokubungaku Kaishaku to Kanshō* 46:8 (August 1981): 94–99.

Yasuda Naomichi. "Kokubunken ni in'yō sareta *Sanbō ekotoba.*" In *Setsuwa bungaku,* ed. Nihon Bungaku Kenkyū Shiryō Kankōkai, pp. 15–42. Tokyo: Gakujutsu Bunken Fukyūkai, 1981.

Yiengpruksawan, Mimi Hall. "One Millionth of a Buddha: The Hyakumantō Darani in the Scheide Library." *Princeton University Library Chronicle* 48 (1986–87): 224–38.

Yoda Tomiko. *Gender and National Literature: Heian Texts in the Constructions of Japanese Modernity.* Durham, NC: Duke University Press, 2004.

"Zuiōji." Available at www2.dokidoki.ne.jp/tomura/zuiouzi.htm (accessed August 8, 2008).

Zumthor, Paul. *Speaking of the Middle Ages,* trans. Sarah White. Lincoln: University of Nebraska Press, 1986.

Index

Abe, Ryūichi, 205n41, 212n13

acceptance, 44–46, 207n62; "accept and hold," 46–50, 207n66, 207–8n67, 208n73, 208n79

accounts of miracles *(yan ji)*, 7, 65

Agni, 185–86

Agui school, 76, 92–93

Ajari Kōunbo, 151–52, 162–63

"all things are impermanent," 127, 128, 129

Ama (The diver), 86–87

Amida, descent of, 191*fig.*

Ānanda: entrusted with propagating the Buddha's teachings, 28–29, 31–32, 203–4n20, 204n21; as ideal dharma vessel, 54–55, 209n89; as interlocutor, 25

anju (dark recitation), 141, 147, 221n11

Ankokuji (Gifu), 183

Annam, 192

anomalies, 11–12

ascetic practices, 120, 157, 222n31. See also *hijiri*

aurality, 81, 214n42

avadāna (karmic biography), 7, 15, 65–66, 114

baskets, 184

Bateson, F. W., 203n14

bathing, 176, 224–25n7

baths, 10, 200n28

Bauman, Richard, 199n15

bodhi (enlightened intuition), 40, 41–42

bodhisattvas, 54, 55

body. *See* Buddha, body of; decomposition; dismemberment; embodiment; *fujōkan;* gifts of the body; putrefaction; self-sacrifice; *shashin;* text-body relationship

book. *See* "cult of the book"; history of the book; text; textual culture

Brahma Net Sutra, 117, 121, 218n31

Buddha: body of, 137–38, 142, 151, 153–55, 166, 172, 220n7; past lives of, 36–37, 128, 219n50; robes of, 151–52; sermons of and light miracles, 186–87, 116n17

Buddhabhadra, 26

Buddhist canon, 192

Buddhist cosmology, 176–77

Buddhist icons, 205n36

Buddhist language, 173–75

Buddhist services, 10, 93–96, 215n52; setsuwa in the context of, 90–92
Buddhist statuary, 134–37, 136*fig.*, 167, 179
Buddhist temple architecture, 181
bunju (receptive listening), 207n62
Buswell, Robert, Jr., 201n32
Bynum, Carolyn Walker, 11, 135, 215n3, 220n3
Byōdōin, 10

cakra, 177, 225n9
calligraphic practices, 3, 4
Camille, Michael, 221n12
Campany, Robert, 11–12, 66, 227n40
Carruthers, Mary, 140, 199n13
chanting, 4, 8. 50–52, 141, 153, 186. *See also* chanting hermits; chanting skulls
chanting hermits, 3, 155
chanting skulls, 156–60, 222n30
charity *(dāna)*, 113, 114, 115, 116
Chartier, Roger, 7, 198n7, 199n14
Childs, Margaret, 210n2
Chingen, 70, 82, 111, 146, 221n15. See also *Miracles of the Lotus Sutra*
Chōbōji, 76
Chōgen (Chōken), 3, 92–93, 224n7
Chōnen, 192
Chūsonji (Hiraizumi), 203n15
circumambulation, 4, 176, 178–79, 180, 192, 194. *See also* circumambulatory reading; revolving sutra libraries
circumambulatory reading, 2, 176, 178–79, 187, 193–95. *See also* circumambulation; revolving sutra libraries
Cole, Alan, 13
Collection of Sand and Pebbles, A (Shasek-ishū): cross-sectarian orientation of, 13; food metaphor in, 80; format of, 77; as last major Buddhist setsuwa collection, 10, 13, 67; as matchmaker, 89, 214n46; metaphor of salt gathering, 86; and preaching, 9, 76, 92, 109, 214n50, 217n21; preface to, 86, 89; presaged later trends, 76; on sutra scrolls and statues, 167; textual history of, 75–76, 213nn28,31; typology of beings who maintain the bodhisattva precepts, 108–9

Collection of Spiritual Awakenings, A (Hosshinshū): authorship and textual history of, 74, 78, 213nn24,25; erotic pursuit and religious awakening in, 105; as go-between, 88–89; language of, 74; preface to, 88–89; stories of devout women, 121, 125; story of Giei, 155–56; story of government steward who witnesses a Buddhist service, 90–91, 214n48; story of Kūya, 134, 152, 153; theme of putrefaction, 105, 109–10; theme of reclusion, 121; theme of self-sacrifice, 120; theme of sutra embodiment, 166
Collection of Treasures, A (Hōbutsushū): authorship of, 77; botanical imagery in, 84–85; medicinal metaphor in, 81; textual history and scholarship on, 72–74; story of Kūya, 152, 153; story of the Unbelieving Man, 163; theme of putrefaction in, 216n11; view of the human body in, 108; *waka* poetry in, 84–85
Companion in Solitude, A: audience for, 9, 212n15; authorship and textual history of, 75, 78, 213n26; erotic pursuit and religious awakening in, 105–6; metaphor of salt gathering in, 85–86; sermonizing in, 9, 91–92; sutra copying in, 120, 216n12; theme of *fujōkan*, 107, 122–23, 129–30; theme of "throwing away the body" and reclusion, 120
companion tales *(otogizōshi)*, 76, 107
concentrated mind *(isshin)*, 199n16
concertina booklets *(orihon)*, 189–90, 193
consciousness, 23–24
containers (for text), 23, 36, 57, 205n37
Contemplation Sutra, 28, 58
Conze, Edward, 206n48
"cult of the book" (Schopen), 3, 4, 21–22, 41, 50, 96, 197n3, 206n53
Cunda, 30

Daianji, 13, 71
Dainihonkoku Hokkekyō Genki. See *Miracles of the Lotus Sutra*
Dalai Lama, 195

Kieschnick, John, 187
Kikai, 1
Kikaigashima, 73
Kitano, 185, 186, 226n24
Kiyomori, 168
Kōbō Daishi. *See* Kūkai
Kohon setsuwashū (A Collection of Setsuwa from Old Books), 212nn15,18
Koizumi Hiroshi, 73–74
Kojidan (Conversations about Ancient Matters), 222n25
Kojima Takayuki, 67
Kokinshū, 85
Kokinwakashū (A Collection of Waka Ancient and Modern), 83
Kokon Chomonjū (A Collection of Old and New Tales Heard), 222n25, 223n33
kokoro (mind), 23–24, 110, 221n14
Komatsu Kazuhiko, 78
Komine Kazuaki, 78, 210n2, 213–14n37
Konishi Jin'ichi, 10, 14, 211n9
Konjaku Monogatari (Tales from Times Now Past), 67, 212n18. See also *Tales from Times Now Past*
konshi kinji kyō (gold-on-blue sutra copying) 142, 143*fig.*, 150
Konta Yōzō, 198n4
Korea, 15, 192
Kornicki, Peter, 189
Kōshin, 160, 161
Kōshō, 135, 136*fig.*
Kōzanji, 120, 197n1
Ksānti, 116–17, 118, 119, 217n27
Kūkai (Kōbō Daishi), 3, 201n39, 219n42, 224n4; nine poems on decomposition, 122–24, 125–27, 128, 129, 131
Kumārajīva, 25, 215n9
kusō (nine stages of degradation), 102
kusō no shi (nine poems on decomposition; Kūkai), 122–24, 125–27, 128, 129, 131, 159
Kūya, 134–35, 152–53; statue at Rokuhara-mitsuji, 134–37, 136*fig.*, 140, 153
kyōgen kigo (use of secular forms of writing to express larger religious truths), 99
Kyōkai (Keikai), 68, 87–88, 104, 211n12.

See also *Wondrous Record of Immediate Karmic Retribution, A*
Kyōshakubō, 62–63, 164

LaFleur, William, 201n35
language and Buddhism, 173–75
Larger Sutra of Immeasurable Life, 58
lay believers, 119, 223n35
Leclercq, Jean, 214n42
Lion's Roar, 26, 31, 54
liturgy, 92, 94–95. *See also* Buddhist services
Liu Dong, 182; *Dijing Jingwulüe*, 183–84
locomotion, 60
Loehr, Max, 220n7
Longfusi, 183–84
Lopez, Donald, 203n18
Lotus Sutra: on acceptance of sutras, 44, 48, 207n65, 208n73; assertion of the scroll as dharma container, 56; burning house parable, 25, 45; compares sutra scrolls to stupa, 178; in *Collection of Treasures*, 73; copying of, 166; cross-sectarian orientation of, 13; "Devadatta" chapter, 115; Dragon King's daughter in, 55–56; edition with characters enclosed in jeweled stupas, 138*fig.*; Ezō and, 144–45; and Fugen's vows, 19–20; and gifts of the body, 121; in the *Heike Nōkyō*, 167–71; intertextual allusions in, 28; Kyōshakubō lectures on, 62–63; "Medicinal Herbs" chapter, 10, 81–82; "Medicine King" chapter, 121, 146–48, 168–71, 169*fig.*; memorization of, 141, 143–49, 145–48, 157; mentioned, 227n44; metaphor of the blind turtle, 215n6; metaphors for preaching in, 224n6; in past lives, 37, 39, 205n40, 205n41; and the physical body of the Buddha, 41, 142, 166–67; "Preachers of Dharma" chapter, 137–38, 151; propagation of, 33, 53; protection of, 62–63; reader-text relationship in, 20; reading of, 152–53, 154; recitation of, 111, 120, 156, 157–60, 164; referenced in *Nirvana Sutra*, 28; scrolls of, 56–57, 191*fig.*; in setsuwa, 24; story of bodhisattva who acknowledged everyone he

met as a future buddha, 116; and *suri-kuyō*, 216n12; symbiotic relationship with human host, 58; textual commands in, 42, 206n55; translations of, 25. See also *Miracles of the Lotus Sutra*

love confession *(iro zange)*, 217n20

lust, 105–7, 110–11

Maeda Ai, 198n4

Mahāsattva, Prince, 121

Mahāyāna Buddhism, 12–13, 20–21, 202nn6,9

Mahāyāna sutras, 13, 27, 28–29. See also sutras

"mainstream Buddhism," 20–21, 202n6

Maitreya, 178–79, 180, 204n21

Man'yōshū (A Collection of Ten Thousand Leaves), 84

Manjuśri, 26, 31–32

mantra, 176, 224n5

mappō (final age of the dharma), 15, 100–102, 226n28

Marra, Michele, 101

matchmaker, setsuwa text as, 88–89

Matsuo Shrine, 152, 153

McGann, Jerome, 198n8

McLaverty, James, 40, 203n14

McMahan, David, 203n19

Medicine King, 121, 146–48, 168–71, 169*fig.*

medieval Christian art, 135

medieval manuscripts, 79

medieval period, 13–15

meditation, 13, 100, 180

Meigetsuki, 214n51

meiryō (to understand clearly or with illumination), 221n11

memorization: goals of, 51; as physical movement, 147–49, 221n15; by reading and reciting, 51–52, 157; and sutra copying, 138–39, 142; of sutra fragments, 48; and textual culture, 4; total recall, 46–48, 50. See also memory

memory: faulty, 140–41, 142–43, 144–50; as requirement of dharma vessel, 54–55; "without impediment," 148, 221n15; and writing, 138–39, 140. See also memorization

Meng Xianzhong, 211n12

metafictional strategies, 3, 23, 26–28, 36–40, 60

metaphor, 9–10, 80, 81, 85–86, 215n6; for the human body, 108, 116, 123–24, 217n26; for preaching, 177, 224n6; for self-sacrifice, 120, 218n38; used to describe setsuwa, 78–80, 90

Minamoto no Takakuni, 72

Minamoto no Tamenori, 69, 80–81, 83, 88, 101. See also *Three Jewels, the*

mind *(kokoro)*, 23–24, 51, 110, 221n14; concentrated mind, 199n16

Mingbao ji (Ming Pao Chi, Records of Supernatural Retribution), 16, 68, 72

miracles, 11–12. See also miracle tales

Miracles of the Lotus Sutra (Hokke Genki): audience for, 70; authorship of, 70, 77–78; chanting skull motif in, 159–60; exchange between Saichō and the deity of the Yahata Shrine, 222n25; scholarship on, 212nn16,17; setsuwa concerning Ezō, 144–45; setsuwa concerning Gyōhan, 146–48, 221n15; setsuwa concerning Kakunen, 141, 142–43; setsuwa concerning Kairen, 149; setsuwa concerning Myōren, 148–49; setsuwa concerning Tenjō, 149; as source for *Tales from Times Now Past*, 72; story of Fujiwara no Kanetaka, 154; story of Giei, 155–56; story of the priest Kōshin, 160; story of the priest Ichiei, 159–60; story of the priest Shunchō, 160; story of Riman, 111; sutra copying in, 216n12; text-body relationship in, 82, 162, 165, 222n28, 223n39

miracle tales, 3, 7, 12, 15–16, 65–66, 211n7

mi wo suteru (throwing away the body), 120. See also gifts of the body; self-sacrifice; *shashin*

monogatari, 211n9

Morrell, Robert, 201n34

Motomichi-Nakamura, Kyoko, 68, 211n12

Mount Daisen, 148

Mount Hiei, 13, 70, 141

Mount Kōya, 119

Mount Kumano, 148
Mount Mitake, 148
Mount Wutai, 183, 188
muga (no self), 161
Mujū Ichien, 76–77, 80, 88, 89; as salt
    gatherer, 86; tetralemma of, 108–9,
    112; *Zōtanshū (A Collection of Casual
    Digressions),* 219n39, 222n25. See also
    Collection of Sand and Pebbles, A
Murogi Mitarō, 210n2
Myōe: devotee of *Flower Ornament Sutra,*
    24; self-sacrifice of, 1–2, 3, 97, 101,
    112, 119, 173; mentioned, 17
Myōren, 148–49

Nāgārjuna, 130, 215n9
Nakao Takashi, 224n7
Nanchansi (Suzhou), 183
narrative drift, 37, 39
Natatomo Chiyoji, 198n4
nativism, 210n3
Nattier, Jan, 21, 202nn6,9
nenbutsu recitation, 13, 134, 135–37
Nichiren, 3, 180; "Minobusan gosho," 118;
    self-sacrifice and dismemberment tales,
    118–19, 120, 218n30
*Nihon Genpō Zen'aku Ryōiki (A Wondrous
    Record of Immediate Karmic Retribu-
    tion for Good and Evil in Japan),* 66,
    67, 68. See also *Wondrous Record of
    Immediate Karmic Retribution, A*
Nihon Shoki (Chronicles of Japan), 101
Nippo Jishō, 74
Nirvana Sutra: and the acceptance of sutras,
    48, 207n65; "all things are imperma-
    nent," 127; as composite document,
    31; definition of "sutra" in, 28; on the
    desecration of sutras, 33, 204n31; en-
    trustment in, 29–32; metafictional
    techniques in, 28, 38; metaphor of the
    blind turtle, 215n6; praise for Ānanda,
    54; and protection of sutras, 34, 59;
    on reading and reciting, 51–52; self-
    sacrifice in, 117, 127–29, 218n31;
    staging of, 25–26; sutra containers in,
    57; symbiotic relationship with human
    host, 58; textual commands in, 42;

women's gifts of the body in, 124–25.
    See also Himalaya Boy
Noh, 184
"no self" doctrine, 161
*Notes on One Hundred Sessions of Sermons.
    See One Hundred Sessions of Sermons*
Nyogen, 120

O'Donnell, James, 195
Ōe no Masafusa, *Gōdanshō,* 8
Ōe no Sadamoto, 105
Ohnuma Reiko, 113, 117
*One Hundred Sessions of Sermons (Hyakuza
    Hōdan Kikigakishō):* authorship and
    textual history of, 70–71, 77–78;
    connection between text and textiles
    in, 151–52; cross-sectarian orientation
    of, 13; mentioned, 107; as record of
    sermons, 9, 73, 90, 95, 200n25; scholar-
    ship on, 71, 212n20; sermons of Ajari
    Kōunbo, 151–52, 162–63; sermon
    of Kyōshakuobō, 164; sutra-keeping
    hermits in, 222n29; story of the Un-
    believing Man, 163; theme of textual
    incorporation, 162–63, 166, 223n39
Onjōji (Yamaguchi), 183
ontology, 4, 5, 6, 173–74
orihon (concertina booklets), 189–90, 193
otogizōshi (companion tales), 76, 107
owari manzai, 76

palm-leaf manuscripts, 187
Pandey, Rajyashree, 14
Panjo Yenchi, 211n12
parable of the burning house, 25, 45
paramitas, 113, 114, 115, 152, 222n23
part-whole relationship, 99, 215n3. *See also*
    fragmentation
Perfection of Wisdom sutras, 176, 224n5
performance studies, 6, 199n15
performative writing, 98–99
Phelan, Peggy, 98–99, 108, 110, 130,
    199n15
poetry, 14, 83–85, 211n9
pravartana (rolling forward), 177
prayer wheels, 182, 194–95
preaching: expectations regarding, 91–92;

false, 109, 217n21; metaphors for, 177, 224n6; standardization of liturgy, 92–93, 94–95. *See also* Buddhist services; sermonizing
public works projects, 10, 200nn28,29
Pure Land, 13, 25, 134, 185, 191*fig.*, 226n25; sutras, 24, 42, 206n55
putrefaction, 100, 102, 103–4; nine stages of, 123, 219n43. *See also* decomposition; *fujōkan*

reading. *See* sutra reading
reclusion, 120–22
"reed hand" technique, 169
rendaikyō (lotus throne sutra), 166
reproduction. *See* sutras, reproduction and propagation of
revelation, 27, 203n19
revolving sutra libraries, 181–87, 182*fig.*, 193, 194, 225nn18,19, 226n20
Riffaterre, Michael, 127, 131
Riman, 113
Rinzai Zen, 13, 76
"Rinzō" (The Revolving Sutra Library; Kanze Nagatoshi), 184–85, 226n26
ritsuryō system, 69
robes, 151–53, 162
Rokuharamitsuji, 134, 153

Saichō, 222n25
Saisen, 122
Sakya, Jidgal Dagchen, 194–95
salt gathering, 85–86, 89–90
Samanthabadra (Fugen), 120, 142–43, 167
Sanbō Ekotoba (*Illustrations and Explanations of the Three Jewels*), 67, 68–69. See also *Three Jewels, the*
Sanshū Shido Dōjō Engi (*The Sacred Origins of the Holy Places of Shido in Sanuki Province*), 87
Sāriputra, 49, 56
Sasaki Shizuka, 202n9
Satō Akio, 71
Satō Akira, 78
Schopen, Gregory, 3, 21, 41, 202n8, 206n53
scrolls: as containers of the dharma, 56–57; described in setsuwa, 190–91, 227n40;

human body as, 17; resilience of, 190, 192–94; as stupas, 178; terminology of, 193–94; and textiles, 223n37; as textual form, 175, 187, 189–90, 227n30
seeds, 83
Seikaku (Shōkaku, Shōgaku), 92–93
Seireishū (Kūkai), 122. See also *kusō no shi*
Seiryōji, 73
sekkyō (sermonizing), 8, 63. *See also* sermonizing
self-ordained monks, 211–12n13
self-sacrifice: in *jātaka* tales, 98, 101; metaphors for, 120, 218n38; in setsuwa, 98, 112, 113–19, 218n29; and textual fragments, 99, 117, 133. *See also* gifts of the body; dismemberment; *shashin*
Senjūshō (*Collected Notes on Selected Tales*), 212n18
sense organs, 23, 126, 219n46
seppō (sermonizing), 8, 63. *See also* sermonizing
sermonizing (*sekkyō, seppō*), 95, 210n2, 212n19; in *Collection of Sand and Pebbles*, 76; in *Collection of Treasures*, 73; in *One Hundred Sessions of Sermons*, 70–71, 73; setsuwa as record of, 8, 63. *See also* Buddhist services; preaching
Sessen Dōji (Himalaya Boy), 15, 82, 127–29, 131, 220–21n10
setsuwa: as articles of faith, 9; and Buddhism as a transcultural phenomenon, 63–64; and Buddhist textual culture, 7–8, 22; in the context of Buddhist services, 90–92; cross-sectarian nature of, 13; as didactic genre, 7, 9; English translations of, 7; as food and medicine, 80–82, 133; and the human body, 11, 63, 64, 82, 89–90, 98–100, 119, 174; humor in, 76; influenced by Indian and Chinese narrative forms, 65–66; as a literary genre, 8, 10, 16; metaphors used to describe, 78–80, 90; origins of, 65, 70; and national identity, 63, 210n3; and poetic composition, 85; as a performance genre, 10, 16, 62–63, 64, 70,

setsuwa *(continued)*
    199n15; as popular genre, 7, 9; taci-
    turn and loquacious, 67; textual cul-
    ture of, 9, 13; use of the term, 8–9,
    200n26; women and, 69, 75, 212n15.
    See also setsuwa collections; setsuwa
    scholarship
setsuwa collections: audience for, 10–11;
    compilation of, 7, 9, 77–78, 80; lit-
    erary antecedents for, 15–16; as
    matchmakers, 88–89; as physical
    proxies for preacher, 87–88; prefaces
    and colophons, 64, 80; as records of
    medieval sermonizing, 8; as seeds
    planted in gardens, 82–85; twelfth-
    century, 212n18; use of metaphor
    in, 9–10. See also *Collection of Sand
    and Pebbles, A; Collection of Spiritual
    Awakenings, A; Collection of Treasures,
    A; Companion in Solitude, A; Miracles
    of the Lotus Sutra; One Hundred
    Sessions of Sermons; Tales from Times
    Now Past; Three Jewels The; Wondrous
    Record of Immediate Karmic Retribu-
    tion, A*
setsuwa scholarship, 7, 63–64, 78, 199n19,
    210n3, 211n9
seven enlightened states, 117, 218n28
seven illusions, 117, 218n28
seven precious jewels, 142
shakyō, 100. *See* sutra copying
Sharf, Robert H., 172
Shasekishū (A Collection of Sand and Pebbles),
    67. See also *Collection of Sand and
    Pebbles, A*
shashin (bodily self-sacrifice), 98, 119, 120,
    128, 130–31, 217n27. *See also* self-
    sacrifice
shikkai juji (completely accepting and
    holding all), 208n73. *See also*
    acceptance
Shillingsburg, Peter, 36, 41, 205n37
Shingon school, 13, 201n39
Shinjō (Shinshō), 93, 94–95, 215n52
Shinran, *Shōzōmatsu wasan*, 218n38
Shinsai, 180

Shinshō, 180
Shinzei, 122
Shōtoku Taishi, 103
Shōzōmatsu wasan (Shinran), 218n38
Shugendō, 222n31
*Shūi Ōjōden (A Gleaning of Tales of Rebirth
    in the Pure Land)*, 221n13
Shunchō, 160
Śibi, King, 114–16, 117, 118, 119, 121,
    122
Śiksānanda, 26
sin and retribution, 145–46, 149
six perfections of the bodhisattva, 112, 113,
    115, 152, 222n23
six sense organs, 23, 126, 219n46
sōji (hold completely), 48
sokushin jōbutsu (idea that a person could
    become a buddha in this very body),
    99
Sōniryō (Regulations for monks and nuns),
    69, 211n13
Sonko, 164
Sonoda Shūe, 71
śrāvaka (individual practitioners), 55
storehouse of the jewels of the dharma, 49
strange tales. See *zhi guai*
Strong, John, 65
stupas, 23, 56–57, 138–39, 178, 188, 220n7
Subhūti, 25, 43, 44
Sudhana, 26, 47, 178–79, 180
Sugawara no Michizane, 226n24
Sumiyoshi Shrine, 148
surikuyō ritual, 104–5, 216n12
sutra chanting. *See* chanting
sutra copying: and the Buddha body, 166,
    172; with characters as jeweled stupa,
    138–39, 138*fig.*, 139*fig.*; characters
    per line, 141; for a dead person, 104–
    5, 216n12; gold on blue, 142, 143*fig.*,
    150; "lotus throne sutra" method, 166;
    merit for, 209n86; official mandate for,
    189; "one-character, one-buddha sutra"
    method, 166; and sutra reading, 154;
    using hair and blood, 119–20; as writ-
    ing, 150. See also *surikuyō*
sutra devotion, 42, 53–54, 206–7n56

sutra embodiment, 161–66, 172, 223n39. *See also* embodiment
sutra-keeping hermits, 155
sutra library, 34–35. *See also* revolving sutra library
sutra memorization. *See* memorization
Sutra of Golden Radiance, 209n86
Sutra of Immeasurable Life, 25, 28
Sutra of Immeasurable Meanings, 167
Sutra of Meditation on the Bodhisattva Universal Virtue, 167
Sutra of Meditation on the Buddha Amitāyus, 13, 25, 32–33, 168, 203–4n20
Sutra of Parables, 188
sutra reading: as chewing, 214n42; Dōgen on, 179–81; forms and technologies for, 17, 175–77, 187–90, 194–95, 224n4; and preaching, 177–78; reader-text relationship, 20, 23–24; "reading and reciting," 50–52, 143–44, 147, 157; and sutra copying, 154; text-body relationship in, 11. *See also* chanting; sutra recitation
sutra recitation: dark, 141, 147, 221n11; and embodiment, 161–62,172; *Lotus Sutra,* 111, 120, 152–53, 157, 159–60; meditation and, 180; "reading and reciting," 50–52, 143–44, 147, 157. *See also* chanting; *Lotus Sutra;* sutra reading
sutras: anthropomorphized, 161, 191; and the body, 23, 24, 54, 60, 133–34, 161; and the body of the Buddha, 41, 137–38, 142, 166–67; introduction to Japan, 8; intertextual references in, 28; meaning of the word, 151, 222n21; meta-fictional techniques in, 16, 177; ontological status of, 40–41; as oral and written texts, 36, 43–44; preservation and protection of, 32–35, 59; reproduction and propagation of, 23, 43–44, 52–54, 60, 209n86; sects and, 13, 24; as source of enlightened intuition, 40, 41–42; textual engagement with, 42–43, 206n55, 206–7n56; what they need, 59–60; what they want, 7, 22–

23, 24, 42–46, 50. *See also* chanting; setsuwa; sutra copying; sutra embodiment; sutra reading; sutra recitation; text-body relationship
symbiotic relationships, 58–61

Tachibana Nankei, *Tōyūki,* 203n15
Taira no Kiyomori, 167
Taira no Yasuyori, 72–73
Tale of Genji, 79, 216n15
Tales from Times Now Past: authorship and textual history of, 71–72, 77, 213n22; chanting skull motif in, 160, 222n30; erotic pursuit and religious awakening in, 105; exchange between Saichō and the deity of the Yahata Shrine, 222n25; as most influential setsuwa, 67; repeats stories from *Wondrous Record of Immediate Karmic Retribution,* 14, 210n100; scope and structure of, 72, 212n21; self-sacrifice setsuwa in, 98, 117; sources for, 66, 72; story of Giei, 155–56; story of the monk Riman, 111; story of the priest Ichiei, 223n33; story of the priest Kōshin, 160; story of the priest Shunchō, 160; story of sutras that take on human form, 162; tale of Ezō, 145; tale of Gyōhan, 146–48, 221n15; tale of Kairen, 149; tale of Kakunen, 143–44; tale of Myōren, 221n16; tale of Tenjō, 149; theme of sutra embodiment, 223n39
Tamamushi no zushi, 98
Tanabe, George, 8
Tanabe, Willa Jane, 120, 142, 171
Tang Lin, 68
Tangut, 192
Tao-chen (Daozhen), 207n66
Tatelman, Joel, 65
Taylor, Diana, 199n15
Teiser, Stephen, 190, 206n56, 207n66
Tendai, 13
tendokue (ritual of reading by turning), 190, 193
Tenjō, 149

waka, 84, 211n9; *waka soku darani,* 99
Warren, Austin, 40
Waugh, Patricia, 27
Wellek, René, 40
wheel of the dharma, 17, 177, 184, 187, 193,
    194. *See also* revolving sutra libraries
Whitman, Walt, 35; "Out of the Cradle
    Endlessly Rocking," 201n39
Wilson, Elizabeth, 106
"wily authors" (Cole), 27, 203n19
women: devout, 9, 69, 121, 125, 212n15;
    "five obstructions" faced by, 75, 213n27;
    gifts of the body by, 124–25; sinful by
    nature, 160
Wondrous Record of Immediate Karmic Retri-
    bution, A: authorship and compilation
    of, 68, 77–78; first Japanese setsuwa
    collection, 13, 66, 67; gender and,
    210n100; as the human body of a
    preacher, 87–88; mention of *mappō,*
    101; motif of chanting skulls, 157–
    58; punishment of sin in, 104; putre-
    faction in, 103; resemblance to *Ming-*
    baoji, 16, 68; and sermonizing, 9–10;
    as source for other collections, 14, 72;
    story of faulty memory, 145; story
    of sutras that take on human form,
    161–62; sutra copying in, 216n12;
    theme of sutra embodiment, 223n39

woodcut illustrations, 188
"work" and "text," 35–36, 41, 47, 140,
    174, 205n36, 220n10
writing, 51, 150, 155; embodied, 137,
    159

Xuanzang (Hsüan-tsang), 206n56
Yahata Shrine, 222n25
Yakushiji, 13
Yamada Shōzen, 73
Yamagishi Tokuhei, 71
Yamashinadera (Kōfukuji), 82
yan ji (accounts of miracles), 7, 65
Yingzao Fashi, 183
Yokoe no omi Naritojime, 103–4
yūya nenbutsu, 200n28

za (seated sermonizing sessions), 212n19
Zen, 13
Zenpachi, 203n15
zhi guai: combined with *avadāna,* 66;
    influence on setsuwa, 7, 15, 65–66;
    mentioned, 12, 211n7
Zhiyi, 130; *Great Calming and Contempla-*
    tion, 215n9, 216n11
Zotanshū (A Collection of Casual Digres-
    sions), 222n25
Zuiōji (Ehime), 183, 226n24
Zumthor, Paul, 79

Text:	11.25/13.5 Adobe Garamond
Display:	Adobe Garamond
Compositor:	Integrated Composition Systems
Indexer:	Susan Stone
Printer and binder:	IBT Global